The Complete

HOME REPAIR

4th Edition

With 350 Projects and Over 2,000 Photos

COOL
SPRINGS
PRESS
Home and Garden Experts™

MINNEAPOLIS, MINNESOTA

Quarto is the authority on a wide range of topics.
Quarto educates, entertains and enriches the lives of
our readers—enthusiasts and lovers of hands-on living.
www.quartoknows.com

First published in 2016 by Cool Springs Press, an imprint of
Quarto Publishing Group USA Inc., 400 First Avenue North,
Suite 400, Minneapolis, MN 55401 USA. Telephone: (612) 344-8100
Fax: (612) 344-8692

quartoknows.com
Visit our blogs at quartoknows.com

Cool Springs Press titles are also available at discounts in bulk
quantity for industrial or sales-promotional use. For details contact
the Special Sales Manager at Quarto Publishing Group USA Inc.,
400 First Avenue North, Suite 400, Minneapolis, MN 55401 USA.

10 9 8 7 6 5 4 3 2 1

ISBN: 978-1-59186-663-3

Library of Congress Cataloging-in-Publication Data

Names: Black & Decker Corporation (Towson, Md.), creator.
Title: The complete photo guide to home repair : with 350 projects
     and over 2,000 photos.
Other titles: Black & Decker the complete photo guide to home
     repair | Home repair
Description: 4th edition. | Minneapolis, Minnesota : Cool Springs
     Press, 2016. | At head of title: Black & Decker.
Identifiers: LCCN 2015043593 | ISBN 9781591866633 (sc)
Subjects: LCSH: Dwellings--Maintenance and repair--
     Amateurs' manuals.
Classification: LCC TH4817.3 .C655 2016 | DDC 643/.7--dc23
LC record available at http://lccn.loc.gov/2015043593

Acquiring Editor: Mark Johanson
Project Manager: Sherry Anisi
Art Director: Brad Springer
Layout: Danielle Smith-Boldt

Printed in China

NOTICE TO READERS

For safety, use caution, care, and good judgment when following the procedures described in this book. The publisher
and BLACK+DECKER cannot assume responsibility for any damage to property or injury to persons as a result of misuse
of the information provided.

The techniques shown in this book are general techniques for various applications. In some instances, additional
techniques not shown in this book may be required. Always follow manufacturers' instructions included with products,
since deviating from the directions may void warranties. The projects in this book vary widely as to skill levels required:
some may not be appropriate for all do-it-yourselfers, and some may require professional help.

Consult your local building department for information on building permits, codes, and other laws as they apply to
your project.

Contents

The Complete Photo Guide to Home Repair

Contents (Cont.)

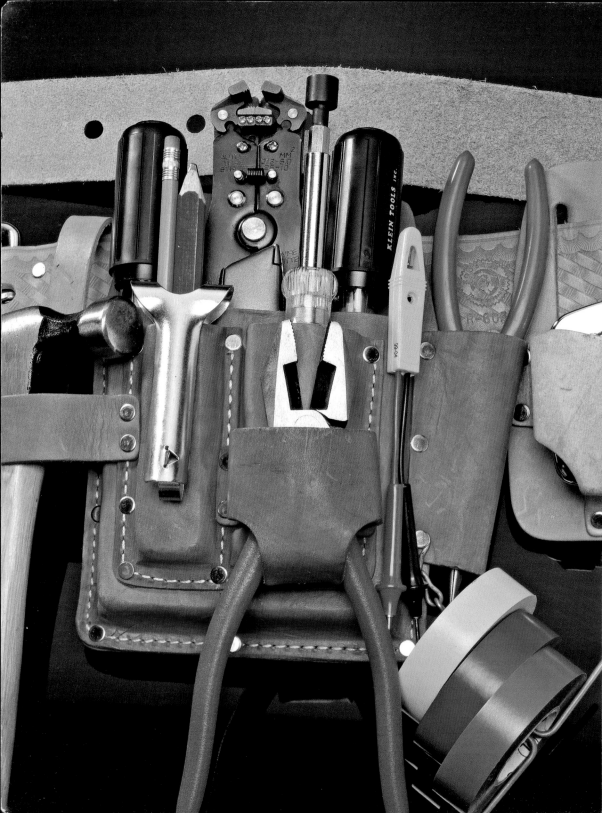

Introduction

Every homeowner needs a big book: A one-stop reference that covers all the fundamental home repair tasks we face on a daily basis. And if that big book is sized so it fits nicely in your tool kit, so much the better. That's why we originally published *BLACK+DECKER The Complete Photo Guide to Home Repair* in its convenient 6½ × 8½–inch trim size. And the fact that building codes change and new tools and techniques are always showing up is the reason we've updated our little big book in this new fourth edition.

On the following pages you'll find clear, step-by-step instructions for repairing and maintaining every major system and surface in and around your house. No filler, nothing you don't need—it's full of hundreds of projects and thousands of photos to help you keep your home in top shape.

This fourth edition includes all the best information from previous editions, as well as new repair projects for every area of the house. Inside you'll find:

- Step-by-step instructions featuring pro tips and techniques. Our home improvement experts give you clear, concise directions to help you from start to finish.
- Color photos of every stage of a project so you'll know exactly what to expect.
- Detailed anatomy photos and illustrations.
- Fully updated information that complies with all current national codes.

Every area of the house is covered. In the interior repairs section, you'll find comprehensive repairs for basements, walls, floors, and ceilings. There's detailed information on minor and major repairs to flooring materials from carpet to laminate. You'll learn everything from how to make your existing windows more energy efficient to how to replace old windows with new, high-efficiency models.

When it comes to exterior repairs, we cover everything from tips for winterizing and improving energy efficiency to repairing flashing, garage door openers, stone walls, and much more. We'll show you how to patch a leaky roof and repair and restore a worn patio, deck, or sidewalk. Repairs to every major siding material are also covered.

Repairs and upgrades to wiring, plumbing, and HVAC systems can be the most intimidating for homeowners, and they're almost always the most expensive to hire out. Armed with this book, you'll have all the information and direction you need to tackle common wiring and plumbing projects with confidence and learn the skills to be prepared for just about any wiring or plumbing emergency.

As a homeowner, you know your home is your biggest investment. *The Complete Photo Guide to Home Repair* is your indispensable resource for protecting that investment.

Interior Repairs

In this chapter:

Repairing Floors

Floor coverings wear out faster than other interior surfaces because they get more wear and tear. Surface damage can affect more than just appearance. Scratches in resilient flooring and cracks in grouted tile joints can let moisture into the floor's underpinnings. Hardwood floors lose their finish and become discolored. Loose boards squeak.

Underneath the finished flooring, moisture ruins wood underlayment and the damage is passed on to the subfloor. Bathroom floors suffer the most from moisture problems. Subflooring can pull loose from joists, causing floors to become uneven and springy.

You can fix these problems yourself, such as squeaks, a broken stair tread, damaged baseboard and trim, and minor damage to floor coverings, with the tools and techniques shown on the following pages.

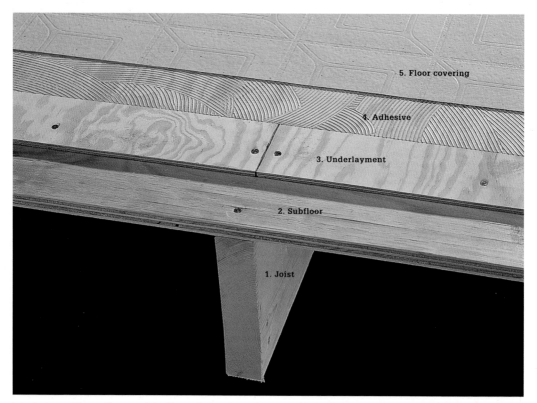

5. Floor covering

4. Adhesive

3. Underlayment

2. Subfloor

1. Joist

A typical wood-frame floor consists of layers that work together to provide the required structural support and desired appearance: 1. At the bottom of the floor are the joists, the 2 × 10 or larger framing members that support the weight of the floor. Joists are typically spaced 16" apart on center. 2. The subfloor is nailed to the joists. Most subfloors installed in the 1970s or later are made of ¾" tongue-and-groove plywood; in older houses, the subfloor often consists of 1"-thick wood planks nailed diagonally across the floor joists. 3. On top of the subfloor, most builders place a ½" plywood underlayment. Some flooring materials, especially ceramic tile, require cementboard for stability. 4. For many types of floor coverings, adhesive or mortar is spread on the underlayment before the floor covering is installed. Carpet rolls generally require tackless strips and cushioned padding. 5. Other materials, such as snap-fit laminate planks or carpet squares, can be installed directly on the underlayment with little or no adhesive.

Tips for Evaluating Floors

When installing new flooring over old, measure vertical spaces to make sure enclosed or under-counter appliances will fit once the new underlayment and flooring are installed. Use samples of the new underlayment and floor covering as spacers when measuring.

High thresholds often indicate that several layers of flooring have already been installed on top of one another. If you have several layers, it's best to remove them before installing the new floor covering.

Buckling in solid hardwood floors indicates that the boards have loosened from the subfloor. Do not remove hardwood floors. Instead, refasten loose boards by drilling pilot holes and inserting flooring nails or screws. New carpet can be installed right over a well-fastened hardwood floor. New ceramic tile or resilient flooring should be installed over underlayment placed on the hardwood flooring.

Loose tiles may indicate widespread failure of the adhesive. Use a wallboard knife to test tiles. If tiles can be pried up easily in many different areas of the room, plan to remove all of the flooring.

Air bubbles trapped under resilient sheet flooring indicate that the adhesive has failed. The old flooring must be removed before the new covering can be installed.

Cracks in grout joints around ceramic tile are a sign that movement of the floor covering has caused, or has been caused by, deterioration of the adhesive layer. If more than 10% of the tiles are loose, remove the old flooring. Evaluate the condition of the underlayment (see opposite page) to determine if it also must be removed.

Repairing Joists

A severely arched, bulged, cracked, or sagging floor joist can only get worse over time, eventually deforming the floor above it. Correcting a problem joist is an easy repair and makes a big difference in your finished floor. It's best to identify problem joists and fix them before installing your underlayment and new floor covering.

One way to fix joist problems is to fasten a few new joists next to a damaged floor joist in a process called sistering. When installing a new joist, you may need to notch the bottom edge so it can fit over the foundation or beam. If that's the case with your joists, cut the notches in the ends no deeper than ⅛" of the actual depth of the joist.

Tools & Materials ▸

4-ft. level	Framing lumber
Reciprocating saw	16d common nails
Hammer	Hardwood shims
Chisel	Metal jack posts
Adjustable wrench	Eye and
Tape measure	ear protection
Ratchet wrench	Work gloves
3" lag screws	
with washers	

How to Repair a Bulging Joist

1 Find the high point of the bulge in the floor using a level. Mark the high point and measure the distance to a reference point that extends through the floor, such as an exterior wall or heating duct.

2 Use the measurement and reference point from the last step to mark the high point on the joist from below the floor. From the bottom edge of the joist, make a straight cut into the joist just below the high point mark using a reciprocating saw. Make the cut ¾ of the depth of the joist. Allow several weeks for the joist to straighten.

3 When the joist has settled, reinforce it by centering a board of the same height and at least 6 ft. long next to it. Fasten the board to the joist by driving 12d common nails in staggered pairs about 12" apart. Drive a row of three nails on either side of the cut in the joist.

How to Repair a Cracked or Sagging Joist

1

Identify the cracked or sagging joist before it causes additional problems. Remove any blocking or bridging above the sill or beam where the sister joist will go.

2

Place a level on the bottom edge of the joist to determine the amount of sagging that has occurred. Cut a sister joist the same length as the damaged joist. Place it next to the damaged joist with the crown side up. If needed, notch the bottom edge of the sister joist so it fits over the foundation or beam.

3

Nail two 6-ft. 2 × 4s together to make a cross beam, then place the beam perpendicular to the joists near one end of the joists. Position a jack post under the beam and use a level to make sure it's plumb before raising it.

4

Raise the jack post by turning the threaded shaft until the cross beam is snug against the joists. Position a second jack post and cross beam at the other end of the joists. Raise the posts until the sister joist is flush with the subfloor. Insert tapered hardwood shims at the ends of the sister joist where it sits on the sill or beam. Tap the shims in place with a hammer and scrap piece of wood until they're snug.

5

Drill pairs of pilot holes in the sister joist every 12", then insert 3" lag screws with washers in each hole. Cut the blocking or bridging to fit and install it between the joists in its original position.

Eliminating Floor Squeaks

Floors squeak when floorboards rub against each other or against the nails securing them to the subfloor. Hardwood floors squeak if they haven't been nailed properly. Normal changes in wood make some squeaking inevitable, although noisy floors sometimes indicate serious structural problems. If an area of a floor is soft or excessively squeaky, inspect the framing and the foundation supporting the floor.

Whenever possible, fix squeaks from underneath. Joists longer than 8 feet should have X-bridging or solid blocking between each pair. If these supports aren't present, install them every 6 feet to stiffen a noisy floor.

Tools & Materials ▸

Drill	Graphite powder
Hammer	Dance-floor wax
Nail set	Pipe straps
Putty knife	Hardwood shims
Wood screws	Wood glue
Flooring nails	Eye and ear protection
Wood putty	Work gloves

How to Eliminate Floor Squeaks

1

If you can access floor joists from underneath, drive wood screws up through the subfloor to draw hardwood flooring and the subfloor together. Drill pilot holes and make certain the screws aren't long enough to break through the top of the floorboards. Determine the combined thickness of the floor and subfloor by measuring at cutouts for pipes.

2

When you can't reach the floor from underneath, surface-nail the floor boards to the subfloor with ring-shank flooring nails. Drill pilot holes close to the tongue-side edge of the board and drive the nails at a slight angle to increase their holding power. Whenever possible, nail into studs. Countersink the nails with a nail set and fill the holes with tinted wood putty.

Eliminate squeaks in a carpeted floor by using a special floor fastening device, called a Squeeeeek No More, to drive screws through the subfloor into the joists. The device guides the screw and controls the depth. The screw has a scored shank, so once it's set, you can break the end off just below the surface of the subfloor.

Eliminate squeaks in hardwood floors with graphite powder, talcum powder, powdered soap, mineral oil, or liquid wax. Remove dirt and deposits from joints, using a putty knife. Apply graphite powder, talcum powder, powdered soap, or mineral oil between squeaky boards. Bounce on the boards to work the lubricant into the joints. Clean up excess powder with a damp cloth. Liquid wax is another option, although some floor finishes, such as urethane and varnish, are not compatible with wax, so check with the flooring manufacturer. Use a clean cloth to spread wax over the noisy joints, forcing the wax deep into the joints.

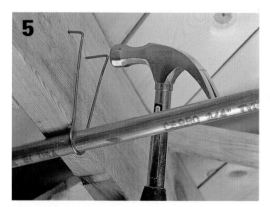

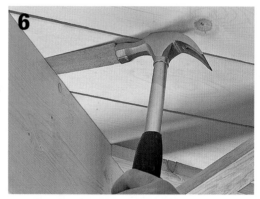

In an unfinished basement or crawl space, copper water pipes are usually hung from floor joists. Listen for pipes rubbing against joists. Loosen or replace wire pipe hangers to silence the noise. Pull the pointed ends of the hanger from the wood, using a hammer or pry bar. Lower the hanger just enough so the pipe isn't touching the joist, making sure the pipe is held firmly so it won't vibrate. Renail the hanger, driving the pointed end straight into the wood.

The boards or sheeting of a subfloor can separate from the joists, creating gaps. Where gaps are severe or appear above several neighboring joists, the framing may need reinforcement, but isolated gapping can usually be remedied with hardwood shims. Apply a small amount of wood glue to the shim and squirt some glue into the gap. Using a hammer, tap the shim into place until it's snug. Shimming too much will widen the gap, so be careful. Allow the glue to dry before walking on the floor.

Replacing Trim Moldings

There's no reason to let damaged trim moldings detract from the appearance of a well-maintained room. With the right tools and a little attention to detail, you can replace or repair them quickly and easily.

Home centers and lumber yards sell many styles of moldings, but they may not stock moldings found in older homes. If you have trouble finding duplicates, check salvage yards in your area. They sometimes carry styles no longer manufactured. You can also try combining several different moldings to duplicate a more elaborate version.

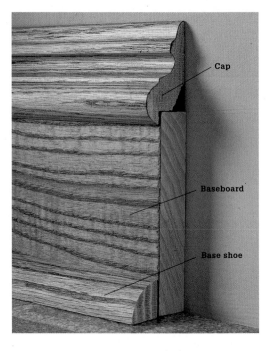

Tools & Materials ▸

Flat pry bars (2)	Wood scraps
Coping saw	Replacement moldings
Miter saw	2d, 4d, and 6d finish nails
Drill	Wood putty
Hammer	Eye and ear protection
Nail set	Work gloves

How to Remove Damaged Trim

Even the lightest pressure from a pry bar can damage wallboard or plaster, so use a large, flat scrap of wood to protect the wall. Insert one bar beneath the trim and work the other bar between the baseboard and the wall. Force the pry bars in opposite directions to remove the baseboard.

To remove baseboards without damaging the wall, use leverage rather than force. Pry off the base shoe first, using a flat pry bar. When you feel a few nails pop, move farther along the molding and pry again.

How to Install Baseboards

1

Scrap baseboard

Start at an inside corner by butting one piece of baseboard securely into the corner. Drill pilot holes, then fasten the baseboard with two 6d finish nails, aligned vertically, at each wall stud. Cut a scrap of baseboard so the ends are perfectly square. Cut the end of the workpiece square. Position the scrap on the back of the workpiece so its back face is flush with the end of the workpiece. Trace the outline of the scrap onto the back of the workpiece.

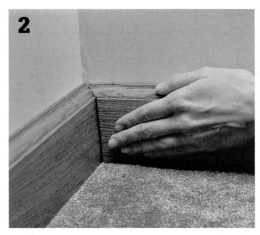

2

Cut along the outline on the workpiece with a coping saw, keeping the saw perpendicular to the baseboard face. Test-fit the coped end. Recut it, if necessary.

3

To cut the baseboard to fit at outside corners, mark the end where it meets the outside wall corner. Cut the end at a 45° angle, using a power miter saw. Lock-nail all miter joints by drilling a pilot hole and driving 4d finish nails through each corner.

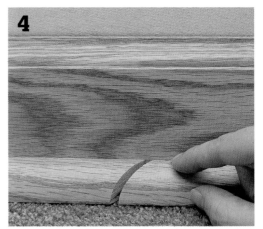

4

Install base shoe molding along the bottom of the baseboards. Make miter joints at inside and outside corners, and fasten base shoe with 2d finish nails. Whenever possible, complete a run of molding using one piece. For long spans, join molding pieces by mitering the ends at parallel 45° angles. Set nail heads below the surface using a nail set, and then fill the holes with wood putty.

Repairing Hardwood

A darkened, dingy hardwood floor may only need a thorough cleaning to reveal an attractive, healthy finish. If you have a fairly new or prefinished hardwood floor, check with the manufacturer or flooring installer before applying any cleaning products or wax. Most prefinished hardwood, for example, should not be waxed.

Water and other liquids can penetrate deep into the grain of hardwood floors, leaving dark stains that are sometimes impossible to remove by sanding. Instead, try bleaching the wood with oxalic acid, available in crystal form at home centers or paint stores. When gouges, scratches, and dents aren't bad enough to warrant replacing a floorboard, repair the damaged area with a latex wood patch that matches the color of your floor.

Identify surface finishes using solvents. In an inconspicuous area, rub in different solvents to see if the finish dissolves, softens, or is removed. Denatured alcohol removes shellac, while lacquer thinner removes lacquer. If neither of those work, try nail polish remover containing acetone, which removes varnish but not polyurethane.

Tools & Materials ▸

Vacuum
Buffing machine
Hammer
Nail set
Putty knife
Cloths

Hardwood cleaning kit
Paste wax or liquid wax
Rubber gloves
Oxalic acid
Wood restorer
Borax

Latex wood patch
Sandpaper
Eye and ear protection

How to Clean & Renew Hardwood

Vacuum the entire floor. Mix hot water and dishwashing detergent that doesn't contain lye, trisodium phosphate, or ammonia. Working on 3-ft.-square sections, scrub the floor with a brush or nylon scrubbing pad. Wipe up the water and wax with a towel before moving to the next section.

If the water and detergent don't remove the old wax, use a hardwood floor cleaning kit. Use only solvent-type cleaners, as some water-based products can blacken wood. Apply the cleaner following the manufacturer's instructions.

When the floor is clean and dry, apply a high-quality floor wax. Paste wax is more difficult to apply than liquid floor wax, but it lasts much longer. Apply the wax by hand, then polish the floor with a rented buffing machine fitted with synthetic buffing pads.

How to Remove Stains

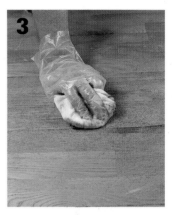

Remove the finish by sanding the stained area with sandpaper. In a disposable cup, dissolve the recommended amount of oxalic acid crystals in water. Wearing rubber gloves, pour the mixture over the stained area, taking care to cover only the darkened wood.

Let the liquid stand for one hour. Repeat the application, if necessary. Wash with 2 tablespoons borax dissolved in one pint water to neutralize the acid. Rinse with water, and let the wood dry. Sand the area smooth.

Apply several coats of wood restorer until the bleached area matches the finish of the surrounding floor.

How to Patch Scratches & Small Holes

Before filling nail holes, make sure the nails are securely set in the wood. Use a hammer and nail set to drive loose nails below the surface. Apply wood patch to the damaged area, using a putty knife. Force the compound into the hole by pressing the knife blade downward until it lies flat on the floor.

Scrape excess compound from the edges, and allow the patch to dry completely. Sand the patch flush with the surrounding surface. Using fine-grit sandpaper, sand in the direction of the wood grain.

Apply wood restorer to the sanded area until it blends with the rest of the floor.

Replacing a Damaged Floorboard

When solid hardwood floorboards are beyond repair, they need to be carefully cut out and replaced with boards of the same width and thickness. Replace whole boards whenever possible. If a board is long, or if part of its length is inaccessible, draw a cutting line across the face of the board, and tape behind the line to protect the section that will remain.

Tools & Materials ▸

Pencil	Flooring nails	Nail set	Wood finish
Framing square	Hammer	Rubber mallet	Wood glue
Drill and bit	Chisel	Wood putty	Eye and ear protection
Tape measure	Pry bar	Putty knife	Work gloves
Masking tape	Speed square	Fine sandpaper	
Circular saw	1½" finish nails	Wood stain	

How to Replace Damaged Floorboards

Draw a rectangle around the damaged area. Determine the minimal number of boards to be removed. To avoid nails, be sure to draw the line ¾" inside the outermost edge of any joints.

Determine the thickness of the boards to be cut. With a drill and ¾"-wide spade bit, slowly drill through a damaged board. Drill until you see the top of the subfloor. Measure the depth. A common thickness is ⅝" and ¾". Set your circular saw to this depth.

3

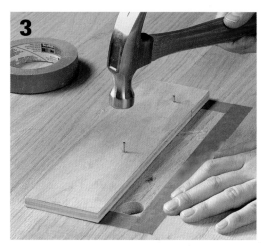

To prevent boards from chipping, place masking tape or painter's tape along the outside of the pencil lines. To create a wood cutting guide, tack a straight wood strip inside the damaged area (for easy removal, allow nails to slightly stick up). Set back the guide the distance between the saw blade and the guide edge of the circular saw.

4

Align the circular saw with the wood cutting guide. Turn on the saw. Lower the blade into the cutline. Do not cut the last ¼" of the corners. Remove cutting guide. Repeat with other sides.

5

Complete the cuts. Use a hammer and sharp chisel to completely loosen the boards from the subfloor. Make sure the chisel's beveled side is facing the damaged area for a clean edge.

6

Remove split boards. Use a scrap 2 × 4 block for leverage and to protect the floor. With a hammer, tap a pry bar into and under the split board. Most boards pop out easily, but some may require a little pressure. Remove exposed nails with the hammer claw.

(continued)

Use a chisel to remove the 2 remaining strips. Again, make sure the bevel side of the chisel is facing the interior of the damaged area. Set any exposed nails with your nail set.

Cut new boards. Measure the length and width of the area to be replaced. Place the new board on a sawhorse, with the section to be used hanging off the edge. Draw a pencil cutline. With saw blade on waste side of mark, firmly press the saw guide against the edge of a speed square. Measure each board separately.

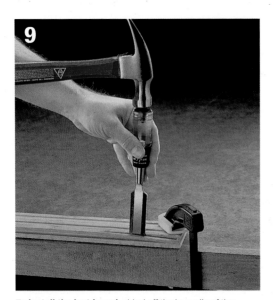

To install the last board, chisel off the lower lip of the groove. Remove the tongue on the end of the board, if necessary. Apply adhesive to the board, and set it in place, tongue first.

Pick a drill bit with a slightly smaller diameter than an 8-penny finish nail, and drill holes at a 45° angle through the corner of the replacement piece's tongue every 3" to 4" along the new board. Hammer a 1½"-long, 8d finish nail through the hole into the subfloor. Use a nail set to countersink nails. Repeat until the last board.

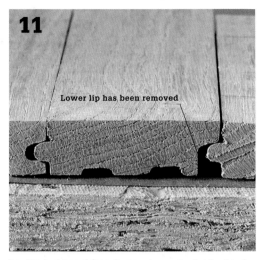

11

Lower lip has been removed

Lay the last board face down onto a protective 2 × 4 and use a sharp chisel to split off the lower lip. This allows it to fit into place.

12

To install the last board, hook the tongue into the groove of the old floor and then use a soft mallet to tap the groove side down into the previous board installed.

13

Drill pilot holes angled outward: two side-by-side holes about ½" from the edges of each board, and one hole every 12" along the groove side of each board. Drive 1½"-long, 8d finish nails through the holes. Set nails with a nail set. Fill holes with wood putty.

14

Once the putty is dry, sand the patch smooth with fine-grit sandpaper. Feather-sand neighboring boards. Vacuum and wipe the area with a clean cloth. Apply matching wood stain or restorer, then apply 2 coats of matching finish.

How to Repair Splinters

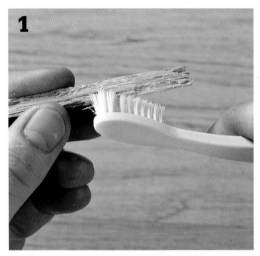

If you still have the splintered piece of wood, but it has been entirely dislodged from the floor, it's a good bet that the hollowed space left by the splinter has collected a lot of dirt and grime. Combine a 1:3 mixture of distilled white vinegar and water in a bucket. Dip an old toothbrush into the solution and use it to clean out the hole left in the floor. While you're at it, wipe down the splinter with the solution, too. Allow the floor and splinter to thoroughly dry.

If the splinter is large, apply wood glue to the hole and splinter. Use a Q-Tip or toothpick to apply small amounts of wood glue under smaller splinters. Soak the Q-Tip in glue; you don't want Q-Tip fuzz sticking out of your floor once the glue dries.

Press the splinter back into place. To clean up the excess glue, use a slightly damp, lint-free cloth. Do not oversoak the cloth with water.

Allow the adhesive to dry. Cover the patch with wax paper and a couple of books. Let the adhesive dry overnight.

How to Patch Small Holes in Wood Floors

Repair small holes with wood putty. Use putty that matches the floor color. Force the compound into the hole with a putty knife. Continue to press the putty in this fashion until the depression in the floor is filled. Scrape excess compound from the area. Use a damp, lint-free cloth while the putty is still wet to smooth the top level with the surrounding floor. Allow to dry.

Sand the area with fine (100- to 120-grit) sandpaper. Sand with the wood grain so the splintered area is flush with the surrounding surface. To better hide the repair, feather sand the area. Wipe up dust with a slightly damp cloth.

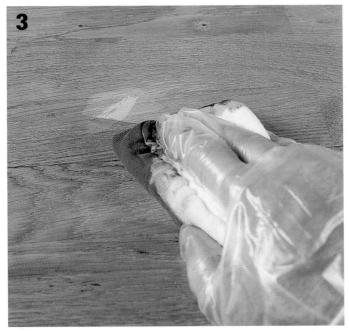

With a clean, lint-free cloth, apply a matching stain (wood sealer or "restorer") to the sanded area. Read the label on the product to make sure it is appropriate for sealing wood floors. Work in the stain until the patched area blends with the rest of the floor. Allow area to completely dry. Apply two coats of finish. Be sure the finish is the same as that which was used on the surrounding floor.

Replacing Sections of Wood Floors

When an interior wall or section of wall has been removed during remodeling, you'll need to patch gaps in the flooring where the wall was located. There are several options for patching floors, depending on your budget and the level of your do-it-yourself skills.

If the existing flooring shows signs of wear, consider replacing the entire flooring surface. Although it can be expensive, an entirely new floor covering will completely hide any gaps in the floor and provide an elegant finishing touch for your remodeling project.

If you choose to patch the existing flooring, be aware that it's difficult to hide patched areas completely, especially if the flooring uses unique patterns or finishes. A creative solution is to intentionally patch the floor with material that contrasts with the surrounding flooring (opposite page).

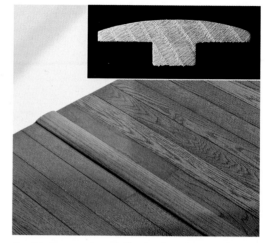

A quick, inexpensive solution is to install T-molding to bridge a gap in a wood strip floor. T-moldings are especially useful when the surrounding boards run parallel to the gap. T-moldings are available in several widths and can be stained to match the flooring.

When patching a wood-strip floor, one option is to remove all of the floor boards that butt against the flooring gap using a pry bar and replace them with boards cut to fit. This may require you to trim the tongues from some tongue-and-groove floorboards. Sand and refinish the entire floor so the new boards match the old.

How to Use Contrasting Flooring Material

Fill gaps in floors with materials that have a contrasting color and pattern. For wood floors, parquet tiles are an easy and inexpensive choice (above, left). You may need to widen the gap with a circular saw set to the depth of the wood covering to make room for the contrasting tiles. To enhance the effect, cut away a border strip around the room and fill these areas with the same contrasting flooring material (above, right).

Tips for Patching Floors ▸

Build up the subfloor in the patch area, using layers of thin plywood and building paper, so the new surface will be flush with the surrounding flooring. You may need to experiment with different combinations of plywood and paper to find the right thickness.

Make a vinyl or carpet patch by laying the patch material over the old flooring, then cutting through both layers. When the cut strip of old flooring is removed, the new patch will fit tightly in its place. If flooring material is patterned, make sure the patterns are aligned before you cut.

Install a carpet patch using heat-activated carpet tape and a rented seam iron. Original carpet remnants are ideal for patching. New carpet, even of the same brand, style and color, will seldom match the original carpet exactly.

Replacing Laminate Flooring

In the event that you need to replace a laminate plank, you must first determine how to remove the damaged plank. If you have a glueless "floating" floor it is best to unsnap and remove each plank starting at the wall and moving in until you reach the damaged plank. However, if the damaged plank is far from the wall, cut out the damaged plank. Fully-bonded laminate planks have adhesive all along the bottom of the plank and are secured directly to the underlayment. When you remove the damaged plank you run the risk of gouging the subfloor, so we recommend calling in a professional if you find that your laminate planks are completely glued to the subfloor.

As indestructible as laminate floors may seem, minor scratches caused by normal day-to-day wear and tear are unavoidable. Whether the damaged plank is close to a wall or in the middle of the floor, this project will show you how to replace it.

Tools & Materials ▸

Circular saw	Rubber mallet
Underlayment	Drawbar
½" spacers	Finish nails
Tapping block	Strap clamps
Scrap foam	Threshold and screws
Speed square	Putty knife
Manufacturer's glue	Floor adhesive
Painter's tape	Notched trowel
Hammer	Soft mallet
Nail set	Pliers
Pry bar	Eye and ear protection
Router	Work gloves
Chisels	

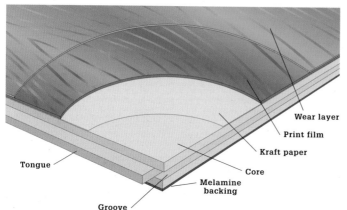

From bottom to top, laminate planks are engineered to resist moisture, scratches, and dents. A melamine base layer protects the inner core layer, which is most often HDF (high-density fiberboard). This is occasionally followed by kraft paper saturated in resins for added protection and durability. The print film is a photographic layer that replicates the look of wood or ceramic. The surface is a highly protective wear layer. The tongue-and-groove planks fit together tightly and may be (according to manufacturer's instructions) glued together for added stability.

Labels: Wear layer, Print film, Kraft paper, Core, Melamine backing, Tongue, Groove

How to Replace Laminate Planks

Draw a rectangle in the middle of the damaged board with a 1½" border between the rectangle and factory edges. At each rectangle corner and inside each corner of the plank, use a hammer and nail set to make indentations. At each of these indentations, drill ³⁄₁₆" holes into the plank. Only drill the depth of the plank.

To protect the floor from chipping, place painter's tape along the cutlines. Now, set the circular saw depth to the thickness of the replacement plank. (If you don't have a replacement plank, see page 20, Step 2 to determine the plank thickness.) To plunge cut the damaged plank, turn on the saw and slowly lower the blade into the cutline until the cut guide rests flat on the floor. Push the saw from the center of the line out to each end. Stop ¼" in from each corner. Use a hammer to tap a pry bar or chisel into the cutlines. Lift and remove the middle section. Place a sharp chisel between the two drill holes in each corner and strike with a hammer to complete each corner cut. Vacuum.

To remove the remaining outer edges of the damaged plank, place a scrap 2 × 4 wood block along the outside of one long cut and use it for leverage to push a pry bar under the flooring. Insert a second pry bar beneath the existing floor (directly under the joint of the adjacent plank) and use a pliers to grab the 1½" border strip in front of the pry bar. Press downward until a gap appears at the joint. Remove the border piece. Remove the opposite strip and then the two short end pieces in the same manner.

Place a scrap of cardboard in the opening to protect the underlayment foam while you remove all of the old glue from the factory edges with a chisel. Vacuum up the wood and glue flakes.

(continued)

5

To remove the tongues on one long and one short end, lay the replacement plank face down onto a protective scrap of plywood (or 2 × 4). Clamp a straight cutting guide to the replacement plank so the distance from the guide causes the bit to align with the tongue and trim it off. Pressing the router against the cutting guide, slowly move along the entire edge of the replacement plank to remove the tongue. Clean the edges with sandpaper.

6

Dry-fit the grooves on the replacement board into the tongues of the surrounding boards and press into place. If the board fits snugly in between the surrounding boards, pry the plank up with a manufacturer suction cup. If the plank does not sit flush with the rest of the floor, check to make sure you routered the edges off evenly. Sand any rough edges that should have been completely removed and try to fit the plank again.

7

Set the replacement plank by applying laminate glue to the removed edges of the replacement plank and into the grooves of the existing planks. Firmly press the plank into place.

8

Clean up glue with a damp towel. Place a strip of wax paper over the new plank and evenly distribute some books on the wax paper. Allow the adhesive to dry for 12 to 24 hours.

Variation: Floating Floors ▸

If your damaged plank is close to the wall and the laminate floor is glueless, follow these steps:

To remove shoe molding, wedge a chisel between the shoe molding and baseboards to create a gap and maintain that gap with wood shims. Continue this process every 6" along the wall. Locate the nails that are holding the shoe to the baseboard and use a pry bar at those locations to gently pull the shoe away from the baseboard (inset).

To remove the first plank closest to the wall, use a pry bar to lift it just enough to get your hands under it and then slowly lift up and away from the adjacent plank. Continue to remove the planks that are between the shoe molding and the damaged plank with your hands. Finally, remove the damaged plank.

Snap in a new replacement plank and then continue to replace the rest of the boards until you reach the wall in the same manner.

Lay the shoe molding back in place along the wall. Using a nail set and hammer, countersink finish nails into the top of the shoe molding every 6 to 12" along the wall. Fill the holes with wood putty.

How to Replace a Parquet Tile

For the initial plunge cut, set the depth of a circular saw to the thickness of the parquet tile. (If you don't know the thickness, see Here's How, this page.) Hold the saw so that only the top of the guide plate touches the surface of the wood; the blade, when lowered, will cut into the damaged wood block. Turn on the saw. Slowly lower the blade into the cutting line until the saw's cut guide rests flat on the floor. Make a series of four plunge cuts into the damaged tile—1" inside each edge—to make a square cutout.

Use a hammer and a sharp, 1"-wide chisel to chip out the cut pieces in the center of the damaged tile. When you're removing the pieces around the edge of the cutout, make sure the beveled side of the chisel is facing the damaged area so that a clean flat edge is left along the adjacent tiles. If you need some elbow grease to remove the center pieces, use a hammer to tap a pry bar under the damaged cutout and then lean it over a scrap of 2 × 4 for leverage.

Use a putty knife to scrape away the remaining adhesive on the underlayment so that the new tile will sit flush with the surrounding floor.

Here's How ▶

If you don't have a replacement tile, and therefore don't know how thick the tiles are, you can determine the thickness by slowly drilling through the damaged tile with a ¾" hole saw or ¾"-wide spade drill bit. Very slowly drill through the damaged tile. Drill only a bit at a time until you bore all the way through the flooring and can see the top of the subfloor, then you can measure the depth of the board with a measuring tape. The depth will range from ⁵⁄₁₆" to ¾" thick.

4

Lower lip
removed

Remove lower lip of groove in replacement tile. If the replacement wood block has a tongue-and-groove structure, remove the lower lip of the groove so that you can press it into place. Lay the replacement block face down onto a protective scrap of wood and use a sharp chisel to split off the lower lip. Lightly sand the edges.

5

Apply adhesive. Use a ⅛" notched trowel to spread a thin layer of floor adhesive onto the back of the replacement tile and the floor. The ridges should be about ⅛" high on the replacement tile. The adhesive on the floor is only to make sure the tiles are completely covered on all edges. You want a secure bond, but you do not want adhesive to squeeze up between the tiles.

Warning ▶

Whenever cutting or drilling wood, be sure to wear protective eyewear. Eyeglasses made of safety glass will suffice as protective eyewear.

6

Install replacement block. Hook the tongue of the replacement block into the groove of an adjacent block and then use a soft mallet to gently tap the groove side of the new block down into place. If adhesive happens to squeeze up onto any of the block, clean it immediately with the cleaning solvent recommended by the adhesive manufacturer. You're done!

Repairing Vinyl Flooring

Repair methods for vinyl flooring depend on the type of floor as well as the type of damage. With sheet vinyl, you can fuse the surface or patch in new material. With vinyl tile, it's best to replace the damaged tiles.

Small cuts and scratches can be fused permanently and nearly invisibly with liquid seam sealer, a clear compound that's available wherever vinyl flooring is sold. For tears or burns, the damaged area can be patched. If necessary, remove vinyl from a hidden area, such as the inside of a closet or under an appliance, to use as patch material.

When vinyl flooring is badly worn or the damage is widespread, the only answer is complete replacement. Although it's possible to add layers of flooring in some situations, evaluate the options carefully. Be aware that the backing of older vinyl tiles made of asphalt may contain asbestos fibers. Consult a professional for their removal.

Tools & Materials ▸

Carpenter's square
Utility knife
Putty knife
Heat gun
J-roller
Notched trowel
Marker
Masking tape
Scrap of
   matching flooring
Mineral spirits
Floor covering
   adhesive
Wax paper

Liquid seam sealer
Flooring scraper
Vacuum
Lacquer thinner
Soft cloth
Eye and ear
   protection
Work gloves

How to Patch Sheet Vinyl

Measure the width and length of the damaged area. Place the new flooring remnant on a surface you don't mind making some cuts on—like a scrap of plywood. Use a carpenter's square for cutting guidance. Make sure your cutting size is a bit larger than the damaged area.

Lay the patch over the damaged area, matching pattern lines. Secure the patch with duct tape. Using a carpenter's square as a cutting guide, cut through the new vinyl (on top) and the old vinyl (on bottom). Press firmly with the knife to cut both layers.

Use tape to mark one edge of the new patch with the corresponding edge of the old flooring as placement marks. Remove the tape around the perimeter of the patch and lift up.

Soften the underlying adhesive with an electric heat gun and remove the damaged section of floor. Work from edges in. When the tile is loosened, insert a putty knife and pry up the damaged area.

(continued)

Scrape off the remaining adhesive with a putty knife or chisel. Work from the edges to the center. Dab mineral spirits (or Goo Gone) or spritz warm water on the floor to dissolve leftover goop, taking care not to use too much; you don't want to loosen the surrounding flooring. Use a razor-edged scraper (flooring scraper) to scrape to the bare wood underlayment.

Apply adhesive to the patch, using a notched trowel (with ⅛" V-shaped notches) held at a 45° angle to the back of the new vinyl patch.

Set one edge of the patch in place. Lower the patch onto the underlayment. Press into place. Apply pressure with a J-roller or rolling pin to create a solid bond. Start at the center and work toward the edges, working out air bubbles. Wipe up adhesive that oozes out the sides with a clean, damp cloth or sponge.

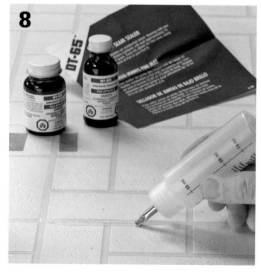

Let the adhesive dry overnight. Use a soft cloth dipped in lacquer thinner to clean the area. Mix the seam sealer according to the manufacturer's directions. Use an applicator bottle to apply a thin bead of sealer onto the cutlines.

How to Replace Resilient Tile

Use an electric heat gun to warm the damaged tile and soften the underlying adhesive. Keep the heat source moving so you don't melt the tile. When an edge of the tile begins to curl, insert a putty knife to pry up the loose edge until you can remove the tile. *Note: If you can clearly see the seam between tiles, first score around the tile with a utility knife. This prevents other tiles from lifting.*

Scrape away remaining adhesive with a putty knife or, for stubborn spots, a floor scraper. Work from the edges to the center so that you don't accidentally scrape up the adjacent tiles. Use mineral spirits to dissolve leftover goop. Take care not to allow the mineral spirits to soak into the floor under adjacent tiles. Vacuum up dust, dirt, and adhesive. Wipe clean.

When the floor is dry, use a notched trowel—with ⅛" V-shaped notches—held at a 45° angle to apply a thin, even layer of vinyl tile adhesive onto the underlayment. *Note: Only follow this step if you have dry-back tiles.*

Set one edge of the tile in place. Lower the tile onto the underlayment and then press it into place. Apply pressure with a J-roller to create a solid bond, starting at the center and working toward the edge to work out air bubbles. If adhesive oozes out the sides, wipe it up with a damp cloth or sponge. Cover the tile with wax paper and some books, and let the adhesive dry for 24 hours.

Repairing Ceramic Tile Floors

Although ceramic tile is one of the hardest floor coverings, problems can occur. Tiles sometimes become damaged and need to be replaced. Usually, this is simply a matter of removing and replacing individual tiles. However, major cracks in grout joints indicate that floor movement has caused the adhesive layer beneath the tile to deteriorate. In this case, the adhesive layer must be replaced in order to create a permanent repair.

Any time you remove tile, check the underlayment. If it's no longer smooth, solid, and level, repair or replace it before replacing the tile. When removing grout or damaged tiles, be careful not to damage surrounding tiles. Always wear eye protection when working with a hammer and chisel. Any time you are doing a major tile installation, make sure to save extra tiles. This way, you will have materials on hand when repairs become necessary.

Tools & Materials ▶

Hammer
Cold chisel
Eye protection
Putty knife
Square-notched
  trowel
Rubber mallet
Level
Needlenose pliers
Screwdriver
Grout float mix
Grout saw
Thin-set mortar
Replacement tile

Tile spacers
Grout
Bucket
Grout pigment
Grout sealer
Grout sponge
Floor-leveling
  compound
Work gloves

How to Replace Ceramic Tiles

With a carbide-tipped grout saw, apply firm but gentle pressure across the grout until you expose the unglazed edges of the tile. Do not scratch the glazed tile surface. If the grout is stubborn, use a hammer and screwdriver to first tap the tile (Step 2).

If the tile is not already cracked, use a hammer to puncture the tile by tapping a nail set or center punch into it. Alternatively, if the tile is significantly cracked, use a chisel to pry up the tile.

Insert a chisel into one of the cracks and gently tap the tile. Start at the center and chip outward so you don't damage the adjacent tiles. Be aware that cement board looks a lot like mortar when you're chiseling. Remove and discard the broken pieces.

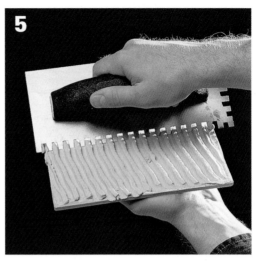

Use a putty knife to scrape away old thinset adhesive; use a chisel for poured mortar installation. If the underlayment is covered with metal lath, you won't be able to get the area smooth; just clean it out the best you can. Once the adhesive is scraped from the underlayment, smooth the rough areas with sandpaper. If there are gouges in the underlayment, fill them with epoxy-based thinset mortar (for cementboard) or a floor-leveling compound (for plywood). Allow the area to dry completely.

Use a ¼" notched trowel to apply thinset adhesive to the back of the replacement tile. Set the tile down into the space, and use plastic spacers around the tile to make sure it is centered within the opening.

Set the tile in position and press down until it is even with the adjacent tiles. Twist it a bit to get it to sit down in the mortar. Use a mallet or hammer and a block of wood covered with cloth or a carpet scrap to lightly tap on the tile, setting it into the adhesive.

Use a putty knife to apply grout to the joints. Fill in low spots by applying and smoothing extra grout with your finger. Use the round edge of a toothbrush handle to create a concave grout line, if desired. You must now grout the joint.

Repairing Carpet

Burns and stains are the most common carpeting problems. You can clip away the burned fibers of superficial burns using small scissors. Deeper burns and indelible stains require patching by cutting away and replacing the damaged area.

Another common problem, addressed on the opposite page, is carpet seams or edges that have come loose. You can rent the tools necessary for fixing this problem.

Tools & Materials ▸

Cookie-cutter tool
Knee kicker
4" wallboard knife
Utility knife
Seam iron
Replacement
 carpeting
Painter's tape

Phillips screwdriver
Double-face
 carpet tape
Seam adhesive
Heat-activated
 seam tape
Boards
Weights

How to Repair Spot Damage

1

2

3

Remove extensive damage or stains with a "cookie-cutter" tool, available at carpeting stores. Press the cutter down over the damaged area and twist it to cut away the carpet.

Using the cookie-cutter tool again, cut a replacement patch from scrap carpeting. Insert double-face carpet tape under the cutout, positioning the tape so it overlaps the patch seams.

Press the patch into place. Make sure the direction of the nap or pattern matches the existing carpet. To seal the seam and prevent unraveling, apply seam adhesive to the edges of the patch.

How to Restretch Loose Carpet

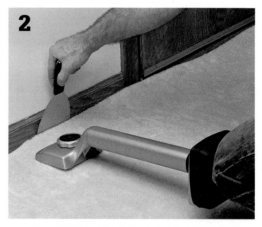

Adjust the knob on the head of the knee kicker so the prongs grab the carpet backing without penetrating through the padding. Starting from a corner or near a point where the carpet is firmly attached, press the knee kicker head into the carpet, about 2" from the wall.

Thrust your knee into the cushion of the knee kicker to force the carpet toward the wall. Tuck the carpet edge into the space between the wood strip and the baseboard using a 4" wallboard knife. If the carpet is still loose, trim the edge with a utility knife and stretch it again.

How to Glue Loose Seams

Remove the old tape from under the carpet seam. Cut a strip of new seam tape and place it under the carpet so it's centered along the seam with the adhesive facing up. Plug in the seam iron and let it heat up.

Pull up both edges of the carpet and set the hot iron squarely onto the tape. Wait about 30 seconds for the glue to melt. Move the iron about 12" farther along the seam. Quickly press the edges of the carpet together into the melted glue behind the iron. Separate the pile to make sure no fibers are stuck in the glue and the seam is tight. Place weighted boards over the seam to keep it flat while the glue sets. Remember, you have only 30 seconds to repeat the process.

How to Patch Major Carpet Damage

Use a utility knife to cut four strips from a carpet remnant, each a little wider and longer than the cuts you plan to make around the damaged part of your carpet. Most wall-to-wall carpet is installed under tension; so to relieve that tension, set the knee kicker 6" to 1 ft. from the area to be cut out and nudge it forward (toward the patch area). If you create a hump in the carpet, you've pushed too hard and need to back off. Now place one of the strips upside down in front of the knee kicker and tack it to the floor at 2" to 4" intervals. Repeat the same process on the other three sides.

Use a marker to draw arrows on tape. Fan the carpet with your hand to see which direction the fibers are woven, and then use the pieces of tape to mark that direction on both the carpet surrounding the damaged area and the remnant you intend to use as a patch. Place a carpet remnant on plywood and cut out a carpet patch slightly larger than the damaged section, using a utility knife. As you cut, use a Phillips screwdriver to push carpet tufts or loops away from the cutting line. Trim loose pile, and then place the patch right side up over the damaged area.

Tool Tip ▸

Knee kickers have teeth that grab the carpet backing. These teeth should be set to grab the backing without grabbing the padding. There is an adjustable knob to do this. You can tell if the knee kicker is grabbing the padding by the increased pressure needed to move it forward. To release the tension just before a damaged area of carpet you intend to patch, place the feet on the floor and use your knee to press it toward the damaged area.

Tack one edge of the patch through the damaged carpet and into the floor, making sure the patch covers the entire damaged area. Use a utility knife to cut out the damaged carpet, following the border of the new patch as a template. If you cut into the carpet padding, use duct tape to mend it. Remove the patch and the damaged carpet square.

Cut four lengths of carpet seam tape, each about 1" longer than an edge of the cut out area, using a utility knife or scissors. Cover half of each strip with a thin layer of seam adhesive and then slip the coated edge of each strip, sticky side up, along the underside edges of the original carpet. Apply more adhesive to the exposed half of tape, and use enough adhesive to fill in the tape weave.

Line up your arrows and press the patch into place. Take care not to press too much, because glue that squeezes up onto the newly laid carpet creates a mess. Use an awl to free tufts or loops of pile crushed in the seam. Lightly brush the pile of the patch to make it blend with the surrounding carpet. Leave the patch undisturbed for 24 hours. Check the drying time on the adhesive used and wait at least this long before removing the carpet tacks.

What If . . . ▸

If you have cushion-backed, fully-bonded carpet, you can follow the instructions above to make a large patch, except:

1. You won't need a knee kicker.
2. You don't need to nail outline strips around the patch area.
3. Use a putty knife to scrape away any dried cement from the hole you make. Some glues may require heat or chemical solvents to effectively remove them.
4. Apply multi-purpose flooring adhesive to the floor with a ³⁄₃₂" trowel.
5. Instead of seam tape, just use a thin bead of cushion-back seam adhesive along the perimeter of the hole.

Sealing Interior Concrete Floors

Concrete is a versatile building material. Most people are accustomed to thinking of concrete primarily as a utilitarian substance, but it can also mimic a variety of flooring types and be a colorful and beautiful addition to any room.

Whether your concrete floor is a practical surface for the garage or an artistic statement of personal style in your dining room, it should be sealed. Concrete is a hard and durable building material, but it is also porous. Consequently, concrete floors are susceptible to staining. Many stains can be removed with the proper cleaner, but sealing and painting prevents oil, grease, and other stains from penetrating the surface in the first place; thus, cleanup is considerably easier.

Prepare the concrete for sealer application by acid etching. Etching opens the pores in concrete surfaces, allowing sealers to bond with it. All smooth or dense concrete surfaces, such as garage floors, should be etched before applying stain. The surface should feel gritty, like 120-grit sandpaper, and allow water to penetrate it. If you're not sure whether your floor needs to be etched or not, it's better to etch. If you don't etch when it is needed, you will have to remove the sealer residue before trying again.

Tools & Materials ▸

Garden hose or pressure washer (for outdoors and garages only)
Stiff bristle broom
Acid-tolerant bucket
Sprinkling can or acid-tolerant pump spray

4"-wide synthetic bristle paint brush
Paint tray
Roller cover with ½" nap
Long-handle paint roller
Wet/dry shop vacuum

Long pants and long-sleeve shirt
Rubber boots
Rubber gloves
Safety goggles
Respirator
Acid etcher

Alkaline-base neutralizer (ammonia, baking soda, or some brand of cleaning solution)
Concrete sealer

Tips for Acid Etching Concrete Floors

A variety of acid etching products is available: Citric acid is a biodegradable acid that does not produce chlorine fumes. It is the safest etcher and the easiest to use, but it may not be strong enough for some very smooth concretes. Sulfamic acid is less aggressive than phosphoric acid or muriatic acid, and it is perhaps the best compromise between strength of solution and safety. Phosphoric acid is a stronger and more noxious acid than the previous two, but it is considerably less dangerous than muriatic acid. It is currently the most popular etching choice. Muriatic acid (hydrochloric acid) is an extremely dangerous acid that quickly reacts and creates very strong fumes. This is an etching solution of last resort. It should only be used by professionals or by the most serious DIYers. Never add water to acid—only add acid to water.

Acids of any kind are dangerous. Use caution when working with acid etches; it is critical that there be adequate ventilation and that you wear protective clothing, including: safety goggles, rubber gloves, rubber boots, long pants, and a long-sleeve shirt. In addition, wear a chlorine respirator—the reaction of any base and acid can release chlorine or hydrogen gas.

Even after degreasing a concrete floor, residual grease or oils can create serious adhesion problems for coatings of sealant or paint. To check whether your floor has been adequately cleaned, pour a glass of water on to the floor. If it is ready for sealing, the water will soak into the surface quickly and evenly. If the water beads, clean the floor again.

How to Acid Etch a Concrete Floor

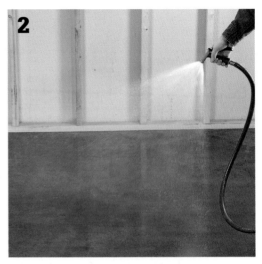

Clean and prepare the surface by first sweeping up all debris. Next, remove all surface muck: mud, wax, and grease. Finally, remove existing paints or coatings.

Saturate the surface with clean water. The surface needs to be wet before acid etching. Use this opportunity to check for any areas where water beads up. If water beads on the surface, contaminants still need to be cleaned off with a suitable cleaner or chemical stripper.

Test your acid-tolerant pump sprayer with water to make sure it releases a wide, even mist. Once you have the spray nozzle set, check the manufacturer's instructions for the etching solution and fill the pump sprayer with the recommended amount of water.

Add the acid etching contents to the water in the acid-tolerant pump sprayer (or sprinkling can). Follow the directions (and mixing proportions) specified by the manufacturer. Use caution.

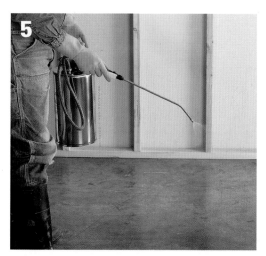

Apply the acid solution. Using the sprinkling can or acid-tolerant pump spray unit, evenly apply the diluted acid solution over the concrete floor. Do not allow acid solution to dry at any time during the etching and cleaning process. Etch small areas at a time, 10 × 10 ft. or smaller. If there is a slope, begin on the low side of the slope and work upward.

Use a stiff bristle broom or scrubber to work the acid solution into the concrete. Let the acid sit for 5–10 minutes, or as indicated by the manufacturer's directions. A mild foaming action indicates that the product is working. If no bubbling or fizzing occurs, stop the process and re-clean the surface thoroughly.

When the fizzing stops, the acid has finished reacting with the alkaline concrete surface. Neutralize any remaining acid by adding a gallon of water to a 5-gallon bucket and then stirring in an alkaline-base neutralizer (options include 1 cup ammonia, 4 cups gardener's lime, a full box of baking soda, or 4 oz. of "Simple Green" cleaning solution).

Use a stiff bristle broom to distribute the neutralizing solution over the entire floor area. Sweep the water around until the fizzing stops and then spray the surface with a hose to rinse it.

(continued)

Use a wet-dry shop vacuum to clean up the rinse water. Although the acid is neutralized, it's a good idea to check your local regulations regarding proper disposal of the neutralized spent acid.

When the floor dries, check for residue by rubbing a dark cloth over a small area of concrete. If any white residue appears, continue the rinsing process. Check for residue again. An inadequate acid rinse is even worse than not acid etching at all when it's time to add the sealant.

If you have any leftover acid you can make it safe for your disposal system by mixing more alkaline solution in the 5-gallon bucket and carefully pouring the acid from the spray unit into the bucket until all of the fizzing stops.

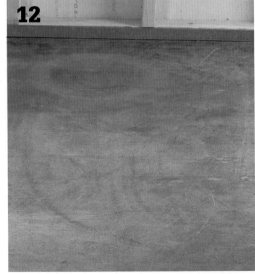

Let the concrete dry for at least 24 hours and sweep it thoroughly. The concrete should now have the texture of 120-grit sandpaper and be able to accept concrete sealant. Mask any exposed sill plates or base trim before sealing.

How to Seal a Concrete Floor

1

Etch, clean, and dry concrete. Mix the sealer in a bucket with a stir stick. Lay painter's tape down for a testing patch. Apply sealer to this area and allow to dry to ensure desired appearance.

2

Use wide painter's tape to protect walls and then, using a good quality 4"-wide synthetic bristle paintbrush, coat the perimeter with sealer.

3

Use a long-handled paint roller with a ½" nap sleeve to apply an even coat to the rest of the surface. Do small sections at a time (about 2 × 3 feet). Work in one orientation. Avoid lap marks by always maintaining a wet edge. Do not work the area once the coating has partially dried. Allow surface to dry, usually 8 to 12 hours.

4

After the first coat has dried, apply the second coat at an orientation 90° from the first coat.

5

Clean tools according to manufacturer's directions.

Salvaging Lumber

Ⓞne of the biggest challenges to home repair is getting rid of things. Rather than hiring a dumpster or cutting the old supplies into little bits and throwing them out with your normal trash stream, consider re-using them. Not only is it cheaper, it's also environmentally friendly.

Any time you do demolition work around your home, you generate plenty of salvageable "waste." In fact, you'll have a wealth of different members and wood pieces from which to select. For instance, plank boards from siding are often milled to add a tongue and groove so that they can be used as flooring. You can use the same process to rip plank flooring down to strips, if that's the look you're after. Looking for 4 × 4s to create a chunky, eye-catching trestle table? If you can't find just the right pieces, consider laminating reclaimed 2 × 4s instead. Keep in mind that much of the older lumber in buildings or salvage yards is not nominal and will be hard to adapt to a project that mixes old and new wood. It's usually best to use reclaimed lumber by itself. Be prepared to change your plans as well, because you may not be able to find certain sizes or species no matter how hard you look. Being adaptable and creative is key to successfully reclaiming any building material, especially wood. You should be ready to take advantage of what you find—even if it isn't necessarily what you were looking for.

Laminated Beams ▸

Separating laminated members is often necessary to salvage pieces for reuse. For instance, delaminating a header of sandwiched 2 × 8s can yield all the usable wood you'll need for a table. Pry laminated pieces apart with long pry or crow bars by simultaneously pushing and pulling to create separation. Separating larger laminated sections will be easier with two people, providing extra muscle to force the pry bars in opposite directions.

The time-tested method of prying nails out with the claw of a claw hammer works as effectively with reclaimed wood as it does with new lumber. Use a scrap of plywood or other soft pad under the head of the hammer to increase leverage and protect the surface of the wood.

Types of Reclaimed Lumber

Timbers and Beams. The most plentiful reclaimed lumber comes in the form of various-sized structural members. The timbers can run 2 foot square or larger and are sometimes 20 feet long. Smaller beams can be just as impressive, and headers 4 to 6 inches thick are common as well. The beauty of large timbers is that they can fill both practical and aesthetic roles. They can be used in their original form for a rough, rustic look or resurfaced and refinished to serve as a sleek exposed structural element in a home. Smaller members are often used for making tables or other furnishings, including built-ins such as bookshelves. Framing members of intriguing wood species can be laminated, sawn, and finished to craft remarkable countertops.

Planks. Wood planks are reclaimed from floors, subfloors, and siding. The planks can be used in a number of ways. Depending on where the planks come from, how they were originally cut, and what surface appearance aging has left on them, the planks can be used as is, lightly surfaced and refinished to retain the marks of age, or completely resurfaced to recapture the original grain pattern and color. Planks are most often squared off or milled shiplap. But plain planks can be milled to serve as tongue-and-groove flooring or paneling. They can also be ripped to produce strip flooring.

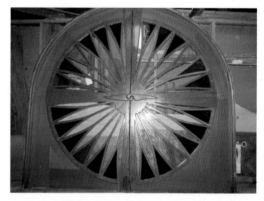

Flooring. Much of the usable wood recovered from older buildings is flooring. Because plank flooring was the more common style prior to the mid-twentieth century, most reclaimed wood flooring comes in the form of planks. The planks can be tongue-and-groove, shiplapped, or butt joined. Shiplapped is more common the older the building is, because it was easier to manufacture. Older, wide planks are also usually longer than today's strips, often running 8 feet or longer. Squared planks such as siding are generally milled with a tongue-and-groove before being used for a new floor. Think twice before ripping planks to create strip floors; the wider surface of a plank allows for more of the grain and coloring to show.

Doors. Reclaimed doors can add flair to different areas of a home, from the kitchen to the front entryway. Doors salvaged from older buildings are usually solid wood, but styles are nearly limitless. Doors to fit more standard openings are available in just about every panel configuration imaginable. You'll find older interior doors as well, including solid pocket doors, and doors with leaded glass inserts. The trick to reusing any found door is choosing one that is the right shape and close to the measurements of the opening you're looking to fill. Then it's just a case of trimming and refitting the door for its new role or enlarging or shrinking the door rough opening. Or, use the door to build a coffee table or other re-purposeful furnishing.

Tips for Removing Nails from Wood

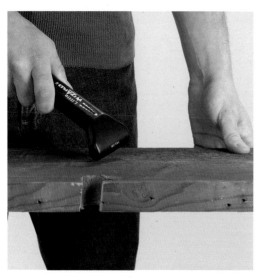

Finding the nail is the first step in removing it. That's why a handheld metal detector is a must for checking reclaimed lumber. A hidden nail or screw can destroy a saw blade and cause serious injury to the operator.

Nippers are a good choice for removing nails carefully, to limit damage to the board face. However, they will not work on sunken nails or flush nail heads because the pinchers need room to close over the nail body to pull it out.

Extractor pulling pliers are specifically designed for maximum leverage. They are quite effective for removing nails and other fasteners with a minimum amount of damage to the face of the wood. They are also easy and quick to use but less effective on stubborn nails in hardwood.

Use a cat's paw for large, stubborn, embedded nails. Tap the slot of the tool under the nail head by rapping on it with a hammer. Pull back on the handle. Use a scrap of wood under the cat's paw head for extra leverage. A cat's paw is a blunt instrument and a last recourse, usually reserved for rough or hand-hewn timbers because it will likely mar the surface.

How to Install Reclaimed Floorboards

Reclaiming some wood building materials directly from an existing structure can be a challenge. Structural members such as timbers and beams must be extracted carefully to prevent wholesale collapse. Others, such as siding, are arduous to remove and will need exceptional amounts of prep to be reused. But wood flooring is one of the easiest and most rewarding materials to salvage. Do it right, and you may not even need to refinish the reclaimed flooring after you re-install it.

The process is fairly straightforward and is basically the reverse of installing a wood floor. Start by clearing the room you're working in and remove shoe or other base moldings. Remove the first and possibly second row of boards on the tongue side of the floor.

This may require destroying one or more boards to gain access. Do that by using a pry bar on damaged flooring, or a circular saw and pry bar, to cut into and tear out boards so that you have clear access for prying out the adjacent rows.

Removing planks from that point is relatively easy. Slide the tongue of a pry bar under the tongue of the plank next to a nail, and pry the nail up. Do this at each nail location until the plank is completely loose. Then pry up and toward you to release it from the next row. Continue removing planks, taking care not to damage the tongues as you remove the boards. Remove all the nails as you work, and check boards for nails before finally placing them neatly in stacks separated by bolsters.

Acclimate Your Flooring ▸

Stack reclaimed flooring neatly, well supported by bolsters. If you are planning on using the flooring with its existing finish intact, separate the layers with building paper.

How to Mill Tongues and Grooves into Reclaimed Planks

1

Blade guard removed for clairty

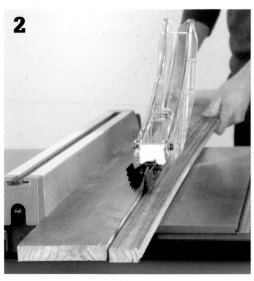

2

Joint one edge of each plank using a jointer. If you don't have a jointer, you can joint the edge using a table saw with a jointer jig. A properly jointed edge will be necessary for the boards to fit snugly together when laid as a floor.

Use your table saw to rip the opposite edge of each board so that it is perfectly parallel to the jointed edge.

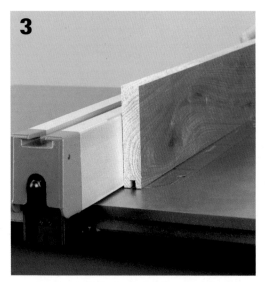

3

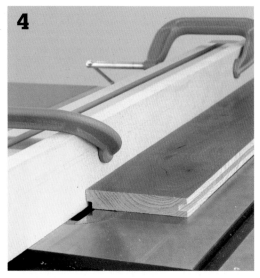

4

Saw the grooves first. Set a dado blade to the appropriate height, and set the table saw fence so that the groove runs along the middle of the edge. Stack dado blades as necessary to cut wider grooves in thicker stock. Cut the first groove in a test piece.

Reset the fence to cut the tongues. Use a short or scrap piece to cut the first tongue. Err on the side of cutting tongues too thick because you can always cut more off, but you'll be in trouble if the tongues do not fit snugly.

5

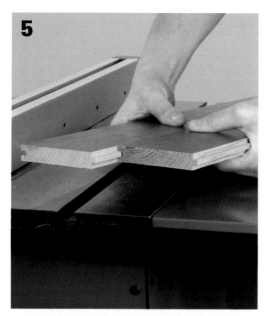

Check the fit of the tongue into the groove, with both pieces lying flat. The fit should be snug enough that you have to apply some force to join the two pieces.

6

Once you're certain that the measurements are all correct, cut all the grooves first. Check each for fit, using the tongue on the scrap piece. Finally, cut all the tongues on the other edges of the planks.

7

Check all the planks one last time, paying special attention to any burrs or imperfections in the tongues and grooves. Sand down any spots that might prove troublesome when installing the floor.

Installing a Reclaimed Floor

Perhaps the most common use for reclaimed wood is as flooring. And the most common type of reclaimed floor is a wide plank floor. In fact, the planks can be as wide as 10 inches. Although this means that the planks can be a little more cumbersome to handle than modern hardwood strip flooring, take heart: wide plank floors go down much quicker than their strip counterparts.

The look of a wide plank floor is impressive. It can make a space seem larger, and a plank floor can visually anchor the room. Keep in mind that each plank presents much more visual area than a strip would. An oddly colored or patterned strip over the span of a wood floor would hardly get noticed; in a plank floor, an odd duck will stick out like a sore thumb. You can minimize the impact any unusual-looking plank has on the floor's overall appearance by shuffling it to an outside edge of the floor. If you're lucky, you may even need to rip it down to fit, minimizing its impact even more.

The finish you choose may affect how you work with the wood during installation. If you're planning on sanding and refinishing the floor entirely, you can proceed to work as quickly and efficiently as possible. However, if you've chosen your planks for their historical finish, you'll want to work with soft gloves and be careful with tools, such as power nailers, which sit right on the surface of planks. Also be careful in moving planks around as you pull them off the stack. Any noticeable scratches will probably rule out keeping the vintage finish.

Lastly, it's a good idea to face-nail and plug wide planks if they were previously pegged, or if you expect that the space will experience regular variations in temperature. A cupped or warping plank floor will not be the showcase for which you chose reclaimed wood in the first place.

Tools & Materials ▶

Tape measure	Pry bar
Staple gun	Flooring planks
Drill/driver	Underlayment (rosin paper)
Chalk line	Nails
Hammer	Scrap wood
Mallet	Eye and ear protection
Flooring nailer	Work gloves
Miter saw	

Salvaged white oak floorboards

8d finish nails

Strip nails for flooring nailer

Salvaged floorboards come in varieties and sizes that can be hard to find in new material, such as the quartersawn white oak flooring seen here. Sanded and finished, it has a rich color (inset).

How to Install Reclaimed Floorboards

Measure the room and double-check that you have all the planks you'll need to cover the surface and account for waste. Make sure the subfloor is clean and free of loose nails or other debris. If the boards have a distinctive pattern or coloration that will affect positioning, decide on the positions and number the planks.

Roll underlayment out to cover the subfloor surface. Staple it to the subfloor with a staple gun. Overlap each strip by several inches, and cut as necessary with a utility knife equipped with a new blade.

Locate floor joists, nail a brad at each end, and snap chalk lines over the centerline of each floor joist. Nail and snap another chalk line perpendicular to these lines, between ¼" and ½" from the edge of the starting wall.

Drill pilot holes every 8" to 10" along the length of the planks that you'll use as a starter row. Drill the holes in the face, along the inside groove edge that will face the wall. This is to prevent any cracking or damage during face-nailing of the first row.

(continued)

5

Ensure that the first plank is properly positioned with its inside edge along the starter chalk line. Hammer finish nails through the pilot holes, until the heads are just above the surface. Sink the nails using a nailset.

6

Drill pilot holes in the first plank's tongue, every 8" to 10" along its length. Drill at a 45˚ angle into the joist locations. Blind nail a finish nail into each hole, and use a nailset to sink it.

7

Snug new rows in place with a scrap piece (milled with a groove slightly larger than the tongues on your planks) set against the tongue. Tap the piece lightly with a wood mallet until the new plank is tight against the existing row.

8

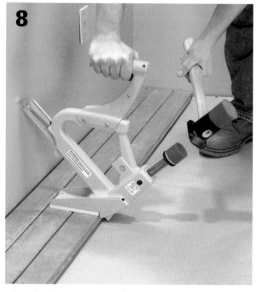

After the first row, nail planks into place with a power nailer. Position the lip over the edge of the plank, and hit the strike button with a rubber mallet.

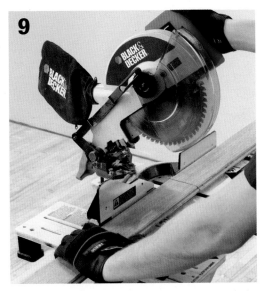

9

Stagger the planks to create a brickwork pattern. Cut planks face up, using a miter saw equipped with an 80-tooth blade. Saw end planks so that the cut end will face the wall.

10

If you encounter a plank that is bowed or warped and won't easily snug up to the preceding row, make a wedge from a scrap 2 × 4 by sawing diagonally from one corner to the other. Nail a 2 × 4 scrap to the floor, and tap the wedge into position to force the plank into place for nailing.

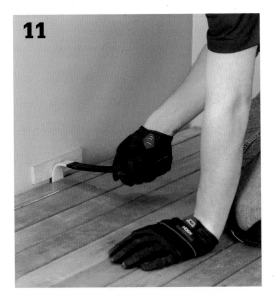

11

Rip final-row planks to the width necessary to fit them between the next-to-last row of planks and the wall, leaving an expansion gap of between ¼" and ½". Pull the plank into place with a pry bar, and then face-nail using the same process you used on the first row.

12

Sand and finish the floor as desired, or leave a pre-finished or distressed surface as is. Stain or finish shoe molding as necessary, and nail it into place around perimeter of room.

Repairing Drywall

Patching holes and concealing popped nails are common drywall repairs. Small holes can be filled directly, but larger patches must be supported with some kind of backing, such as plywood. To repair holes left by nails or screws, dimple the hole slightly with the handle of a utility knife or drywall knife and fill it with spackle or joint compound.

Use joint tape anywhere the drywall's face paper or joint tape has torn or peeled away. Always cut away any loose drywall material, face paper, or joint tape from the damaged area, trimming back to solid drywall material.

All drywall repairs require three coats of joint compound, just like in new installations. Lightly sand your repairs before painting, or adding texture.

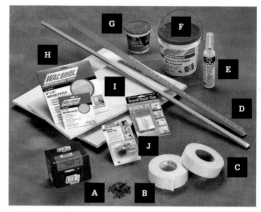

Most wallboard problems can be remedied with basic wallboard materials and specialty materials: (A) wallboard screws; (B) paper joint tape; (C) self-adhesive fiberglass mesh tape; (D) corner bead; (E) paintable latex or silicone caulk; (F) all-purpose joint compound; (G) lightweight spackling compound; (H) wallboard repair patches; (I) scraps of wallboard; (J) and wallboard repair clips.

Tools & Materials ▸

Drill or screwgun	Hacksaw	150-grit sandpaper	Self-adhesive
Hammer	Fine metal file	Wood scraps	fiberglass mesh
Utility knife	1¼" wallboard	Paper joint tape	joint tape
Wallboard knives	screws	Drywall wet-sander	Wallboard repair patch
Framing square	All-purpose	Plywood or lumber strips	Wallboard repair clips
Wallboard saw	joint compound	Studs	Latex or silicone caulk
Rasp	Lightweight spackle	Metal corner beads	Caulk gun

To repair a popped nail, drive a wallboard screw 2" above or below the nail, so it pulls the panel tight to the framing. Scrape away loose paint or compound, then drive the popped nail ⅟₁₆" below the surface. Apply three coats of joint compound to cover the holes.

If wallboard is dented, without cracks or tears in the face paper, just fill the hole with lightweight spackling or all-purpose joint compound, let it dry, and sand it smooth.

How to Repair Cracks & Gashes

Use a utility knife to cut away loose drywall or face paper and widen the crack into a "V"; the notch will help hold the joint compound.

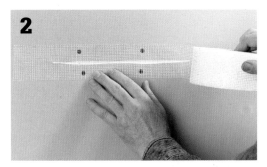

Push along the sides of the crack with your hand. If the drywall moves, secure the panel with 1¼" drywall screws driven into the nearest framing members. Cover the crack and screws with self-adhesive mesh tape.

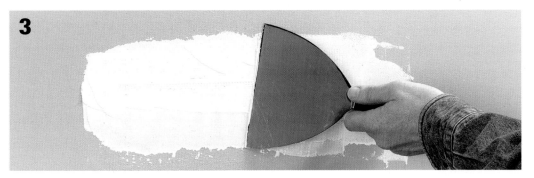

Cover the tape with compound, lightly forcing it into the mesh, then smooth it off, leaving just enough to conceal the tape. Add two more coats, in successively broader and thinner coats to blend the patch into the surrounding area.

For cracks at corners or ceilings, cut through the existing seam and cut away any loose drywall material or tape, then apply a new length of tape or inside-corner bead and two coats of joint compound.

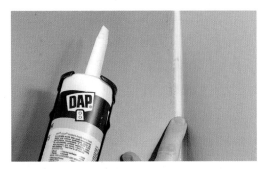

Variation: For small cracks at corners, apply a thin bead of paintable latex or silicone caulk over the crack, then use your finger to smooth the caulk into the corner.

How to Patch Small Holes in Drywall

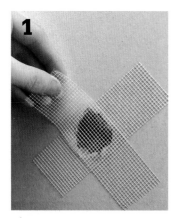

1

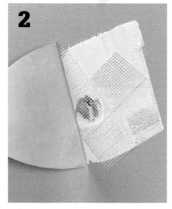

2

3

Trim away any broken drywall, face paper, or joint tape around the hole, using a utility knife. Cover the hole with crossed strips of self-adhesive mesh tape.

Cover the tape with all-purpose joint compound, lightly forcing it into the mesh, then smooth it off, leaving just enough to conceal the tape.

Add two more coats of compound in successively broader and thinner coats to blend the patch into the surrounding area. Use a drywall wet sander to smooth the repair area.

Other Options for Patching Small Holes in Drywall

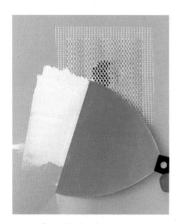

Drywall repair patches: Cover the damaged area with the self-adhesive patch; the thin metal plate provides support and the fiberglass mesh helps hold the joint compound.

Beveled drywall patch: Bevel the edges of the hole with a drywall saw, then cut a drywall patch to fit. Trim the beveled patch until it fits tight and flush with the panel surface. Apply plenty of compound to the beveled edges, then push the patch into the hole. Finish with paper tape and three coats of compound.

Drywall paper-flange patch: Cut a drywall patch a couple inches larger than the hole. Mark the hole on the backside of the patch, then score and snap along the lines. Remove the waste material, keeping the face paper "flange" intact. Apply compound around the hole, insert the patch, and embed the flange into the compound. Finish with two additional coats.

How to Patch Large Holes in Drywall

1

2

3

Outline the damaged area, using a framing square. (Cutting four right angles makes it easier to measure and cut the patch.) Use a drywall saw to cut along the outline.

Cut plywood or lumber backer strips a few inches longer than the height of the cutout. Fasten the strips to the back side of the drywall, using 1¼" drywall screws.

Cut a drywall patch ⅛" smaller than the cutout dimensions, and fasten it to the backer strips with screws. Apply mesh joint tape over the seams. Finish the seams with three coats of compound.

How to Patch Large Holes with Repair Clips

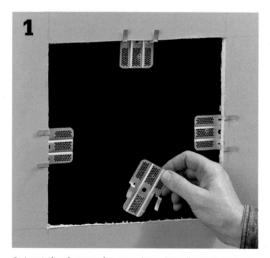

1

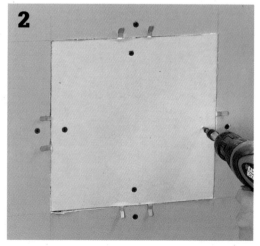

2

Cut out the damaged area, using a drywall saw. Center one repair clip on each edge of the hole. Using the provided drywall screws, drive one screw through the wall and into the clips; position the screws from the edge and centered between the clip's tabs.

Cut a new drywall patch to fit in the hole. Fasten the patch to the clips, placing drywall screws adjacent to the previous screw locations and ¾" from the edge. Remove the tabs from the clips, then finish the joints with tape and three coats of compound.

How to Patch Over a Removed Door or Window

1

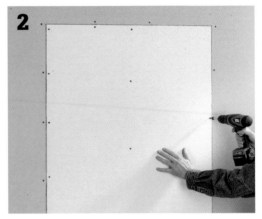

2

Frame the opening with studs spaced 16" O.C. and partially beneath the existing drywall—the new joints should break at the center of framing. Secure the existing drywall to the framing with screws driven every 12" around the perimeter. If the wall is insulated, fill the stud cavity with insulation.

Using drywall the same thickness as the existing wall, cut the patch piece about ¼" shorter than the opening. Position the patch against the framing so there is a ⅛" joint around the perimeter, and fasten in place with drywall screws every 12". Finish the butt joints with paper tape and three coats of compound.

How to Repair Metal Corner Bead

1

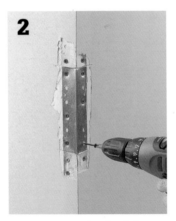

2

3

Secure the bead above and below the damaged area with 1¼" drywall screws. To remove the damaged section, cut through the spine and then the flanges, using a hacksaw held parallel to the floor. Remove the damaged section, and scrape away any loose drywall and compound.

Cut a new corner bead to fit the opening exactly, then align the spine perfectly with the existing piece and secure with drywall screws driven ¼" from the flange edge; alternate sides with each screw to keep the piece straight.

File the seams with a fine metal file to ensure a smooth transition between pieces. If you can't easily smooth the seams, cut a new replacement piece and start over. Hide the repair with three coats of drywall compound.

Repairing Plaster

Plaster walls are created by building up layers of plaster to form a hard, durable wall surface. Behind the plaster itself is a gridlike layer of wood, metal, or rock lath that holds the plaster in place. Keys, formed when the base plaster is squeezed through the lath, hold the dried plaster to the ceiling or walls.

Before you begin any plaster repair, make sure the surrounding area is in good shape. If the lath is deteriorated or the plaster is soft, call a professional.

Use a latex bonding liquid to ensure a good bond and a tight, crack-free patch. Bonding liquid also eliminates the need to wet the plaster and lath to prevent premature drying and shrinkage, which could ruin the repair.

Tools & Materials ▸

Wallboard knives
Paintbrush
Utility knife
Lightweight spackle
All-purpose
   joint compound
Patching plaster

Fiberglass mesh tape
Latex bonding liquid
150-grit sandpaper
Paint
Wallboard for patches
Wire mesh
Aviation snips

Spackle is used to conceal cracks, gashes, and small holes in plaster. Some new spackling compounds start out pink and dry white so you can see when they're ready to be sanded and painted. Use lightweight spackle for low-shrinkage and one-application fills.

How to Fill Dents & Small Holes in Plaster

1

Scrape or sand away any loose plaster or peeling paint to establish a solid base for the new plaster.

2

Fill the hole with lightweight spackle. Apply the spackle with the smallest knife that will span the damaged area. Let the spackle dry, following the manufacturer's instructions.

3

Sand the patch lightly with 150-grit production sandpaper. Wipe the dust away with a clean cloth, then prime and paint the area, feathering the paint to blend the edges.

How to Patch Large Holes in Plaster

Sand or scrape any texture or loose paint from the area around the hole to create a smooth, firm edge. Use a wallboard knife to test the plaster around the edges of the damaged area. Scrape away all loose or soft plaster.

Apply latex bonding liquid liberally around the edges of the hole and over the base lath to ensure a crack-free bond between the old and new plaster.

Mix patching plaster as directed by the manufacturer, and use a wallboard knife or trowel to apply it to the hole. Fill shallow holes with a single coat of plaster.

For deeper holes, apply a shallow first coat, then scratch a crosshatch pattern in the wet plaster. Let it dry, then apply second coat of plaster. Let the plaster dry, and sand it lightly.

Use texture paint or wallboard compound to recreate any surface texture. Practice on heavy cardboard until you can duplicate the wall's surface. Prime and paint the area to finish the repair.

Variation: Holes in plaster can also be patched with wallboard. Score the damaged surface with a utility knife and chisel out the plaster back to the center of the closest framing members. Cut a wallboard patch to size, then secure in place with wallboard screws driven every 4" into the framing. Finish joints as you would standard wallboard joints.

How to Patch Holes Cut in Plaster

Cut a piece of wire mesh larger than the hole, using aviation snips. Tie a length of twine at the center of the mesh and insert the mesh into the wall cavity. Twist the wire around a dowel that is longer than the width of the hole, until the mesh pulls tight against the opening. Apply latex bonding liquid to the mesh and the edges of the hole.

Apply a coat of patching plaster, forcing it into the mesh and covering the edges of the hole. Scratch a cross-hatch pattern in the wet plaster, then allow it to dry. Remove the dowel and trim the wire holding the mesh. Apply a second coat, filling the hole completely. Add texture. Let dry, then scrape away any excess plaster. Sand, prime, and paint the area.

How to Repair Cracks in Plaster

Scrape away any texture or loose plaster around the crack. Using a utility knife, cut back the edges of the crack to create a keyway (inset).

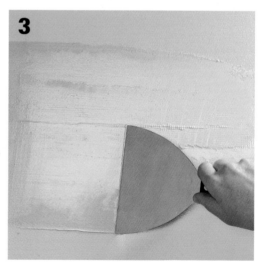

Work joint compound into the keyway using a 6" knife, then embed mesh tape into the compound, lightly forcing the compound through the mesh. Smooth the compound, leaving just enough to conceal the tape.

Add two more coats of compound, in successively broader and thinner coats, to blend the patch into the surrounding area. Lightly sand, then retexture the repair area to match the wall. Prime and paint it to finish the repair.

Replacing Paneling

Despite its durability, prefinished sheet paneling occasionally requires repairs. Many scuff marks can be removed with a light coat of paste wax, and most small scratches can be disguised with a touchup stick.

Paneling manufacturers do not recommend trying to spot-sand or refinish prefinished paneling.

The most common damage to paneling are water damage and punctures. The only way to repair major damage is to replace the affected sheets.

If the paneling is more than a few years old, it may be difficult to locate matching pieces. If you can't find any at lumber yards or building centers, try salvage yards. Buy the panels in advance so that you can condition them to the room before installing them. To condition the paneling, place it in the room, standing on its long edge. Place spacers between the sheets so air can circulate around each one. Let the paneling stand for 24 hours if it will be installed above grade, and 48 hours if it will be installed below grade.

Before you go any further, find out what's behind the paneling. Building Codes often require that paneling be backed with wallboard. The support provided by the wallboard keeps the paneling from warping and provides an extra layer of sound protection. However, if there is wallboard behind the paneling, it may need repairs as well, particularly if you're dealing with water damage. And removing damaged paneling may be more difficult if it's glued to wallboard or a masonry wall. In any case, it's best to have a clear picture of the situation before you start cutting into a wall.

Finally, turn off the electricity to the area and remove all receptacle covers and switch plates on the sheets of paneling that need to be replaced.

Most scuffs in paneling can be polished out using paste wax. To use, make sure the panel surface is clean and dust free, then apply a thin even coat of paste wax using a clean soft cloth. Work in small areas using a circular motion. Allow to dry until a paste becomes hazy (5 to 10 minutes), then buff with a new cloth. Apply a second coat if necessary.

Touch-up and fill sticks can help hide most scratches in prefinished paneling. Wax touch-up sticks are like crayons—simply trace over the scratch with the stick. To use a fill stick, apply a small amount of the material into the surface and smooth it over the scratch using a flexible putty knife. Wipe away excess fill with a clean, soft cloth.

Tools & Materials ▸

Wallboard knife	Spray paint
Putty knife	Panel adhesive
Flat pry bar	Color-matched
Framing square	paneling nails
Linoleum knife	Shims
Hammer	Finish nails
Chisel	Putty sticks
Caulk gun	Wood filler
Rubber mallet	Paste wax
Nail set	Eye and ear protection
Replacement panels	Work gloves

How to Replace a Strip of Paneling

Carefully remove the baseboard and top moldings. Use a wallboard or putty knife to create a gap, then insert a pry bar and pull the trim away from the wall. Remove all the nails.

Draw a line on the panel from top to bottom, 3-in. to 4-in. from each edge of the panel. Hold a framing square along the line and cut with a linoleum knife. Using a fair amount of pressure, you should cut through the panel within two passes. If you have trouble, use a hammer and chisel to break the panel along the scored lines.

Insert a pry bar under the panel at the bottom, and pull up and away from the wall, removing nails as you go. Once the center portion of the panel is removed, scrape away any old adhesive, using a putty knife. Repair the vapor barrier if damaged; below-grade applications may require a layer of 4mil polyethylene between outside walls and paneling. Measure and cut the new panel, including any necessary cutouts, and test-fit the panel.

On the back of the panel, apply zigzag beads of panel adhesive from top to bottom every 16", about 2" in from each edge, and around cutouts. Tack the panel into position at the top, using color-matched paneling nails. When the adhesive has set up, press the panel to the wall and tap along stud lines with a rubber mallet, creating a tight bond between the adhesive and wall. Drive finish nails at the base of the panel to hold it while the adhesive dries. Replace all trim pieces and fill nail holes with wood filler.

Maintaining Wall Tile

As we've said throughout this book, ceramic tile is durable and nearly maintenance-free, but like every other material in your house, it can fail or develop problems. The most common problem with ceramic tile involves damaged grout. Failed grout is unattractive, but the real danger is that it offers a point of entry for water. Given a chance to work its way beneath grout, water can destroy a tile base and eventually wreck an entire installation. It's important to regrout ceramic tile as soon as you see signs of damage.

Another potential problem for tile installations is damaged caulk. In tub and shower stalls and around sinks and backsplashes, the joints between the tile and the fixtures are sealed with caulk. The caulk eventually deteriorates, leaving an entry point for water. Unless the joints are recaulked, seeping water will destroy the tile base and the wall.

In bathrooms, towel rods, soap dishes, and other accessories can work loose from walls, especially if they weren't installed correctly or aren't supported properly. For maximum holding power, anchor new accessories to wall studs or blocking. If no studs or blocking are available, use special fasteners, such as toggle bolts or molly bolts, to anchor the accessories directly to the surface of the underlying wall. To hold screws firmly in place in ceramic tile walls, drill pilot holes and insert plastic sleeves, which expand when screws are driven into them.

Tools & Materials ▸

Awl	Tile adhesive
Utility knife	Masking tape
Trowel	Grout
Grout float	Cloth or rag
Hammer	Rubbing alcohol
Chisel	Mildew remover
Small pry bar	Silicone or latex caulk
Eye protection	Sealer
Replacement tile	Sponge

How to Regrout Wall Tile

Use an awl or utility knife to scrape out the old grout completely, leaving a clean bed for the new grout.

Clean and rinse the grout joints, then spread grout over the entire tile surface, using a rubber grout float or sponge. Work the grout well into the joints and let it set slightly.

Wipe away excess grout with a damp sponge. When the grout is dry, wipe away the residue and polish the tiles with a dry cloth.

How to Recaulk a Joint

Start with a completely dry surface. Scrape out the old caulk and clean the joint with a cloth dipped in rubbing alcohol. If this is a bathtub or sink, fill it with water to weight it down.

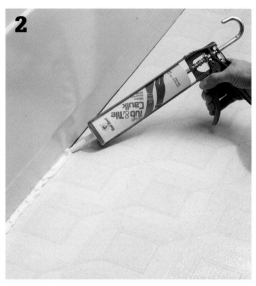

Cut the tip off caulk cartridges at a 45° angle and then make a flat cut at the top with a utility knife. This will allow you to deliver a smooth bead that is not too thin or too heavy.

Clean the joint with a product that kills mildew spores; let it dry. Fill the joint with silicone or latex caulk.

Wet your fingertip with cold water, then use your finger to smooth the caulk into a cove shape. After the caulk hardens, use a utility knife to trim away any excess.

How to Replace Built-in Wall Accessories

Carefully remove the damaged accessory. Scrape away any remaining adhesive or grout. Apply dry-set tile adhesive to the back side of the new accessory, then press it firmly in place.

Use masking tape to hold the accessory in place while the adhesive dries. Let the mortar dry completely (12 to 24 hours), then grout and seal the area.

How to Replace Surface-mounted Accessories

Lift the accessory up and off the mounting plate. If the mounting plate screws are driven into studs or blocking, simply hang the new accessory. If not, add hardware such as molly bolts, toggle bolts, or plastic anchor sleeves.

Put a dab of silicone caulk over the pilot holes and the tips of the screws before inserting them. Let the caulk dry, then install the new fixture on the mounting plate.

How to Remove & Replace Broken Wall Tiles

1

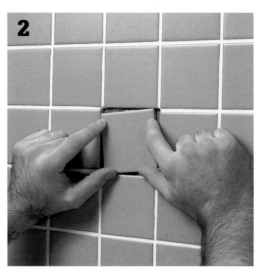

2

Carefully scrape away the grout from the surrounding joints, using a utility knife or an awl. Break the damaged tile into small pieces, using a hammer and chisel. Remove the broken pieces, then scrape away debris or old adhesive from the open area.

If the tile to be replaced is a cut tile, cut a new one to match. Test-fit the new tile and make sure it sits flush with the field. Spread adhesive on the back of the replacement tile and place it in the hole, twisting it slightly. Use masking tape to hold the tile in place for 24 hours so the adhesive can dry.

3

4

Remove the tape, then apply premixed grout, using a sponge or grout float. Let the grout set slightly, then tool it with a rounded object such as a toothbrush handle. Wipe away excess grout with a damp cloth.

Let the grout dry for an hour, then polish the tile with a clean, dry cloth.

Repairing Wallcoverings

oosened seams and bubbles are common wallcovering problems, but both are easy to remedy using a little adhesive and a sponge. For papers that are compatible with water, use a clean, damp sponge. For other types of papers (grasscloth or flocked wallcoverings, for example), clean fingers are probably the best choice.

Scratches, tears or obvious stains can be patched so successfully that the patch is difficult to spot. Whenever you hang wallcoverings, save remnants for future repairs. It's also a good idea to record the name of the manufacturer as well as the style and run numbers of the wallcoverings. Write this information on a piece of masking tape and put it on the back of a switchplate in the room.

If you need to patch an area of wallcovering but don't have remnants available, you can remove a section of wallcovering from an inconspicuous spot, such as inside a closet or behind a door. You can camouflage the spot by painting the hole with a color that blends into the background of the wallcovering.

Tools & Materials ▸

Edge roller
Syringe-type
   adhesive applicator
Sponge
Utility knife

Adhesive
Removable tape
Wallcovering
   remnants
Eye protection

How to Fix a Bubble

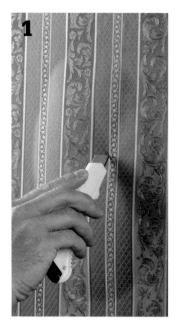

Cut a slit through the bubble, using a sharp razor knife. If there is a pattern in the wallcovering, cut along a line in the pattern to hide the slit.

Insert the tip of a glue applicator through the slit and apply adhesive sparingly to the wall under the wallcovering.

Press the wallcovering gently to rebond it. Use a clean, damp sponge to press the flap down and wipe away excess glue.

How to Patch Wallcovering

1

Fasten a scrap of matching wallcovering over the damaged portion with drafting tape, so that the patterns match.

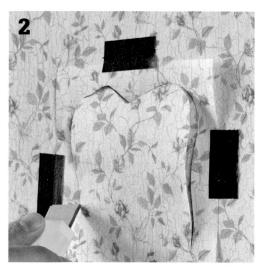

2

Holding a utility knife blade at a 90° angle to the wall, cut through both layers of wallcovering. If the wallcovering has strong pattern lines, cut along the lines to hide the seams. With less definite patterns, cut irregular lines.

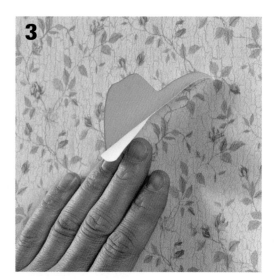

3

Remove the scrap and patch, then peel away the damaged wallcovering. Apply adhesive to the back of the patch and position it in the hole so that the pattern matches. Rinse the patch area with a damp sponge.

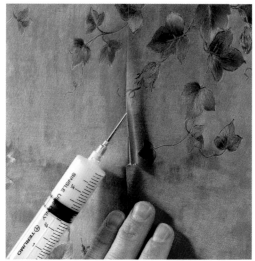

VARIATION: Lift the edge of the wallcovering seam and insert the tip of a glue applicator under it. Squirt adhesive onto the wall and gently press the seam flat. Let the repair stand for ½ hour, then smooth the seam lightly with a seam roller. Wipe the seam lightly with a damp sponge.

Repairing Ceilings

Most ceiling repairs are relatively simple: the techniques used to repair wallboard walls apply to ceilings as well, while sagging panels can be refastened or replaced easily; the edges of acoustical tiles make it easy to remove and replace a single tile; and textures can be matched with a little practice on a scrap of cardboard or simply removed altogether.

However, plaster, by contrast, is difficult to work with, and replastering is not an option for most homeowners. While minor repairs are manageable, widespread failure can be dangerous. If you find large spongy areas or extensive sags consult a professional.

Aerosol touch-up products are available for small repairs to ceilings with popcorn and orange peel textures. Use a wallboard knife to scrap away the existing texture at the damaged area and slightly around it. Make any necessary repairs, then spray on the aerosol texture carefully to blend the new texture with the existing ceiling.

Tools & Materials ▸

Texture touch-up product	Pressure sprayer	Acoustic ceiling tile	Drywall screws and washers
Eye protection	Wallboard knife	Construction adhesive	Work gloves
Sheet plastic	Masking tape	Caulk gun	
	Utility knife	Drill and bit	

How to Remove Popcorn Ceiling Texture

To protect floors and ease cleanup later, line floors with 6-mil plastic, then cover with corrugated cardboard to provide a non-slip surface. Caution: Popcorn ceilings in houses built prior to 1980 may contain asbestos. Contact your local building department for regulations governing asbestos removal.

Using a pressure sprayer, dampen the ceiling with a mixture of a teaspoon of liquid detergent per gallon of water. Allow 20 minutes for the mixture to soak in, rewetting as necessary.

Scrape texture from the ceiling using a 6-in. wallboard knife. Be careful not to cut into the wallboard surface. After all texture is removed, sand rough spots, then carefully roll up and dispose of the plastic and debris. Patch any damaged areas with joint compound, then prime and paint.

How to Replace Acoustical Ceiling Tile

Cut out the center section of the damaged tile with a utility knife. Slide the edges away from the surrounding tiles.

Trim the upper lip of the grooved edges of the new tile, using a straightedge. If necessary, also remove one of the tongues.

At the ceiling, apply construction adhesive to the furring strips. Install the new tile, tongue first, and press it into the adhesive. *TIP: To hold large tiles in place while the glue dries, lay a flat board across the tile, then prop a 2 × 4 post between the board and the floor.*

How to Raise a Sagging Wallboard Ceiling

Position a T-brace under the lowest point of the sagging area with the bottom end on a piece of plywood or hardboard on the floor. Nudge it forward until the sagging panels are tight to the joists. If fasteners pop through the surface, drive them back in.

Remove loose tape and compound at joints between loose panels. Starting at one end, drive wallboard screws with broad, thin washers every 4" through the center of the joint and into the joists. In the field of panel, drive screws 2" from existing fasteners.

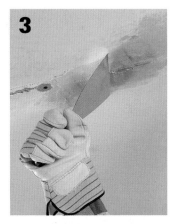

When the area is securely fastened, remove the T-brace. Scrape off any loose chips of paint or wallboard around joints and screws, then fill with compound. Cover large cracks or gaps with fiberglass tape before applying the compound.

Repairing Water-damaged Walls & Ceilings

A sure sign of a water problem is discoloration and bubbling on the ceiling surface. Water from a leaky roof or pipe above will quickly find a low spot or a joint between wallboard panels, soaking through to a visible surface in a matter of minutes. Water in joints is especially damaging because it ruins the edges of two panels at once. If you have a water problem, be sure to fix the leak and allow the damaged wallboard to dry thoroughly before making any repairs.

Whenever water or moisture infiltrates a house, there is always a concern regarding mold. Mold grows where water and nutrients are present—damp wallboard paper can provide such an environment. You can use a damp rag and baking soda or a small amount of detergent to clean up small areas of mold (less than one square yard), though you should wear goggles, rubber gloves, and a dust mask to prevent contact with mold spores. If mold occupies more area than this, you may have a more serious problem. Contact a mold abatement specialist for assessment and remediation. To help prevent mold growth, use exhaust fans and dehumidifiers to rid your home of excess moisture and repair plumbing leaks as soon as they are found.

If damaged wallboard requires extensive repair, resurfacing walls and ceiling with a layer of new wallboard may be the best option. Resurfacing is essentially the same installation as hanging multiple layers of wallboard, and results in a smooth, flat surface. However, the added wall thickness can affect the appearance of window and door trim, which may need to be extended. Use ⅜" wallboard for resurfacing—while ¼" wallboard is thinner, it's fragile and can be difficult to work with.

Tools & Materials ▸

Utility saw
Utility knife
Drill or screwgun
Wallboard knives
150-grit sandpaper
Paint roller and tray
Wallboard screws
Wallboard

Construction adhesive
Stain-blocking primer
Paper tape
Joint compound
Paint
Eye and ear protection
Work gloves

How to Repair Water Damaged Wallboard

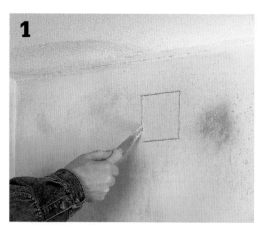

After the source for the water leak has been fixed, cut 4-in. holes at each end of joist and stud bays to help ventilation. Where possible, remove wet or damp insulation to dry out. Use fans and dehumidifiers to help speed up the drying process.

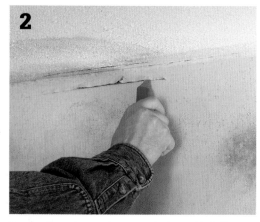

Remove loose tape and compound using a utility knife. Cut back areas of soft wallboard to solid material. To prevent sagging, prop waterlogged ceiling panels against joists with T-braces.

3

Once wallboard is dry, refasten ceiling panels to framing or remove panels that are excessively bowed. Reinforce damaged wall panels with wallboard screws driven 2 in. from the existing fasteners.

Tip ▶

If wallboard contains small areas (less than one square yard) of mold on the panel surface, clean with a damp rag and baking soda or detergent. Allow to dry, then continue the repair. Wear protective eyewear, rubber gloves, and a disposable dust mask when cleaning mold. *Caution: Larger areas containing mold must be evaluated and treated by a mold abatement specialist.*

4

Patch all vent holes and damaged areas with wallboard and replace insulation. Apply a quality stain-blocking primer/sealer to the affected area. Use an oil-based sealer; latex-based sealers may allow water stains to bleed through.

5

After the primer/sealer has dried, finish all joints and repairs with paper tape and three coats of compound. If water stains bleed through, reseal prior to final priming and painting.

Removing Wall & Ceiling Surfaces

If a wall or ceiling surface is damaged or deteriorated beyond repair or if your remodeling project requires framing alterations or additional utility lines, you may need to remove the wall and ceiling surfaces.

Removing any wall surface is a messy job, but it's not a difficult one. But before you tear into a wall with a hammer or power saw, you need to know what lies inside. Start by checking for hidden mechanicals in the project area. Wiring that's in the way can be moved fairly easily, as can water supply pipes and drain vents. If it's gas piping, drain pipe, or ducting, however, you'll probably have to call a professional before you can move to the next step.

When you're ready to begin demolition, prepare the work area to help contain dust and minimize damage to flooring and other surfaces—tearing out wallboard and plaster creates a very fine dust that easily finds its way into neighboring rooms. Cover doorways (even closed ones) and openings with plastic sheeting. Tape plastic over HVAC registers to prevent dust from circulating through the system. Protect floors with cardboard or hardboard and plastic or drop cloths. Also, carefully remove any trim from the project area, cutting painted joints with a utility knife to reduce the damage to the finish.

As an added precaution, turn off the power to all circuits in the work area, and shut off the main water supply if you'll be making cuts near water pipes.

Locate framing members using a stud finder or by knocking on the wall and feeling for solid points. Verify the findings by driving finish nails through the wall surface. After finding the center of one stud, measure over 16" to locate neighboring studs.

Tools & Materials ▸

Utility knife
Pry bar
Circular saw
Straightedge
Maul
Masonry chisel
Stud finder
Wallcovering
 remover fluid
Wallpaper scorer
Heavy tarp

Reciprocating saw
 with bimetal blade
Hammer
Eye and ear
 protection
Dust mask
Heavy work gloves
Pressure sprayer
Wallboard knife
Aviation snips

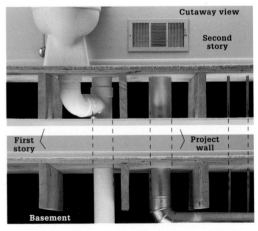

Check for hidden plumbing lines, ductwork, wiring, and gas pipes before cutting into a wall. To locate the lines, examine the areas directly below and above the project wall. In most cases, pipes, utility lines, and ductwork run through the wall vertically between floors. Original blueprints for your house should show the location of many of the utility lines.

Lead Paint ▸

Before removing any surface in a home built before 1980, test for lead, a hazardous substance. (Lead paint additives were banned in 1978, but supplies on hand were sold and used beyond that time.) You can find inexpensive test kits at hardware stores and home centers. If tests indicate lead, get expert advice. Most paint stores and the paint department in larger home centers carry free brochures on what's known as "lead abatement procedures." You can also find information at www.epa.gov.

How to Remove Wallcovering

Find a loose edge and try to strip off the wallcovering. Vinyls often peel away easily. If the wallcovering does not strip by hand, cover the floor with layers of newspaper. Add wallcovering remover fluid to a bucket of water, as directed by the manufacturer.

Pierce the wallcovering surface with a wallpaper scorer (inset) to allow remover solution to enter and soften the adhesive. Use a pressure sprayer, paint roller, or sponge to apply the remover solution. Let it soak into the covering, according to the manufacturer's directions.

Peel away loosened wallcovering with a 6-in. wallboard knife. Be careful not to damage the plaster or wallboard. Remove all backing paper. Rinse adhesive residue from the wall with remover solution. Rinse with clear water and let the walls dry completely.

How to Remove Ceramic Wall Tile

Be sure the floor is covered with a heavy tarp, and the electricity and water are shut off. Knock a small starter hole into the bottom of the wall, using a maul and masonry chisel.

Begin cutting out small sections of the wall by inserting a reciprocating saw with a bimetal blade into the hole, and cutting along grout lines. Be careful when sawing near pipes and wiring.

Cut the entire wall surface into small sections, removing each section as it is cut. Be careful not to cut through studs.

How to Remove Wallboard

1

Remove baseboard and other trim, and prepare the work area. Set a circular saw to the thickness of the wallboard, then cut from floor to ceiling. Use a utility knife to finish the cuts at the top and bottom and to cut through the taped horizontal seam where the wall meets the ceiling surface.

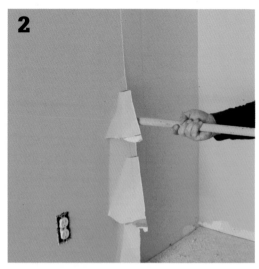

2

Insert the end of a pry bar into the cut, near a corner of the opening. Pull the pry bar until the wallboard breaks, then tear away the broken pieces. Take care to avoid damaging the wallboard outside the planned rough opening.

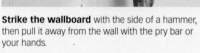

Tip ▶

Strike the wallboard with the side of a hammer, then pull it away from the wall with the pry bar or your hands.

3

Remove nails, screws, and any remaining wallboard from the framing members, using a pry bar or drill (or screwgun). Check any vapor barrier and insulation for damage and replace if necessary.

How to Remove Plaster

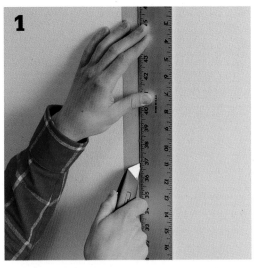

1

Remove baseboards and other trim and prepare the work area. Score the cutting line several times with a utility knife, using a straightedge as a guide. The line should be at least ⅛" deep.

2

Break the plaster along the edges by holding a scrap piece of 2 × 4 on edge just inside the scored lines, and rapping it with a hammer. Use a pry bar to remove the remaining plaster.

3

Cut through the lath along the edges of the plaster, using a reciprocating saw or jigsaw. Remove the lath from the studs using a pry bar. Pry away any remaining nails. Check the vapor barrier and insulation for damage and replace if necessary.

VARIATION: If the wall has metal lath laid over the wood lath, use aviation snips to clip the edges of the metal lath. Press the jagged edges of the lath flat against the stud. The cut edges of metal lath are very sharp; be sure to wear heavy work gloves.

Final Inspection & Fixing Problems

After the final coat of joint compound has dried but before you begin sanding, inspect the entire finish job for flaws. If you discover scrapes, pitting, or other imperfections, add another coat of joint compound. Repair any damaged or overlooked areas such as cracked seams and over-cut holes for electrical boxes prior to sanding.

During your inspection, make sure to check that all seams are acceptably feathered out. To check seams, hold a level or 12-in. taping knife perpendicularly across the seam; fill concave areas with extra layers of compound and correct any convex seams that crown more than $\frac{1}{16}$".

Tools & Materials ▸

6" and 12" taping knives	Self-adhesive fiberglass mesh tape
Sanding block or pole sander	220-grit sanding screen or 150-grit sandpaper
All-purpose joint compound	Eye and ear protection
Level	

How to Fix Common Taping Problems

Pitting occurs when compound is overmixed or applied with too little pressure to force out trapped air bubbles. Pitting can be corrected easily with a thin coat of compound. If trapped air bubbles are present, sand lightly before covering with compound.

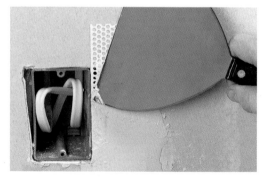

Mis-cut holes for electrical boxes can be flat-taped. Cover the gap with self-adhesive mesh tape and cover with three coats of all-purpose compound. Pre-cut repair patches are also available.

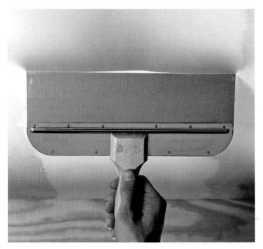

Concave seams can be filled with an extra layer or two of all-purpose compound. Let dry and sand lightly between coats.

For seams crowned more than ¹⁄₁₆", carefully sand along the center, but do not expose the tape.Check the seam with a level. If it's still crowned, add a layer of compound with a 12" knife, removing all of it along the seam's center and feathering it out toward the outside edges. After it dries, apply a final coat, if necessary.

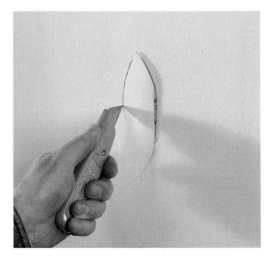

Bubbled or loose tape occurs when the bed layer is too thin, which causes a faulty bond between the tape and compound. Cut out small, soft areas with a utility knife and retape. Large runs of loose tape will have to be fully removed before retaping.

Cracked seams are often the result of compound that has dried too quickly or shrunk. Retape the seam if the existing tape and compound is intact; otherwise, cut out any loose material. In either case, make sure to fill the crack with compound.

Ladders

Two quality stepladders and an extension plank are all you need to paint most interior surfaces. For painting high areas, build a simple scaffold by running the plank through the steps of two stepladders. It can be easy to lose your balance or step off the plank, so choose tall ladders for safety; the upper part of the ladders can help you balance and will keep you from stepping off the ends of the plank. Buy a strong, straight 2" × 10" board no more than 12 feet long, or rent a plank from a material dealer or rental outlet.

A manufacturer's sticker provides weight ratings and instructions for the correct use of the ladder. Read it carefully when shopping for a ladder. Choose a ladder that will easily accommodate your weight plus the additional weight of any tools or materials you plan to carry up the ladder.

Rent extension planks from a paint dealer or from a rental center.

Keep steps tight by periodically checking them and tightening the braces when they need it.

Keep the ladder in front of you when working. Lean your body against the ladder for balance.

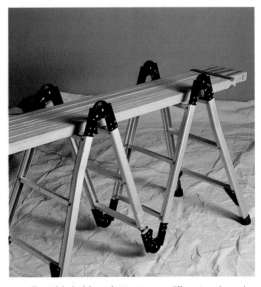

An adjustable ladder adapts to many different work needs. It can be used as a straight ladder, a stepladder, or a base for scaffold planks.

Paint Safety

Always read and follow the label information on paint and solvent containers. Chemicals that pose a fire hazard are listed (in order of flammability) as: combustible, flammable, or extremely flammable. Use caution when using these products and remember that the fumes are also flammable.

The warning "use with adequate ventilation" means that there should be no more vapor buildup than there would be if you were using the material outside. Open doors and windows, use exhaust fans, and wear an approved respirator if you can't provide adequate ventilation.

Save a small amount of paint for touchups and repairs, and then safely dispose of the remainder. Dispose of alkyd (oil-based) paint according to local regulations regarding hazardous materials; if possible, recycle latex paint at your local hazardous waste disposal facility or allow it to dry out completely and set it out with your regular trash.

Paint chemicals do not store well. Buy only as much as is needed for the project and keep them away from children and pets.

Read label information. Chemicals that are poisonous or flammable are labeled with warnings and instructions for safe handling.

Wear safety goggles when using chemical stripper or cleaning products. Use goggles when painting overhead.

Do not use chemicals that are listed as combustible or flammable, such as paint strippers, near an open flame. Store paint chemicals out of the reach of children and away from appliances with pilot lights, such as a furnace or gas oven.

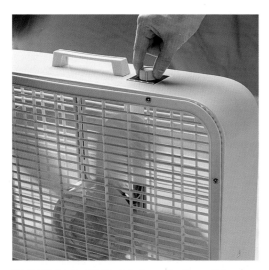

Open windows and doors and use a fan for ventilation when painting indoors. If a product label has the warning "harmful or fatal if swallowed," assume that the vapors are dangerous to breathe.

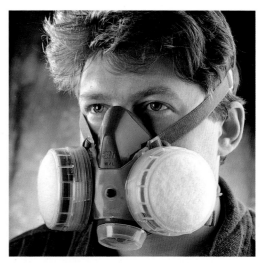

Wear a respirator to filter vapors if you cannot ventilate a work area adequately. If you can smell vapors, the ventilation is not adequate.

Pour paint thinner into a clear jar after use. When the solid material settles out, pour off the clear thinner and save it to reuse later. Dispose of the sediment as hazardous waste.

Dispose of leftover latex primers and paint safely. Let the container stand uncovered until the paint dries completely. In most communities, dried latex paint can be put into the regular trash. (Alkyd primers and paint must be disposed of as hazardous waste.)

Preparation Tools & Materials

It's as simple as it is unavoidable: Good preparation produces a professional-looking job. In the old days, preparation could be difficult and time consuming, but with the help of the new tools and materials on the market today, it's easier than ever.

New cleaners and removal agents help prepare surfaces for paint and wallcovering; new patching products help you create virtually invisible wall repairs; ingenious new masking and draping materials take the tedium out of keeping the paint where it belongs; primers and sealers provide good coverage and help paint bond properly. While you're in the planning stages of a painting or decorating project,

take a stroll down the aisles at a local home center or hardware store. Consider the project ahead of you and evaluate which products will make the job simpler and more enjoyable.

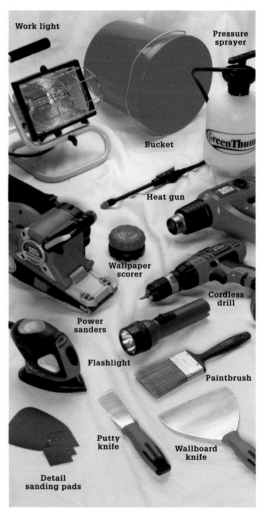

Smooth, even surfaces are easy to achieve with tools such as these: sanding sponges (A), sandpaper (B), sanding block (C), a drywall-corner sanding sponge (D), microfiber tack cloth (E), and synthetic steel wool (F).

Tools for preparation include some ordinary home workshop tools and some specialty items. All are available at home improvement centers, as well as at better decorating supply stores.

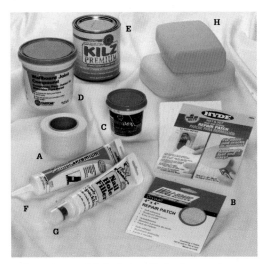

Wall repair materials include: self-adhesive seam tape (A), hole-patching kits (B), crack-repair compound (C), joint compound (D), stainblocking primer/sealer (E), and sink and tub caulk (F). Some new spackling compounds (G) start out pink and dry white so you can see when they're ready to be sanded and painted. Sponges (H) are useful for smoothing damp joint compound to reduce the amount of sanding that's necessary later.

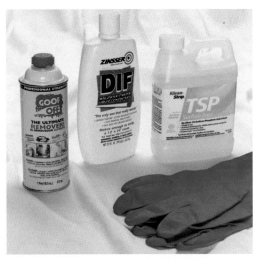

Walls must be clean, smooth, and free of grease before a painting project. If wallpaper is to be removed, a wallpaper removal agent is extremely helpful. Clockwise from top left are: cleanup solution to remove old drips and splatters, wallcovering remover to strip old wallcoverings, trisodium phosphate (TSP) for washing the walls, and rubber gloves, which should be worn when using chemicals such as these.

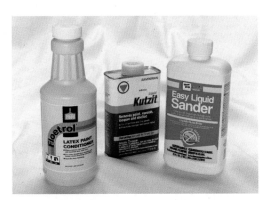

Preparation liquids include latex bonding agent for plaster repairs; paint remover; and liquid deglosser, for dulling glossy surfaces prior to painting.

Primers provide maximum adhesion for paint on any surface. There are many specialty primers available, including mold-resistant primers that are especially useful in areas that tend to be damp, such as bathrooms (A), primers made for plaster and new drywall (B), stainblocking primers (C), and tinted primers that reduce the need for multiple coats of paint (particularly for deep colors) (D).

Room Preparation

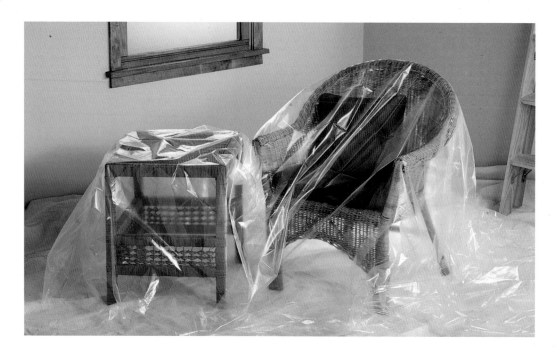

Before painting, your first step is to protect everything that could be covered by dust or splattered by paint. Remove all window and door hardware, light fixtures, and coverplates on outlets and wall switches. Drape furniture and cover the floors. Remove heating and air conditioning duct covers. Mask off wood moldings with self-adhesive paper or masking tape. Painting time can be a good opportunity to upgrade with new hardware, like window pulls and cabinet knobs.

Tip ▸

When removing hardware, mark the pieces with masking tape for identification so that they can easily be replaced.

How to Prepare a Room

Remove all hardware, such as window handles and cabinet catches, from surfaces to be painted. If you will be installing new hardware, buy it now and drill new screw holes if needed.

2

Remove all nails, screws, and picture hangers from surfaces to be painted. To prevent damage to the plaster or wallboard, use a block of wood under the head of the hammer.

3

Remove covers from heating and air-conditioning ducts to protect them from splatters. Remove thermostats, or use masking tape to protect them against paint drips.

4

Move furniture to the center of the room and cover it with plastic sheets. In large rooms, leave an alley through the center for access if you are painting the ceiling. Cover floors with 9-ounce canvas drop cloths. Canvas absorbs paint spills.

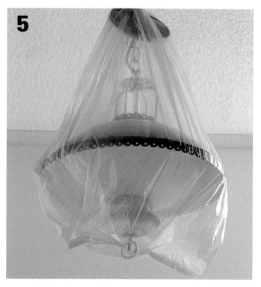

5

Turn off the electricity. Remove the coverplates from outlets and switches, then replace the cover screws. Lower light fixtures away from electrical boxes, or remove the fixtures. Cover hanging fixtures with plastic bags.

Primers & Sealers

A sealer should be applied to wood surfaces before they are varnished. Wood often has both hard and soft grains, as well as a highly absorbent end grain. Applying a sealer helps close the surface of the wood so the varnish is absorbed evenly in different types of wood grain. If the wood is not sealed, the varnish may dry to a mottled finish.

Primers are used to seal surfaces that will be painted. Wallboard seams and patched areas absorb paint at a different rate than surrounding areas. Joints and patch areas often show or "shadow" through the finished paint if the walls are not adequately primed.

Choose a primer designed for the project: mildew-resistant primers are excellent for bathrooms and laundry rooms, stain-blocking primers cover smoke and other hard-to-cover stains, and tinted primers provide good bases for deep colors, such as red or purple.

Tinted primers provide an excellent base for finish coats, especially for deep colors that might otherwise require several coats to cover adequately. Color base is available to tint white primers if necessary.

Tips for Priming & Sealing ▸

Seal raw wood by applying a primer before painting or a clear sealer before varnishing. Unsealed wood can produce a spotty finish.

Roughen gloss surfaces with fine sandpaper, then prime them to provide good bonding between the new and the old paint. Primers provide "tooth" for the new coat of paint.

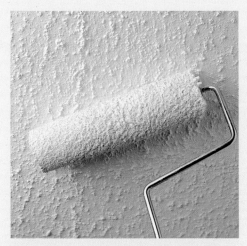

Seal textured surfaces with a PVA or alkyd primer, then apply a finish coat with a long-nap roller. Textured walls and ceilings soak up a lot of paint and make it difficult to apply paint evenly.

Prime repair areas on plaster with high-quality primer.

How to Use a Paint Roller

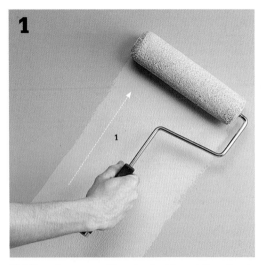

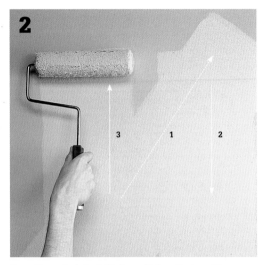

Wet the roller cover with water (for latex paint) or mineral spirits (for alkyd enamel), to remove lint and prime the cover. Squeeze out excess liquid. Dip the roller fully into the paint pan reservoir and roll it over the textured ramp to distribute the paint evenly. The roller should be full, but not dripping. Make an upward diagonal sweep about 4 ft. long on the surface, using a slow stroke to avoid splattering.

Draw the roller straight down (2) from the top of the diagonal sweep made in step 1. Lift and move the roller to the beginning of the diagonal sweep and roll up (3) to complete the unloading of the roller.

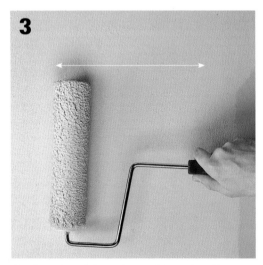

Distribute the paint over the rest of the section with horizontal back-and-forth strokes.

Smooth the area by lightly drawing the roller vertically from the top to the bottom of the painted area. Lift the roller and return it to the top of the area after each stroke.

How to Use a Paintbrush

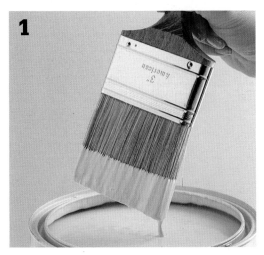

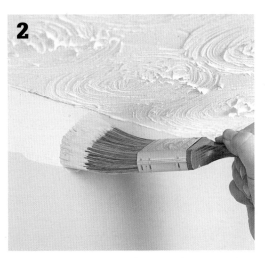

Dip the brush into the paint, loading one-third of its bristle length. Tap the bristles against the side of the can to remove excess paint, but do not drag the bristles against the lip of the can.

Paint along the edges (called "cutting in") using the narrow edge of the brush, pressing just enough to flex the bristles. Keep an eye on the paint edge, and paint with long, slow strokes. Always paint from a dry area back into wet paint to avoid lap marks.

Brush wall corners using the wide edge of the brush. Paint open areas with a brush or roller before the brushed paint dries.

To paint large areas with a brush, apply the paint with 2 or 3 diagonal strokes. Hold the brush at a 45° angle to the work surface, pressing just enough to flex the bristles. Distribute the paint evenly with horizontal strokes.

Smooth the surface by drawing the brush vertically from the top to the bottom of the painted area. Use light strokes and lift the brush from the surface at the end of each stroke. This method is best for slow-drying alkyd enamels.

Trim Painting Techniques

When painting an entire room, paint the wood trim first, then paint the walls. Start by painting the inside portions of the trim, and work out toward the walls. On windows, for instance, first paint the edges close to the glass, then paint the surrounding face trim.

Doors should be painted quickly because of the large surface. To avoid lap marks, always paint from dry surfaces back into wet paint. On baseboards, cut in the top edge and work down to the flooring. Plastic floor guards or a wide broadknife can help shield carpet and wood flooring from paint drips.

Alkyds and latex enamels may require two coats. Always sand lightly between coats and wipe with a tack cloth so that the second coat bonds properly.

How to Paint a Window

1

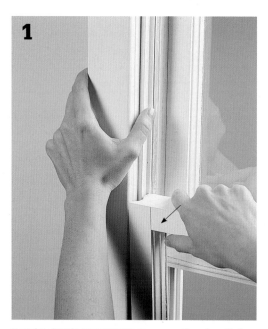

To paint double-hung windows, remove them from their frames if possible. Newer, spring-mounted windows are released by pushing against the frame (see arrow).

2

Drill holes and insert two 2" nails into the legs of a wooden step ladder. Mount the window easel-style for easy painting. Or, lay the window flat on a bench or sawhorses. Do not paint the sides or bottom of the window sashes.

3

Using a tapered sash brush, begin by painting the wood next to the glass. Use the narrow edge of the brush, and overlap the paint onto the glass to create a weatherseal.

4

Remove excess paint from the glass with a putty knife wrapped in a clean cloth. Rewrap the knife often so that you always wipe with clean fabric. Overlap paint from the sash onto the glass by 1/16".

5

Case molding

Sash

Sill

Apron

Paint all flat portions of the sashes, then the case moldings, sill, and apron. Use slow brush strokes, and avoid getting paint between the sash and the frame.

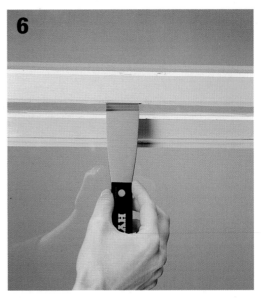

6

If you must paint windows in place, move the painted windows up and down several times during the drying period to keep them from sticking. Use a putty knife to avoid touching the painted surfaces.

How to Paint Doors

Remove the door by driving out the lower hinge pin with a screwdriver and hammer. Have a helper hold the door in place. Then, drive out the middle and upper hinge pins.

Place the door flat on sawhorses for painting. On paneled doors, paint in the following order, using a brush rather than a roller: 1) recessed panels, 2) horizontal rails, and 3) vertical stiles.

Let the painted door dry. If a second coat of paint is needed, sand the first coat lightly and wipe the door with tack cloth before repainting.

Seal the unpainted edges of the door with a clear wood sealer to prevent moisture from entering the wood. Water can cause wood to warp and swell.

Tips for Painting Trim ▶

Protect wall and floor surfaces with a wide wallboard knife or a plastic shielding tool.

Wipe all of the paint off of the wallboard knife or shielding tool each time it is moved.

Paint both sides of cabinet doors. This provides an even moisture seal and prevents warping.

Paint deep patterned surfaces with a stiff-bristled brush, like this stenciling brush. Use small circular strokes to penetrate recesses.

Ceiling & Wall Painting Techniques

For a smooth finish on large wall and ceiling areas, paint in small sections. It's best to paint both the edges and expanses of each wall, one at a time, rather than edge the entire room before rolling. First use a paintbrush to cut in the edges, then immediately roll the section while it is still wet before moving on. If brushed edges dry before the area is rolled, lap marks will be visible on the finished wall. Working in natural light makes it easier to spot missed areas.

Choose high-quality paint and tools and work with a full brush or roller to avoid lap marks and to ensure full coverage. Roll slowly to minimize splattering.

Tips for Painting Ceilings & Walls ▸

Paint to a wet edge. Cut in the edges on small sections with a paintbrush, then immediately roll the section. (Using a corner roller makes it unnecessary to cut in inside corners.) With two painters, have one cut in with a brush while the other rolls the large areas.

Minimize brush marks. Slide the roller cover slightly off of the roller cage when rolling near wall corners or a ceiling line. Brushed areas dry to a different finish than rolled paint.

How to Paint Ceilings

Paint ceilings with a roller handle extension. Use eye protection while painting overhead. Start at the corner farthest from the entry door. Paint the ceiling along the narrow end in 3 × 3' sections, cutting in the edges with a brush before rolling. Apply the paint with a diagonal stroke. Distribute the paint evenly with back-and-forth strokes. For the final smoothing strokes, roll each section toward the wall containing the entry door, lifting the roller at the end of each sweep.

How to Paint Walls

Paint walls in 2 × 4' sections. Start in an upper corner, cutting in the ceiling and wall corners with a brush, then rolling the section. Make the initial diagonal roller stroke from the bottom of the section upward, to avoid dripping paint. Distribute the paint evenly with horizontal strokes, then finish with downward sweeps of the roller. Next, cut in and roll the section directly underneath. Continue with adjacent areas, cutting in and rolling the top sections before the bottom sections. Roll all finish strokes toward the floor.

Painting Cabinets

If your kitchen cabinets are in good shape structurally and you are happy with their configuration but not their appearance, a coat of paint may be all it takes to update your kitchen in a dramatic way. You can brighten dark wood, freshen up previously painted cabinet surfaces, or create a new look with faux finish techniques. Any wood, metal or previously painted cabinets can be painted.

As with any painting project, your final results depend on careful and thorough preparation and use of high-quality products. Remove doors, drawers, and all hardware so you can paint the surfaces in a flat position, eliminating many drips and sags.

Choose a high-quality enamel paint in satin, low-luster, or semi-gloss finish. A high gloss finish will highlight surface defects and create glare. Latex paint is suitable for this project. Using an alkyd (oil-based) paint may result in a smoother finish with fewer brush marks, but the cleanup is more involved and the fumes may require that you wear a respirator.

Cabinets with matte surfaces in good condition need only be washed with trisodium phosphate (TSP) or another appropriate detergent for preparation. But if the surface is smooth or glossy, as when varnished or painted with a gloss enamel, you'll need to sand and/or chemically degloss before you apply paint. An undercoat of primer improves adhesion and reduces stain-through. If the previous paint was dark or a highly saturated color, or bare wood has been exposed, an undercoat is also necessary. Do not spot-prime because the top coat will not cover evenly in those areas. Avoid applying two layers of top coat, but if you do, make sure to sand or degloss the first coat to get good adhesion of the second coat.

If you are also changing hardware, determine whether you will be using the same screw holes. If not, fill the existing holes with wood putty before sanding.

Painted cabinets are re-emerging as a popular design element in kitchens. Bright paint adds liveliness and fun, while more neutral tones are soothing and let other kitchen elements have the spotlight.

How to Paint Cabinets

Tools & Materials ▸

Screwdriver
Hand sander
Brushes
TSP or other degreaser
Sandpaper

Masking tape
Primer
Enamel paint
Eye and ear
    protection

Shopping Tips ▸

- Always buy the highest quality brush.
- Use synthetic-bristle brushes for latex paint. Look for soft, flagged tips.
- Natural-bristle brushes should only be used for oil-based paints.
- Use a nylon brush for fine work.
- An angled sash brush gives you more control for painting face frames.

Remove doors and drawers. Wash all surfaces to be painted with TSP or other degreaser. Scrape off any loose paint. Sand or chemically degloss all surfaces. Wipe away sanding dust and prime varnished surfaces, dark colors, or bare wood with primer.

Remove shelves, when possible, to create access for painting cabinet interiors. Paint the cabinet backs first, followed by the tops, sides and then the bottoms. Paint the face frames last (so you won't need to reach over them when painting the interior).

Paint both sides of doors beginning with the interior surfaces. With raised panel doors, paint the panel inserts first, then the horizontal rails. Paint the vertical stiles last.

Tips for Repairing Wood Cabinets ▸

You never have too much storage. That reality was as true in years gone by as it is today, which is why you'll find a large selection of wood cabinets in salvage shops and yards. Depending on how old they are, these salvaged units are often unique wood species, with wonderful period features such as tip-out bins and spice rack drawers. Unlike modern particleboard versions, most older cabinets—and any that date back before the 1950s—are solid-wood construction. This construction is key to their longevity.

Like other reclaimed materials, cabinetry often represents a good bargain. The biggest costs—the materials and craftsmanship—have already been accounted for by the original owner. But a bargain is only a bargain if you can really make use of what you're buying. When it comes to reclaimed cabinetry, planning a whole kitchen remodel may be overreaching. It's unlikely that you'll find exactly the number and size of cabinets that fit your space. In addition, cabinet styles of decades past differ from contemporary styles. For instance, most modern kitchens incorporate recessed kickboards under bottom cabinets and leave an open space above top-mounted units, whereas the carcasses of older cabinetry often ran to the floor or all the way to the ceiling. You can modify reclaimed cabinets for your purposes, or take the easier route and use salvaged cabinets as focal points for a kitchen or dining room, or simply incorporate them into work areas as handsome utility cabinets.

In any case, you'll probably have to do some amount of refurbishing to any older cabinet you purchase. This can range from simply cleaning the unit thoroughly, to refinishing, to correcting more serious structural problems. Whatever work needs to be done, it's always easier to do it before you mount the cabinet.

You can start with the finish. As with other types of reclaimed wood, you may want to stabilize and preserve the existing finish. If the cabinet is painted, it's probably worth sanding down a small inconspicuous section underneath or inside the cabinet to determine if the wood is unique enough to merit refinishing natural. However, painted cabinets are often sanded lightly to remove loose paint and sprayed with a polyurethane sealer to fix the surface and give the cabinets an attractive distressed look. Other finishes can be removed to allow for a brand look.

Before you work on the finish of the cabinet, however, you should thoroughly inspect the structure to identify any structural problems. This will entail removing doors and drawers, and all hardware.

The best cabinets are made of dovetailed joints, and those are likely to still be in good shape. Box or butt joints are more common but less secure and chances are, if the cabinet is fairly old, you'll need to reinforce the joints to one degree or another. You may also need to square up the cabinet so that it doesn't sag or hang out of true.

BRACING CORNERS

There are many different options for reinforcing wobbly cabinet joints, and you can use a combination of them if necessary. Corner braces, also known as glue blocks, are effective solutions for a cabinet that is out of square, and once in place they reinforce the entire cabinet box structure. They are also simple to make and simple to install. Cut a 2"-square piece of 1" nominal board (hardwood is preferable) and saw the square in half diagonally. Use bar clamps to square up the cabinet, checking the corners for square with a carpenter's square. Coat the edges of the block with wood glue and position it in the corner of the cabinet, on level with the top edge

Use L-braces to stiffen corners. There are many, but a quick and easy solution for functional utility cabinets is to brace the corners with metal L-brackets or angle braces. Screw the braces into place with ½" screws.

of the cabinet. Brace all four corners of the cabinet, and allow the glue to dry completely before removing the bar clamps. Where the cabinet structure is very tenuous, you can drill pilot holes through the blocks and nail them into place for additional strength. A quicker and easier solution for functional utility cabinets is to brace the corners with steel angle braces. Screw the braces into place with ½" screws. Steel corner plates are a way to secure the corners without marring the interior look of the cabinet. To install corner plates, use a chisel to create a mortise in the corner down into which the corner plate will be screwed.

RECONSTITUTING JOINTS

Some well-made cabinets will be joined with dovetail joints that can withstand gravity and the ravages of time virtually unscathed. But more commonly, cabinets are joined with box joints or simple butt joints. These can separate as adhesive degrades and fasteners loosen over time.

SALVAGE WISDOM

Nailed joints are susceptible to time, gravity, and wear and tear, just as glued joints are. If you are reviving a reclaimed cabinet and find that nails are missing or are too loose in their holes, the best idea is to replace them with screws.

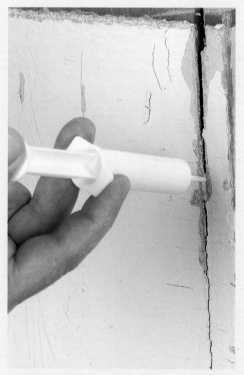

If a joint in the face frame or carcass of a cabinet has separated slightly, you can restore it by using a glue syringe to inject wood glue into the joint and then clamping the joint until the adhesive dries. This method can also be used to renew the joints in a cabinet drawer.

To reinforce nailed joints, drill countersunk holes for the screws over the nail holes, and plug the holes after you've installed the screws. Where screws have stripped in their holes, you can glue a dowel into the hole and then screw into the dowel.

Eliminating Stair Squeaks

This staircase has center stringers to help support the treads. The 2 × 4s nailed between the outside stringers and the wall studs serve as spacers that allow room for the installation of skirt boards and wall finishes.

Like floors, stairs squeak when the lumber becomes warped or loose boards rub together. The continual pounding of foot traffic takes its toll on even the best built staircases. An unstable staircase is as unsafe as it is unattractive. Problems related to the structure of a staircase, such as severe sagging, twisting, or slanting, should be left to a professional. However, you can easily complete many common repairs.

Squeaks are usually caused by movement between the treads and risers, which can be alleviated from above or below the staircase.

Tools & Materials ▸

Drill
Screwdriver
Hammer
Utility knife
Nail set
Wood screws
Wood putty
Caulk gun
Hardwood shims
Wood blocks
Wood plugs

Wood glue
Quarter-round molding
Finish nails
Construction adhesive
Caulk gun
Eye and ear protection

How to Eliminate Squeaks from Below the Stairs

Glue wood blocks to the joints between the treads and risers with construction adhesive. Once the blocks are in place, drill pilot holes and fasten them to the treads and risers with wood screws. If the risers overlap the back edges of the treads, drive screws through the risers and into the treads to bind them together.

Fill the gaps between stair parts with tapered hardwood shims. Coat the shims with wood glue and tap them into the joints between treads and risers until they're snug. Shimming too much will widen the gap. Allow the glue to dry before walking on the stairs.

How to Eliminate Squeaks from Above the Stairs

When the underside of a staircase is inaccessible, silence noisy stairs from above. Drill pilot holes and drive screws down through stair treads into the risers. Countersink the screws and fill the holes with putty or wood plugs.

Support the joints between treads and risers by attaching quarter-round molding. Drill pilot holes and use finish nails to fasten the molding. Set the nails with a nail set.

Tap glued wood shims under loose treads to keep them from flexing. Use a block to prevent splitting, and drive the shim just until it's snug. When the glue dries, cut the shims flush, using a utility knife.

Replacing a Broken Stair Tread

A broken stair tread is hazardous because we often don't look at steps as we climb them. Replace a broken step right away. The difficulty of this job depends on the construction of your staircase and the accessibility of the underside. It's better to replace a damaged tread than to repair it. A patch could create an irregular step that surprises someone unfamiliar with it.

Tools & Materials ▸

Flat pry bar	Stair tread
Hammer	Construction
Combination square	adhesive
Circular saw	Screws
Drill	Wood putty
Nail set	Finish nails
Caulk gun	Nail set

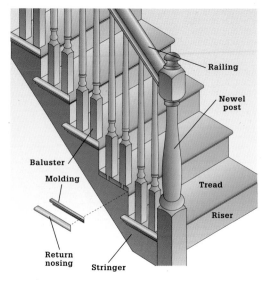

Railing

Newel post

Baluster

Molding

Tread

Riser

Return nosing

Stringer

How to Replace a Broken Stair Tread

Carefully remove any decorative elements attached to the tread. Pull up carpeting and roll it aside. Remove trim pieces on or around the edges of the tread. Remove the balusters by detaching the top ends from the railing and separating the joints in the tread. Some staircases have a decorative hardwood cap inlaid into each tread. Remove these with a flat pry bar, taking care to pry from underneath the cap to avoid marring the exposed edges.

If possible, hammer upward from underneath the stairs to separate the tread from the risers and stringers. Otherwise, use a hammer and pry bar to work the tread loose, pulling nails as you go. Once the tread is removed, scrape the exposed edges of the stringers to remove old glue and wood fragments.

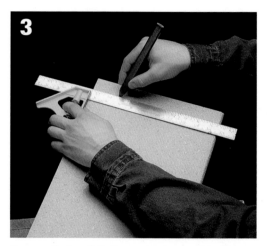

Measure the length for the new tread and mark it with a combination square so the cut end will be square and straight. If the tread has a milled end for an inlay, cut from the plain end. Cut the new tread to size, using a circular saw, and test-fit it carefully.

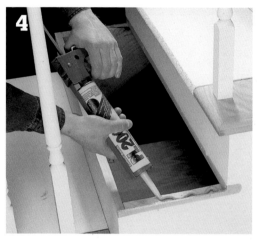

Apply a bead of construction adhesive to the exposed tops of the stringers. The adhesive will strengthen the bond between the tread and stringer and will cushion the joint, preventing the parts from squeaking.

Set the tread in place. If you have access to the step from underneath, secure the tread to the riser above it by driving screws through the riser into the back edge of the tread. To fasten it from the top side, drill and countersink pilot holes and drive two or three screws through the tread into the top edge of each stringer. Also drive a few screws along the front edge of the tread into the riser below it. Fill the screw holes in the tread with wood putty or plugs.

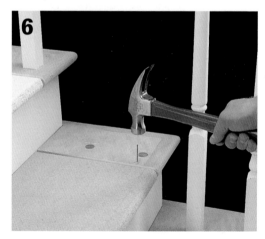

Reinstall any decorative elements, using finish nails. Set the nails with a nail set. Reinstall the balusters, if necessary.

Windows & Doors

In this chapter:

Solving Common Door Problems

The most common door problems are caused by loose hinges. When hinges are loose, the door won't hang right, causing it to rub and stick and throw off the latch mechanism. The first thing to do is check the hinge screws. If the holes for the hinge screws are worn and won't hold the screws, try the repair on the next page.

If the hinges are tight but the door still rubs against the frame, sand or plane down the door's edge. If a door doesn't close easily, it may be warped; use a long straightedge to check for warpage. You may be able to straighten a slightly warped door using weights, but severe warpage can't be corrected. Instead of buying a new door, remove the doorstop and reinstall it following the curve of the door.

Door latch problems occur for a number of reasons: loose hinges, swollen wood, sticking latchbolts, and paint buildup. If you've addressed those issues and the door still won't stay shut, it's probably because the door frame is out of square. This happens as a house settles with age; you can make minor adjustments by filing the strike plate on the door frame. If there's some room between the frame and the door, you can align the latchbolt and strike plate by shimming the hinges. Or, drive a couple of extra-long screws to adjust the frame slightly.

Common closet doors, such as sliding and bifold types, usually need only some minor adjustments and lubrication to stay in working order.

Door locksets are very reliable, but they do need to be cleaned and lubricated occasionally. One simple way to keep an entry door lockset working smoothly is to spray a light lubricant into the keyhole, then move the key in and out a few times. Don't use graphite in locksets, as it can abrade some metals with repeated use.

Tools & Materials ▸

Screwdrivers	Spray lubricant
Nail set	Wooden golf tees
Hammer	or dowels
Drill	Wood glue
Utility knife	Cardboard shims
Metal file	3" wood screws
Straightedge	Finish nails
Pry bar	Paint or stain
Plane	Sandpaper
Paintbrush	Wood sealer

Tip ▸

Latchbolts stick when they are dirty or in need of lubrication. Clean and lubricate locksets, and make sure the connecting screws aren't too tight—another cause of binding.

A misaligned latchbolt and strike plate will prevent the door from latching. Poor alignment may be caused by loose hinges, or the door frame may be out of square.

Sticking doors usually leave a mark where they rub against the door frame. Warped doors may resist closing and feel springy when you apply pressure. Check for warpage with a straightedge.

How to Remove a Door

Drive the lower hinge pin out using a screwdriver and hammer. Have a helper hold the door in place, then drive out the upper (and center, if applicable) hinge pins. To help get the screwdriver tip under the pin head, use a nail set or small punch to tap the pin up from underneath.

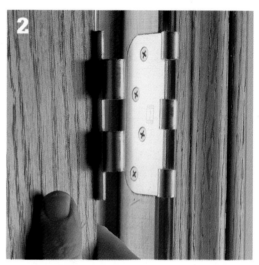

Remove the door and set it aside. Clean and lubricate the hinge pins before reinstalling the door.

How to Tighten a Loose Hinge Plate

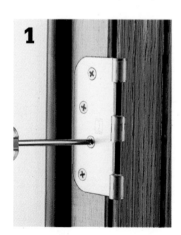

Remove the door from the hinges. Tighten any loose screws. If the wood won't hold the screws tightly, remove the hinges.

Coat wooden golf tees or dowels with wood glue, and drive them into the worn screw holes. If necessary, drill out the holes to accept dowels. Let the glue dry, then cut off excess wood.

Drill pilot holes in the new wood, and reinstall the hinge.

Check the door for a square fit. If the door is far out of square with the frame, remove it and shim the top or bottom hinge (right). Or, drive long screws into one of the hinges (below).

Install a thin cardboard shim behind the bottom hinge to raise the position of the latchbolt. To lower the latchbolt, shim behind the top hinge.

Remove two hinge screws from the top or bottom hinge, and drive a 3" wood screw into each hole. The screws will reach the framing studs in the wall and pull the door jamb upward, changing the angle of the door. Add long screws to the top hinge to raise the latchbolt or to the bottom hinge to lower it.

Fix minor alignment problems by filing the strike plate until the latchbolt fits.

How to Straighten a Warped Door

1

Check the door for warpage using a straightedge. Or, close the door until it hits the stop and look for a gap (see below). The amount of gap between the door and the stop reveals the extent of the warpage. The stop must be straight for this test, so check it with a straightedge.

2

If the warpage is slight, you can straighten the door using weights. Remove the door, and rest the ends of the door on sawhorses. Place heavy weights on the bowed center of the door, using cardboard to protect the finish. Leave the weights on the door for several days, and check it periodically with a straightedge.

How to Adjust for a Severely Warped Door

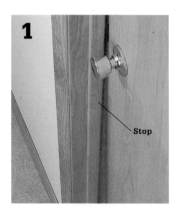

1

Stop

A severe warp cannot be corrected. Instead, you can adjust the doorstop to follow the shape of the door. If you touch up the door jamb with paint or stain after you've finished, no one will notice the repair.

2

Remove the doorstop using a small pry bar. If it's painted, cut the paint film first with a utility knife to prevent chipping. Avoid splintering by removing nails from the stop by pulling them through the back side of the piece. Pull all nails from the door jamb.

3

Close the door and latch it. Starting at the top, refasten the stop, keeping the inside edge flush against the door. Drive finish nails through the old holes, or drill new pilot holes through the stop. Set the nails with a nail set after you've checked the door's operation.

How to Free a Sticking Door

Tighten all of the hinge screws. If the door still sticks, use light pencil lines to mark the areas where the door rubs against the door jamb.

During dry weather, remove the door. If you have to remove a lot of material, you can save time by planing the door (step 3). Otherwise, sand the marked areas with medium-grit sandpaper. Make sure the door closes without sticking, then smooth the sanded areas with fine-grit sandpaper.

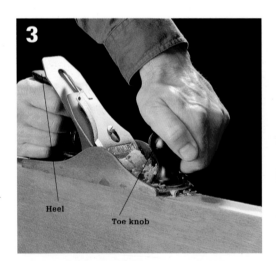

Heel

Toe knob

Secure the door on-edge. If the door has veneered surfaces, cut through the veneers with a utility knife to prevent splintering. Operate the plane so the wood grain runs "uphill" ahead of the plane. Grip the toe knob and handle firmly, and plane with long, smooth strokes. To prevent dipping, press down on the toe at the start of the stroke, and bear down on the heel at the end of the stroke. Check the door's fit, then sand the planed area smooth.

Apply clear sealer or paint to the sanded or planed area and any other exposed surfaces of the door. This will prevent moisture from entering the wood and is especially important for entry doors.

How to Maintain a Sliding Door

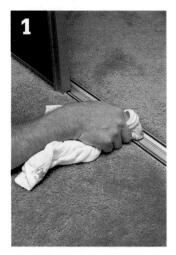

Clean the tracks above and below the doors with a toothbrush and a damp cloth or a hand vacuum.

Spray a greaseless lubricant on all the rollers, but do not spray the tracks. Replace any bent or worn parts.

Check the gap along the bottom edge of the door to make sure it is even. To adjust the gap, rotate the mounting screw to raise or lower the door edge.

How to Maintain a Bifold Door

Open or remove the doors and wipe the tracks with a clean rag. Spray the tracks and rollers or pins with greaseless lubricant.

Check closed doors for alignment within the door frame. If the gap between the closed doors is uneven, adjust the top pivot blocks with a screwdriver or wrench.

Adjustable pivot blocks are also found at the bottom of some door models. Adjust the pivot blocks until the gap between the door and the frame is even.

Weatherizing Basics

No matter whether you live in a hot or a cold climate, weatherizing your home's windows and doors can pay off handsomely. Heating and cooling costs may account for over half of the total household energy bill.

Before buying a basement window well cover, measure the widest point of the window well and note its shape.

Since most weatherizing projects are relatively inexpensive, you can recover your investment quickly. In fact, in some climates, you can pay back the cost of a weatherproofing project in one season.

If you live in a cold climate, you probably already understand the importance of weatherizing. The value of keeping warm air inside the house during a cold winter is obvious. From the standpoint of energy efficiency, it's equally important to prevent warm air from entering the house during summer.

Weatherizing your home is an ideal do-it-yourself project, because it can be done a little at a time, according to your schedule. In cold climates, the best time of the year to weatherize is the fall, before it turns too cold to work outdoors.

Whether you're concerned about the environment or want to spend less on your utility bills, some simple adjustments around your home can help you accomplish your goal.

Most weatherizing projects deal with windows and doors, because these are the primary areas of heat loss in most homes. Here are a few simple

Use a caulk that matches your home exterior to seal the window and door frames.

A felt door sweep can seal out drafts, even if you have an uneven floor or a low threshold.

suggestions you might consider for the exterior of your home:

Minimize heat loss from basement window wells by covering them with plastic window well covers (opposite page, top). Most window well covers have an upper flange designed to slip under the siding. Slip this in place, then fasten the cover to the foundation with masonry anchors and weigh down the bottom flange with stones. For extra weatherizing, seal the edges with caulk.

Adding caulk is a simple way to fill narrow gaps in interior or exterior surfaces. It's also available in a peelable form that can be easily removed at the end of the season.

When buying caulk, estimate half a cartridge per window or door, four for an average-sized foundation sill, and at least one more to close gaps around vents, pipes, and other openings.

Caulk around the outside of the window and door frames to seal any gaps. For best results, use a caulk that matches or blends with the color of your siding.

There are many different types of caulk and weather stripping materials. All are inexpensive and easy to use, but it's important to get the right materials for the job, as most are designed for specific applications.

Generally, metal and metal-reinforced weather stripping is more durable than products made of plastic, rubber, or foam. However, even plastic, rubber, and foam weather stripping products have a wide range of quality. The best rubber products are those made from neoprene rubber—use this whenever it's available.

A door sweep (previous page, bottom) attaches to the inside bottom of the door to seal out drafts. A felt or bristle sweep is best if you have an uneven floor or a low threshold. Vinyl and rubber models are also available.

A threshold insert fits around the base of the door. Most have a sweep on the interior side and a drip edge on the exterior side to direct water away from the threshold.

A threshold insert seals the gap between the door and the threshold. These are made from vinyl or rubber and can be easily replaced.

Self-adhesive foam strips (below) attach to sashes and frames to seal the air gaps at windows and doors. Reinforced felt strips have a metal spine that adds rigidity in high-impact areas, such as doorstops.

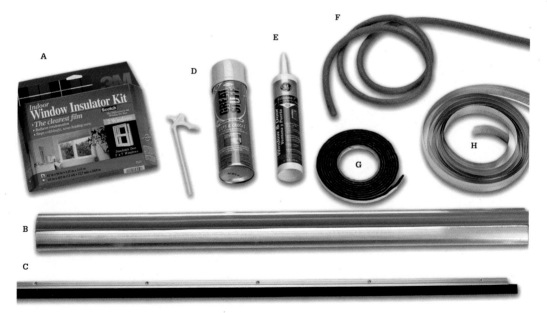

Weatherizing products commonly found in home centers include: A clear film, heat-shrink window insulator kit (A); an aluminum door threshold with vinyl weatherstripping insert (B); a nail-on, rubber door sweep (C); minimal expanding spray foam (D); silicone window and door caulk (E); open-cell foam caulk-backer rod (F); self-adhesive, closed-cell foam weatherstripping coil (G); flexible brass weatherstripping coil, also called V-channel, (H).

Tips for Weatherizing Doors ▸

Door weather stripping is prone to failure because it undergoes constant stress. Use metal weather stripping that is tacked to the surfaces whenever you can—especially around door jambs. It is much more durable than self-adhesive products. If your job calls for flexible weather stripping, use products made from neoprene rubber, not foam. Replace old door thresholds or threshold inserts as soon as they begin to show wear.

Install a storm door to decrease drafts and energy loss through entry doors. Buy an insulated storm door with a continuous hinge and seamless exterior surface.

Adjust the door frame to eliminate large gaps between the door and jamb. Remove the interior case molding and drive new shims between the jamb and framing member on the hinge side, reducing the size of the door opening. Close the door to test fit, and adjust as needed before reattaching the case molding.

Patio door: Use rubber compression strips to seal the channels in patio door jambs, where movable panels fit when closed. Also install a patio door insulator kit (plastic sheeting installed similarly to plastic sheeting for windows) on the interior side of the door.

Garage door: Attach a new rubber sweep to the bottom outside edge of the garage door if the old sweep has deteriorated. Also check the door jambs for drafts, and add weather stripping, if needed.

How to Weatherize an Exterior Door

Cut two pieces of metal tension strip or V-channel the full height of the door opening, and cut another to full width. Use wire brads to tack the strips to the door jambs and door header on the interior side of the doorstops. *TIP: Attach metal weather stripping from the top down to help prevent buckling.* Flare out the tension strips with a putty knife to fill the gaps between the jambs and the door when the door is in the closed position (do not pry too far at a time).

Add reinforced felt strips to the edge of the doorstop on the exterior side. The felt edge should form a close seal with the door when closed. *TIP: Drive fasteners only until they are flush with the surface of the reinforcing spine—overdriving will cause damage and buckling.*

Attach a new door sweep to the bottom of the door on the interior side (felt or bristle types are better choices if the floor is uneven). Before fastening it permanently, tack the sweep in place and test the door swing to make sure there is enough clearance.

Tip ▸

Fix any cracks in wooden door panels with epoxy wood filler or caulk to block air leaks. If the door has a stain finish, use tinted wood putty, filling from the interior side. Sand and touch up with paint or stain.

Tips for Weatherizing a Window ▸

Sliding windows: Treat side-by-side sliding windows as if they were double-hung windows turned 90°. For greater durability, use metal tension strips, rather than self-adhesive compressible foam, in the sash track that fit against the edge of the sash when the window is closed.

Casement windows: Attach self-adhesive foam or rubber compression strips on the outside edges of the window stops.

Storm windows: Create a tight seal by attaching foam compression strips to the outside of storm window stops. After installing the storm window, fill any gaps between the exterior window trim and the storm window with caulk backer rope (left). Check the inside surface of the storm window during cold weather for condensation or frost buildup. If moisture is trapped between the storm window and the permanent window, drill one or two small holes through the bottom rail (right) to allow moist air to escape. Drill at a slightly upward angle.

How to Weatherstrip a Window

Cut metal V-channel to fit in the channels for the sliding sash, extending at least 2" past the closed position for each sash (do not cover sash-closing mechanisms). Attach the V-channel by driving wire brads (usually provided by the manufacturer) with a tack hammer. Drive the fasteners flush with the surface so the sliding sash will not catch on them.

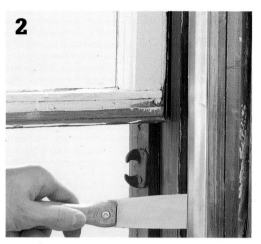

Flare out the open ends of the V-channels with a putty knife so the channel is slightly wider than the gap between the sash and the track it fits into. Avoid flaring out too much at one time—it is difficult to press V-channel back together without causing some buckling.

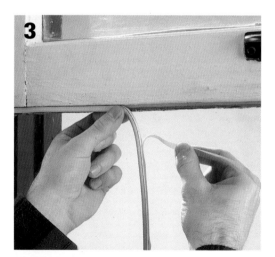

Wipe down the underside of the bottom window sash with a damp rag, and let it dry; then attach self-adhesive compressible foam or rubber to the underside of the sash. Use high-quality hollow neoprene strips, if available. This will create an airtight seal when the window is locked in position.

Bottom sash (raised)

Top sash (lowered)

Seal the gap between the top sash and the bottom sash on double-hung windows. Lift the bottom sash and lower the top sash to improve access, and tack metal V-channel to the bottom rail of the top sash using wire brads. *TIP: The open end of the "V" should be pointed downward so moisture cannot collect in the channel. Flare out the V-channel with a putty knife to fit the gap between the sash.*

Shortening Interior Doors

There should be a ⅜ to ¾" gap between the bottom of interior doors and the finished floor. This lets the door swing without binding on new carpet or other floor coverings. But eventually, you may decide to recarpet or add new tile or wood flooring beneath an existing door, and you'll need to shorten the door to create the proper gap again. If you own a circular saw with a fine-tooth blade, it's a simple project for a do-it-yourselfer.

Most newer homes have solid-wood interior doors these days, but hollow-core doors are still fairly common, and they're typical on older homes. Shortening either door type is a similar task, but hollow-core doors will require a few more steps because the door consists of multiple pieces (see page 129).

(see page 129)

Tools & Materials ▸

Hammer
Screwdriver
Utility knife
Sawhorses
Circular saw with fine-tooth blade
Straightedge
Clamps
File
Sanding block
Scrap plywood
Wood glue

Changing a floor covering is a great way to update the look of a room, but if the new floor covering is thicker than the old one, you can impede door swing. The solution is to shorten the door.

How to Shorten a Solid Wood Door

Set a strip of scrap plywood on the floor against the door, and trace along the plywood to create a reference line for cutting. The thickness of the plywood will set the amount of door gap, and it will help establish an even gap line. Do not press the plywood down into the carpet when drawing the line. If the flooring is uneven, open the door to where it rubs the most and use this spot to mark the gap.

Remove the door from the jamb by tapping out the hinge pins with a hammer and flat-blade screwdriver. If the hinge pins are fixed, you'll need to unscrew the hinge leaves from the jamb instead.

To prevent the saw from chipping the wood as it cuts, use a sharp utility knife to score along the cutting line. Guide the knife against a metal straightedge. Score both door faces and the edges.

(continued)

Clamp a straightedge to the door so the saw blade will cut about ¹⁄₁₆" on the waste side of your score line. The straightedge provides a guide for the edge of the saw base. Use the saw with a fine-tooth blade installed to check your setup.

Set the blade so the teeth project about ¼" below the door, and guide the saw along the straightedge to saw off the door bottom. Use steady feed pressure, and slow down your cutting rate at the end to prevent splintering the door edge.

Use a file to soften the sharp edges of the cut and to form a very slight chamfer all around the door bottom. Switch to a sanding block and medium-grit sandpaper to smooth away any blade marks and roughness.

With the door in place, measure ⅜" up from the top of the floor covering and mark the door. Remove the door from the hinges by tapping out the hinge pins with a screwdriver and a hammer.

Mark the cutting line. Cut through the door veneer with a sharp utility knife to prevent it from chipping when the door is sawed.

Lay the door on sawhorses and clamp a straightedge to the door as a cutting guide. Saw off the bottom of the door. The hollow core of the door may be exposed.

To reinstall a cutoff frame piece in the bottom of the door, chisel the veneer from both sides of the removed portion.

Apply wood glue to the cutoff piece. Insert the frame piece into the opening of the door and clamp it. Wipe away any excess glue and let the door dry overnight.

Replacing Thresholds

While construction varies from home to home, the part of a door that is generally referred to as the "threshold" is actually made up of two separate components: a sill, which serves as the bottom of the door frame and diverts water and dirt away from the home, and the threshold or saddle, which is attached to the sill and helps to seal the air space under a door. Due to constant traffic and exposure to the elements, sills and saddles may eventually require replacing.

Modern prehung doors often have a cast metal sill with an integrated saddle and are installed directly on top of the subfloor. Older homes often have thick wooden sills that are installed lower than metal sills, flush with the floor framing, with a separate saddle bridging the gap between the sill and the finished floor. Saddles are available in several styles and materials, such as wood, metal, and vinyl. Because the design of entry thresholds can vary, it is important to examine the construction of your door threshold to determine your needs. In this project, we replaced a deteriorating wooden sill and saddle with a new oak sill and a wooden weatherstripped saddle.

Besides replacing a deteriorating threshold, you might also choose to replace an existing threshold for increased accessibility. While standard thresholds are designed to keep mud and dirt out of a home, they deny access to people in wheelchairs and can cause people to trip if they are unsteady on their feet. See page 133 for tips on making thresholds accessible.

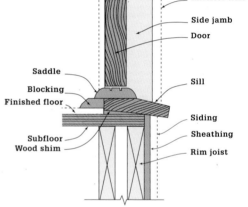

Tools & Materials ▸

Reciprocating saw	3" galvanized screws
Pry bar	or 10d galvanized
Hammer	casing nails
Chisel	1½" galvanized
Drill with	screws or 8d
countersink bit	galvanized nails
Pencil	Silicone caulk
Shims	Sealer/protectant
Putty	Tape measure

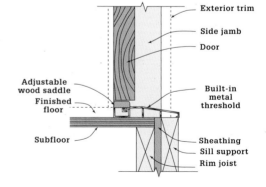

How to Replace an Exterior Door Threshold

Remove the old saddle. This may be as easy as unscrewing the saddle and prying it out. If necessary, cut the old saddle in two using a reciprocating saw, then pry out the saddle. Be careful not to damage the flooring or door frame. Note which edge of the saddle is more steeply beveled; the new saddle should be installed the same way.

Examine the sill for damage or deterioration. If it needs replacing, use a reciprocating saw to cut the sill into three pieces, cutting as close to the jambs as possible. Pry out the center piece, then use a hammer and chisel to split out the pieces directly beneath the jambs. Remove any remaining nails from beneath the jambs using a reciprocating saw with a metal cutting blade.

Measure and cut the new sill to size. If possible, use the salvaged end pieces from the old sill as a template to mark the notches on the new sill. Cut the notches using a jigsaw.

Test-fit the new sill, tapping it into place beneath the jambs using a hammer and wood block to protect the sill. Remove the sill and, if necessary, install long wood strips (or tapered shims) beneath the sill so it fits snugly beneath the jambs with a gentle slope away from the home.

(continued)

Apply several beads of caulk to the area beneath the sill. Tap the sill back in place. Drill countersunk pilot holes every 4 to 5" and fasten the sill with 10d galvanized casing nails or 3" screws.

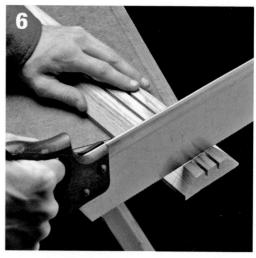

Measure the distance between the jambs and cut the new saddle to length. Test-fit the saddle. Mark the ends and cut notches to fit around the door jamb stops using a jigsaw. Apply caulk to the bottom of the saddle and position it so it covers the gap between the sill and the finished floor. Fasten the saddle using 1½" galvanized screws.

Variation ▸

If you are installing a metal saddle, instead of cutting notches in the saddle, use a hammer and chisel to notch the jamb stops to fit.

Waterproofing Tip ▸

A threshold insert seals the gap between the door and the saddle. A door sweep attaches to the door bottom to help seal out drafts.

Variation: Making Thresholds Accessible ▸

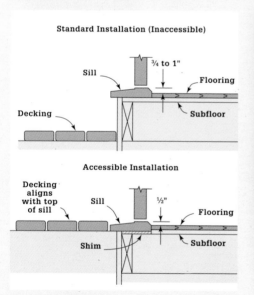

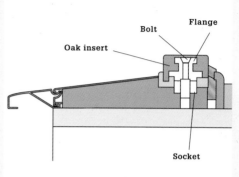

Adjustable sills: Many prehung doors have an aluminum sill with an adjustable wood saddle. Some versions can be made accessible without additional modification by lowering the saddle as far as possible. Other types can be adapted by recessing the sill into the subfloor.

Accessible thresholds: There are many ways to modify standard thresholds for accessibility. Often, the first step is to raise the exterior surface or decking to the same level as the threshold. Entry thresholds should be no higher than ¼" for square-edged sills and ½" high for beveled sills.

Mini-ramps: The slide channels on most sliding glass doors present a major obstacle for wheelchair users. The height difference can be as much as 2" from the bottom to the top of the track. Commercially available mini-ramps can make standard sliding glass door thresholds accessible.

Improving Window Operation

Many of us have experienced difficulty with opening windows due to swelled wood or painted channels. Almost as frequent, windows won't stay open because of a broken sash cord or chain. To avoid difficulties with windows, regular maintenance is crucial. Double-hung windows with spring-loaded sash tracks require cleaning and an occasional adjustment of the springs in (or behind) the tracks. Casement windows are often faulty at the crank mechanisms. If cleaning doesn't fix the problem, the crank mechanism must be replaced. For storm windows, the window track must be clean, and greaseless lubricant must be applied each time the windows and screens are removed.

Windows endure temperature extremes, house setting, and all sorts of wear and tear. Sooner or later you'll need to perform a bit of maintenance to keep them working properly.

Tools & Materials ▸

Heat gun	Work gloves	Scrap wood
Putty knife	Screwdrivers	Toothbrush
Linseed oil,	Paint zipper	Paint solvent
or primer	or utility knife	Rags
Glazing compound	Hammer	Sash cord
Glazier's points	Vacuum	Lubricant
Razor blade	Small pry bar	Wax candle
Paint scraper	Scissors	String
Eye protection	Stiff brush	All-purpose grease

How to Adjust Windows

Spring-loaded windows have an adjustment screw on the track insert. Adjust both sides until the window is balanced and opens and closes smoothly.

Spring-lift windows operate with the help of a spring-loaded lift rod inside a metal tube. Adjust them by unscrewing the top end of the tube from the jamb, then twisting the tube to change the spring tension: clockwise for more lifting power; counterclockwise for less. Maintain a tight grip on the tube at all times to keep it from unwinding.

Tips for Freeing Sticking Windows ▸

Cut the paint film if the window is painted shut. Insert a paint zipper or utility knife between the window stop and the sash, and slide it down to break the seal.

Place a block of scrap wood against the window sash. Tap lightly with a hammer to free the window.

Clean the tracks on sliding windows and doors with a hand vacuum and a toothbrush. Dirt buildup is common on storm window tracks.

Clean weatherstrips by spraying with a cleaner and wiping away dirt. Use paint solvent to remove paint that may bind windows. Then apply a small amount of lubricant to prevent sticking.

Lubricate wood window channels by rubbing them with a white candle, then open and close the window a few times. Do not use liquid lubricants on wood windows.

How to Replace Broken Sash Cords

Cut any paint seal between the window frame and stops with a utility knife or paint zipper. Pry the stops away from the frame, or remove the molding screws.

Bend the stops out from the center to remove them from the frame. Remove any weatherstripping that's in the way.

Slide out the lower window sash. Pull knotted or nailed cords from holes in the sides of the sash (see step 9).

Pry out or unscrew the weight pocket cover in the lower end of the window channel. Pull the weight from the pocket, and cut the old sash cord from the weight.

Tie one end of a piece of string to a nail and the other end to the new sash cord. Run the nail over the pulley and let it drop into the weight pocket. Retrieve the nail and string through the pocket.

Pull on the string to run the new sash cord over the pulley and through the weight pocket. Make sure the new cord runs smoothly over the pulley.

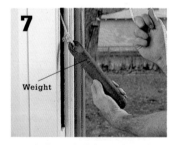

Attach the end of the sash cord to the weight using a tight double knot. Set the weight in the pocket. Pull on the cord until the weight touches the pulley.

Rest the bottom sash on the sill. Hold the sash cord against the side of the sash, and cut enough cord to reach 3" past the hole in the side of the sash.

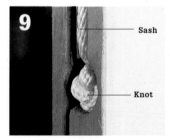

Knot the sash cord and wedge the knot into the hole in the sash. Replace the pocket cover. Slide the window and any weatherstripping into the frame, then attach the stops in the original positions.

How to Clean & Lubricate a Casement Window Crank

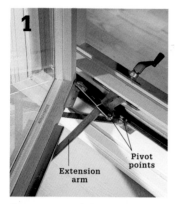

1

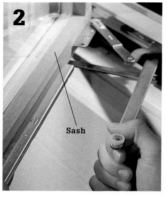

2

3

Labels on image 1: Pivot points, Extension arm

Label on image 2: Sash

Labels on image 3: Channel knob, WD-40

If a casement window is hard to crank, clean the accessible parts. Open the window until the roller at the end of the extension arm is aligned with the access slot in the window track.

Disengage the extension arm by pulling it down and out of the track. Clean the track with a stiff brush, and wipe the pivoting arms and hinges with a rag.

Lubricate the track and hinges with spray lubricant or household oil. Wipe off excess lubricant with a cloth, then reattach the extension arm. If that doesn't solve the problem, repair or replace the crank assembly (below).

How to Repair a Casement Window Crank Assembly

1

2

3

Label on image 6: white lithium grease

Disengage the extension arm from the window track, then remove the molding or cap concealing the crank mechanism. Unhinge any pivot arms connected to the window.

Remove the screws securing the crank assembly, then remove the assembly and clean it thoroughly. If the gears are badly worn, replace the assembly. Check a home center or call the manufacturer for new parts. Note which way the window opens— to the right or left—when ordering replacement parts.

Apply an all-purpose grease to the gears, and reinstall the assembly. Connect the pivot arms, and attach the extension arm to the window. Test the window operation before installing the cap and molding.

How to Fix a Broken Windowpane

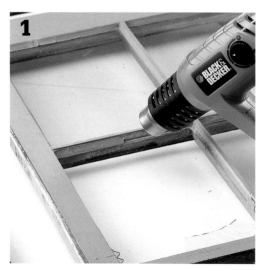

Wearing heavy leather gloves, remove the broken pieces of glass. Then, soften the old glazing compound using a heat gun or a hair dryer. Don't hold the heat gun too long in one place because it can be hot enough to scorch the wood or crack adjacent panes of glass.

Once a section of compound is soft, remove it using a putty knife. Work carefully to avoid gouging the wood frame. If a section is difficult to scrape clean, reheat it with the heat gun. Soft compound is always easy to remove.

Once the wood opening is scraped clean, seal the wood with a coat of linseed oil or primer. If the wood isn't sealed, the dry surface will draw too much moisture from the glazing compound and reduce its effectiveness.

Apply a thin bed of glazing compound to the wood frame opening and smooth it in place with your thumb.

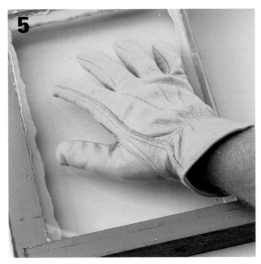

5

Press the new pane into the opening, making sure to achieve a tight seal with the compound on all sides. Wiggle the pane from side to side and up and down until the pane is seated. There will be some squeeze-out, but do not press all the compound out.

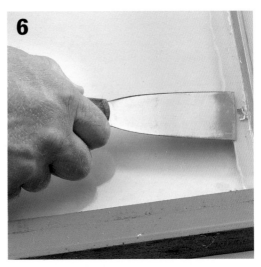

6

Drive glazier's points into the wood frame to hold the pane in place. Use the tip of a putty knife to slide the point against the surface of the glass. Install at least 2 points on each side of the pane.

7

Make a rope of compound (about ½" dia.) by rolling it between your hands. Then press it against the pane and the wood frame. Smooth it in place by drawing a putty knife, held at a 45° angle, across its surface. Scrape off excess.

8

Allow the glazing compound at least one week to dry completely. Then prime and paint it to match the rest of the sash. Be sure to spread the paint over the joint between the compound and the glass. This will seal the joint completely. When the paint is dry, scrape off the extra with a razor blade paint scraper.

Fixing Storm Windows & Doors

Compared to removable wood storm windows and screens, repairing combination storm windows is a little more complex. But there are several repairs you can make without too much difficulty, as long as you find the right parts. Take the old corner keys, gaskets, or other original parts to a hardware store that repairs storm windows so the clerk can help you find the correct replacement parts. If you cannot find the right parts, have a new sash built.

Tools & Materials ▸

Tape measure
Screwdriver
Scissors
Drill
Utility knife
Spline roller
Nail set

Hammer
Spline cord
Screening, glass
Rubber gasket
Replacement hardware
Lubricant

Remove the metal storm window sash by pressing in the release hardware in the lower rail then lifting the sash out. Sash hangers on the corners of the top rail should be aligned with the notches in the side channels before removal.

How to Replace Screening in a Metal Storm Window

Pry the vinyl spline from the groove around the edge of the frame with a screwdriver. Retain the old spline if it is still flexible, or replace it with a new spline.

Stretch the new screen tightly over the frame so that it overlaps the edges of the frame. Keeping the screen taut, use the convex side of a spline roller to press the screen into the retaining grooves.

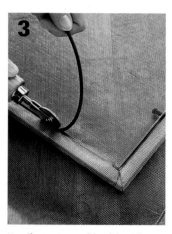

Use the concave side of the spline roller to press the spline into the groove (it helps to have a partner for this). Cut away excess screen using a utility knife.

How to Replace Glass in a Metal Storm Window

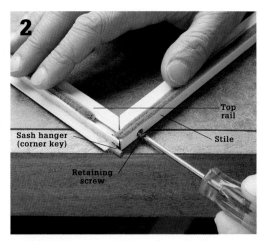

Remove the sash frame from the window, then completely remove the broken glass from the sash. Remove the rubber gasket that framed the old glass pane and remove any glass remnants. Find the dimensions for the replacement glass by measuring between the inside edges of the frame opening, then adding twice the thickness of the rubber gasket to each measurement.

Set the frame on a flat surface, and disconnect the top rail. Remove the retaining screws in the sides of the frame stiles where they join the top rail. After unscrewing the retaining screws, pull the top rail loose, pulling gently in a downward motion to avoid damaging the L-shaped corner keys that join the rail and the stiles. For glass replacement, you need only disconnect the top rail.

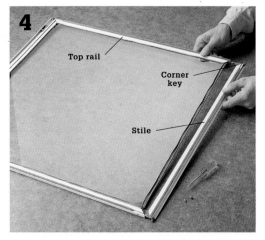

Fit the rubber gasket (buy a replacement if the original is in poor condition) around one edge of the replacement glass pane. At the corners, cut the spine of the gasket partway so it will bend around the corner. Continue fitting the gasket around the pane, cutting at the corners, until all four edges are covered. Trim off any excess gasket material.

Slide the glass pane into the channels in the stiles and bottom rail of the sash frame. Insert corner keys into the top rail, then slip the other ends of the keys into the frame stiles. Press down on the top rail until the mitered corners are flush with the stiles. Drive the retaining screws back through the stiles and into the top rail to join the frame together. Reinsert the frame into the window.

How to Disassemble & Repair a Metal Sash Frame

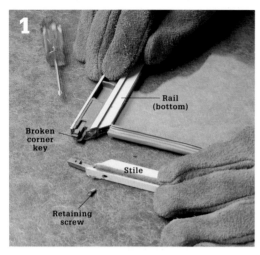

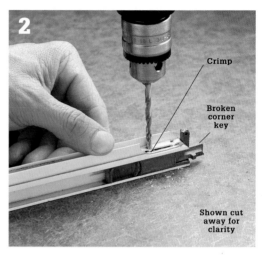

Metal window sash are held together at the corner joints by L-shaped pieces of hardware that fit into grooves in the sash frame pieces. To disassemble a broken joint, start by disconnecting the stile and rail at the broken joint—there is usually a retaining screw driven through the stile that must be removed.

Corner keys are secured in the rail slots with crimps that are punched into the metal over the key. To remove keys, drill through the metal in the crimped area using a drill bit the same diameter as the crimp. Carefully knock the broken key pieces from the frame slots with a screwdriver and hammer.

Locate matching replacement parts for the broken corner key, which is usually an assembly of two or three pieces. There are dozens of different types, so it is important that you save the old parts for reference.

Insert the replacement corner key assembly into the slot in the rail. Use a nail set as a punch, and rap it into the metal over the corner key, creating a new crimp to hold the key in place.

Insert the glass and gasket into the frame slots, then reassemble the frame and drive in retainer screws (for screen windows, replace the screening).

Tips for Maintaining Storm Windows & Doors ▸

Replace turnbuttons and window clips that do not hold storm windows tightly in place. Fill old screw holes with wood dowels and glue before driving the screws.

Lubricate the sliding assemblies on metal-framed combination storm windows or doors once a year using penetrating lubricant.

Replace deteriorated glazing around glass panes in wood-framed windows. Sound glazing makes windows more energy-efficient and more attractive.

Tighten storm door latches by redriving loose screws in the strike plate. If the latch does not catch on the strike plate, loosen the screws on the strike plate, insert thin wood shims between the plate and the jamb, and retighten the screws.

Add a wind chain if your storm door does not have one. Wind chains prevent doors from blowing open too far, causing damage to the door hinges or closer. Set the chain so the door will not open more than 90°.

Adjust the door closer so it has the right amount of tension to close the door securely, without slamming. Most closers have tension-adjustment screws at the end of the cylinder farthest from the hinge side of the door.

Installing Replacement Windows

If you're looking to replace or improve old single- or double-hung windows, consider using sash-replacement kits. They can give you energy-efficient, maintenance-free windows without changing the outward appearance of your home or breaking your budget.

Unlike prime window replacement, which changes the entire window and frame, or pocket window replacement, in which a complete window unit is set into the existing frame, sash replacement uses the original window jambs, eliminating the need to alter exterior or interior walls or trim. Installing a sash-replacement kit involves little more than removing the old window stops and sashes and installing new vinyl jamb liners and wood or vinyl sash. And all of the work can be done from inside your home.

Most sash-replacement kits offer tilt features and other contemporary conveniences. Kits are available in vinyl, aluminum, or wood construction with various options for color and glazing, energy efficiency, security features, and noise reduction.

Nearly all major window manufacturers offer sash-replacement kits designed to fit their own windows. You can also order custom kits that are sized to your specific window dimensions. A good fit is essential to the performance of your new windows. Review the tips shown on the next page for measuring your existing windows, and follow the manufacturer's instructions for the best fit.

Tools & Materials ▸

Sill-bevel gauge
Flat pry bar
Scissors
Screwdriver
Nail set
Sash-replacement kit
1" galvanized roofing nails

Fiberglass insulation
Finish nails
Wood-finishing materials
Torpedo level
Eye and ear protection
Work gloves

Upgrade old, leaky windows with new, energy-efficient sash-replacement kits. Kits are available in a variety of styles to match your existing windows or to add a new decorative accent to your home. Most kits offer natural or painted interior surfaces and a choice of outdoor surface finishes.

How to Install a New Window Sash

Measure the width of the existing window at the top, middle, and bottom of the frame. Use the smallest measurement, then reduce the figure by ⅜". Measure the height of the existing window from the head jamb to the point where the outside edge of the bottom sash meets the sill. Reduce the figure by ⅜". *NOTE: Manufacturers' specifications for window sizing may vary.*

Check for a straight, level, and plumb sill, side, and head jambs using a torpedo level. Measure the frame diagonally to check for square (if the diagonal measurements are equal, the frame is square). If the frame is not square, check with the sash-kit manufacturer. Most window kits can accommodate some deviation in frame dimensions.

Carefully remove the interior stops from the side jambs, using a putty knife or pry bar. Save the stops for reinstallation.

With the bottom sash down, cut the cord holding the sash, balancing weight on each side of the sash. Let the weights and cords fall into the weight pockets.

(continued)

Lift out the bottom sash. Remove the parting stops from the head and side jambs. (The parting stops are the strips of wood that separate the top and bottom sash.) Cut the sash cords for the top sash, then lift out the top sash. Remove the sash-cord pulleys. If possible, pull the weights from the weight pockets at the bottom of the side jambs, then fill the weight pockets with fiberglass insulation. Repair any parts of the jambs that are rotted or damaged.

Position the jamb-liner brackets, and fasten them to the jambs with 1" galvanized roofing nails. Place one bracket approximately 4" from the head jamb and one 4" from the sill. Leave 1/16" clearance between the blind stop and the jamb-liner bracket. Install any remaining brackets, spacing them evenly along the jambs.

Position any gaskets or weatherstripping provided for the jamb liners. Carefully position each liner against its brackets and snap it into place. When both liners are installed, set the new parting stop into the groove of the existing head jamb, and fasten it with small finish nails. Install a vinyl sash stop in the interior track at the top of each liner to prevent the bottom sash from being opened too far.

Set the sash control mechanism, using a slotted screwdriver. Gripping the screwdriver firmly, slide down the mechanism until it is about 9" above the sill, then turn the screwdriver to lock the mechanism and prevent it from springing upward. The control mechanisms are spring-loaded—do not let them go until they are locked in place. Set the mechanism in each of the four sash channels.

Install the top sash into the jamb liners. Set the cam pivot on one side of the sash into the outside channel. Tilt the sash, and set the cam pivot on the other side of the sash. Make sure both pivots are set above the sash control mechanisms. Holding the sash level, tilt it up, depress the jamb liners on both sides, and set the sash in the vertical position in the jamb liners. Once the sash is in position, slide it down until the cam pivots contact the locking terminal assemblies.

Install the bottom sash into the jamb liners, setting it into the inside sash channels. When the bottom sash is set in the vertical position, slide it down until it engages the control mechanisms. Open and close both sashes to make sure they operate properly.

Reinstall the stops that you removed in step 3. Fasten them with finish nails, using the old nail holes, or drill new pilot holes for the nails.

Check the tilt operation of the bottom sash to make sure the stops do not interfere. Remove the labels, and clean the windows. Paint or varnish the new sash as desired.

Securing Windows & Doors

Securing windows and doors is often simply a matter of having the right hardware pieces. But skimping on strength or quality with any of them will undermine the security of the whole system.

Glass is both the strength and weakness of windows, in terms of security. An intruder can easily break the glass, but may not, since the noise it would make is likely to draw attention. Aside from installing metal bars, there's no way to secure the glass, so make sure your windows can't be opened from the outside.

Entry doors should be metal or solid wood—at least 1¾" thick—and each one in the home should have a deadbolt lock, as doorknob locks provide little security. Lock quality varies widely; just make sure to choose one that has a bolt (or bolt core) of hardened steel and a minimum 1" throw— the distance the bolt protrudes from the door when engaged.

Door hinges are easy to secure. Manufacturers offer a variety of inexpensive devices that hold a door in place even when the hinge pins are removed.

Garage doors are structurally secure, but their locking devices can make them easy targets. When you're away from home, place a padlock in the roller track. If you have an automatic door opener, make sure the remote transmitter uses a rolling code system, which prevents thieves from copying your signal. An electronic keypad can make your garage door as secure and easy to use as your front door.

Tools & Materials ▸

Hammer	Plywood shims
Drill	Casing nails
Hole saw	Board
Spade bit	Eye bolts
Awl	Hinge
Screwdriver	Screws
Chisel	Dowel
Utility knife	Security devices

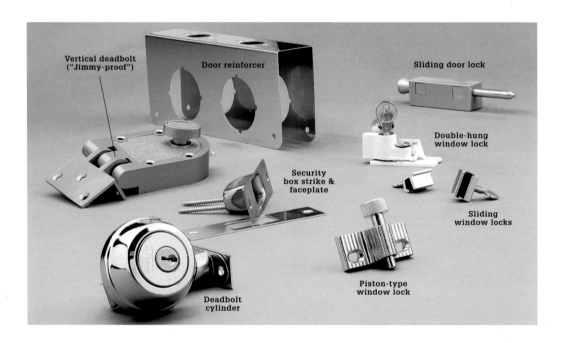

Vertical deadbolt ("Jimmy-proof")

Door reinforcer

Sliding door lock

Double-hung window lock

Security box strike & faceplate

Sliding window locks

Deadbolt cylinder

Piston-type window lock

Tips for Securing Windows

Pin together sashes of single- and double-hung windows with ¼ × 3" eye bolts. With the window closed, drill a ¼"-dia. hole, at a slight downward angle, through the top rail of the bottom sash and into the bottom rail of the top sash. Avoid hitting the glass, and stop the hole about ¾ of the way through the top sash. To lock the window in open positions, drill holes along the sash stiles (vertical pieces) instead.

Drive screws into the top channel of sliding windows to prevent intruders from lifting the window sash out of the lower channel. The screws should just clear the top of the window and not interfere with its operation. Use sturdy screws, and space them about 6" apart.

Block sash channels on sliding windows with a narrow board or a thick dowel.

Use auxiliary locks on sliding windows when a dowel or board won't work. Most types can be installed on the upper or lower window track.

Replace old sash locks on double-hung windows with keyed devices. Traditional sash locks can be highly vulnerable—especially on old windows. Be sure to store a key nearby, for emergency exits.

(continued)

Removing the handles from casement and awning windows keeps intruders from cranking the window open after breaking the glass.

Security bars or gates can be installed in ground-floor windows to prevent intruders from gaining entry to your home.

Tips for Securing Sliding Glass Doors

Make a custom lock for your door track, using a thick board and a hinge. Cut the board to fit behind the closed door, then cut it again a few inches from one end. Install a hinge so you can flip up the end and keep the door secure while it's ajar. Attach knobs to facilitate use.

Drive screws into the upper track to keep the sliding panel from being pried up and out of the lower track. Use sturdy pan-head screws, spaced about every 8", and drive them so their heads just clear the top of the door. For metal door frames, use self-tapping screws and a low drill speed.

Attach a sliding-door lock to the frame of the sliding panel. Drill a hole for the deadbolt into the upper track. Then drill an additional hole a few inches away so you can lock the door in an open position.

Tips for Securing Doors

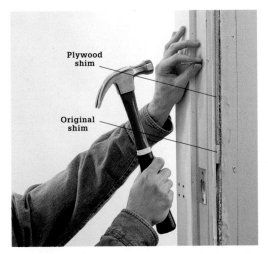

Install plywood shims in the gaps between the door frame and wall studs, to prevent pry-bar attacks. Remove the casing molding on the inside of the frame and inspect the gap; if it's wider than ¼", install new plywood shims in the spaces between the original shims. Be sure to shim directly above, below, and behind the strike plate. Drill pilot holes, and secure the shims with 10d casing nails.

Replace short hinge screws with longer screws (3" or 4") that extend through the door jamb and into the wall studs. This helps resist door kick-ins. Tighten the screws snug, but avoid overtightening them, which can pull the frame out of square.

Add metal door reinforcers to strengthen the areas around locks and prevent kick-ins. Remove the lockset and slip the reinforcer over the door's edge. Be sure to get a reinforcer that is the correct thickness for your door.

Add a heavy-duty latch guard to reinforce the door jamb around the strike plate. For added protection, choose a guard with a flange that resists pry-bar attacks. Install the guard with long screws that reach the wall studs.

(continued)

Have lock cylinders re-keyed to ensure that lost or stolen keys can't be used by unwanted visitors. Remove cylinder, leaving bolt mechanism in door, and take it to a locksmith.

Putting a peephole into an exterior door is a quick and easy security measure. Simply drill a hole at the appropriate height, then screw the two halves of the peephole together.

How to Install a Security Box Strike

Mark the horizontal center of the deadbolt on the door jamb and tape the box strike template to the jamb, aligning the center marks. Use an awl to mark the drilling points, then use a utility knife to score a ⅛"-deep line around the outside of the template.

Drill pilot holes for the faceplate screws, and bore holes for the box mortise, using the recommended spade bit. To chisel the faceplate mortise, make parallel cuts ⅛" deep, holding the chisel at a 45° angle with the bevel side in. Flip the chisel over, and drive it downward to remove the material.

Insert the box strike into the mortise and install the screws inside the box. Angle the screws slightly toward the center of the wall stud, to increase their holding power. Position the faceplate and install the screws.

How to Install a Deadbolt Lock

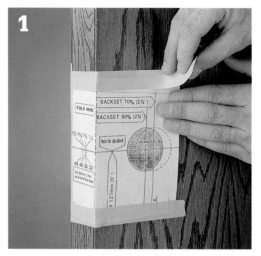

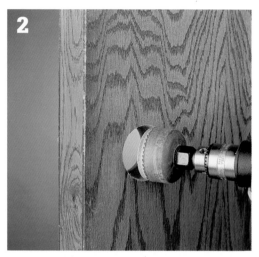

Measure up from the floor or existing lockset to locate the lock. Its center should be at least 3½" from the lockset center. Tape the template (supplied with lock) to the door. Use an awl to mark the center-points of the cylinder and deadbolt holes on the door. Close the door and use the template to mark the centerline for the deadbolt hole in the door jamb.

Bore the cylinder hole with a hole saw and drill. To avoid splintering the door, drill through one side until the hole saw pilot (mandrel) just comes out the other side. Remove the hole saw, then complete the hole from the opposite side of the door.

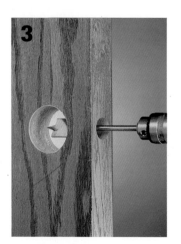

Use a spade bit to bore the deadbolt hole from the edge of the door into the cylinder hole. Be sure to keep the drill perpendicular to the door edge while drilling.

Insert the deadbolt into the edge hole. Fit the two halves of the lock into the door, aligning the cylinder tailpiece and connecting screw fittings with the proper holes in the deadbolt. Secure the two halves together with the connecting screws.

Use the centerline mark on the jamb to locate the hole for the deadbolt. Bore the hole, then chisel a mortise for the strike plate. Install the strike plate. Or, for greater security, install a security box strike, instead of the standard strike plate.

Tuning Up Garage Doors

Imagine this: You're driving home late at night, it's pouring outside, and you're shivering because you've got the flu. Then, you turn into your driveway, punch a little button, and your garage door opens, a light comes on, you pull in, and you're HOME. You didn't have to get drenched, or lift a door that felt like heavy metal, or scream at the heavens for making you so miserable. Thanks to a well-maintained garage door and opener, you escaped all of this, and that is a good thing.

Unfortunately, over time, many good things become bad things, especially if they aren't well-maintained. An overhead garage door is no exception. To keep everything running smoothly requires effort on three fronts: the door, the opener, and the opener's electronic safety sensors. Here's what you need to know to keep all three in tiptop shape.

Tools & Materials ▶

Mineral spirits
Graphite spray lubricant
Garage door weather-stripping
Level
Soft-faced mallet
Penetrating lubricant
Toweling
Socket wrenches
Lightweight oil
Pliers
Open-end wrenches
Old paintbrush or toothbrush
Screwdriver
Eye and ear protection
Work gloves

A bit of routine maintenance now and again will help keep your garage door working exactly as it should, rain or shine.

How to Tune-Up a Garage Door

Begin the tune-up by lubricating the door tracks, pulleys, and rollers. Use a lightweight oil, not grease, for this job. The grease catches too much dust and dirt.

Remove clogged or damaged rollers from the door by loosening the nuts that hold the roller brackets. The roller will come with the bracket when the bracket is pulled free.

Mineral spirits and kerosene are good solvents for cleaning roller bearings. Let the bearing sit for a half hour in the solvent. Then brush away the grime build-up with an old paintbrush or toothbrush.

(continued)

4

If the rollers are making a lot of noise as they move over the tracks, the tracks are probably out of alignment. To fix this, check the tracks for plumb. If they are out of plumb, the track mounting brackets must be adjusted.

5

To adjust out-of-plumb tracks, loosen all the track mounting brackets (usually 3 or 4 per track) and push the brackets into alignment.

6

It's often easier to adjust the brackets by partially loosening the bolts and tapping the track with a soft-faced mallet. Once the track is plumb, tighten all the bolts.

Sometimes the door lock bar opens sluggishly because the return spring has lost its tension. The only way to fix this is to replace the spring. One end is attached to the body of the lock; the other end hooks onto the lock bar.

If a latch needs lubrication, use graphite in powder or liquid form. Don't use oil because it attracts dust that will clog the lock even more.

ALTERNATIVE: Sometimes the lock bar won't lock the door because it won't slide into its opening on the door track. To fix this, loosen the guide bracket that holds the lock bar and move it up or down until the bar hits the opening.

(continued)

Worn or broken weather stripping on the bottom edge of the door can let in a lot of cold air and stiff breezes. Check to see if this strip is cracked, broken, or has holes along its edges. If so, remove the old strip and pull any nails left behind.

Measure the width of your garage door, then buy a piece of weather stripping to match. These strips are standard lumber-yard and home center items. Sometimes they are sold in kit form, with fasteners included. If not, just nail the stripping in place with galvanized roofing nails.

If the chain on your garage door opener is sagging more than ½" below the bottom rail, it can make a lot of noise and cause drive sprocket wear. Tighten the chain according to the directions in the owner's manual.

On openers with a chain, lubricate the entire length of the chain with lightweight oil. Do not use grease. Use the same lubricant if your opener has a drive screw instead.

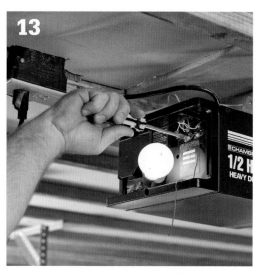

Test the door's closing force sensitivity and make adjustments at the opener's motor case if needed. Because both the sensitivity and the adjustment mechanism vary greatly between opener models, you'll have to rely on your owner's manual for guidance. If you don't have the owner's manual, you can usually download one from the manufacturer's website.

Check for proper alignment on the safety sensors near the floor. They should be pointing directly at one another and their lenses should be clean of any dirt and grease.

Make sure that the sensors are "talking" to the opener properly. Start to close the door, then put your hand down between the two sensors. If the door stops immediately and reverses direction, it's working properly. If it's not, make the adjustment recommended in the owner's manual. If that doesn't do the trick, call a professional door installer and don't use the door until it passes this test.

Installing Garage Doors

Your sectional garage door will bear the brunt of everything Mother Nature and an active household throws at it—seasonal temperature swings, moisture, blistering sunlight, and the occasional misfired half-court jump shot. If that isn't enough, the average sectional garage door cycles up and down at least four times per day, which totals up to around 1,300 or more uses every year. For all of these reasons, it pays to install a high-quality door on your new garage so you can enjoy a long service life from it.

These days, you don't have to settle for a drab, flat-panel door. Door manufacturers provide many options for cladding colors, panel texture and layout, exterior hardware, and window styles. Today's state-of-the-art garage doors also benefit from improved material construction, more sophisticated safety features, and enhanced energy efficiency. When you order your new door, double-check your garage's rough opening and minimum ceiling height to be sure the new door will fit the space properly.

Installing a sectional garage door is easier than you might think, and manufacturers make the process quite accessible for average do-it-yourselfers. With a helper or two, you should have little difficulty installing a new garage door in a single day. The job is really no more complex than other window and door replacements if you work carefully and exercise good judgment. Garage door kits come with all the necessary hardware and detailed step-by-step instructions. Since garage door styles vary, the installation process for your new door may differ from the photo sequence you see here, so always defer to the manufacturer's instructions. This will ensure the door is installed correctly and the manufacturer will honor the product warranty.

Tools & Materials ▸

Work gloves & eye
  protection
Tape measure
Long level
Drill with nut drivers
Stepladder
Ratchet wrench with
  sockets

Adjustable wrench
Hammer
Sectional garage
  door with tracks
  & mounting
  brackets
16d nails
Doorstop molding

The sectional garage door you choose for your garage will go a long way toward defining the building's appearance and giving you trouble-free performance day in and day out.

Measure for the door. Measure the width of the header, the headroom clearance to the rafter collar ties (or bottom truss chords), and the inside opening of the doorway. Check these measurements against the minimum requirements outlined in the instruction manual that comes with your sectional garage door.

Assemble door tracks. Working on the floor, lay out and assemble the vertical tracks, jamb brackets, and flag angle hardware. Install the door bottom seal and the roller and hinge hardware on the bottom door section.

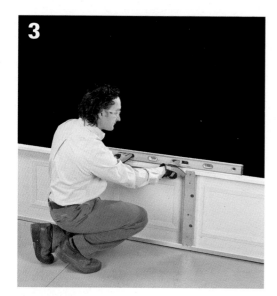

Install the first section. Set the bottom door section into position against the side jambs, and adjust it left or right until the side jambs overlap it evenly. Check the top of the door section for level. Place shims beneath the door to level it, if necessary. Have a helper hold the door section in place against the jambs until it is secured in the tracks.

Attach the tracks. Slip a vertical track over the door section rollers and against the side jamb. Adjust it for plumb, then fasten the jamb brackets to the side jamb blocking with lag screws. Carefully measure, mark, and install the other vertical track as well.

(continued)

Attach the lift cables. Depending on your door design, you may need to attach lift cables to the bottom door section at this time. Follow the instructions that come with your door to connect these cables correctly.

Install the door hinges. Fasten the end and intermediate hinges to the bottom door section, and then install roller brackets and hinges on the other door sections. Attach hinges to the top edges of each door section only. This way you'll be able to stack one section on top of the next during assembly.

Add next sections. Slip the next door section into place in the door tracks and on top of the first section. Connect the bottom hinges (already attached to the first section) to the second door section. Repeat the process until you have stacked and installed all but the top door section.

OPTION: The top door section may require additional bracing, special top roller brackets, and a bracket for securing a garage door opener. Install these parts now following the door manufacturer's instructions.

Install the top section. Set the top door section in place and fasten it to the hinges on the section below it. Support the door section temporarily with a few 16d nails driven into the door header blocking and bent down at an angle.

Complete track installation. Fasten the horizontal door tracks to the flag angle brackets on top of the vertical track sections. Temporarily suspend the back ends of the tracks with rope so they are level.

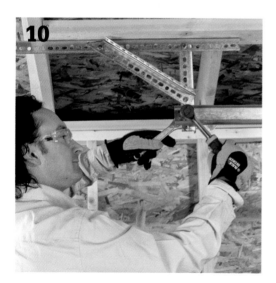

Install rear hanger brackets. This step will vary among door opener brands. Check your door instruction manual for the correct location of rear hanger brackets that will hold the horizontal door tracks in position. Measure, cut, and fasten sections of perforated angle iron together with bolts, washers, and nuts to form two Y-shaped door track brackets. Fasten the brackets to the collar tie or bottom truss chord with lag screws and washers following the door manufacturer's recommendations.

Attach the extension springs. The door opener here features a pair of smaller springs that run parallel to the horizontal door tracks, not parallel to the door header as larger torsion springs are installed. The springs are attached to cables that attach to the rear door hanger brackets.

(continued)

12

13

Test to make sure the door tracks properly. Raise it about halfway first. You'll need at least one helper here. Slide a sturdy support underneath the door bottom to hold the door and then inspect to make sure the rollers are tracking and the tracks are parallel.

Attach the spring cables. The door should be fully raised and held in place with C-clamps tightened onto the tracks to prevent it from slipping down. The tension in the springs should be relieved. The cables in this case are tied off onto a 3-hole clip that is then hooked onto the horizontal angle bracket near the front of the tracks.

14

15

Attach the doorstop molding. Measure, cut, and nail sections of doorstop molding to the door jambs on the outside of the door to seal out weather. A rolled vinyl doorstop may come with your door kit. If not, use strips of 1 × 2 treated wood or cedar for this purpose.

Attach a new rubber sweep to the bottom outside edge of the garage door. Also check the door jambs for drafts, and add weather stripping, if needed.

Garage Door Openers

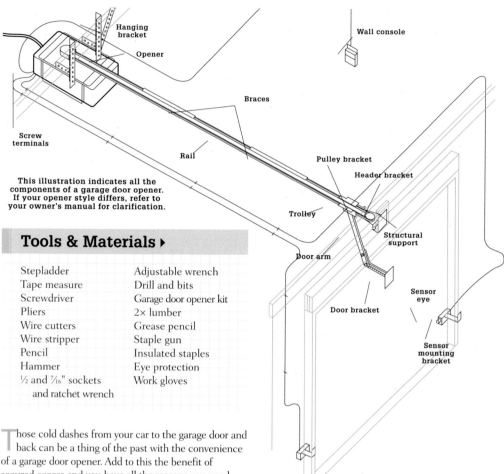

Hanging bracket

Opener

Wall console

Braces

Screw terminals

Rail

Pulley bracket

Header bracket

This illustration indicates all the components of a garage door opener. If your opener style differs, refer to your owner's manual for clarification.

Trolley

Structural support

Door arm

Sensor eye

Door bracket

Sensor mounting bracket

Tools & Materials ▶

Stepladder	Adjustable wrench
Tape measure	Drill and bits
Screwdriver	Garage door opener kit
Pliers	2× lumber
Wire cutters	Grease pencil
Wire stripper	Staple gun
Pencil	Insulated staples
Hammer	Eye protection
½ and ⁷⁄₁₆" sockets and ratchet wrench	Work gloves

Those cold dashes from your car to the garage door and back can be a thing of the past with the convenience of a garage door opener. Add to this the benefit of secured access and you have all the reasons you need to install an automatic garage door opener. Garage door openers come in three basic models, each with its own benefits and drawbacks, but this project shows the basic steps for installing a chain-drive system—the most common and least expensive type—on a sectional door in a garage with exposed joists. If you have a one-piece door, a lightweight metal or glass-paneled door, or a garage with a finished ceiling, consult the manufacturer's directions for alternative installation procedures.

Before you begin, read all of the manufacturer's instructions. Then make sure your garage door is properly balanced and moves smoothly. Open and

close the door to see if it sticks or binds at any point. Release the door in the half-open position. It should stay in place supported by its own springs. If your door is not balanced or sticks at any point, call a garage door service professional before installing the opener.

Most garage door openers plug into a standard grounded receptacle located near the unit. Some local codes may require openers to be hard-wired into circuits. Consult the manufacturer's directions for hard-wiring procedures.

How to Install a Garage Door Opener

Start by aligning the rail pieces in proper order and securing them with the included braces and bolts. Screw the pulley bracket to the door end of the rail and slide the trolley onto the rail. Make sure the pulley and all rail pieces are properly aligned and that the trolley runs smoothly without hitting any hardware along the rail. Remove the two screws from the top of the opener, then attach the rail to the opener using these screws (inset).

The drive chain/cable should be packaged in its own dispensing carton. Attach the cable loop to the front of the trolley using the included linking hardware. Wrap the cable around the pulley, then wrap the remaining chain around the drive sprocket on the opener. Finally, attach it to the other side of the trolley with linking hardware. Make sure the chain is not twisted, then attach the cover over the drive sprocket. Tighten the chain by adjusting the nuts on the trolley until the chain is ½" above the base of the rail.

To locate the header bracket, first extend a vertical line from the center of the door onto the wall above. Raise the door and note the highest point the door reaches. Measure from the floor to this point. Add 2" to this distance and mark a horizontal line on the front wall where it intersects the centerline. If there is no structural support behind the cross point, fasten 2× lumber across the framing. Then fasten the header bracket to the structural support with the included screws.

Support the opener on the floor with a board or box to prevent stress and twisting to the rail. Attach the rail pulley bracket to the header bracket above the door with the included clevis pin. Then place the opener on a stepladder so it is above the door tracks. Open the door and shim beneath the opener until the rail is 2" above the door.

Hang the opener from the ceiling joists with the included hanging brackets and screws. Angle at least one of the hanging brackets to increase the stability of the unit while in operation. Attach the manual release cord and handle to the release arm of the trolley.

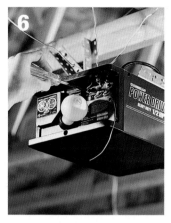

Strip ¼" of sheathing from the wall-console bell wire. Connect the wire to the screw terminals on the console, then attach it to the inside wall of the garage with the included screws. Run the wires up the wall and connect them to the proper terminals on the opener. Secure the wire to the wall with insulated staples, being careful not to pierce the wire. Install the light bulbs and lenses.

Install the sensor-eye mounting brackets at each side of the garage door, parallel to each other, about 4 to 6" from the floor. The sensor brackets can be attached to the door track, the wall, or the floor, depending upon your garage layout. See the manufacturer's directions for the best configuration for your garage.

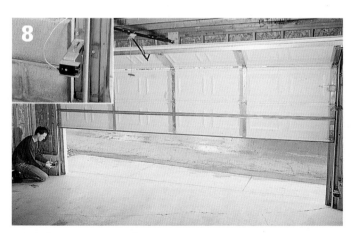

Attach the sensor eyes to the brackets with the included wing nuts, but do not tighten the nuts completely. Make sure the path of the eyes is unobstructed by the door tracks. Run wires from both sensors to the opener unit and connect the wires to the proper terminals. Plug the opener into a grounded receptacle and adjust the sensors until the indicator light shows the correct eye alignment (inset), then tighten the wing nuts. Unplug the unit and attach the sensor wires to the walls with insulated staples.

Center the door bracket 2 to 4" below the top of the door. Drill holes and attach the bracket with the included carriage bolts. Connect the straight and curved arm sections with the included bolts. Attach the arm to the trolley and door bracket with the included latch pins. Plug the opener into a grounded receptacle and test the unit. See the manufacturer's directions for adjustment procedures.

Removing Windows & Doors

If your remodeling project requires removing old windows and doors, do not start this work until all preparation work is finished and the interior wall surfaces and trim have been removed. You will need to close up the wall openings as soon as possible, so make sure you have all the necessary tools, framing lumber, and new window or door units before starting the final stages of demolition. Be prepared to finish the work as quickly as possible.

Windows and doors are removed using the same basic procedures. In many cases, old units can be salvaged for resale or later use, so use care when removing them.

Tools & Materials ▶

Utility knife
Flat pry bar
Hammer
Reciprocating saw
Plywood
Masking tape

Removing windows or doors is a similar process and often easier with a helper. Use care when removing large windows or patio doors, which can be very heavy.

Masking tape used to keep windows from shattering

How to Remove Doors

1

Using a pry bar and hammer, gently remove the interior door trim. Save the trim to use after the new door is installed.

2

Cut away the old caulk between the exterior siding and the brick molding on the door frame using a utility knife.

3

Use a flat pry bar or a cat's paw to remove the casing nails securing the door jambs to the framing. Cut stubborn nails with a reciprocating saw (see step 2, below). Remove the door from the opening.

How to Remove Windows

1

Carefully pry off the interior trim around the window frame. For double-hung windows with sash weights, remove the weights by cutting the cords and pulling the weights from the weight pockets near the bottom of the side jambs.

2

Cut through the nails holding the window jambs to the framing members using a reciprocating saw. Place tape over the windowpanes to prevent shattering, then remove the window unit from the opening.

Nailing flange

Variation: For windows and doors attached with nailing flanges, cut or pry loose the siding material, then remove the nails holding the unit to the sheathing. See pages 202 to 203 for more information on removing siding.

Installing Prehung Interior Doors

Install prehung interior doors after the framing work is complete and the drywall has been installed. If the rough opening for the door has been framed accurately, installing the door takes about an hour.

Standard prehung doors have 4½-inch-wide jambs and are sized to fit walls with 2 × 4 construction and ½-inch wallboard. If you have 2 × 6 construction or thicker wall surface material, you can special-order a door to match, or you can add jamb extensions to a standard-sized door (photo, below).

Tools & Materials ▸

Level	8d casing nails
Hammer	Glue
Handsaw	Eye and ear
Prehung interior door	protection
Wood shims	Work gloves

Tip: Jamb Extensions ▸

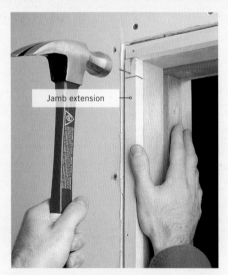

Jamb extension

If your walls are built with 2 × 6 studs, you'll need to extend the jambs by attaching wood strips to the edges of the jamb before the door is installed. Use glue and 4d casing nails when attaching jamb extensions.

How to Install a Prehung Interior Door

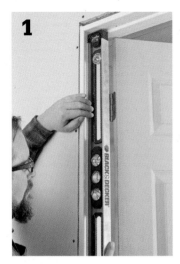

1

Slide the door unit into the framed opening so the edges of the jambs are flush with the wall surface and the hinge-side jamb is plumb.

2

Insert pairs of wood shims driven from opposite directions into the gap between the framing members and the hinge-side jamb, spaced every 12". Check the hinge-side jamb to make sure it is still plumb and does not bow.

3

Anchor the hinge-side jamb with 8d casing nails driven through the jamb and shims and into the jack stud.

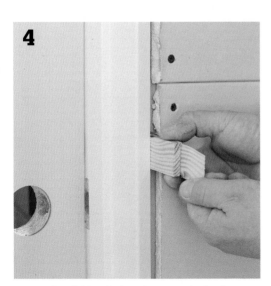

4

Insert pairs of shims in the gap between the framing members and the latch-side jamb and top jamb, spaced every 12". With the door closed, adjust the shims so the gap between door edge and jamb is ⅛" wide. Drive 8d casing nails through the jambs and shims, into the framing members.

5

Cut the shims flush with the wall surface, using a handsaw. Hold the saw vertically to prevent damage to the door jamb or wall. Finish the door and install the lockset as directed by the manufacturer. Install trim around the door.

How to Install a Replacement Window with a Nailing Flange

1

Remove the existing window (see pages 145 to 146), and set the new window into the rough opening. Center it left to right, and shim beneath the sill to level it. On the exterior side, measure out from the window on all sides, and mark the siding for the width of the brick molding you'll install around the new window. Extend layout lines to mark where you'll cut the siding.

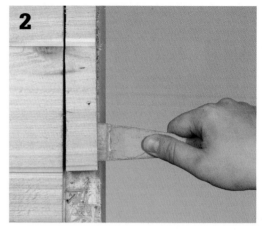

2

Remove exterior siding around the window area to expose the wall sheathing. Use a zip tool to separate vinyl siding for removal or use a pry bar and hammer to remove wood clapboard. For more on removing exterior surfaces, see pages 181 and 203.

3

Cover the sill and rough opening framing members with self-adhesive, rolled flashing. Apply additional strips of flashing behind the siding and up the sill flashing. Finish flashing with a strip along the header. The flashing should cover the front edges and sides of the opening members.

4

Apply a bead of silicone caulk around the back face of the window flange, then set it into the rough opening, centering it side-to-side in the opening. Tack the window in place by driving one roofing nail partway through the top flange. On the interior side, level and plumb the window, using shims to make any necessary adjustments.

Tack the window to the header at one end of the nailing flange, using a 1" galvanized roofing nail. Drive a roofing nail through the other top corner of the flange to hold the window in place, then secure the flange all around the window with more roofing nails. Apply strips of rolled, self-adhesive flashing to cover the window flanges. Start with a strip that covers the bottom flange, then cover the side flanges, overlapping the bottom flashing and extending 8 to 10" above the window. Complete the flashing with a strip along the top, overlapping the side flashing.

Install a piece of metal drip edge behind the siding and above the window. Secure it with silicone caulk only.

Cut and attach brick molding around the window, leaving a slight gap between the brick molding and the window frame. Use 8d galvanized casing nails driven into pilot holes to secure the brick molding to the rough framing. Miter the corner joints. Reinstall the siding in the window installation area, trimming as needed.

Use high-quality caulk to fill the gap between the brick molding and the siding. On the interior side, fill gaps between the window frame and surrounding framing with foam backer rod, low-expansion foam, or fiberglass insulation. Install the interior casing.

Installing Storm Doors

Storm doors are important features for energy efficiency as well as for protecting your entry door. In harsh climates, storm doors protect the entry door from driving rain or snow. They create a dead air buffer between the two doors that acts like insulation. When the screen panels are in place, the door provides great ventilation on a hot day. And, they deliver added security, especially when outfitted with a lockset and a deadbolt lock.

If you want to install a new storm door or replace an old one that's seen better days, your first job is to go shopping. Storm doors come in many different styles to suit just about anyone's design needs. And they come in different materials, including aluminum, vinyl, and even fiberglass. (Wood storm doors are still available but they must be trimmed and fit by hand, as they're not sold in prehung kits.) Most units feature a prehung door in a frame that is mounted on the entry door casing boards. Depending on the model you buy, installation instructions can vary. Be sure to check the directions that come with your door before starting the job.

Once purely utilitarian, today's storm doors can be an important design element of your home. Do your research carefully, and choose a door that complements both the entry door and other trim on your home.

Tools & Materials ▸

Drill/driver
Tape measure
Finish nails
Screwdriver
Paintbrush
Masking tape
Hacksaw
Level
Primer
Paint
Eye protection
Work gloves

A quality storm door helps seal out cold drafts, keeps rain and snow off your entry door, and lets a bug-free breeze into your home when you want one.

How to Install a Storm Door

Test-fit the door in the opening. If it is loose, add a shim to the hinge side of the door. Cut the piece with a circular saw and nail it to the side of the jamb, flush with the front of the casing.

Install the drip edge molding at the top of the door opening. The directions for the door you have will explain exactly how to do this. Sometimes it's the first step, like we show here; otherwise it's installed after the door is in place.

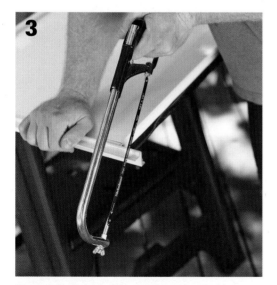

Measure the height of the opening and cut the hinge flange to match this measurement. Use a hacksaw and work slowly so the saw won't hop out of the cut and scratch a visible area of the hinge.

Lift the door and push it tightly into the opening. Partially drive one mounting screw near the bottom and another near the top. Check the door for plumb, and when satisfied, drive all the mounting screws tight to the flange.

Hanging a New Door in an Old Jamb

If you've got an unsightly or damaged door to replace but the jamb and trimwork are in good condition, there's no need to remove the jambs. Instead, buy a slab door and hang it in the existing jamb. It's an excellent way to preserve existing moldings and trim, especially if you live in an old home, and you won't have to color-match a new jamb to its surroundings.

If the hinges are also in good condition, you can reuse them as well. This may be particularly desirable in a historic home with ornate hinges. Most home centers stock six-panel slab doors, or you can order them in a variety of styles and wood types. For aesthetic and practical reasons, choose a door size as close to the original door as possible.

The process for hanging the door involves shimming the door into position in the jamb, scribing the ends and edges, and trimming or planing it to fit the opening. You'll also need to chisel hinge mortises in the door edge to accommodate the jamb hinge positions.

This is a project where patience and careful scribing will pay dividends in the end. Have a helper on hand to hold the door in position as you scribe and fit the door in place.

Tools & Materials ▶

Colored masking tape	Power plane or
Straightedge	hand plane
Door shims	Chisel
Tape measure	Drill/driver
Compass	Hole saw
Combination square	Spade bit
Utility knife	Slab door
Circular saw	Hinge screws
C-clamps	Eye and ear protection
Self-centering drill bit	Work gloves
Hammer	

Before

After

Installing a new door in an old jamb dramatically updates the curb appeal of your home.

How to Hang a New Door in an Old Jamb

Have a helper hold the new door in place against the jamb from inside the room. Slide a pair of thick shims under the door to raise it up slightly off the floor or threshold. Move the shims in or out until the door's top and side rails are roughly even with the jamb so it looks balanced in the opening, then make a mark along the top edge of the door.

Use pieces of colored masking tape to mark the outside of the door along the hinge edge. This will help keep the door's orientation clear throughout the installation process.

Use a pencil compass, set to an opening of 3/16", to scribe layout lines along both long edges of the door and across the top. These lines will create a clear space for the hinges and door swing. If the bottom of the door will close over carpet, set the dividers for 1/2" and scribe the bottom edge. Remove the door and transfer these scribe lines to the other door face.

Lay the door on a sturdy bench or across a pair of sawhorses with the tape side facing up. Score the top and bottom scribe lines with a utility knife to keep the wood fibers from splintering when you cut across the ends.

(continued)

Trim the door ends with a circular saw equipped with a fine-cutting blade. Run the saw base along a clamped straightedge with the blade cutting ⅟₁₆" on the waste side of the layout lines. Check to make sure the blade is set square to the saw base before cutting. Use a power planer or hand plane to plane the door ends to the layout lines.

Stand the door on edge and use a power plane or hand plane to plane down to the edge of the scribe lines. Set the tool for a fine cut; use a ⅟₁₆" cutting depth for power planing and a shallower cutting depth for a hand plane. Try to make each planing pass in long strokes from one end of the door to the other.

Shim the door back into position in the jamb with a helper supporting it from behind. Set the door slightly out from the doorstop moldings so you can mark the hinge locations on the door face.

Use a combination square or one of the hinge leaves to draw hinge mortise layout lines on the door edge. Score the layout lines with a utility knife.

Cut shallow hinge leaf mortises in the door edge with a sharp chisel and hammer. First score the mortise shape with a straightedge and utility knife or a chisel, then make a series of shallow chisel cuts inside the hinge leaf area. Pare away this waste so the mortise depth is slightly deeper than the hinge leaf thickness.

Set the hinges in the door mortises, and drill pilot holes for the hinge screws. Attach the hinges to the door.

Hang the door in the jamb by tipping it into place so the top hinge leaf rests in the top mortise of the jamb. Drive one screw into this mortise. Then set the other leaves into their mortises and install the remaining hinge screws.

Bore holes for the lockset and bolt using a hole saw and spade bit. If you're reusing the original hardware, measure the old door hole sizes and cut matching holes in the new door, starting with the large lockset hole. For new locksets, use the manufacturer's template and hole sizing recommendations to bore the holes. Install the hardware.

Installing Entry Doors

Few parts of a house have a more dramatic effect on the way your home is perceived than the main entry door. A lovely, well-maintained entryway that is tastefully matched architecturally to the house can utterly transform a home's appearance. In fact, industry studies have suggested that upgrading a plain entry door to a higher-end entry door system can pay back multiple times in the resale of your house. But perhaps more importantly, depending on your priorities, it makes a great improvement in how you feel about your home. Plus, it usually pays benefits in home security and energy efficiency as well.

If you are replacing a single entry door with a double door or a door with a sidelight or sidelights, you will need to enlarge the door opening. Be sure to file your plans with your local building department and obtain a permit. You'll need to provide temporary support from the time you remove the wall studs in the new opening until you've installed and secured a new door header that's approved for the new span distance.

The American Craftsman style door with sidelights installed in this project has the look and texture of a classic wood door, but it is actually created from fiberglass. Today's fiberglass doors are quite convincing in their ability to replicate wood grain, while still offering the durability and low maintenance of fiberglass.

Tools & Materials ▸

Tape measure
Level
Reciprocating saw
Caulk & caulk gun
Hammer
Shims
Framing nails

Finish nails
Nail set
Finishing materials
Metal drip cap molding
Eye and ear protection
Work gloves

After

Before

Replacing an ordinary entry door with a beautiful new upgrade has an exceptionally high payback in increased curb appeal and in perceived home value, according to industry studies.

How to Replace an Entry Door

1

Remove the old entry door by cutting through the fasteners driven into the jamb with a reciprocating saw. If the new door or door system is wider, mark the edges of the larger rough opening onto the wall surface. If possible, try to locate the new opening so one edge will be against an existing wall stud. Be sure to include the thickness of the new framing you'll need to add when removing the wall coverings.

2

Frame in the new rough opening for the replacement door. The instructions that come with the door will recommend a rough opening size, which is usually sized to create a ½" gap between the door and the studs and header. Patch the wall surfaces.

3

Cut metal door drip cap molding to fit the width of the opening and tuck the back edge up behind the wallcovering at the top of the door opening. Attach the drip cap with caulk only–do not use nails or screws.

4

Unpack the door unit and set it in the rough opening to make sure it fits correctly. Remove it. Make sure the subfloor is clean and in good repair, and then apply heavy beads of caulk to the underside of the door sill and to the subfloor in the sill installation area. Use plenty of caulk.

(continued)

5

Set the door sill in the threshold and raise the unit up so it fits cleanly in the opening, with the exterior trim flush against the wall sheathing. Press down on the sill to seat it in the caulk and wipe up any squeeze-out with a damp rag

6

Use a 6-ft. level to make sure the unit is plumb and then tack it to the rough opening stud on the hinge side, using pairs of 10d nails driven partway through the casing on the weatherstripped side of the door (or the sidelight). On single, hinged doors, drive the nails just above the hinge locations. *NOTE: Many door installers prefer deck screws over nails when attaching the jambs. Screws offer more gripping strength and are easier to adjust, but covering the screw heads is more difficult than filling nail holes.*

7

Drive wood shims between the jamb and the wall studs to create an even gap. Locate the shims directly above the pairs of nails you drove. Doublecheck the door with the level to make sure it is still plumb.

8

Drive shims between the jamb on the latch side of the unit and into the wall stud. Only drive the nails part way. Test for plumb again and then add shims at nail locations (you may need to double-up the shims, as this gap is often wider than the one on the hinge side). Check to make sure the door jamb is not bowed.

9

Drive finish nails at all remaining locations, following the nailing schedule in the manufacturer's installation instructions.

10

Use a nail set to drive the nail heads below the wood surface. Fill the nail holes with wood putty (you'll get the best match if you apply putty that's tinted to match the stained wood after the finish is applied). The presence of the wood shims at the nail locations should prevent the jamb from bowing as you nail.

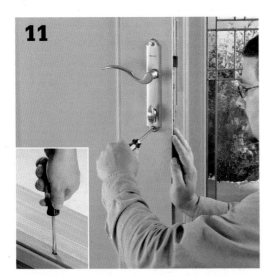

11

Install the lockset, strikeplates, deadbolts or multipoint locks, and any other door hardware. If the door finish has not been applied, you may want to do so first, but generally it makes more sense to install the hardware right away so the door can be operated and locked. Attach the door sill to the threshold and adjust it as needed, normally using the adjustment screws (inset).

12

Apply your door finish if it has not yet been applied. Read the manufacturer's suggestions for finishing very closely and follow the suggested sequences. Some manufacturers offer finish kits that are designed to be perfectly compatible with their doors. Install interior case molding and caulk all the exterior gaps after the finish dries.

Installing Bifold Doors

Bifold doors provide easy access to a closet without requiring much clearance for opening. Most home centers stock kits that include two pairs of prehinged doors, a head track, and all the necessary hardware and fasteners. Typically, the doors in these kits have predrilled holes for the pivot and guide posts. Hardware kits are also sold separately for custom projects. There are many types of bifold door styles, so be sure to read and follow the manufacturer's instructions for the product you use.

Tools & Materials ▸

Tape measure	Hacksaw
Level	Prehinged bifold doors
Circular saw	Head track
Straightedge	Mounting hardware
(optional)	Panhead screws
Drill	Flathead screws
Plane	Eye and ear protection
Screwdriver	

A variety of designer bifold doors are available for installation between rooms and closets. They provide the same attractive appearance as French doors but require much less floor space.

How to Install Bifold Doors

Cut the head track to the width of the opening using a hacksaw. Insert the roller mounts into the track, then position the track in the opening. Fasten it to the header using panhead screws.

Measure and mark each side jamb at the floor for the anchor bracket so the center of the bracket aligns exactly with the center of the head track. Fasten the brackets in place with flathead screws.

Check the height of the doors in the opening, and trim if necessary. Insert pivot posts into predrilled holes at the bottoms and tops of the doors. Insert guide posts at the tops of the leading doors. Make sure all posts fit snugly.

Fold one pair of doors closed and lift into position, inserting the pivot and guide posts into the head track. Slip the bottom pivot post into the anchor bracket. Repeat for the other pair of doors. Close the doors and check alignment along the side jambs and down the center. If necessary, adjust the top and bottom pivots following the manufacturer's instructions.

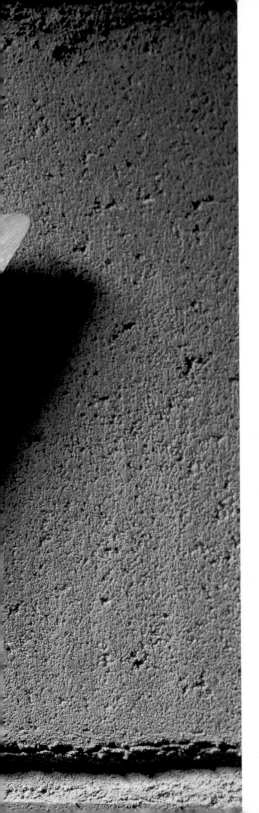

Exterior Repairs

In this chapter:

Inspecting & Repairing a Roof

A roof system is composed of several elements that work together to provide three basic, essential functions for your home: shelter, drainage, and ventilation. The roof covering and flashing are designed to shed water, directing it to gutters and downspouts. Air intake and outtake vents keep fresh air circulating below the roof sheathing, preventing moisture and heat buildup.

When your roof system develops problems that compromise its ability to protect your home—cracked shingles, incomplete ventilation, or damaged flashing—the damage quickly spreads to other parts of your house. Routine inspections are the best way to make sure the roof continues to do its job effectively.

Tools & Materials ▸

Tape measure	Replacement flashing
Wire brush	Replacement shingles
Aviation snips	Roofing cement
Trowel	Roofing nails
Flat pry bar	Double-headed nails
Hammer	Rubber-gasket nails
Utility knife	Chisel
Caulk gun	Eye and ear protection
Plywood	Work gloves

Ice dams above entries pose a danger to everyone entering and leaving the house. To permanently solve ice damming problems, like the one shown here, improve roof ventilation to reduce attic temperatures.

Tips for Identifying Roofing Problems ▸

Ice dams occur when melting snow refreezes near the eaves, causing ice to back up under the shingles, where it melts onto the sheathing and seeps into the house.

Inspect both the interior and the exterior of the roof to spot problems. From inside the attic, check the rafters and sheathing for signs of water damage. Symptoms will appear in the form of streaking or discoloration. A moist or wet area also signals water damage.

Shingle Maintenance Tips

Buckled and cupped shingles are usually caused by moisture beneath the shingles. Loosened areas create an entry point for moisture and leave shingles vulnerable to wind damage.

Dirt and debris attract moisture and decay, which shorten a roof's life. To protect shingles, carefully wash the roof once a year, using a pressure washer. Pay particular attention to areas where moss and mildew may accumulate.

In damp climates, it's a good idea to nail a zinc strip along the center ridge of a roof, under the ridge caps. Minute quantities of zinc wash down the roof each time it rains, killing moss and mildew.

Overhanging tree limbs drop debris and provide shade that encourages moss and mildew. To reduce chances of decay, trim any limbs that overhang the roof.

How to Locate & Evaluate Leaks

If you have an unfinished attic, examine the underside of your roof with a flashlight on a rainy day. If you find wetness, discoloration, or other signs of moisture, trace the trail up to where the water is making its entrance.

Water that flows toward a wall can be temporarily diverted to minimize damage. Nail a small block of wood in the path of the water, and place a bucket underneath to catch the drip. On a dry day, drive a nail through the underside of the roof decking to mark the hole.

If the leak is finding its way to a finished ceiling, take steps to minimize damage until the leak can be repaired. As soon as possible, reduce the accumulation of water behind a ceiling by poking a small hole in the wallboard or plaster and draining the water.

Once you mark the source of a leak from inside, measure from that spot to a point that will be visible and identifiable from outside the house, such as a chimney, vent pipe, or the peak of the roof. Get up on the roof and use that measurement to locate the leak.

How to Make Emergency Repairs

If your roof is severely damaged, the primary goal is to prevent additional damage until permanent repairs are made. Nail a sheet of plywood to the roof to serve as emergency cover to keep out the wind and water.

Cover the damaged area by nailing strips of lath around the edges of a plastic sheet or tarp. *TIP: For temporary repairs, use double-headed nails, which can be easily removed. Fill nail holes with roofing cement when the repair is complete.*

How to Make Spot Repairs with Roofing Cement

To reattach a loose shingle, wipe down the felt paper and the underside of the shingle. Let each dry, then apply a liberal coat of roofing cement. Press the shingle down to seat it in the bed of cement.

Tack down buckled shingles by cleaning below the buckled area. Fill the area with roofing cement, then press the shingle into the cement. Patch cracks and splits in shingles with roofing cement.

Check the joints around flashing, which are common places for roof leaks to occur. Seal any gaps by cleaning out and replacing any failed roofing cement. *TIP: Heat softens the roof's surface, and cold makes it brittle. If needed, warm shingles slightly with a hair dryer to make them easier to work with and less likely to crack.*

How to Replace Asphalt Shingles

Pull out damaged shingles, starting with the uppermost shingle in the damaged area. Be careful not to damage surrounding shingles that still are in good condition.

Remove old nails in and above the repair area, using a flat pry bar. Patch damaged felt paper with roofing cement.

Install the replacement shingles, beginning with the lowest shingle in the repair area. Nail above the tab slots, using ⅞" or 1" roofing nails.

Install all but the top shingle with nails, then apply roofing cement to the underside of the top shingle, above the seal line.

Slip the last shingle into place, under the overlapping shingle. Lift the shingles immediately above the repair area, and nail the top replacement shingle.

How to Replace Wood Shakes & Shingles

To age new shakes and shingles so they match existing ones, dissolve 1 pound of baking soda in 1 gallon of water. Brush the solution onto the shakes or shingles, then place them in direct sunlight for four to five hours. Rinse them thoroughly and let dry. Repeat this process until the color closely matches the originals.

Split the damaged shakes or shingles, using a hammer and chisel. Remove the pieces. Slide a hacksaw blade under the overlapping shingles and cut the nail heads. Pry out the remaining pieces of the shakes or shingles.

Gently pry up, but don't remove, the shakes or shingles above the repair area. Cut new pieces for the lowest course, leaving a ⅜" gap between pieces. Nail replacements in place with ring-shank siding nails. Fill in all but the top course in the repair area.

Cut the shakes or shingles for the top course. Because the top course can't be nailed, use roofing cement to fasten the pieces in place. Apply a coat of roofing cement where the shakes or shingles will sit, then slip them beneath the overlapping pieces. Press down to seat them in the roofing cement.

How to Patch Valley Flashing

Measure the damaged area and mark an outline for the patch. Cut a patch wide enough to fit under shingles on both sides of the repair area, and tapered to a point at one end. Using a trowel or flat pry bar, carefully break the seal between the damaged flashing and surrounding shingles.

Scrub the damaged flashing with a wire brush, and wipe it clean. Apply a heavy bead of roofing cement to the back of the patch. Cut a slit in the old flashing. Insert the tapered end of the patch into the slit, and slip the side edges under the shingles. *TIP: Use the same material for your patch as the original flashing. When dissimilar materials are joined, corrosion accelerates.*

Rest the square end of the patch on top of the old flashing, and press it firmly to seal the roofing cement joint. Add roofing cement to the exposed seams. Using a trowel, feather out the cement to create a smooth path for water flow.

How to Replace Vent Flashing

Sleeve

Remove the shingles above and on the sides of the vent pipe. Remove the old vent flashing, using a flat pry bar. Apply a heavy, double bead of roofing cement along the bottom edge of the flange of the new flashing. Set the new flashing in place so it covers at least one course of shingles. Nail around the perimeter of the flange, using rubber-gasket nails.

Cut the shingles to fit around the neck of the flashing so they lie flat against the flange. Apply roofing cement to the shingle and flashing joints, and cover any exposed nail heads.

How to Replace Step Flashing

Carefully bend up the counterflashing or the siding covering the damaged flashing. Cut any roofing cement seals, and pull back the shingles. Use a flat pry bar to remove the damaged flashing. *TIP: When replacing flashing around masonry, such as a chimney, use copper or galvanized steel. Lime from mortar can corrode aluminum.*

Cut the new flashing to fit, and apply roofing cement to all unexposed edges. Slip the flashing in place, making sure it's overlapped by the flashing above and overlaps the flashing and shingle below.

Drive one roofing nail through the flashing, at the bottom corner, and into the roof deck. Do not fasten the flashing to the vertical roof element, such as the chimney.

Reposition the shingles and counterflashing, and seal all joints with roofing cement.

Repairing Wood Fascia & Soffits

Fascia and soffits add a finished look to your roof and promote a healthy roof system. A well-ventilated soffit system prevents moisture from building up under the roof and in the attic.

Most fascia and soffit problems can be corrected by cutting out sections of damaged material and replacing them. Joints between fascia boards are lock-nailed at rafter locations, so you should remove whole sections of fascia to make accurate bevel cuts for patches. Soffits can often be left in place for repairs.

Tools & Materials ▸

Circular saw	Replacement materials
Jigsaw	Nailing strips
Drill	2" and 2½" galvanized
Putty knife	deck screws
Hammer	4d galvanized casing nails
Flat pry bar	Acrylic caulk
Nail set	Primer
Chisel	Paint
Caulk gun	Eye and ear protection
Paintbrush	Work gloves

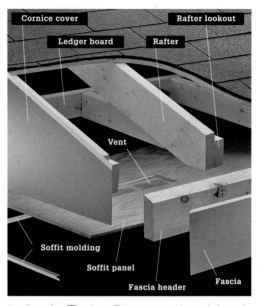

Fascia and soffits close off the eaves area beneath the roof overhang. The fascia covers the ends of rafters and rafter lookouts, and provides a surface for attaching gutters. Soffits are protective panels that span the area between the fascia and the side of the house.

How to Repair Wood Fascia

Remove gutters, shingle moldings, and any other items mounted on the fascia. Carefully pry off the damaged fascia board, using a pry bar. Remove the entire board and all old nails.

Set your circular saw for a 45° bevel, and cut off the damaged portion of the fascia board. Reattach the undamaged original fascia to the rafters or rafter lookouts, using 2" deck screws. Bevel-cut a patch board to replace the damaged section.

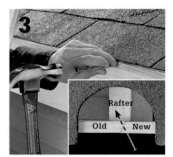

Set the patch board in place. Drill pilot holes through both fascia boards into the rafter. Drive nails in the holes to create a lock-nail joint (inset). Replace shingle moldings and trim pieces, using 4d casing nails. Set the nail heads. Prime and paint the new board.

How to Repair Wood Panel Soffits

In the area where soffits are damaged, remove the support moldings that hold the soffits in place along the fascia and exterior wall. Drill entry holes, then use a jigsaw to cut out the damaged soffit area. *TIP: Cut soffits as close as possible to the rafters or rafter lookouts. Finish cuts with a chisel, if necessary.*

Remove the damaged soffit section, using a pry bar. Cut nailing strips the same length as the exposed area of the rafters, and fasten them to the rafters or rafter lookouts at the edges of the openings, using 2½" deck screws.

Using soffit material similar to the original panel, cut a replacement piece ⅛" smaller than the opening. If the new panel will be vented, cut the vent openings.

Attach the replacement panel to the nailing strips, using 2" deck screws. If you are not going to paint the entire soffit after the repair, prime and paint the replacement piece before installing it.

Reattach the soffit molding, using 4d casing nails. Set the nail heads.

Using siliconized acrylic caulk, fill all nail holes, screw holes, and gaps. Smooth out the caulk with a putty knife until the caulk is even with the surface. Prime and paint the soffit panels.

Repairing Gutters

Gutters perform the important task of channeling water away from your house. A good gutter system prevents damage to your siding, foundation, and landscaping, and it helps prevent water from leaking into your basement. When gutters fail, evaluate the type and extent of damage to select the best repair method. Clean your gutters and downspouts as often as necessary to keep the system working efficiently.

Tools & Materials ▸

Flat pry bar
Hacksaw
Caulk gun
Pop rivet gun
Drill
Hammer
Stiff-bristled brush
Putty knife
Steel wool
Aviation snips
Level
Paintbrush
Trowel
Garden hose
Chalk line

Wood scraps
Replacement
   gutter materials
Siliconized
   acrylic caulk
Roofing cement
Metal flashing
Sheet-metal screws
   or pop rivets
Gutter hangers
Primer and paint
Gutter patching kit
Gutter guards
Eye and ear protection
Work gloves

Use a trowel to clean leaves, twigs, and other debris out of the gutters before starting the repairs.

Keep gutters and downspouts clean so rain falling on the roof is directed well away from the foundation. Nearly all wet basement problems are caused by water collecting near the foundation, a situation that can frequently be traced to clogged and overflowing gutters and downspouts.

How to Unclog Gutters

Flush clogged downspouts with water. Wrap a large rag around a garden hose and insert it in the downspout opening. Arrange the rag so it fills the opening, then turn on the water full force.

Check the slope of the gutters, using a level. Gutters should slope slightly toward the downspouts. Adjust the hangers, if necessary.

Place gutter guards over the gutters to prevent future clogs.

How to Rehang Sagging Gutters & Patch Leaks

For sagging gutters, snap a chalk line on the fascia that follows the correct slope. Remove hangers in and near the sag. Lift the gutter until it's flush with the chalk line. *TIP: A good slope for gutters is a ¼" drop every 10 ft. toward the downspouts.*

Reattach hangers every 24", and within 12" of seams. Use new hangers, if necessary. Avoid using the original nail holes. Fill small holes and seal minor leaks, using gutter caulk.

Use a gutter patching kit to make temporary repairs to a gutter with minor damage. Follow manufacturer's directions. For permanent repairs, see pages 200 to 201.

How to Repair Leaky Joints

Drill out the rivets or unfasten the metal screws to disassemble the leaky joint. Scrub both parts of the joint with a stiff-bristled brush. Clean the damaged area with water, and allow to dry completely.

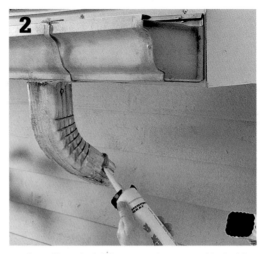

Apply caulk to the joining parts, then reassemble the joint. Secure the connection with pop rivets or sheet-metal screws.

How to Patch Metal Gutters

Clean the area around the damage with a stiff-bristled brush. Scrub it with steel wool or an abrasive pad to loosen residue, then rinse it with water.

Apply a ⅛"-thick layer of roofing cement evenly over the damage. Spread the roofing cement a few inches past the damaged area on all sides.

Cut and bend a piece of flashing to fit inside the gutter. Bed the patch in the roofing cement. Feather out the cement to reduce ridges so it won't cause significant damming. *TIP: To prevent corrosion, make sure the patch is the same type of metal as the gutter.*

How to Replace a Section of Metal Gutter

Remove gutter hangers in and near the damaged area. Insert wood spacers in the gutter, near each hanger, before prying. *TIP: If the damaged area is more than 2 ft. long, replace the entire section with new material.*

Slip spacers between the gutter and fascia, near each end of the damaged area, so you won't damage the roof when cutting the gutter. Cut out the damaged section, using a hacksaw.

Cut a new gutter section at least 4" longer than the damaged section.

Clean the cut ends of the old gutter, using a wire brush. Caulk the ends, then center the gutter patch over the cutout area and press into the caulk.

Secure the gutter patch with pop rivets or sheet-metal screws. Use at least three fasteners at each joint. On the inside surfaces of the gutter, caulk over the heads of the fasteners.

Reinstall gutter hangers. If necessary, use new hangers, but don't use old holes. Prime and paint the patch to match the existing gutter.

Removing Exterior Siding

Although it's sometimes possible to install new siding over old if the old siding is solid and firmly attached to the house, it's often better to remove the siding, especially if it's damaged. Taking off the old siding allows you to start with a flat, smooth surface. And because the overall thickness of the siding will remain unchanged, you won't have to add extensions to your window and door jambs.

There's no "right" way to remove siding. Each type of siding material is installed differently, and consequently, they have different removal techniques. A couple of universal rules do apply, however. Start by removing trim that's placed over the siding, and work from the top down. Siding is usually installed from the bottom up, and working in the opposite direction makes removal much easier. Determine the best removal method for your project based on your type of siding.

Strip one side of the house at a time, then re-side that wall before ripping the siding off another section. This minimizes the amount of time your bare walls are exposed to the elements. Take care not to damage the sheathing. If you can't avoid tearing the housewrap, it can easily be replaced, but the sheathing is another story.

While the goal is to remove the siding quickly, it's also important to work safely. Take care when working around windows so the siding doesn't crack or break the glass. Invest the necessary time to protect the flowers and shrubs before starting the tear-off.

Renting a dumpster will expedite the cleanup process. It's much easier to dispose of the siding as soon as it's removed. When you're finished with your cleanup, use a release magnet to collect the nails on the ground.

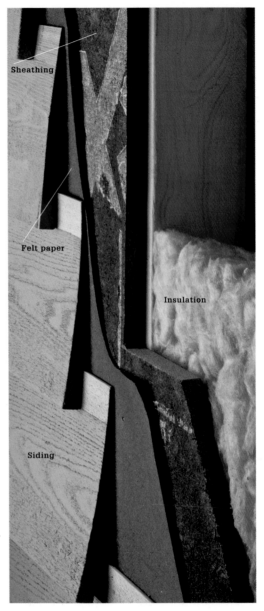

The **exterior wall** is composed of siding, housewrap or felt paper, and sheathing. Remove the siding without disturbing or damaging the sheathing.

Tools & Materials ▸

Cat's paw	Masonry-cutting blade
Flat pry bar	Masonry bit
Zip-lock tool	Aviation snips
Drill	Roofing shovel
Circular saw	Release magnet
Cold chisel	Eye and ear protection
Hammer	Work gloves

Brick molding comes preattached to most wood-frame window and door units. To remove the molding, pry along the outside of the frame to avoid marring the exposed parts of the jambs and molding.

Lap siding is nailed at the top, then covered by the next course. Pry off the trim at the top of the wall to expose the nails in top row. Remove the nails using a cat's paw, and work your way down the wall.

Shakes and shingles are best removed with a roofing shovel. Use the shovel to pry the siding away from the wall. Once the siding is removed, use the shovel or a hammer to pull out remaining nails.

Board and batten siding is removed by prying off the battens from over the boards. Use a pry bar or cat's paw to remove the nails from the boards.

Siding shown cutaway for clarity

Vinyl siding has a locking channel that fits over the nailing strip of the underlying piece. To remove, use a zip-lock tool to separate the panels, and use a flat pry bar or hammer to remove the nails.

Building paper

Sheathing

Metal lath

Stucco

Stucco siding is difficult to remove. It's usually much easier to apply the new siding over the stucco than to remove it. If you're determined to take it off, use a cold chisel and hammer to break it into pieces, and aviation snips to cut the lath.

Replacing Wall Sheathing

After removing the old siding, inspect the sheathing to make sure it's still in good condition. If water penetrated behind the siding, there's a good chance the sheathing is warped, rotted, or otherwise damaged, and will need to be replaced. You'll only need to replace the section of sheathing that's damaged. Before cutting into the wall, make sure there are no wires, cables, or pipes under the sheathing.

Older homes typically have planks or plywood sheathing, while new homes may have a nonstructural sheathing. The replacement material doesn't have to be the same material as the original sheathing, but it does have to be the same thickness.

Tools & Materials ▸

Hammer	3" deck screws
Circular saw	2¼" deck screws
Tape measure	Drill
Chalk line	Eye and ear
Pry bar	protection
Sheathing	Work gloves
2 × 4	

Although the sheathing isn't visible, a smooth, solid sheathing installation is essential to a professional looking siding finish.

How to Replace Wall Sheathing

1

Snap chalk lines around the area of damaged sheathing, making sure the vertical lines are next to wall studs. Remove any nails or staples in your path. Set the depth of the circular saw blade to cut through the sheathing, but not cut the studs.

2

Pry off the damaged sheathing. Remove any remaining nails or staples in the studs. Measure the opening, subtract ⅛" from each side, then cut a piece of sheathing to size.

3

Align 2 × 4 nailing strips with the edges of the wall studs. Fasten the strips in place, using 3" deck screws.

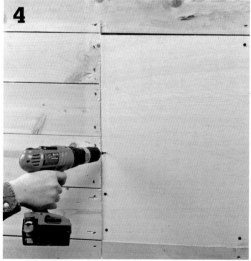

4

Place the new piece of sheathing in the opening, keeping a ⅛" gap on each side to allow for expansion. Attach the sheathing to the nailing strips and studs, using 2¼" deck screws driven every 12".

Repairing Siding

Damage to siding is fairly common, but fortunately, it's also easy to fix. Small to medium holes, cracks, and rotted areas can be repaired with filler or by replacing the damaged sections with matching siding.

If you cannot find matching siding for repairs at building centers, check with salvage yards or siding contractors. When repairing aluminum or vinyl siding, contact the manufacturer or the contractor who installed the siding to help you locate matching materials and parts. If you're unable to find an exact match, remove a section of original siding from a less visible area of the house, such as the back of the garage, and use it for the patch. Cover the gap in the less visible area with a close matching siding, where the mismatch will be less noticeable.

Tools & Materials ▸

Aviation snips	Trowel	Epoxy wood filler	Replacement siding,
Caulk gun	Screwdrivers	Epoxy glue	shakes, or shingles
Drill	Hacksaw	Galvanized ring-shank	End caps
Flat pry bar	Circular saw	siding nails	Wood preservative
Hammer	Jigsaw	Siliconized	Primer
Straightedge	Keyhole saw	acrylic caulk	Paint or stain
Tape measure	Flat pry bar	Roofing cement	Metal sandpaper
Utility knife	Nail set	Sheathing	Eye and ear protection
Zip-lock tool	Stud finder	Trim	Work gloves
Chisel	Paintbrush		

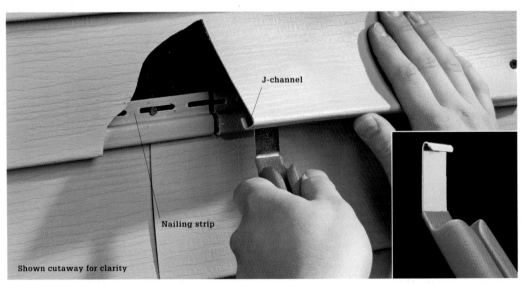

J-channel

Nailing strip

Shown cutaway for clarity

Vinyl and metal siding panels have a locking J-channel that fits over the bottom of the nailing strip on the underlying piece. Use a zip-lock tool (inset) to separate panels. Insert the tool at the seam nearest the repair area. Slide it over the J-channel, pulling outward slightly, to unlock the joint from the siding below.

How to Repair Vinyl Siding

Starting at the seam nearest the damaged area, unlock interlocking joints, using a zip-lock tool. Insert spacers between the panels, then remove the fasteners in the damaged siding, using a flat pry bar. Cut out the damaged area, using aviation snips. Cut a replacement piece 4" longer than the open area, and trim 2" off the nailing strip from each end. Slide the piece into position.

Insert siding nails in the nailing strip, then position the end of a flat pry bar over each nail head. Drive the nails by tapping on the neck of the pry bar with a hammer. Place a scrap piece of wood between the pry bar and siding to avoid damaging the siding. Slip the locking channel on the overlapping piece over the nailing strip of the replacement piece. *TIP: If the damaged panel is near a corner, door, or window, replace the entire panel. This eliminates an extra seam.*

How to Patch Aluminum Siding

Cut out the damaged area, using aviation snips. Leave an exposed area on top of the uppermost piece to act as a bonding surface. Cut a patch 4" larger than the repair area. Remove the nailing strip. Smooth the edges with metal sandpaper.

Nail the lower patch in place by driving siding nails through the nailing flange. Apply roofing cement to the back of the top piece, then press it into place, slipping the locking channel over the nailing strip of the underlying piece. Caulk the seams.

How to Replace Aluminum End Caps

Remove the damaged end cap. If necessary, pry the bottom loose, then cut along the top with a hacksaw blade. Starting at the bottom, attach the replacement end caps by driving siding nails through the nailing tabs and into the framing members.

Trim the nailing tabs off the top replacement cap. Apply roofing cement to its back. Slide the cap over the locking channels of the siding panels. Press the top cap securely in place.

How to Replace Board & Batten Siding

1

Remove the battens over the damaged boards. Pry out the damaged boards in their entirety. Inspect the underlying housewrap, and patch if necessary.

2

Cut replacement boards from the same type of lumber, allowing a ⅛" gap at the side seams. Prime or seal the edges and the back side of the replacement boards. Let them dry.

3

Nail the new boards in place, using ring-shank siding nails. Replace the battens and any other trim. Prime and paint or stain the new boards to blend with the surrounding siding.

How to Replace Wood Shakes & Shingles

1

Split damaged shakes or shingles with a hammer and chisel, and remove them. Insert wood spacers under the shakes or shingles above the repair area, then slip a hacksaw blade under the top board to cut off any remaining nail heads.

2

Cut replacement shakes or shingles to fit, leaving a ⅛"- to ¼"-wide gap at each side. Coat all sides and edges with wood preservative. Slip the patch pieces under the siding above the repair area. Drive siding nails near the top of the exposed area on the patches. Cover nail heads with caulk. Remove the spacers.

How to Replace Lap Siding

1

If the damage is caused by water, locate and repair the leak or other source of the water damage.

2

Mark the area of siding that needs to be replaced. Make the cutout lines over the center of the framing members on each side of the repair area, staggering the cuts to offset the joints. *TIP: Use an electronic studfinder to locate framing members, or look for the nail heads.*

3

Insert spacers beneath the board above the repair area. Make entry cuts at the top of the cutting lines with a keyhole saw, then saw through the boards and remove them. Pry out any nails or cut off the nail heads, using a hacksaw blade. Patch or replace the sheathing and building paper, if necessary.

4

Measure and cut replacement boards to fit, leaving an expansion gap of ⅛" at each end. Use the old boards as templates to trace cutouts for fixtures and openings. Use a jigsaw to make the cutouts. Apply wood sealer or primer to the ends and backs of the boards. Let them dry.

5

Nail the new boards in place with siding nails, starting with the lowest board in the repair area. At each framing member, drive nails through the bottom of the new board and the top of the board below. *TIP: If you removed the bottom row of siding, nail a 1 × 2 starter strip along the bottom of the patch area.*

6

Fill expansion joints with caulk (use paintable caulk for painted wood or tinted caulk for stained wood). Prime and paint or stain the replacement boards to match the surrounding siding.

Repairing Exterior Trim

Some exterior trim serves as decoration, like gingerbread and ornate cornice moldings. Other trim, such as brick molding and end caps, works with siding to seal your house from the elements. Damaged brick molding and corner boards should be patched with stock material similar to the original.

If you cannot find matching replacement parts for decorative trim at home improvement stores, check salvage shops or contact a custom millworker.

Tools & Materials ▸

Hammer
Chisel
Circular saw
Nail set
Putty knife
Utility knife
Paintbrush
Flat pry bar
Caulk gun
Epoxy wood filler
Epoxy glue
Panel adhesive

Caulk
10d galvanized casing nails
Galvanized ring-shank
   siding nails
Sandpaper
Primer
Paint
Building paper
Drip edge
Replacement trim
Eye and ear protection
Work gloves

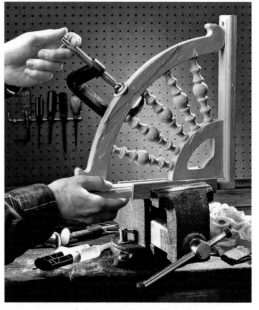

Repair delicate or ornamental trim molding in your workshop, whenever possible. You'll get better results than if you try repairing it while it's still attached.

Tips for Repairing & Replacing Trim ▸

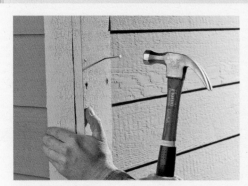

Reattach loose trim with new ring-shank siding nails driven near old nail locations. Fill old nail holes with paintable caulk, and touch up caulk and new nail heads with paint to match the surrounding surface.

Repair decorative trim molding with epoxy glue or wood filler. For major repairs, make your own replacement parts, or take the trim to a custom millwork shop.

How to Replace Brick Molding

Pry off old brick molding around windows and doors, using a flat pry bar. Remove any old drip edge. Inspect and repair the building paper.

Hold a replacement piece of brick molding, slightly longer than the original piece, across the opening. Mark cutting lines to fit the opening. Cut the replacement molding at the marks, matching any miter cuts.

Cut a 3"-wide piece of flashing to fit between the jambs, then bend it in half lengthwise to form the new drip edge (preformed drip edge is also available). Slip it between the siding and building paper, above the door or window. Do not nail the drip edge in place.

Test-fit the replacement piece of brick molding, then apply exterior-grade panel adhesive to the back side. Follow the manufacturer's directions for allowing the adhesive to set.

Nail the brick molding to the door header, using 10d galvanized casing nails. Lock-nail the miter joints, and set all nail heads. Seal joints, and cover nail holes with caulk. Prime and paint when the caulk dries.

Identifying Exterior Paint Problems

Two enemies work against painted surfaces—moisture and age. A simple leak or a failed vapor barrier inside the house can ruin even the finest paint job. If you notice signs of paint failure, such as blistering or peeling, take action to correct the problem right away. If the surface damage is discovered in time, you may be able to correct it with just a little bit of touch-up painting.

Evaluating the painted surfaces of your house can help you identify problems with siding, trim, roofs, and moisture barriers. The pictures on these two pages show the most common forms of paint failure, and how to fix them. Be sure to fix any moisture problems before repainting.

Evaluate exterior painted surfaces every year, starting with areas sheltered from the sun. Paint failure will appear first in areas that receive little or no direct sunlight and is a warning sign that similar problems are developing in neighboring areas.

Common Forms of Paint Failure

Blistering appears as a bubbled surface. It results from poor preparation or hurried application of primer or paint. The blisters indicate trapped moisture is trying to force its way through the surface. To fix isolated spots, scrape and touch up. For widespread damage, remove paint down to bare wood, then apply primer and paint.

Peeling occurs when paint falls away in large flakes. It's a sign of persistent moisture problems, generally from a leak or a failed vapor barrier. If the peeling is localized, scrape and sand the damaged areas, then touch up with primer and paint. If it's widespread, remove the old paint down to bare wood, then apply primer and paint.

Alligatoring is widespread flaking and cracking, typically seen on surfaces that have many built-up paint layers. It can also be caused by inadequate surface preparation or by allowing too little drying time between coats of primer and paint. Remove the old paint, then prime and repaint.

Localized blistering and peeling indicates that moisture, usually from a leaky roof, gutter system, or interior pipe, is trapped under the paint. Find and eliminate the leak, then scrape, prime, and repaint the area.

Clearly defined blistering and peeling occurs when a humid room has an insufficient vapor barrier. If there's a clear line where an interior wall ends, remove the siding and replace the vapor barrier.

Mildew forms in cracks and in humid areas that receive little direct sunlight. Wash mildewed areas with a 1:1 solution of household chlorine bleach and water, or with trisodium phosphate (TSP).

Rust occurs when moisture penetrates paint on iron or steel. Remove the rust and loose paint with a drill and wire brush attachment, then prime and repaint.

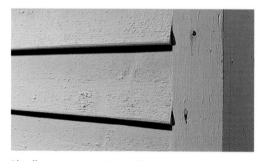

Bleeding spots occur when nails in siding begin to rust. Remove the nails, sand out the rust, then drive in galvanized ring-shank nails. Apply metal primer, then paint to blend in with the siding.

Efflorescence occurs in masonry when minerals leech through the surface, forming a crystalline or powdery layer. Use a scrub brush and a muriatic acid solution to remove efflorescence before priming and painting.

Preparing to Paint Your House

The key to an even paint job is to work on a smooth, clean, dry surface. Generally, the more preparation work you do, the smoother the final finish will be and the longer it will last.

For the smoothest finish, sand all the way down to the bare wood with a power sander. For a less time-consuming (but rougher) finish, scrape off any loose paint, then spot-sand rough areas. Pressure washing will remove some of the flaking paint, but by itself, won't create a smooth surface for painting.

Tools & Materials ▸

Pressure washer	Caulk gun
Scrapers	Heat gun
Power sander	80-, 120-, and
Sanding block	150-grit sandpaper
Putty knife	Putty
Paint scraper	Paintable
Stiff-bristled brush	siliconized caulk
Wire brush	Muriatic acid
Steel wool	Sealant
Coarse abrasive pad	Epoxy wood filler
Drill	Eye and ear protection
Wire-wheel attachment	Work gloves

Sanded to bare wood

Scraped and spot-sanded

Pressure-washed only

The amount of surface preparation you do will largely determine the final appearance of your paint job. Decide how much sanding and scraping you're willing to do to obtain a finish you'll be happy with.

How to Remove Paint

Use a heat gun to loosen thick layers of old paint. Aim the gun at the surface, warm the paint until it starts to bubble, then scrape the paint as soon as it releases.

To remove large areas of paint on wood lap siding, use a siding sander with a disk that's as wide as the reveal on your siding.

How to Prepare Surfaces for Paint

Clean the surface and remove loose paint by pressure washing the house. As you work, direct the water stream downward, and don't get too close to the surface with the sprayer head. Allow all surfaces to dry thoroughly before continuing.

Scrape off loose paint, using a paint scraper. Be careful not to damage the surface by scraping too hard.

Smooth out rough paint with a finishing sander and 80-grit sandpaper. Use sanding blocks and 80- to 120-grit sandpaper to sand hard-to-reach areas of trim. *TIP: You can make sanding blocks from dowels, wood scraps, or garden hoses.*

Use detail scrapers to remove loose paint in hard-to-reach areas. Some of these scrapers have interchangeable heads that match common trim profiles.

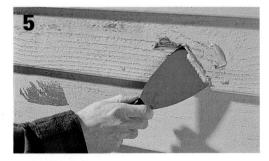

Inspect all surfaces for cracks, rot, and other damage. Mark affected areas with colored push pins or tape. Fill the holes and cracks with epoxy wood filler.

Use a finishing sander with 120-grit sandpaper to sand down repaired areas, ridges, and hard edges left from the scraping process, creating a smooth surface.

How to Prepare Trim Surfaces for Paint

Scuff-sand glossy surfaces on doors, window casings, and all surfaces painted with enamel paint. Use a coarse abrasive pad or 150-grit sandpaper.

Fill cracks in siding and gaps around window and door trim with paintable siliconized acrylic caulk.

How to Remove Clear Finishes

Pressure-wash stained or unpainted surfaces that have been treated with a wood preservative or protectant before recoating them with fresh sealant.

Use a stiff-bristled brush to dislodge any flakes of loosened surface coating that weren't removed by pressure washing. Don't use a wire brush on wood surfaces.

How to Prepare Metal & Masonry for Paint

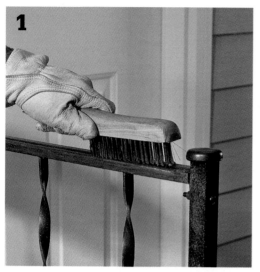

Remove rust and loose paint from metal hardware, such as railings and ornate trim, using a wire brush. Cover the surface with metal primer immediately after brushing to prevent the formation of new rust.

Scuff-sand metal siding and trim with medium-coarse steel wool or a coarse abrasive pad. Wash the surface and let dry before priming and painting.

Remove loose mortar, mineral deposits, or paint from mortar lines in masonry surfaces with a drill and wire-wheel attachment. Clean broad, flat masonry surfaces with a wire brush. Correct any minor damage before repainting.

Dissolve rust on metal hardware with diluted muriatic acid solution. When working with muriatic acid, it's important to wear safety equipment, work in a well-ventilated area, and follow all manufacturer's directions and precautions.

Painting Your House

Schedule priming and painting tasks so that you can paint within two weeks of priming surfaces. If more than two weeks pass, wash the surface with soap and water before applying the next coat.

Check the weather forecast and keep an eye on the sky while you work. Damp weather or rain within two hours of application will ruin a paint job. Don't paint when the temperature is below 50° or above 90°F. Avoid painting on windy days—it's dangerous to be on a ladder in high winds, and wind blows dirt onto the fresh paint.

Plan each day's work so you can follow the shade. Prepare, prime, and paint one face of the house at a time, and follow a logical painting order. Work from the top of the house down to the foundation, covering an entire section before you move the ladder or scaffolding.

Tools & Materials ▸

Paintbrushes
Paint rollers
Sash brush
Scaffolding
Ladders
Primer

House paint
Trim paint
Cleanup materials
Masking tape
Eye and ear protection
Work gloves

Paint in a logical order, starting from the top and working your way down. Cover as much surface as you can reach comfortably without moving your ladder or scaffolding. After the paint or primer dries, touch up any unpainted areas that were covered by the ladder or ladder stabilizer.

Tips for Applying Primer & Paint ▸

Use the right primer and paint for each job. Always read the manufacturer's recommendations.

Plan your painting sequence so you paint the walls, doors, and trim before painting stairs and porch floors. This prevents the need to touch up spills.

Tips for Selecting Brushes & Rollers ▸

Wall brushes, which are thick, square brushes 3" to 5" wide, are designed to carry a lot of paint and distribute it widely. *TIP: It's good to keep a variety of clean brushes on hand, including 2½", 3", and 4" flat brushes, 2" and 3" trim brushes, and tapered sash brushes.*

Trim and tapered sash brushes, which are 2" to 3" wide, are good for painting doors and trim, and for cutting-in small areas.

Paint rollers work best for quickly painting smooth surfaces. Use an 8" or 9" roller sleeve for broad surfaces.

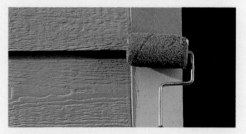

Use a 3" roller to paint flat-surfaced trim, such as end caps and corner trim.

Tips for Loading & Distributing Paint ▸

Load your brush with the right amount of paint for the area you're covering. Use a full load of paint for broad areas, a moderate load for smaller areas and feathering strokes, and a light load when painting or working around trim.

Hold the brush at a 45° angle and apply just enough downward pressure to flex the bristles and squeeze the paint from the brush.

How to Use a Paintbrush

Load the brush with a full load of paint. Starting at one end of the surface, make a long, smooth stroke until the paint begins to feather out. *TIP: Paint color can vary from one can to the next. To avoid problems, pour all of your paint into one large container and mix it thoroughly. Pour the mixed paint back into the individual cans and seal them carefully. Stir each can before use.*

At the end of the stroke, lift the brush without leaving a definite ending point. If the paint appears uneven or contains heavy brush marks, smooth it out without overbrushing.

Reload the brush and make a stroke from the opposite direction, painting over the feathered end of the first stroke to create a smooth, even surface. If the junction of the two strokes is visible, rebrush with a light coat of paint. Feather out the starting point of the second stroke.

Tips for Using Paint Rollers ▸

Wet the roller nap, then squeeze out the excess water. Position a roller screen inside a five-gallon bucket. Dip the roller into the paint, then roll it back and forth across the roller screen. The roller sleeve should be full, but not dripping, when lifted from the bucket.

Cone-shaped rollers work well for painting the joints between intersecting surfaces.

Doughnut-shaped rollers work well for painting the edges of lap siding and moldings.

Tips for Cleaning Painting Tools ▸

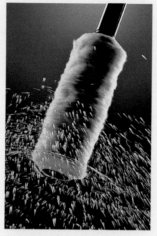

Scrape paint from roller covers with the curved side of a cleaner tool.

Use a spinner tool to remove paint and solvent from brushes and roller covers.

Comb brushes with the spiked side of a cleaner tool to properly align bristles for drying.

How to Paint Fascia, Soffits & Trim

Prime all surfaces to be painted, and allow ample drying time. Paint the face of the fascia first, then cut in paint at the bottom edges of the soffit panels. *TIP: Fascia and soffits are usually painted the same color as the trim.*

Paint the soffit panels and trim with a 4" brush. Start by cutting in around the edges of the panels, using the narrow edge of the brush, then feather in the broad surfaces of the soffit panels with full loads of paint. Be sure to get good coverage in the grooves.

Paint any decorative trim near the top of the house at the same time you paint the soffits and fascia. Use a 2½" or 3" paintbrush for broader surfaces, and a sash brush for more intricate trim areas.

How to Paint Siding

1

Paint the bottom edges of lap siding by holding the paintbrush flat against the wall. Paint the bottom edges of several siding pieces before returning to paint the faces of the same boards.

2

Paint the broad faces of the siding boards with a 4" brush, using the painting technique shown on page 204. Working down from the top of the house, paint as much surface as you can reach without leaning beyond the sides of the ladder.

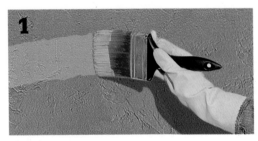

3

Paint the siding all the way down to the foundation, working from top to bottom. Shift the ladder or scaffolding, then paint the next section. *TIP: Paint up to the edges of end caps and window or door trim that will be painted later. If you're not planning to paint the trim, mask it off or use a paint shield.*

4

On board and batten or vertical panel siding, paint the edges of the battens, or top boards, first. Paint the faces of the battens before the sides dry, then use a roller with a ⅝"-nap sleeve to paint the large, broad surfaces between the battens.

How to Paint Stucco Walls

1

Using a large paintbrush, paint the foundation with anti-chalking masonry primer, and let it dry. Using concrete paint and a 4" brush, cut in the areas around basement windows and doors.

2

Apply concrete paint to board surfaces with a paint roller and a ⅝"-nap sleeve. Use a 3" trim roller or a 3" paintbrush for trim.

How to Paint Doors, Windows & Trim

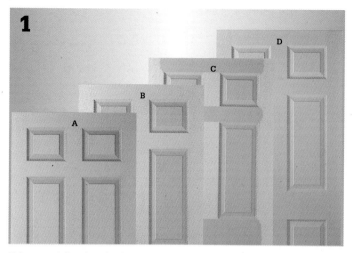

Using a sash brush, paint doors in this sequence: beveled edges of raised door panels (A), panel faces (B), horizontal rails (C), and vertical stiles (D).

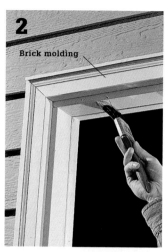

For trim, use a trim brush or sash brush and a moderate load of paint to paint the inside edges of door and window jambs, casings, and brick molding. *TIP: Paint surfaces on the interior side of the door-stop to match the interior trim.*

Mask off the siding—if freshly painted, make sure it's completely dry first. Paint the outside edges of casings and brick molding. Work paint all the way into the corners created by the siding's profile.

Paint the faces of door jambs, casings, and brick molding, feathering fresh paint around the previously painted edges.

Paint wood door thresholds and porch floors with specially formulated enamel floor paint.

Using Paint-spraying Equipment

Spray equipment can make quick work of painting, but it still requires the same careful preparation work as traditional brush and roller methods. Part of that prep work involves using plastic to completely cover doors, windows, and other areas that you don't want painted, rather than just taping them off.

Spray equipment can be purchased or rented at hardware and home improvement stores. There are several types and sizes of spray equipment, including high-volume low-pressure (HVLP), airless, air-assisted airless, and electrostatic enhanced. They all work the same way—by atomizing paint and directing it to a work surface in a spray or fan pattern. For our project, we used an HVLP sprayer, which we recommend because it produces less overspray and more efficient paint application than other sprayers.

Be sure to read and follow all safety precautions for the spray equipment. Since the paint is under a lot of pressure, it can not only tear the skin, but it can inject toxins into the blood stream if used incorrectly. Wear the proper safety protection, such as safety glasses and a respirator, when spray painting the house.

As with other paint applications, pay close attention to the weather. Don't spray if rain is likely, and don't spray on windy days, since the wind can carry the paint particles away from the siding.

Tools & Materials ▸

Paint sprayer	Plastic
Utility knife	Cardboard
Spray equipment	Cheesecloth
Paint	5-gallon bucket
Paintbrushes	Eye and ear protection
Respirator	Work gloves
Masking tape	

Paint sprayers allow you to cover large areas of siding and trim in a short amount of time. They also make it easier to paint areas that are hard to reach with a brush or roller.

How to Paint Using a Paint Sprayer

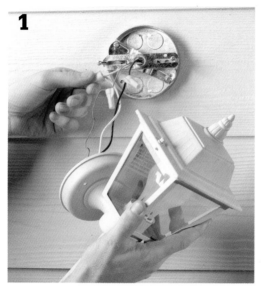

1

Remove outside light fixtures, window and door screens, and other detachable items that you don't want painted.

2

Cover doors, windows, and any other areas you don't want painted, using plastic and masking tape.

3

Strain the paint through cheesecloth to remove particles and debris. Mix the paint together in a 5-gallon bucket. Fill the sprayer container.

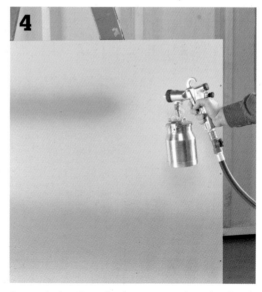

4

Spray a test pattern of paint on a scrap piece of cardboard. Adjust the pressure until you reach an even "fan" without any thick lines along the edge of the spray pattern.

(continued)

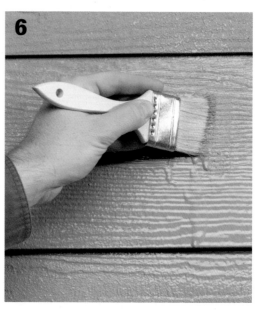

Cut-in around doors and windows with the paint. Spray the paint along each side of the doors and windows, applying the paint evenly.

If you happen to spray an excessive amount of paint in an area and it starts to run, stop the sprayer. Use a paintbrush to spread out the paint and eliminate the runs.

Hold the spray gun perpendicular to the house, approximately 12" from the wall. Start painting near the top of the wall, close to a corner. Move your entire arm, rather than just the wrist, in a steady, side-to-side motion. Do not wave your arm in an arc. Start your arm movement, then start the gun.

8

Spray the paint in an even motion, being careful not to tilt the gun. As you sweep your arm back and forth, overlap each coat of paint by 20 to 30 percent, working your way down the wall. When stopping, release the trigger before discontinuing your motion.

How to Paint Doors Using a Paint Sprayer

1

2

Remove the door by taking off the hinges. Remove all hardware from the door, such as handles and locks. If the door contains glass, you can either tape it off, or allow paint to get on the glass and then scrape it off with a razor after it's dry.

Prop up the door so it stands vertically. Starting at the top of the door, spray on the paint. As you make passes across the door, slightly go past the edges before sweeping back in the opposite direction. Wait until the paint is completely dry, then turn the door around and paint the other side.

Staining Siding

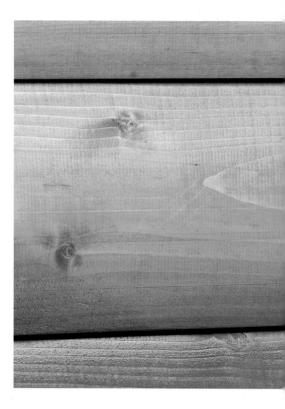

Stain lends color to wood siding, but because it is partially transparent, it also allows the natural beauty of the wood grain to show through. Water-based stains are applied with an acrylic or synthetic brush. Oil-based stains are usually applied with a natural-bristle brush.

Work in small sections at a time. Complete an entire length of board without stopping in the middle. Unlike paint, stain can darken or leave streaks if you go back over an area after it dries. Save the trim until the end, then stain it separately to get an even coverage.

Staining requires the same careful preparation work as painting. The surface must be clean and dry. Avoid working in direct sunlight so the stain doesn't dry too quickly. Check manufacturer's recommendations before staining. Some stains cannot be applied in temperatures below 50°F.

Tools & Materials ▸

Paintbrush
  or foam brush
Cloths

Stain
Eye and ear protection
Work gloves

How to Stain Log Cabin Siding

1

Load the brush with stain. Starting at a corner, move the brush across the siding with a long, smooth stroke. Cover the entire width of the log with stain, reloading the brush as needed, applying stain in the same direction. *TIP: Mix the stain thoroughly and often as it's being applied.*

2

Wipe away excess stain with a clean cloth. Keep applying stain until you reach the opposite corner or an edge. Once the top course is stained, go back to the corner and start on the next row of siding, using the same technique. If the run of siding is short, such as between windows, apply stain to two rows at a time. Stain remaining courses the same way.

How to Stain Shingle Siding

Load the brush with stain. Starting at the top of a wall by a corner, apply stain to the shingles, using smooth, downward strokes. Wipe off excess stain with a cloth. Cover the face of the shingle and stain the bottom edge before moving on to the next one. Apply stain to one or two courses at a time, moving across the wall as you go. Never stop in the middle of a shingle. When you reach the opposite corner, start over on the next set of shingles. Stain remaining rows the same way.

Once all of the shingles are stained, apply stain to the trim. Move the brush in the same direction as the wood grain, then wipe away excess with a cloth.

Repairing Stucco

Although stucco siding is very durable, it can be damaged, and over time it can crumble or crack. The directions given below work well for patching small areas less than 2 sq. ft. For more extensive damage, the repair is done in layers, as shown on the opposite page.

Tools & Materials ▸

Caulk gun
Putty knife
Mason's trowel
Square-end trowel
Hammer
Whisk broom
Wire brush
Masonry chisel
Aviation snips
Scratching tool
Metal primer
Stucco patching
 compound
Stucco mix

Masonry paint
1½" roofing nails
15# building paper
Self-furring
 metal lath
Masonry caulk
Tint
Metal stop bead
Eye and ear
 protection
Work gloves

Fill thin cracks in stucco walls with masonry caulk. Overfill the crack with caulk, and feather until it's flush with the stucco. Allow the caulk to set, then paint it to match the stucco. Masonry caulk stays semiflexible, preventing further cracking.

How to Patch Small Areas

Remove loose material from the repair area, using a wire brush. Use the brush to clean away rust from any exposed metal lath, then apply a coat of metal primer to the lath.

Apply premixed stucco repair compound to the repair area, slightly overfilling the hole, using a putty knife or trowel. Read manufacturer's directions, as drying times vary.

Smooth the repair with a putty knife or trowel, feathering the edges to blend into the surrounding surface. Use a whisk broom or trowel to duplicate the original texture. Let the patch dry for several days, then touch it up with masonry paint.

How to Repair Large Areas

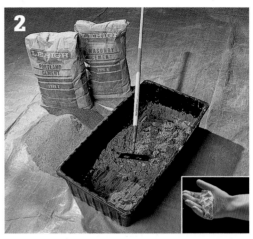

Make a starter hole with a drill and masonry bit, then use a masonry chisel and hammer to chip away stucco in the repair area. *NOTE: Wear safety glasses and a particle mask or respirator when cutting stucco. Cut self-furring metal lath to size with aviation snips and attach it to the sheathing, using roofing nails. Overlap pieces by 2". If the patch extends to the base of the wall, attach a metal stop bead at the bottom.*

To mix your own stucco, combine three parts sand, two parts portland cement, and one part masonry cement. Add just enough water so the mixture holds its shape when squeezed (inset). Mix only as much as you can use in one hour. *TIP: Premixed stucco works well for small jobs, but for large ones, it's more economical to mix your own.*

Apply a ⅜"-thick layer of stucco directly to the metal lath. Push the stucco into the mesh until it fills the gap between the mesh and the sheathing. Score horizontal grooves into the wet surface, using a scratching tool. Let the stucco dry for two days, misting it with water every two to four hours.

Apply a second, smooth layer of stucco. Build up the stucco to within ¼" of the original surface. Let the patch dry for two days, misting every two to four hours.

Combine finish-coat stucco mix with just enough water for the mixture to hold its shape. Dampen the patch area, then apply the finish coat to match the original surface. Dampen the patch periodically for a week. Let it dry for several more days before painting.

Repairing Concrete

Concrete is one of the most durable building materials, but it still requires occasional repair and maintenance. Freezing and thawing, improper finishing techniques, a poor subbase, or lack of reinforcement all can cause problems with concrete. By addressing problems as soon as you discover them, you can prevent further damage that may be difficult or impossible to fix.

Concrete repairs fall into a wide range, from simple cleaning and sealing, to removing and replacing whole sections. Filling cracks and repairing surface damage are the most common concrete repairs.

Another effective repair is resurfacing—covering an old concrete surface with a layer of fresh concrete. It's a good solution to spalling, crazing, or popouts—minor problems that affect the appearance more than the structure. These problems often result from inadequate preparation or incorrect finishing techniques.

As with any kind of repair, the success of the project depends largely on good preparation and the use of the best repair products for the job. Specially formulated repair products are manufactured for just about every type of concrete repair. Be sure to read the product-use information before purchasing any products; some products need to be used in combination with others.

A good repair can outlast the rest of the structure in some cases, but if structural damage has occurred, repairing the concrete is only a temporary solution. By using the right products and techniques, however, you can make cosmetic repairs that improve the appearance of the surface and keep damage from becoming worse.

Probably the most important point to remember when repairing concrete is that curing makes repairs last longer. That means covering repaired surfaces with plastic sheeting and keeping them damp for at least a week. In dry, hot weather, lift the plastic occasionally, and mist with water.

Before   After

Good repairs restore both the appearance and the function to failing concrete structures and surfaces. Careful work can produce a well-blended, successful repair like the one shown above.

Concrete Repair Products

Concrete repair products include: vinyl-reinforced concrete patch (A) for filling holes, popouts, and larger cracks; hydraulic cement (B) for repairing foundations, retaining walls, and other damp areas; quick-setting cement (C) for repairing vertical surfaces and unusual shapes; anchoring cement (D) for setting hardware in concrete; concrete sealing products (E); masonry paint (F); concrete recoating product (G) for creating a fresh surface on old concrete; joint-filler caulk (H); pour-in crack sealer (I); concrete cleaner (J); concrete fortifier (K) to strengthen concrete; bonding adhesive (L) to prepare the repair area; and concrete sand mix (M) for general repairs and resurfacing.

Tips for Disguising Repairs ▸

Add concrete pigment or liquid cement color to concrete patching compound to create a color that matches the original concrete. Experiment with different mixtures until you find a matching color. Samples should be dry to show the actual colors.

Use masonry paint to cover concrete repairs. Paint can be used on vertical or horizontal surfaces, but high-traffic surfaces will require more frequent touch-up or repainting.

Identifying Problems with Concrete

There are two general types of concrete failure: structural failure, usually resulting from outside forces like freezing water; and surface damage, most often caused by improper finishing techniques or concrete mixtures that do not have the right ratio of water to cement. Surface problems sometimes can be permanently repaired if the correct products and techniques are used. More significant damage can be patched for cosmetic purposes and to resist further damage, but the structure will eventually need to be replaced.

Common Concrete Problems

Sunken concrete is usually caused by erosion of the subbase. Some structures, like sidewalks, can be raised to repair the subbase, then relaid. A more common (and more reliable) solution is to hire a mudjacking contractor to raise the surface by injecting fresh concrete below the surface.

Frost heave is common in colder climates. Frozen ground forces concrete slabs upward, and sections of the slab can pop up. The best solution is to break off and remove the affected section or sections, repair the subbase, and pour new sections that are set off by isolation joints.

Moisture buildup occurs in concrete structures, like foundations and retaining walls, that are in constant ground contact. To identify the moisture source, tape a piece of foil to the wall. If moisture collects on the outer surface of the foil, the source likely is condensation, which can be corrected by installing a dehumidifier. If moisture is not visible on the foil, it is likely seeping through the wall. Consult a professional mason.

Staining can ruin the appearance of a concrete surface or structure. Stains can be removed with commercial-grade concrete cleaner or a variety of other chemicals. For protection against staining, seal masonry surfaces with clear sealant.

Widespread cracks all the way through the surface, and other forms of substantial damage, are very difficult to repair effectively. If the damage to the concrete is extensive, remove and replace the structure.

Isolated cracks occur on many concrete building projects. Fill small cracks with concrete caulk or crack-filler, and patch large cracks with vinyl-reinforced patching material.

Popouts can be caused by freezing moisture or stress, but very often they occur because the concrete surface was improperly floated or cured, causing the aggregate near the surface of the concrete to loosen. A few scattered popouts do not require attention, but if they are very large or widespread, you can repair them as you would repair holes.

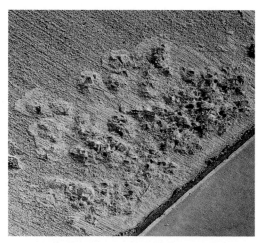

Spalling is surface deterioration of concrete. Spalling is caused by overfloating, which draws too much water to the surface, causing it to weaken and peel off over time. When spalling occurs, it is usually widespread, and the structure may need resurfacing.

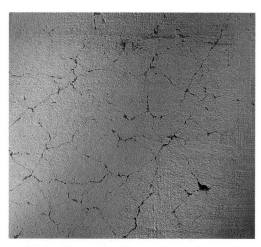

Crazing is widespread hairline cracks, usually caused by overfloating or too much portland cement in the concrete. Clean and seal the surface to help prevent further crazing. For a long-term solution, resurface.

Patching Holes in Concrete

Large and small holes are treated differently when repairing concrete. The best product for filling in smaller holes (less than ½" deep) is vinyl-reinforced concrete patcher, which is often sold in convenient quart of gallon containers of dry powder. Reinforced repair products should be applied only in layers that are ½" thick or less.

For deeper holes, use sand-mix concrete with an acrylic or latex fortifier, which can be applied in layers up to 2" thick. This material is sold in 60- or 80-pound bags of dry mix.

Patches in concrete will be more effective if you create clean, backward-angled cuts (page 240) around the damaged area, to create a stronger bond. For extensive cutting of damaged concrete, it's best to score the concrete first with a circular saw equipped with a masonry blade. Use a chisel and maul to complete the job.

Tools & Materials ▶

Trowels	Vegetable oil or
Drill with masonry-	commercial release
grinding disc	agent
Circular saw with	Hydraulic cement
masonry-cutting	Latex bonding agent
blade	Vinyl-reinforced
Masonry chisel	patching compound
Hand maul	Sand-mix concrete
Paintbrush	Concrete fortifier
Screed board	Plastic sheeting
Float	Floor scraper
Scrap lumber	Concrete primer
Vacuum	Paint roller
Hammer	Floor leveler
Eye and ear protection	Gauge rake or spreader
Work gloves	

Use hydraulic cement or quick-setting cement for repairing holes and chip-outs in vertical surfaces. Because they set up in just a few minutes, these products can be shaped to fill holes without the need for forms. If the structure is exposed constantly to moisture, use hydraulic cement.

How to Patch Large Areas

Mark straight cutting lines around the damaged area, then cut with a circular saw equipped with a masonry-cutting blade. Set the foot of the saw so the cut bevels away from the damage at a 15° angle. Chisel out any remaining concrete within the repair area. *TIP: Set the foot of the saw on a thin board to protect it from the concrete.*

Tip ▶

You can enhance the appearance of repaired vertical surfaces by painting with waterproof concrete paint once the surface has cured for at least a week. Concrete paint is formulated to resist chalking and efflorescence.

Mix sand-mix concrete with concrete acrylic fortifier, and fill the damaged area slightly above the surrounding surface.

Smooth and feather the repair with a float until the repair is even with the surrounding surface. Re-create any surface finish, like brooming, used on the original surface. Cover the repair with plastic and protect from traffic for at least one week.

How to Caulk Gaps around Masonry

Cracks between a concrete walk and foundation may result in seepage, leading to a wet basement. Repair cracks with caulk-type concrete patcher.

Caulk around the mud sill, the horizontal wooden plate where the house rests on the foundation. This area should be recaulked periodically to prevent heat loss.

How to Patch Small Holes

Cut out around the damaged area with a masonry-grinding disc mounted on a portable drill (or use a hammer and stone chisel). The cuts should bevel about 15° away from the center of the damaged area. Chisel out any loose concrete within the repair area. Always wear gloves and eye protection.

Apply a thin layer of latex bonding agent. The adhesive will bond with the damaged surface and create a strong bonding surface for the patching compound. Wait until the latex bonding agent is tacky (no more than 30 minutes) before proceeding to the next step.

Fill the damaged area with vinyl-reinforced patching compound, applied in ¼ to ½" layers. Wait about 30 minutes between applications. Add layers of the mixture until the compound is packed to just above surface level. Feather the edges smooth, cover the repair with plastic, and protect from traffic for at least one week.

How to Patch Concrete Floors

Clean the floor with a vacuum, and remove any loose or flaking concrete with a masonry chisel and hammer. Mix a batch of vinyl floor patching compound following manufacturer's directions. Apply the compound using a smooth trowel, slightly overfilling the cavity. Smooth the patch flush with the surface.

After the compound has cured fully, use a floor scraper to scrape the patched areas smooth.

How to Apply Floor Leveler

Remove any loose material and clean the concrete thoroughly; the surface must be free of dust, dirt, oils, and paint. Apply an even layer of concrete primer to the entire surface, using a long-nap paint roller. Let the primer dry completely.

Following the manufacturer's instructions, mix the floor leveler with water. The batch should be large enough to cover the entire floor area to the desired thickness (up to 1"). Pour the leveler over the floor.

Distribute the leveler evenly using a gauge rake or spreader. Work quickly: the leveler begins to harden in 15 minutes. You can use a trowel to feather the edges and create a smooth transition with an uncovered area. Let the leveler dry for 24 hours.

Filling Cracks in Concrete

The materials and methods for repairing cracks in concrete depend on the location and size of the crack. For small cracks (less than ¼" wide), you can use gray-tinted concrete caulk for a quick fix. For more permanent solutions, use pourable crack filler or fortified patching cements. The patching cements are polymer compounds that increase the bonding properties and allow some flexibility. For larger cracks on horizontal surfaces, use fortified sand-mix concrete; for cracks on vertical surfaces, use hydraulic or quick-setting cement. Thorough preparation is essential for creating a good bonding surface.

Tools & Materials ▸

Wire brush
Drill with wire
    wheel attachment
Stone chisel
Hand maul
Paint brush
Trowel
Latex bonding agent
Work gloves

Vinyl-reinforced
    patching compound
Concrete caulk
Fortified sand-mix
    concrete
Plastic sheeting
Pourable crack filler
Hydraulic or quick-
    setting cement

Use concrete repair caulk for quick-fix repairs to minor cracks. Although convenient, repair caulk should be viewed only as a short-term solution to improve appearance and help prevent further damage from water penetration.

Tips for Preparing Cracked Concrete for Repair ▸

Clean loose material from the crack using a wire brush or a portable drill with a wire wheel attachment. Loose material or debris left in the crack will result in a poor bond and an ineffective repair.

Chisel out the crack to create a backward-angled cut (wider at the base than at the surface), using a stone chisel and hammer. The angled cutout shape prevents the repair material from pushing out of the crack.

How to Repair Small Cracks

Prepare the crack for the repair (opposite page), then apply a thin layer of latex bonding agent to the entire repair area, using a paint brush. The latex bonding agent helps keep the repair material from loosening or popping out of the crack.

Mix vinyl-reinforced patching compound, and trowel it into the crack. Feather the repair with a trowel, so it is even with the surrounding surface. Cover the surface with plastic and protect it from traffic for at least a week.

Variations for Repairing Large Cracks

Sand

Shown cut away

Horizontal surfaces: Prepare the crack (opposite page), then pour sand into the crack to within ½" of the surface. Prepare sand-mix concrete, adding a concrete fortifier, then trowel the mixture into the crack. Feather until even with the surface, using a trowel.

Vertical surfaces: Prepare the crack (opposite page). Mix vinyl-reinforced concrete or hydraulic cement, then trowel a ¼"- to ½"-thick layer into the crack until the crack is slightly overfilled. Feather the material even with the surrounding surface, then let it dry. If the crack is over ½" deep, trowel in consecutive layers. Let each layer dry before applying another.

How to Seal Cracks in Concrete Foundation Walls

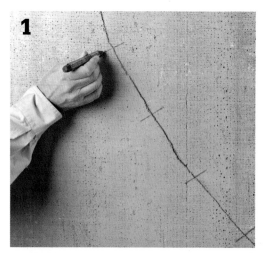

1

To determine if a foundation crack is stable, you need to monitor it over the course of several months, particularly over the fall and spring seasons. Draw marks across the crack at various points, noting the length as well as its width at the widest gaps. If the crack moves more than ⅟₁₆", consult a building engineer or foundation specialist.

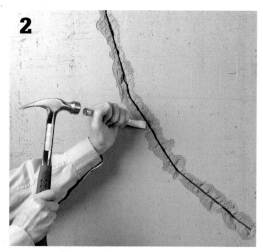

2

To repair a stable crack, use a chisel to cut a keyhole cut that's wider at the base then at the surface, and no more than ½" deep. Clean out the crack with a wire brush.

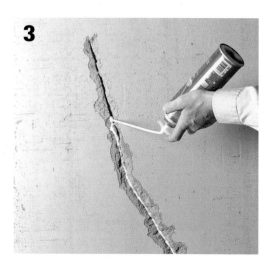

3

To help seal against moisture, fill the crack with expanding insulating foam, working from bottom to top.

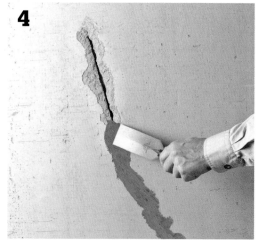

4

Mix hydraulic cement according to the manufacturer's instructions, then trowel it into the crack, working from the bottom to top. Apply cement in layers no more than ½" thick, until the patch is slightly higher than the surrounding area. Feather cement with the trowel until it's even with the surface and allow to dry thoroughly.

Repairing Concrete Steps

Steps require more maintenance and repair than other concrete structures around the house because heavy use makes them more susceptible to damage. Horizontal surfaces on steps can be treated using the same products and techniques used on other masonry surfaces. For vertical surfaces, use quick-setting cement, and shape it to fit.

Tools & Materials ▸

Trowel	Latex bonding agent
Wire brush	Vinyl-reinforced
Paintbrush	patching
Circular saw with	compound
masonry-cutting blade	Quick-setting cement
Chisel	Plastic sheeting
Float	Tape
Edger	Heavy block
Scrap lumber	Eye and ear
Vegetable oil or	protection
commercial	Work gloves
release agent	

Isolated damage to step surfaces, like the deep popout being repaired above, can be fixed to renew your steps. If damage is extensive, you may need to replace the steps.

Damaged concrete steps are an unsightly and unsafe way to welcome visitors to your home. Repairing cracks as they develop not only keeps the steps in a safer and better looking condition, it prolongs their life.

How to Replace a Step Corner

Retrieve the broken corner, then clean it and the mating surface with a wire brush. Apply latex bonding agent to both surfaces. If you do not have the broken piece, you can rebuild the corner with patching compound (below).

Spread a heavy layer of fortified patching compound on the surfaces to be joined, then press the broken piece into position. Lean a heavy brick or block against the repair until the patching compound sets (about 30 minutes). Cover the repair with plastic and protect it from traffic for at least one week.

How to Patch a Step Corner

Clean chipped concrete with a wire brush. Brush the patch area with latex bonding agent.

Mix patching compound with latex bonding agent, as directed by the manufacturer. Apply the mixture to the patch area, then smooth the surfaces and round the edges, as necessary, using a flexible knife or trowel.

Tape scrap lumber pieces around the patch as a form. Coat the insides with vegetable oil or commercial release agent so the patch won't adhere to the wood. Remove the wood when the patch is firm. Cover with plastic and protect from traffic for at least one week.

How to Patch Step Treads

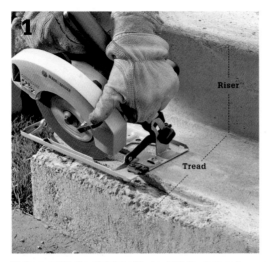

Make a cut in the stair tread just outside the damaged area, using a circular saw with a masonry-cutting blade. Make the cut so it angles toward the back of the step. Make a horizontal cut on the riser below the damaged area, then chisel out the area in between the two cuts.

Cut a form board the same height as the step riser. Coat one side of the board with vegetable oil or commercial release agent to prevent it from bonding with the repair, then press it against the riser of the damaged step, and brace it in position with heavy blocks. Make sure the top of the form is flush with the top of the step tread.

Apply latex bonding agent to the repair area with a clean paint brush, wait until the bonding agent is tacky (no more than 30 minutes), then press a stiff mixture of quick-setting cement into the damaged area with a trowel.

Smooth the concrete with a float, and let it set for a few minutes. Round over the front edge of the nose with an edger. Use a trowel to slice off the sides of the patch, so it is flush with the side of the steps. Cover the repair with plastic and wait a week before allowing traffic on the repaired section.

Miscellaneous Concrete Repairs

There are plenty of concrete problems you may encounter around your house that are not specifically addressed in many repair manuals. These miscellaneous repairs include such tasks as patching contoured objects that have been damaged and repairing masonry veneer around the foundation of your house. You can adapt basic techniques to make just about any type of concrete repair. Remember to dampen concrete surfaces before patching so that the moisture from concrete and other patching compounds is not absorbed into the existing surface. Be sure to follow the manufacturer's directions for the repair products you use.

Tools & Materials ▶

Putty knife	Soft-bristle brush
Trowel	Quick-setting cement
Hand maul	Emery paper
Chisel	Wire lath
Wire brush	Masonry anchors
Aviation snips	Concrete acrylic fortifier
Drill	Sand-mix concrete

Concrete slabs that slant toward the house can lead to foundation damage and a wet basement. Even a level slab near the foundation can cause problems. Consider asking a concrete contractor to fix it by mud-jacking, forcing wet concrete underneath the slab to lift the edge near the foundation.

How to Repair Shaped Concrete

Scrape all loose material and debris from the damaged area, then wipe down with water. Mix quick-setting cement and trowel it into the area. Work quickly—you only have a few minutes before concrete sets up.

Use the trowel or a putty knife to mold the concrete to follow the form of the object being repaired. Smooth the concrete as soon as it sets up. Buff with emery paper to smooth out any ridges after the repair dries.

How to Repair Masonry Veneer

Chip off the crumbled, loose, or deteriorated veneer from the wall, using a cold chisel and maul. Chisel away damaged veneer until you have only good, solid surface remaining. Use care to avoid damaging the wall behind the veneer. Clean the repair area with a wire brush.

Old metal lath

New metal lath

Clean up any metal lath in the repair area if it is in good condition. If not, cut it out with aviation snips. Add new lath where needed, using masonry anchors to hold it to the wall.

Mix fortified sand-mix concrete (or specialty concrete blends for wall repair), and trowel it over the lath until it is even with the surrounding surfaces.

Recreate the surface texture to match the surrounding area. For our project, we used a soft-bristled brush to stipple the surface. To blend in the repair, add pigment to the sand mixture or paint the repair area after it dries.

Resurfacing a Concrete Walkway

Concrete that has surface damage but is still structurally sound can be preserved by resurfacing—applying a thin layer of new concrete over the old surface. If the old surface has deep cracks or extensive damage, resurfacing will only solve the problem temporarily. Because new concrete will bond better if it is packed down, use a dry, stiff concrete mixture that can be compacted with a shovel.

Tools & Materials ▸

Shovel	Rubber mallet
Wood float	Level
Broom	Mortar bag
Circular saw	Stakes
Maul	2 × 4 lumber
Drill	Vegetable oil or commercial
Paint brush	release agent
Paint roller and tray	4" drywall screws
Wheelbarrow	Sand-mix concrete
Screed board	Bonding adhesive
Groover	Plastic sheets
Edger	Brick pavers
Hose	Type N mortar
Bricklayer's trowel	Eye and ear protection
Jointer	Work gloves

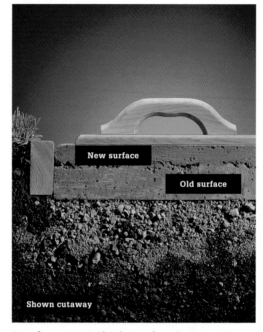

New surface

Old surface

Shown cutaway

Resurface concrete that has surface damage, such as spalling or popouts. Because the new surface will be thin (1" to 2"), use sand-mix concrete. If you are having ready-mix concrete delivered by a concrete contractor, make sure they do not use aggregate larger than ½" in the mixture.

How to Resurface Using Fresh Concrete

Clean the surface thoroughly. If the surface is flaking or spalled, scrape it with a spade to dislodge as much loose concrete as you can, then sweep the surface clean.

Dig a 6"-wide trench around the surface on all sides to create room for 2 × 4 forms.

Stake 2 × 4 forms flush against the sides of the concrete slabs, 1" to 2" above the surface (make sure height is even). Drive stakes every 3 ft. and at every joint in forms. Mark control joint locations onto the outside of the forms directly above existing control joints. Coat the inside edges of the forms with vegetable oil or commercial release agent.

Apply a thin layer of bonding adhesive over the entire surface. Follow the directions on the bonding adhesive product carefully. Instructions for similar products may differ slightly.

Mix concrete, using sand-mix concrete. Make the mixture slightly stiffer (drier) than normal concrete. Spread the concrete, then press down on the concrete with a shovel or 2 × 4 to pack the mixture into the forms. Smooth the surface with a screed board.

Float the concrete with a wood float, then tool with an edger, and cut control joints in the original locations. Recreate any surface treatment, such as brooming, used on the original surface. Let the surface cure for one week, covered with plastic. Seal the concrete.

Building Concrete Steps

Designing steps requires some calculations and some trial and error. As long as the design meets safety guidelines, you can adjust elements such as the landing depth and the dimensions of the steps. Sketching your plan on paper will make the job easier.

Before demolishing your old steps, measure them to see if they meet safety guidelines. If so, you can use them as a reference for your new steps. If not, start from scratch so your new steps do not repeat any design errors.

For steps with more than two risers, you'll need to install a handrail. Ask a building inspector about other requirements.

Tools & Materials ▸

Tape measure	2 × 4 lumber
Sledge hammer	Steel rebar grid
Shovel	Wire
Drill	Bolsters
Reciprocating saw	Construction adhesive
Level	Compactible gravel
Mason's string	Fill material
Hand tamper	Exterior-grade
Mallet	¾" plywood
Concrete	2" deck screws
Concrete mixing tools	Isolation board
Screed board	#3 rebar
Jigsaw	Stakes
Clamps	Latex caulk
Ruler or	Vegetable oil
framing square	or commercial
Float	release agent
Step edger	Eye and ear protection
Broom	Work gloves

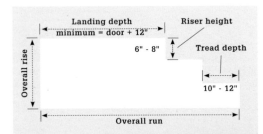

New concrete steps give a fresh, clean appearance to your house. And if your old steps are unstable, replacing them with concrete steps that have a non-skid surface will create a safer living environment.

How to Design Steps

Attach a mason's string to the house foundation,
1" below the bottom of the door threshold. Drive a stake
where you want the base of the bottom step to fall. Attach the
other end of the string to the stake and use a line level to level
it. Measure the length of the string—this distance is the overall
depth, or run, of the steps.

Measure down from the string to the bottom of the stake
to determine the overall height, or rise, of the steps. Divide
the overall rise by the estimated number of steps. The rise of
each step should be between 6" and 8". For example, if the
overall rise is 21" and you plan to build three steps, the rise of
each step would be 7" (21 divided by 3), which falls within the
recommended safety range for riser height.

Measure the width of your door and add at least 12"; this
number is the minimum depth you should plan for the landing
area of the steps. The landing depth plus the depth of each
step should fit within the overall run of the steps. If necessary,
you can increase the overall run by moving the stake at
the planned base of the steps away from the house, or by
increasing the depth of the landing.

Sketch a detailed plan for the steps, keeping these
guidelines in mind: each step should be 10" to 12" deep, with
a riser height between 6" and 8", and the landing should be
at least 12" deeper than the swing radius (width) of your door.
Adjust the parts of the steps as needed, but stay within the
given ranges. Creating a final sketch will take time, but it is
worth doing carefully.

How to Build Concrete Steps

Remove or demolish existing steps; if the old steps are concrete, set aside the rubble to use as fill material for the new steps. Wear protective gear, including eye protection and gloves, when demolishing concrete.

Dig 12"-wide trenches to the required depth for footings. Locate the trenches perpendicular to the foundation, spaced so the footings will extend 3" beyond the outside edges of the steps. Install steel rebar grids for reinforcement. Affix isolation boards to the foundation wall inside each trench, using a few dabs of construction adhesive.

Mix the concrete and pour the footings. Level and smooth the concrete with a screed board. You do not need to float the surface afterwards.

When bleed water disappears, insert 12" sections of rebar 6" into concrete, spaced at 12" intervals and centered side to side. Leave 1 ft. of clear space at each end.

Let the footings cure for two days, then excavate the area between them to 4" deep. Pour in a 5"-thick layer of compactible gravel subbase and tamp until it is level with the footings.

6

Make slopes
⅛" per foot

7

Bevel

Transfer the measurements for the side forms from your working sketch onto ¾" exterior-grade plywood. Cut out the forms along the cutting lines, using a jigsaw. Save time by clamping two pieces of plywood together and cutting both side forms at the same time. Add a ⅛" per foot back-to-front slope to the landing part of the form.

Cut form boards for the risers to fit between the side forms. Bevel the bottom edges of the boards when cutting to create clearance for the float at the back edges of the steps. Attach the riser forms to the side forms with 2" deck screws.

8

Cleats

Riser
support

9

Cut a 2 × 4 to make a center support for the riser forms. Use 2" deck screws to attach 2 × 4 cleats to the riser forms, then attach the support to the cleats. Check to make sure all corners are square.

Cut an isolation board and glue it to the house foundation at the back of the project area. Set the form onto the footings, flush against the isolation board. Add 2 × 4 bracing arms to the sides of the form, attaching them to cleats on the sides and to stakes driven into the ground.

(continued)

Fill the form with clean fill (broken concrete or rubble). Stack the fill carefully, keeping it 6" away from the sides, back, and top edges of the form. Shovel smaller fragments onto the pile to fill the void areas.

Lay pieces of #3 metal rebar on top of the fill at 12" intervals, and attach them to bolsters with wire to keep them from moving when the concrete is poured. Keep rebar at least 2" below the top of the forms. Mist the forms and the rubble with water.

Coat the forms with vegetable oil or a commercial release agent, then mist them with water so concrete won't stick to the forms. Mix concrete and pour steps one at a time, beginning at the bottom. Settle and smooth the concrete with a screed board. Press a piece of #3 rebar 1" down into the "nose" of each tread for reinforcement.

Float the steps, working the front edge of the float underneath the beveled edge at the bottom of each riser form.

14

Pour concrete into the forms for the remaining steps and the landing. Press rebar into the nose of each step. Keep an eye on the poured concrete as you work, and stop to float any concrete as soon as the bleed water disappears.

Shown cut away for clarity

OPTION: For railings with mounting plates that attach to sunken J-bolts, install the bolts before the concrete sets. Otherwise, choose railings with surface-mounted hardware (see step 16) that can be attached after the steps are completed.

15

Once the concrete sets, shape the steps and landing with a step edger. Float the surface. Sweep with a stiff-bristled broom for maximum traction.

16

Mounting plate

Remove the forms as soon as the surface is firm to the touch, usually within several hours. Smooth rough edges with a float. Add concrete to fill any holes. If forms are removed later, more patching may be required. Backfill the area around the base of the steps, and seal the concrete. Install a grippable hand railing that is securely anchored to the steps and the wall.

Resurfacing a Concrete Patio

Patio tile is most frequently applied over a concrete subbase—either an existing concrete patio, or a new concrete slab. A third option, which we show you on the following pages, is to pour a new tile subbase over an existing concrete patio. This option involves far less work and expense than removing an old patio and pouring a new slab. And it ensures that your new tiled patio will not develop the same problems that may be present in the existing concrete surface.

See the following photographs to help you determine the best method for preparing your existing concrete patio slab. To resurface a concrete sidewalk, see pages 248 to 249.

New subbase

Old patio

Tools & Materials ▶

Basic hand tools	Margin trowel
Shovel	30# building paper
Maul	Plastic sheeting
Straightedge	2 × 4 and 2 × 2 lumber
Aviation snips	2½" and 3" deck screws
Masonry hoe	⅜" stucco lath
Mortar box	Roofing cement
Hand tamper	Floor-mix concrete
Magnesium float	Screed board
Concrete edger	Eye and ear protection
Utility knife	Work gloves

How to Install a Subbase for Patio Tile

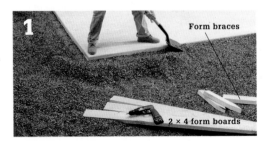

1

Form braces

2 × 4 form boards

Dig a trench at least 6" wide, and no more than 4" deep, around the patio to create room for 2 × 4 forms. Clean dirt and debris from the exposed sides of the patio. Cut and fit 2 × 4 frames around the patio, joining the ends with 3" deck screws. Cut wood stakes from 2 × 4s and drive them next to the forms, at 2-ft. intervals.

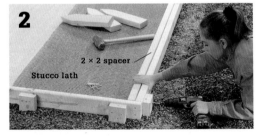

2

2 × 2 spacer

Stucco lath

Adjust the form height: set stucco lath on the surface, then set a 2 × 2 spacer on top of the lath (their combined thickness equals the thickness of the subbase). Adjust the form boards so the tops are level with the 2 × 2, and screw the stakes to the forms with 2½" deck screws.

3

Building paper
"bond-breaker"

Remove the 2 × 2 spacers and stucco lath, then lay strips of 30# building paper over the patio surface, overlapping seams by 6", to create a bond-breaker for the new surface. Crease the building paper at the edges and corners, making sure the paper extends past the tops of the forms. Make a small cut in the paper at each corner for easier folding.

4

Lay strips of stucco lath over the building-paper bond-breaker, overlapping seams by 1". Keep the lath 1" away from forms and the wall. Use aviation snips to cut the stucco lath (wear heavy gloves when handling metal).

5

Screed board

Build temporary 2 × 2 forms to divide the project into working sections and provide rests for the screed board used to level and smooth the fresh concrete. Make the sections narrow enough that you can reach across the entire section (3-ft. to 4-ft. sections are comfortable for most people). Screw the ends of the 2 × 2s to the form boards so the tops are level.

6

Mix dry floor-mix concrete with water in a mortar box, blending with a masonry hoe, according to the manufacturer's directions, or use a power mixer.

(continued)

NOTE: The mixture should be very dry when prepared so it can be pressed down into the voids in the stucco lath with a tamper.

Fill one working section with floor-mix concrete, up to the tops of the forms. Tamp the concrete thoroughly with a lightweight tamper to help force it into the voids in the lath and into corners. The lightweight tamper shown above is made from a 12" × 12" piece of ¾" plywood, with a 2 × 4 handle attached.

Level off the surface of the concrete by dragging a straight 2 × 4 screed board across the top, with the ends riding on the forms. Move the 2 × 4 in a sawing motion as you progress, creating a level surface and filling any voids in the concrete. If voids or hollows remain, add more concrete and smooth it off.

Use a magnesium float to smooth the surface of the concrete. Applying very light pressure, move the float back and forth in an arching motion, tipping the lead edge up slightly to avoid gouging the surface.

Pour and smooth out the next working section, repeating steps 7 to 9. After floating this section, remove the 2 × 2 temporary form between the two sections. Fill the void left behind with fresh concrete. Float the fresh concrete with the magnesium float until the concrete is smooth and level and blends into the working section on each side. Pour and finish the remaining working sections one at a time, using the same techniques.

Let the concrete dry until pressing the surface with your finger does not leave a mark. Cut contours around all edges of the subbase with a concrete edger. Tip the lead edge of the edger up slightly to avoid gouging the surface. Smooth out any marks left by the edger using a float.

Cover the concrete with sheets of plastic, and cure for at least three days (see manufacturer's directions for recommended curing time). Weight down the edges of the sheeting. After curing is compete, remove the plastic and disassemble and remove the forms.

Trim off the building paper around the sides of the patio using a utility knife. Apply roofing cement to the exposed sides of the patio, using a trowel or putty knife to fill and seal the seam between the old and new surfaces. After the roofing cement dries, shovel dirt or ground cover back into the trench around the patio.

Identifying Brick & Block Problems

Inspect damaged brick and block structures closely before you begin any repair work. Accurately identifying the nature and cause of the damage is an important step before choosing the best solution for the problem and preventing the problems from recurring in the future.

Look for obvious clues, like overgrown tree roots, or damaged gutters that let water drain onto masonry surfaces. Also check the slope of the adjacent landscape; it may need to be regraded to direct water away from a brick or block wall. Water is the most common cause of problems, but major cracks that recur can be a sign of serious structural problems that should be examined by an engineer.

Repairs fail when the original source of the problem is not eliminated prior to making the repair. When a concrete patch separates, for example, it means that the opposing stresses causing the crack are still at work on the structure. Find and correct the cause (often a failing subbase or stress from water or freezing and thawing), then redo the repair.

Types of Brick & Block Problems

Deteriorated mortar joints are common problems in brick and block structures—mortar is softer than most bricks or blocks and is more prone to damage. Deterioration is not always visible, so probe surrounding joints with a screwdriver to see if they are sound.

Major structural damage, like the damage to this brick porch, usually requires removal of the existing structure, improvements to the subbase, and reconstruction of the structure. Projects of this nature should only be attempted by professional masons.

Damage to concrete blocks often results from repeated freezing and thawing of moisture trapped in the wall or in the blocks themselves. Instead of replacing the whole block, chip out the face of the block and replace it with a concrete paver with the same dimensions as the face of the block (page 266).

Spalling occurs when freezing water or other forces cause enough directional pressure to fracture a brick. The best solution is to replace the entire brick (pages 264 to 265) while eliminating the source of the pressure, if possible. *TIP: Chip off a piece of the damaged brick to use as a color reference when looking for a replacement.*

Damaged mortar caps on chimneys allow water into the flue area, where it can damage the chimney and even the roof or interior walls. Small-scale damage (top photo) can be patched with fire-rated silicone caulk. If damage is extensive (bottom photo), repair or replace the mortar cap.

Stains and discoloration can be caused by external sources or by minerals leeching to the surface from within the brick or block (called efflorescence). If the stain does not wash away easily with water, use a cleaning solution.

Repairing Brick & Block Walls

The most common brick and block wall repair is tuck-pointing, the process of replacing failed mortar joints with fresh mortar. Tuck-pointing is a highly useful repair technique for any homeowner. It can be used to repair walls, chimneys, brick veneer, or any other structure where the bricks or blocks are bonded with mortar.

Minor cosmetic repairs can be attempted on any type of wall, from free-standing garden walls to block foundations. Filling minor cracks with caulk or repair compound, and patching popouts or chips are good examples of minor repairs. Consult a professional before attempting any major repairs, like replacing brick or blocks, or rebuilding a structure—especially if you are dealing with a load-bearing structure.

Basement walls are a frequent trouble area for homeowners. Constant moisture and stress created by ground contact can cause leaks, bowing, and paint failure. Small leaks and cracks can be patched with hydraulic cement. Masonry-based waterproofing products can be applied to give deteriorated walls a fresh appearance. Persistent moisture problems are most often caused by improper grading of soil around the foundation or a malfunctioning downspout and gutter system.

NOTE: The repairs shown in this section feature brick and block walls. The same techniques may be used for other brick and block structures.

Tools & Materials ▸

Raking tool	Drill with masonry disc
Mortar hawk	and bit
Tuck-pointer	Mortar
Jointing tool	Gravel
Bricklayer's hammer	Scrap of metal flashing
Mason's trowel	Concrete fortifier
Mason's or	Replacement bricks
stone chisel	or blocks
Pointing trowel	Eye and ear protection
Stiff-bristle brush	Work gloves

Make timely repairs to brick and block structures. Tuck-pointing deteriorated mortar joints is a common repair that, like other types of repair, improves the appearance of the structure or surface and helps prevent further damage.

How to Tuck-point Mortar Joints

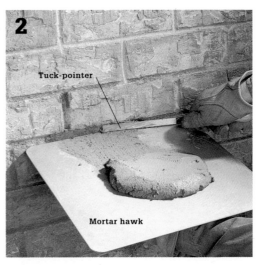

Clean out loose or deteriorated mortar to a depth of ¼" to ¾". Use a mortar raking tool (top) first, then switch to a masonry chisel and a hammer (bottom) if the mortar is stubborn. Clear away all loose debris, and dampen the surface with water before applying fresh mortar.

Mix the mortar, adding concrete fortifier; add tint if necessary. Load mortar onto a mortar hawk, then push it into the horizontal joints with a tuck-pointer. Apply mortar in ¼"-thick layers, and let each layer dry for 30 minutes before applying another. Fill the joints until the mortar is flush with the face of the brick or block.

Apply the first layer of mortar into the vertical joints by scooping mortar onto the back of a tuck-pointer, and pressing it into the joint. Work from the top downward.

After the final layer of mortar is applied, smooth the joints with a jointing tool that matches the profile of the old mortar joints. Tool the horizontal joints first. Let the mortar dry until it is crumbly, then brush off the excess mortar with a stiff-bristle brush.

How to Replace a Damaged Brick

Score the damaged brick so it will break apart more easily for removal: use a drill with a masonry-cutting disc to score lines along the surface of the brick and in the mortar joints surrounding the brick.

Use a mason's chisel and hammer to break apart the damaged brick along the scored lines. Rap sharply on the chisel with the hammer, being careful not to damage surrounding bricks. *TIP: Save fragments to use as a color reference when you shop for replacement bricks.*

Chisel out any remaining mortar in the cavity, then brush out debris with a stiff-bristle or wire brush to create a clean surface for the new mortar. Rinse the surface of the repair area with water.

Mix the mortar for the repair, adding concrete fortifier to the mixture, and tint if needed to match old mortar. Use a pointing trowel to apply a 1"-thick layer of mortar at the bottom and sides of the cavity.

Dampen the replacement brick slightly, then apply mortar to the ends and top of the brick. Fit the brick into the cavity and rap it with the handle of the trowel until the face is flush with the surrounding bricks. If needed, press additional mortar into the joints with a pointing trowel.

Scrape away excess mortar with a masonry trowel, then smooth the joints with a jointing tool that matches the profile of the surrounding mortar joints. Let the mortar set until crumbly, then brush the joints to remove excess mortar.

Tips for Removing & Replacing Several Bricks ▸

For walls with extensive damage, remove bricks from the top down, one row at a time, until the entire damaged area is removed. Replace bricks using the techniques shown above and in the section on building with brick and block. *Caution: Do not dismantle load-bearing brick structures like foundation walls—consult a professional mason for these repairs.*

For walls with internal damaged areas, remove only the damaged section, keeping the upper layers intact if they are in good condition. Do not remove more than four adjacent bricks in one area—if the damaged area is larger, it will require temporary support, which is a job for a professional mason.

How to Reface a Damaged Concrete Block

Cores (hollow)

Drill several holes into the face of the deteriorated block at the cores (hollow spots) of the block using a drill and masonry bit. Wear protective eye covering when drilling or breaking apart concrete.

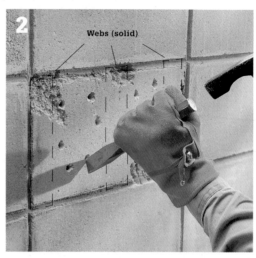

Webs (solid)

Using the holes as starting points, chip away the face of the block over the core areas, using a chisel and hammer. Be careful not to damage surrounding blocks and try to leave the block face intact in front of the solid web areas.

Use a stone chisel to carefully chip out a 2"-deep recess in the web areas. Mark and score cutting lines 2" back from the block face, then chisel away the block in the recess area. Avoid deepening the recess more than 2" because the remaining web sections provide a bonding surface for the concrete paver that will be installed to replace the face of the concrete block.

Mix mortar, then apply a 1"-thick layer to the sides and bottom of the opening, to the webs, and to the top edge and web locations on the paver (use an 8 × 16" paver to fit standard blocks). Press the paver into the cavity, flush with the surrounding blocks. Add mortar to the joints if needed, then prop a 2 × 4 against the paver until the mortar sets. Finish the joints with a jointing tool.

How to Reinforce a Section of Refaced Blocks

Reinforce repair areas spanning two or more adjacent block faces. Start by drilling a few holes in a small area over a core in the block located directly above the repair area. Chip out the block face between the holes with a cold chisel.

Prepare a thin mortar mix made from 1 part gravel and 2 parts dry mortar, then add water. The mixture should be thin enough to pour easily, but not soupy. *NOTE: Adding small amounts of gravel increases the strength of the mortar and increases the yield of the batch.*

Pour the mortar/gravel mixture into the hole above the repair area, using a piece of metal flashing as a funnel. Continue mixing and filling the hole until it will not accept any more mortar. The mortar will dry to form a reinforcing column that is bonded to the backs of the pavers used to reface the blocks.

Patch the hole above the repair area by using a pointing trowel to fill the hole with plain mortar mix. Smooth the surface with the pointing trowel. When the mortar resists finger pressure, finish the joint below the patch with a jointing tool.

Painting Brick & Block

Check brick and block surfaces annually and remove stains or discoloration. Most problems are easy to correct if they are treated in a timely fashion. Regular maintenance will help brick and block structures remain attractive and durable for a long time. Refer to the information below for cleaning tips that address specific staining problems.

Painted brick and block structures can be spruced up by applying a fresh coat of paint. As with any other painting job, thorough surface preparation and a quality primer are critical to a successful outcome.

Many stains can be removed easily, using a commercial brick and block detergent, available at home centers, but remember:

- Always test cleaning solutions on a small inconspicuous part of the surface and evaluate the results.
- Some chemicals and their fumes may be harmful. Be sure to follow manufacturer's safety and use recommendations. Wear protective clothing.
- Soak the surface to be cleaned with water before you apply any solutions. This keeps solutions from soaking in too quickly. Rinse the surface thoroughly after cleaning to wash off any remaining cleaning solution.

Use a pressure washer to clean large brick and block structures. Pressure washers can be rented from most rental centers. Be sure to obtain detailed operating and safety instructions from the rental agent.

Solvent Solutions for Common Brick & Block Blemishes ▸

- Egg splatter: Dissolve oxalic acid crystals in water, following manufacturer's instructions, in a nonmetallic container. Brush onto the surface.
- Efflorescence: Scrub surface with a stiff-bristled brush. Use a household cleaning solution for surfaces with heavy accumulation.
- Iron stains: Spray or brush a solution of oxalic acid crystals dissolved in water, following manufacturer's instructions. Apply directly to the stain.
- Ivy: Cut vines away from the surface (do not pull them off). Let remaining stems dry up, then scrub them off with a stiff-bristled brush and household cleaning solution.
- Oil: Apply a paste made of mineral spirits and an inert material like sawdust.
- Paint stains: Remove new paint with a solution of trisodium phosphate (TSP) and water, following manufacturer's mixing instructions. Old paint can usually be removed with heavy scrubbing or sandblasting.
- Plant growth: Use weed killer according to manufacturer's directions.
- Smoke stains: Scrub surface with household cleanser containing bleach, or use a mixture of ammonia and water.

Tips for Cleaning Brick & Block Surfaces ▸

Mix a paste made from cleaning solvents (chart, opposite page) and talcum or flour. Apply paste directly to stain, let it dry, then scrape it off with a vinyl or plastic scraper.

Use a nylon scraper or a thin block of wood to remove spilled mortar that has hardened. Avoid using metal scrapers, which can damage masonry surfaces.

Mask off windows, siding, decorative millwork, and other exposed nonmasonry surfaces before cleaning brick and block. Careful masking is essential if you are using harsh cleaning chemicals, such as muriatic acid.

Tips for Painting Masonry ▸

Clean mortar joints, using a drill with a wire wheel attachment before applying paint. Scrub off loose paint, dirt, mildew, and mineral deposits so the paint will bond better.

Apply masonry primer before repainting brick or block walls. Primer helps eliminate stains and prevent problems such as efflorescence.

Repairing Stonework

Damage to stonework is typically caused by frost heave, erosion or deterioration of mortar, or by stones that have worked out of place. Dry-stone walls are more susceptible to erosion and popping, while mortared walls develop cracks that admit water, which can freeze and cause further damage.

Inspect stone structures once a year for signs of damage and deterioration. Replacing a stone or repointing crumbling mortar now will save you work in the long run.

A leaning stone column or wall probably suffers from erosion or foundation problems, and can be dangerous if neglected. If you have the time, you can tear down and rebuild dry-laid structures, but mortared structures with excessive lean need professional help.

Tools & Materials ▸

Maul	Wood shims
Chisel	Trowels for mixing and pointing
Camera	Carpet-covered 2 × 4
Shovel	Chalk
Hand tamper	Compactible gravel
Level	Replacement stones
Batter gauge	Type M mortar
Stiff-bristle brush	Mortar tint
Mortar bag	Eye and ear protection
Masonry chisels	Work gloves

Stones in a wall can become dislodged due to soil settling, erosion, or seasonal freeze-thaw cycles. Make the necessary repairs before the problem migrates to other areas.

Tips for Replacing Popped Stones ▸

Return a popped stone to its original position. If other stones have settled in its place, drive shims between neighboring stones to make room for the popped stone. Be careful not to wedge too far.

Use a 2 × 4 covered with carpet to avoid damaging the stone when hammering it into place. After hammering, make sure a replacement stone hasn't damaged or dislodged the adjoining stones.

How to Rebuild a Dry-stone Wall Section

Before you start, study the wall and determine how much of it needs to be rebuilt. Plan to dismantle the wall in a "V" shape, centered on the damaged section. Number each stone and mark its orientation with chalk so you can rebuild it following the original design. *TIP: Photograph the wall, making sure the markings are visible.*

Capstones are often set in a mortar bed atop the last course of stone. You may need to chip out the mortar with a maul and chisel to remove the capstones. Remove the marked stones, taking care to check the overall stability of the wall as you work.

Rebuild the wall, one course at a time, using replacement stones only when necessary. Start each course at the ends and work toward the center. On thick walls, set the face stones first, then fill in the center with smaller stones. Check your work with a level, and use a batter gauge to maintain the batter of the wall. If your capstones were mortared, re-lay them in fresh mortar. Wash off the chalk with water and a stiff-bristle brush.

Tip ▶

If you're rebuilding because of erosion, dig a trench at least 6" deep under the damaged area, and fill it with compactible gravel. Tamp the gravel with a hand tamper. This will improve drainage and prevent water from washing soil out from beneath the wall.

Tint mortar for repair work so it blends with the existing mortar. Mix several samples of mortar, adding a different amount of tint to each, and allow them to dry thoroughly. Compare each sample to the old mortar, and choose the closest match.

Use a mortar bag to restore weathered and damaged mortar joints over an entire structure. Remove loose mortar (see below) and clean all surfaces with a stiff-bristle brush and water. Dampen the joints before tuck-pointing, and cover all of the joints, smoothing and brushing as necessary.

How to Repoint Mortar Joints

Carefully rake out cracked and crumbling mortar, stopping when you reach solid mortar. Remove loose mortar and debris with a stiff-bristle brush. *TIP: Rake the joints with a chisel and maul, or make your own raking tool by placing an old screwdriver in a vice and bending the shaft about 45°.*

Mix type M mortar, then dampen the repair surfaces with clean water. Working from the top down, pack mortar into the crevices, using a pointing trowel. Smooth the mortar when it has set up enough to resist light finger pressure. Remove excess mortar with a stiff-bristle brush.

How to Replace a Stone in a Mortared Wall

1

2

Remove the damaged stone by chiseling out the surrounding mortar, using a masonry chisel or a modified screwdriver (opposite page). Drive the chisel toward the damaged stone to avoid harming neighboring stones. Once the stone is out, chisel the surfaces inside the cavity as smooth as possible.

Brush out the cavity to remove loose mortar and debris. Test the surrounding mortar, and chisel or scrape out any mortar that isn't firmly bonded.

3

4

Dry-fit the replacement stone. The stone should be stable in the cavity and blend with the rest of the wall. You can mark the stone with chalk and cut it to fit, but excessive cutting will result in a conspicuous repair.

Mist the stone and cavity lightly, then apply type M mortar around the inside of the cavity, using a trowel. Butter all mating sides of the replacement stone. Insert the stone and wiggle it forcefully to remove any air pockets. Use a pointing trowel to pack the mortar solidly around the stone. Smooth the mortar when it has set up.

Pressure Washing Masonry

To clean the masonry and stonework surfaces around the outside of your home, there is nothing that works faster or more effectively than a pressure washer. A typical residential-grade unit can be as much as 50 times more powerful than a standard garden hose, while using up to 80% less water.

Pressure washing is quite simple: firmly grasp the spray wand with both hands, depress the trigger and move the nozzle across the surface to be cleaned. Although different surfaces require different spray patterns and pressure settings, it is not difficult to determine the appropriate cleaning approach for each project. The nozzle is adjustable—from a low-pressure, wide-fan spray for general cleaning and rinsing, to a narrow, intense stream for stubborn stains. But the easiest way to control the cleaning is to simply adjust the distance between the nozzle and the surface—move the nozzle back to reduce the pressure; move the nozzle closer to intensify it.

To successfully clean any masonry or stone surface using a pressure washer, follow these tips:

- When cleaning a new surface, start in an inconspicuous area, with a wide spray pattern and the nozzle 4- to 5-ft. from the surface. Move closer to the surface until the desired effect is achieved.

- Keep the nozzle in constant motion, spraying at a steady speed with long, even strokes to ensure consistent results.
- Maintain a consistent distance between the nozzle and the cleaning surface.
- When cleaning heavily soiled or stained surfaces, use cleaning detergents formulated for pressure washers. Always rinse the surface before applying the detergent. On vertical surfaces, apply detergent from bottom to top, and rinse from top to bottom. Always follow the detergent manufacturer's directions.
- After pressure washing, always seal the surface with an appropriate surface sealer (e.g., concrete sealer for cement driveways), following the product manufacturer's instructions.

Tools & Materials ▸

Pressure sprayer
Cleaning solution
Eye and ear protection
Work gloves

Pressure Washer Safety ▸

- Always wear eye protection.
- Do not wear open-toed shoes.
- Make sure the unit is on a stable surface and the cleaning area has adequate slopes and drainage to prevent puddles.
- Assume a solid stance, and firmly grasp the spray gun with both hands to avoid injury if the gun kicks back.
- Always keep the high-pressure hose connected to both the pump and the spray gun while the system is pressurized.
- Never aim the nozzle at people or animals— the high-pressure stream of water can cause serious injury.

Tips for Pressure Washing Masonry ▸

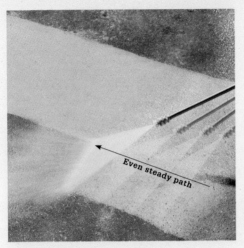

Always keep the nozzle in motion, spraying at a steady speed and using long, even strokes. Take multiple passes over heavily soiled areas. Take care not to dwell on one spot for too long, especially when using narrow, high-pressure spray patterns.

Hold the spray wand so that the nozzle distributes the spray pattern across the surface evenly. Holding the nozzle at too low an angle can cause an uneven spray pattern, resulting in "zebra striping." Also, maintain a consistent distance between the nozzle and the cleaning surface to ensure consistent results and help flush dirt and debris from the area.

Work in identifiable sections, such as the area between the expansion joints in concrete. If there is a slope, work downhill to promote drainage and help flush away dirt and debris. Wet entire surface to prevent streaking.

To prevent streaks on vertical surfaces, always begin pressure washing or applying cleaning detergent at the bottom of the surface, then work upward. When rinsing, start at the top and work downward—gravity will help the clean water flush away dirt, debris, and detergent residue.

Repairing an Asphalt Driveway

The two most popular hard surface driveway materials are asphalt and concrete. Both are used, almost interchangeably, throughout the country in cold and hot climates. But there are some basic differences. Concrete generally costs more to install and asphalt generally costs more to maintain as the years go by. And, concrete doesn't always perform well in cold areas. It's susceptible to damage from the freeze-and-thaw cycle and it can be damaged by exposure to road salt. Asphalt, on the other hand, doesn't always perform well in hot climates. It absorbs a lot of heat from the sun and tends to stay soft during very hot periods. And, of course, when the surface is soft, it can wear more quickly.

A typical asphalt driveway is formed by pouring and compressing a layer of hot asphalt over a subbase of compacted gravel.

Tools & Materials ▸

Driveway cleaner or detergent	Cold chisel	Asphalt patching compound	Caulk gun
Brushes	Hammer	Trowel	Driveway sealer
	Vacuum	Asphalt crack filler	Squeegee brush

How to Repair an Asphalt Driveway

Carefully inspect the asphalt surface for any oil and grease stains. Then remove them with driveway cleaner or household detergent. Scrub the cleaner into the surface with a soft brush and rinse the area clean with a garden hose. Repeat until the stain is gone. If using driveway cleaner, wear the recommended safety equipment.

Once the stains are removed, thoroughly rinse the entire driveway with a garden hose and nozzle. The goal is to wash away any debris and to remove the dust and dirt from the surface cracks.

Repair the small cracks first. Chip out any loose debris with a cold chisel and hammer. Then clean out all debris with a wire brush. Remove all the dust with a shop vacuum. A crevice tool on the end of the hose will do the best job.

Place asphalt patching compound in the holes with a small trowel. Overfill the hole so the patch material is about ½" higher than the surrounding asphalt surface.

Compact the patch material with a small piece of 2 × 4. Tamp the board up and down with your hand, or strike the board with a hammer. Keep working until you can't compress the patch any more.

Finish the patch by covering it with a piece of 2 × 6 and striking it with a hammer or mallet. Work back and forth across the board to smooth out the entire patch and make it flush to the surrounding surface.

(continued)

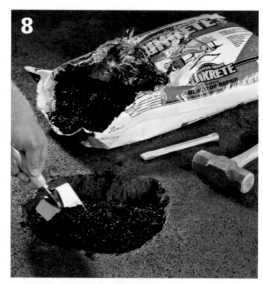

On narrower patches, the compound can be smoothed with a small trowel. Just move the tool across the surrounding surface and then over the patch. This should flatten the patch. Finish up by compressing the compound by pushing it down with the trowel.

Prepare larger potholes by undercutting the edges with a cold chisel and a hammer. Then, remove all the debris and fill the hole with cold-patch asphalt mix. Working directly from the bag, fill the hole about 1 in. higher than the surrounding surface. Then compact it with a 2 × 4, as before.

One great way to compress cold-patch asphalt is to cover the patch with a piece of plywood. Then, drive your car onto the plywood and stop when one tire is centered on the panel. Wait a few minutes, then move the car back and forth a few times.

Once the hole patching is done, fill the routine cracks (less than ¼" wide) with asphalt crack filler. This material comes in a caulk tube, which makes it very easy to apply. Just clean the crack with a wire brush and a vacuum, then squeeze the filler into the crack.

After the crack filler has cured for about 10 or 15 minutes, smooth it out with a putty knife as you force the filler down into the crack. If this creates small depressions, fill these with a second application of filler.

Driveway sealer should always be mixed thoroughly before use. Take a 2× stir stick that's about 30 in. long and stir the sealer until it has a uniform consistency. Pour out enough to cover a strip across the driveway that's about 3-ft. or 4-ft. wide.

Spread the sealer with the squeegee side of the application brush. Try to keep this coat as uniform as possible. Work the sealer into the small cracks and pull it gently over the big patches.

Flip the squeegee over to the brush side and smooth out the lap marks and other irregularities that were left from the application coat. Work at right angles to the first pass.

Maintaining a Deck

Inspect your deck once each year. Replace loose or rusting hardware or fasteners, and apply fresh finish to prevent water damage.

Look carefully for areas that show signs of damage. Replace or reinforce damaged wood as soon as possible.

Restore an older, weathered deck to the original wood color with a deck-brightening solution. Brighteners are available at any home improvement store.

Tools & Materials ▸

Flashlight	Eye and ear protection
Awl or screwdriver	Pressure sprayer
Screwgun	2½" corrosion-
Putty knife	resistant
Scrub brush	deck screws
Rubber gloves	Deck brightener

Inspect hidden areas regularly for signs of rotted or damaged wood. Apply a fresh coat of finish yearly.

Tips for Maintaining an Older Deck ▸

Use an awl or screwdriver to check deck for soft, rotted wood. Replace or reinforce damaged wood.

Clean debris from cracks between decking boards with a putty knife. Debris traps moisture, and can cause wood to rot.

How to Renew a Deck

Drive new fasteners to secure loose decking to joists. If using the old nail or screw holes, new fasteners should be slightly longer than the originals.

Mix deck-brightening solution as directed by manufacturer. Apply solution with pressure sprayer. Let solution set for 10 minutes.

Scrub deck thoroughly with a stiff scrub brush. Wear rubber gloves and eye protection.

Rinse deck with clear water. If necessary, apply a second coat of brightener to extremely dirty or stained areas. Rinse and let dry. Apply a fresh coat of sealer or stain.

Painting Metal Sheds

Metal sheds sometimes age ungracefully. Aluminum panels can become chalky and dull. Steel panels, if scratched, can begin to rust. The aluminum can be treated with an aluminum siding brightener, which can yield a nice result without painting. If the shed is rusty steel, painting is the answer. If the shed has been waxed, you will need to clean it with automotive wax remover or aluminum siding cleaner.

Tools & Materials ▸

Cleaner
Metal primer
Exterior metal paint
Paint spraying equipment
  or roller and brushes

Ladder
Wax remover
Work gloves
Eye protection

Metal sheds rust and become damaged. Proper repairs and preparation followed by a coat of fresh paint improves the appearance and extends shed life.

How to Paint a Metal Shed

Clear all debris from the shed. If the shed has been waxed, clean thoroughly with automotive wax remover or aluminum siding cleaning solution.

Sand, clean and prime all rusted areas with a primer rated for exterior metal.

Paint the shed. The best possible surface will be obtained using a paint sprayer, which can be rented at a rental center. If you do not want to spray, use a short nap roller.

Metal Shed Maintenance ▸

- Trim shrubs and tree branches
- Inspect roof for rust
- Sweep leaves and twigs off roof
- Inspect siding for scratches or rust
- Inspect flooring for damage or rot
- Clean debris from door tracks
- Lubricate door slides or wheel axles with silicone lubricant
- Wash and wax with high-quality auto wax
- Check tightness of cable anchors

Jacking Up a Shed

The sinking shed is a common problem. Unless a shed is built on cement piers that extend below the frost line, it is likely that sooner or later the shed will sink if the ground is subject to freeze/thaw cycles. Usually one side or one corner will sink faster. The easiest solution is to jack up that side or corner of the shed and add some shimming material to level it. Ground contact lumber or cement blocks can be used as shims. You may decide to add another set of support blocks or skids. Remove heavy items from the shed before beginning; no need to jack up the riding mower!

If the skids or joists have rotted, they should be replaced. This is an involved process and not covered here.

Tools & Materials ▸

Bottle jack
Scrap plywood
2 × 4 or 2 × 6 lumber
Pressure treated lumber
Concrete block or brick
Shovel
Hammer
Nails
String level

Work gloves
Eye protection

Before

After

Leveling a sunken shed is a surprisingly simple fix.

How to Jack Up a Shed

Using nails and hammer, install a masonry string level across the base of the shed. Nails should be equidistant from the top and bottom of the baseboards.

Excavate the area around the shed base to expose the foundation, and clear the area to determine the problem; sometimes a sinking shed is due to rotting skids, not settling soil. Remove debris or dirt so you have a clear view of the foundation materials. Depending on the landscape, you may have to dig out an additional area to install the jack.

Dig a trench if you will need room to maneuver a jack handle. The jack needs a firm surface beneath it to dissipate the pressure. Stack two 12 × 12" squares of plywood under the jack. Make sure the wood above the jack is solid. Place a chunk of 2 × 4 or 2 × 6 lumber on top of the jack. Slowly pump up the jack. It is best not to move structures more than ¼" at a time. Allow the structure to rest for a day after each raising.

When the string reads level, insert the appropriate shimming material between the skid or joists and the gravel or concrete base. Ground-contact treated lumber or solid cement bricks or blocks are good alternatives.

Safety Tip ▸

To avoid crushing and related injuries, never work on, under or around a load supported only by a jack. Always use jack stands, or solid cement bricks or blocks to support the shed.

Install New Shed Doors

One of the frustrations of metal shed ownership is that the doors seem to expire long before the shed. Most inexpensive metal sheds have doors that slide on plastic slides—not even wheels! It seems like the doors quickly become catawampus, and no longer slide well in their tracks or cheap slides.

One answer is to create a set of new wood doors for the shed.

Tools & Materials ▸

Cordless drill
2 × 4 lumber
Plywood siding
Deck screws
Sheet metal screws

Angle brackets
Galvanized
  butt hinges
Work gloves
Eye and ear protection

Steel shed doors often expire long before the shed itself. A new set of wood doors is an opportunity for a stylish upgrade.

How to Install Wooden Barn Doors on a Steel Shed

Sliding doors are typically removed by unfastening the screws attaching the door to the top slides then tilting back and lifting the door out of the bottom track.

Use 2 × 4s to frame a door opening. Measure and cut two boards to the height of the opening. Align them in the shed door opening, and use blocking to attach these at the top to the roof beams. Attach a 2 × 4 between the two sides as a header. Attach the base of the side 2 × 4s to the bottom door track, using angle brackets and sheet metal screws.

Measure the opening, and create two doors of equal size to fit into it. Use 2 × 4s for framing, with a diagonal brace, and cover with plywood siding. Attach the doors to the frame using galvanized butt hinges. The old metal doors may be used, but you will need to cut them down to size. They may also be mounted on galvanized butt hinges. Attach hardware.

Replacing Shed Siding

Sometimes even the best maintenance doesn't stop shed siding from rotting or deteriorating. Powerful sun rays on southern exposures can wreak havoc on even the best maintained shed. Woodpiles, shrubs, or snow piles can lead to contact rot that might not be noticed until too late. A poorly designed shed that includes horizontal members that are not protected by flashing will collect leaves and water, leading to rot. The best approach is to totally replace the siding. The amount of work for partial replacement is equivalent to full replacement, so the only savings might be in material costs.

Remember that siding is typically not rated for ground contact, so make sure siding is not in contact with the ground. If it is, dig out the dirt and perhaps create a drainage feature around the shed to direct water away from the shed. Splashing water from the roof can also age the shed more quickly.

Here, a 1 × 6 base trim board was attached over the oriented strand board siding, creating a ledge on the top of the trim board that ultimately led to rot in the panel. Battens made from 1 × 2 were run vertically to cover vertical seams and at each stud location to create a board-and-batten effect.

Tools & Materials ▸

Circular saw	Siding
Pry bar	Exterior caulk
Hammer	Chalk line
Galvanized siding nails	Pneumatic nailer
Flashing	Work gloves
Drill	Eye and ear
Deck screws	protection

Partial Replacement ▸

Alternately, you could remove only the bottom, rotted portion of the siding. This is only a short term fix, as this partial job is susceptible to future problems. Remove trim boards and mark a level, horizontal line about 6" above the rotted area. Use a circular saw set to the thickness of the siding and saw along the line. Remove the rotted wood. Cut a new piece of siding to fit. Insert a piece of Z flashing under the old siding. Slide the new siding under the flashing and nail to studs. Replace the trim.

Before

Accumulating rot defaces and devalues your shed; fortunately there's a quick fix.

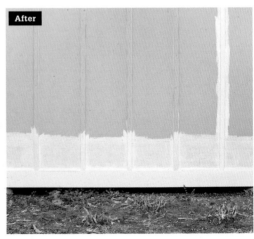

After

Replacing rotting siding is a common fix for wooden sheds. After painting it will look as good as new.

How to Replace Shed Siding

Remove the trim boards and/or batten with a pry bar and hammer to gain access to the rotting portion. The corner boards may also have to be removed.

Determine where the damaged or rotted material ends and snap a chalk line at least 6" past that point to serve as your cutting line. Where possible, snap chalk lines that fall midway across a framing member.

Use a circular saw to make a straight cut along the chalk line. The saw setting should be just slightly deeper than the width of the panel (usually about a ½"). It is easiest and safest to make the cuts before removing the fasteners which hold the panels in place. Finish the cut with a jigsaw or handsaw where the circular saw cannot reach. Remove any screws if present and pry off the damaged material.

Cut 2 × 4 blocking to support the wall studs along the cutout lines. To secure the blocking, use a handheld drill and drive deck screws toe-nail style into the studs. The backers will be used to secure the replacement patch.

Measure and cut replacement panels using the same size and type material. To allow for expansion and contraction, leave no more than ⅛" gap between the patch board and the original siding. Use screws or nails to fasten the patch. Screws provide better holding power but are more difficult to conceal. Reattach trim and then prime and paint all exposed wood surfaces.

TIP: Make corrective repairs to fix problems so they don't recur. Use a pneumatic nailer to secure appropriate molding to the ledge of the base trim. Here, pieces of ¾ × ¾" quarter-round molding are set into thick beds of caulk on the top edges of the base trim and then secured with finish nails. This creates a surface that sheds water instead of allowing it to accumulate.

Plumbing

In this chapter:

The Home Plumbing System

Because most of a plumbing system is hidden inside walls and floors, it may seem to be a complex maze of pipes and fittings. But spend a few minutes with us and you'll gain a basic understanding of your system. Understanding how home plumbing works is an important first step toward doing routine maintenance and money-saving repairs.

A typical home plumbing system includes three basic parts: a water supply system, a fixture and appliance set, and a drain system. These three parts can be seen clearly in the photograph of the cut-away house on the opposite page.

Fresh water enters a home through a main supply line (1). This fresh water source is provided by either a municipal water company or a private underground well. If the source is a municipal supplier, the water passes through a meter (2) that registers the amount of water used. A family of four uses about 400 gallons of water each day.

Immediately after the main supply enters the house, a branch line splits off (3) and is joined to a water heater (4). From the water heater, a hot water line runs parallel to the cold water line to bring the water supply to fixtures and appliances throughout the house. Fixtures include sinks, bathtubs, showers, and laundry tubs. Appliances include water heaters, dishwashers, clothes washers, and water softeners. Toilets and exterior sillcocks are examples of fixtures that require only a cold water line.

The water supply to fixtures and appliances is controlled with faucets and valves. Faucets and valves have moving parts and seals that eventually may wear out or break, but they are easily repaired or replaced.

Waste water then enters the drain system. It first must flow past a drain trap (5), a U-shaped piece of pipe that holds standing water and prevents sewer gases from entering the home. Every fixture must have a drain trap.

The drain system works entirely by gravity, allowing waste water to flow downhill through a series of large-diameter pipes. These drain pipes are attached to a system of vent pipes. Vent pipes (6) bring air into the drain system to prevent suction or pressure that might allow the trap to lose its water seal. Vent pipes usually exit the house at a roof vent (7).

All waste water eventually reaches a drainage stack or a building drain (8).

NOTE: *In a two or more story house there is usually more than one drainage stack. There is no stack in a one-story house. The stack or building drain becomes a sewer line (9) that exits the house near the foundation. In a municipal system, this sewer line joins a main sewer line located near the street. Where sewer service is not available, waste water empties into a septic system.*

Water meters and main shutoff valves are located where the main water supply pipe enters the house. The water meter is the property of your local municipal water company. If the water meter leaks, or if you suspect it is not functioning properly, call your water company for repairs.

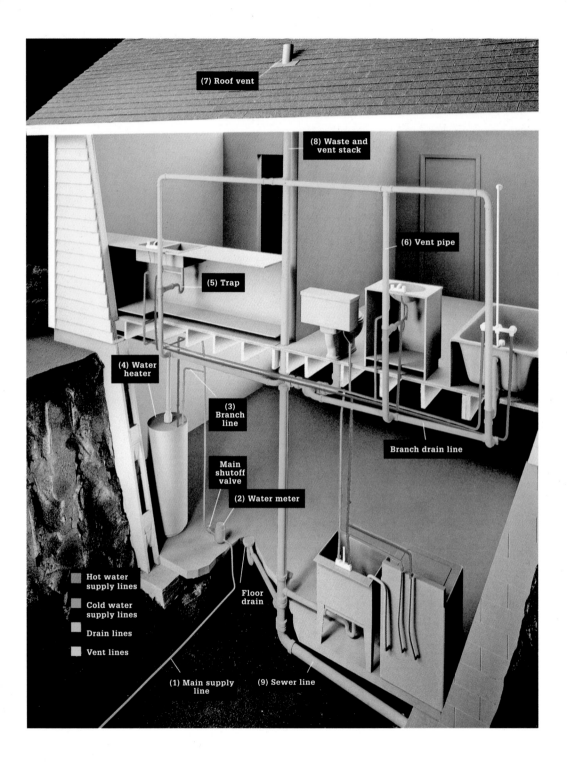

(7) Roof vent

(8) Waste and vent stack

(6) Vent pipe

(5) Trap

(4) Water heater

(3) Branch line

Main shutoff valve

(2) Water meter

Branch drain line

Hot water supply lines

Cold water supply lines

Drain lines

Vent lines

Floor drain

(1) Main supply line

(9) Sewer line

Shutting Off the Water

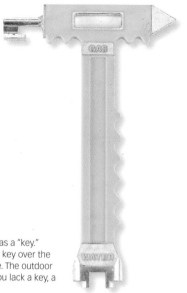

In case an emergency requires you to replace or repair a faucet, fixture, or appliance, knowing how to shut off the water is imperative. The photos on this page show the most common types of shutoffs. If you don't feel completely confident about finding your home's shutoff points or how to turn them off, contact your local water company for information.

There are two basic types of valves, which shut off in two different ways. To turn off many older valves, rotate the handle clockwise (remember "lefty loosey; righty tighty") until it stops. To turn off many newer valves, rotate the handle one-quarter turn only.

Some outdoor shutoffs require the use of a special tool, often referred to as a "key." Keep your key within easy reach in case of an emergency. To turn off, slip the key over the valve and rotate one quarter turn, so the handle is at a right angle to the pipe. The outdoor main shutoff shown below is an example of a shutoff that requires a key. If you lack a key, a meter valve can usually be turned with a wrench or channel-type pliers.

Meter

Key-operated shutoff (open)

An outdoor main shutoff may be as simple as an exposed valve that you turn by hand. Or it may be buried in a housing that is sometimes called a Buffalo box. In this example, both the meter and the main shutoff are housed in the Buffalo box; in other cases, the meter is located inside the house.

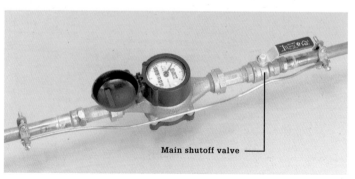

Main shutoff valve

You may have an inside main shutoff, usually located near the point where the main supply pipe enters the house near the water meter. Many homes have both a Buffalo box and an indoor main shutoff. There may be a valve on each side of the meter; turn off either one of them to shut off water to the house.

Partial-house shutoffs are often found in medium- to large-size homes. They control water flow to large areas of the house. They are found in pairs, one for hot and one for cold water. Turning off a pair of these may shut off water to a floor or to an entire bathroom or kitchen.

Fixture shutoff valves, also called stop valves, control water to a specific faucet, toilet, or fixture. They are also usually found in pairs, one for hot and one for cold. However, toilets, icemakers, and other cold-water-only fixtures will have only one stop valve. If you live in an older home that lacks stop valves, it's a good idea to install them.

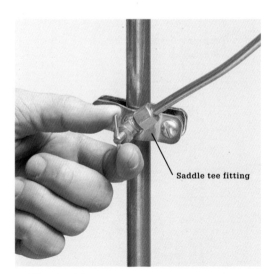

Saddle tee fitting

Saddle valves often are used to tap into a water supply pipe to bring water to a low-demand fixture, such as an ice maker or a hot water dispenser. Some municipalities do not endorse saddle valves, but most do (although the vast majority of professional plumbers do not like to install them because they tend to leak). The saddle valve handle appears to be a shutoff but it is not—if a leak develops at or downline from a saddle valve, find the closest shutoff valve between the water supply and the saddle if you need to stop the water flow.

Built-in shutoff valves

Integral shutoffs are sometimes found on tub-and-shower faucets and other fixtures. This arrangement allows water to be turned off to the fixture only, so water remains available for the rest of the house.

Plumbing Tools

Many plumbing projects and repairs can be completed with basic hand tools you probably already own. Adding a few simple plumbing tools will prepare you for all the projects in this book. Specialty tools, such as a snap cutter or appliance dolly, are available at rental centers. When buying tools, invest in quality products.

Always care for tools properly. Clean tools after using them, wiping them free of dirt and dust with a soft rag. Prevent rust on metal tools by wiping them with a rag dipped in household oil. If a metal tool gets wet, dry it immediately, and then wipe it with an oiled rag. Keep toolboxes and cabinets organized. Make sure all tools are stored securely.

Caulk gun & all purpose caulk

Utility knife

Non-contact volt meter

Head lamp

Wire brush

Hacksaw

Cold chisel

Ratchet wrench and sockets

Metal files

Tape measure

Strainer wrench

Seat wrench

Adjustable wrenches

Screwdriver

Putty knife

Channel-type
pliers

Needlenose pliers

Basin wrench

Level

(continued)

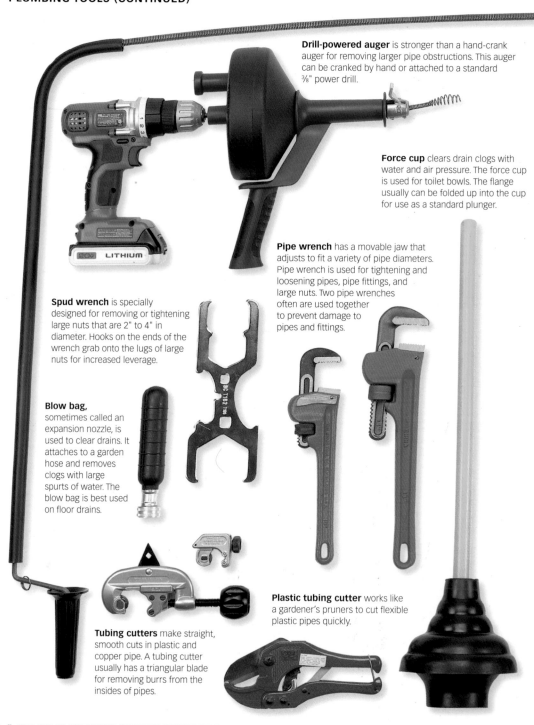

Drill-powered auger is stronger than a hand-crank auger for removing larger pipe obstructions. This auger can be cranked by hand or attached to a standard ⅜" power drill.

Force cup clears drain clogs with water and air pressure. The force cup is used for toilet bowls. The flange usually can be folded up into the cup for use as a standard plunger.

Pipe wrench has a movable jaw that adjusts to fit a variety of pipe diameters. Pipe wrench is used for tightening and loosening pipes, pipe fittings, and large nuts. Two pipe wrenches often are used together to prevent damage to pipes and fittings.

Spud wrench is specially designed for removing or tightening large nuts that are 2" to 4" in diameter. Hooks on the ends of the wrench grab onto the lugs of large nuts for increased leverage.

Blow bag, sometimes called an expansion nozzle, is used to clear drains. It attaches to a garden hose and removes clogs with large spurts of water. The blow bag is best used on floor drains.

Plastic tubing cutter works like a gardener's pruners to cut flexible plastic pipes quickly.

Tubing cutters make straight, smooth cuts in plastic and copper pipe. A tubing cutter usually has a triangular blade for removing burrs from the insides of pipes.

Closet auger is used to clear toilet clogs. It is a slender tube with a crank handle on one end of a flexible auger cable. A special bend in the tube allows the auger to be positioned in the bottom of the toilet bowl. The bend is usually protected with a rubber sleeve to prevent scratching the toilet.

MAPP torch (left) is used for soldering fittings to copper pipes. Light the torch quickly and safely using a spark lighter.

Rental tools may be needed for large jobs and special situations. A power miter saw makes fast, accurate cuts in a wide variety of materials, including plastic pipes. A motorized drain auger clears tree roots from sewer service lines. Use an appliance dolly to move heavy objects like water heaters. A snap cutter is designed to cut tough cast-iron pipes. The right-angle drill is useful for drilling holes in hard-to-reach areas.

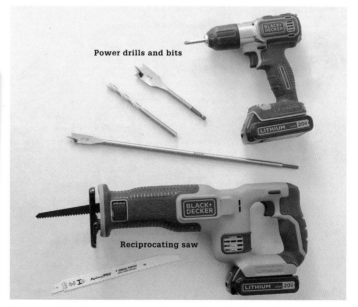

Flame-resistant pad helps keep wood and other underlying materials safe from the torch's flame.

Power hand tools can make any job faster, easier, and safer. Cordless power tools offer added convenience. Use a cordless ⅜" power drill for virtually any drilling task.

Plumbing Materials

Common Pipe & Tube Types ▸

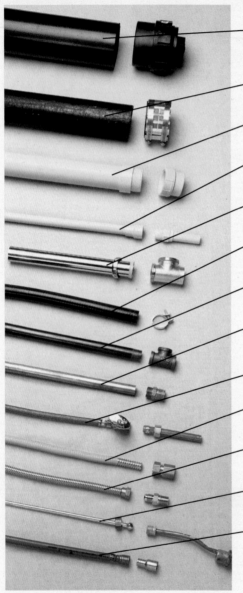

BENEFITS & CHARACTERISTICS

ABS (acrylonitrile butadiene styrene) ABS is an approved DWV pipe (although it has its detractors) and is commonly used in many markets, especially in the western U.S.

Cast iron is strong but hard to work with. Repairs should be made with plastic pipe, if allowed.

PVC (polyvinyl chloride) is rigid plastic that resists heat and chemicals. Schedule 40 is the minimum thickness for use as DWV pipe and water service pipe.

CPVC (chlorinated polyvinyl chloride) rigid plastic is inexpensive and withstands high temperature and pressure.

Chromed brass has an attractive shiny surface and is used for drain traps where appearance is important.

PE (polyethylene) plastic is a black or bluish flexible pipe sometimes used for main water service lines as well as irrigation systems.

Black pipe (iron pipe) generally is threaded at the ends to accept female-threaded fittings. Not for potable water.

Rigid copper is used for water supply pipes. It resists corrosion and has smooth surfaces for good water flow.

Braided metal is used for water supply tubes that connect shutoff valves to fixtures.

Flexible stainless-steel (protective coated) connectors are used to attach gas appliances to supply stopcocks.

Flexible stainless-steel (uncoated) connectors are used to attach gas appliances to supply stopcocks

Chromed copper supply tube is used in areas where appearance is important. Easy to bend and fit.

PEX (cross-linked polyethylene) is flexible and is approved by major building codes for water supply.

Flexible copper tubing (not shown) bends easily and requires fewer couplings than rigid copper.

COMMON USES	LENGTHS	DIAMETERS	FITTING METHODS	TOOLS USED FOR CUTTING
DWV pipes, sewer pipes, drain traps	10 ft.	1¼, 1½, 2, 3, 4"	Solvent cement or threaded fittings	Tubing cutter, miter box or hacksaw
DWV pipes, sewer pipes	5 ft., 10 ft.	1½, 2, 3, 4"	Oakum & lead, banded neoprene couplings	Snap cutter or hacksaw
DWV pipes, sewer pipes, drain traps	10 ft., 20 ft.; or sold by linear ft.	1¼", 1½", 2", 3", 4"	Solvent cement, threaded fittings	Tubing cutter, miter box, or hacksaw
Hot & cold water supply pipes	10 ft.	⅜", ½", ¾", 1"	Solvent cement and plastic fittings, or with compression fittings	Tubing cutter, miter box, or hacksaw
Valves & shutoffs; drain traps, supply risers	Lengths vary	1¼", ½", ¾", 1¼", 1½"	Compression fittings, or with metal solder	Tubing cutter, hacksaw, or reciprocating saw
Outdoor cold water supply pipes	Sold in coils of 25 to hundreds of ft.	¼" to 1"	Rigid PVC fittings and stainless steel hose clamps	Ratchet-style plastic pipe cutter or miter saw
Gas supply pipe	Sold in lengths up to 10 ft.	⅜, 1, 1¼, 1½"	Threaded connectors	Hacksaw, power cutoff saw or reciprocating saw with bi-metal blade
Hot & cold water supply pipes	10 ft., 20 ft.; or sold by linear ft.	⅜", ½", ¾", 1"	Metal solder, compression fittings, threaded fittings, press connect fittings, push connect fittings, flared fittings	Tubing cutter, hacksaw, or jigsaw
Supply tubes	12" or 20"	⅜, ½, ¾"	Attached threaded fittings	Do not cut
Gas ranges, dryers, water heaters	12" to 60"	⅝", ½" (OD)	Attached threaded fittings	Do not cut
Gas ranges, dryers, water heaters	12" to 60"	⅝", ½" (OD)	Attached threaded fittings	Do not cut
Supply tubing	12", 20", 30"	⅜"	Brass compression fittings	Tubing cutter or hacksaw
Hot & cold water supply; PEX-AL-PEX (usually orange) is used in radiant floors	Sold in coils of 25 ft. to hundreds of ft.	¼" to 1"	Crimp fittings, push connect fittings	Tubing cutter
Gas supply; hot & cold water supply	30-ft., 60-ft. coils; or by ft.	¼", ⅜", ½", ¾", 1"	Brass flare fittings, solder, compression fittings	Tubing cutter or hacksaw

Copper Tubing

Copper is an ideal material for water supply pipes. It resists corrosion and has smooth surfaces that provide good water flow. Copper pipes are available in several diameters, but most home water supply systems use ½" or ¾" pipe. Copper pipe is manufactured in rigid and flexible forms.

Rigid copper, sometimes called hard copper, is approved for home water supply systems by all local codes. It comes in three wall-thickness grades: Types M, L, and K. Type M is the thinnest, the least expensive, and a good choice for do-it-yourself home plumbing.

Rigid Type L usually is required by code for commercial plumbing systems. Because it is strong and solders easily, Type L may be preferred by some professional plumbers and do-it-yourselfers for home use. Type K has the heaviest wall thickness and is used most often for underground water service lines.

Flexible copper, also called soft copper, comes in two wall-thickness grades: Types L and K. Both are approved for most home water supply systems, although flexible Type L copper is used primarily for gas service lines. Because it is bendable and will resist a mild frost, Type L may be installed as part of a water supply system in unheated indoor areas, like crawl spaces. Type K is used for underground water service lines.

A third form of copper, called DWV, is used for drain systems. Because most codes now allow low-cost plastic pipes for drain systems, DWV copper is seldom used.

Copper pipes are connected with soldered, compression, or flare fittings (see chart below). Always follow your local code for the correct types of pipes and fittings allowed in your area.

Soldered fittings, also called sweat fittings, often are used to join copper pipes. Correctly soldered fittings are strong and trouble-free. Copper pipe can also be joined with compression fittings or flare fittings. See chart below.

Copper Pipe & Fitting Chart ▸

FITTING METHOD	RIGID COPPER			FLEXIBLE COPPER		GENERAL COMMENTS
	TYPE M	TYPE L	TYPE K	TYPE L	TYPE K	
Soldered	yes	yes	yes	yes	yes	Inexpensive, strong, and trouble-free fitting method. Requires some skill.
Compression	yes	not applicable		no	no	Makes repairs and replacement easy. More expensive than solder. Best used on flexible copper.
Flare	no	no	no	yes	yes	Use only with flexible copper pipes. Usually used as a gas-line fitting. Requires some skill.
Push-connect fittings	no	yes	yes	no	no	

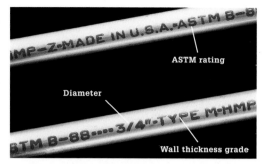

Grade stamp information includes the pipe diameter, the wall-thickness grade, and a stamp of approval from the ASTM (American Society for Testing and Materials). Type M pipe is identified by red lettering, Type L by blue lettering.

Bend flexible copper pipe with a coil-spring tubing bender to avoid kinks. Select a bender that matches the outside diameter of the pipe. Slip bender over pipe using a twisting motion. Bend pipe slowly until it reaches the correct angle, but not more than 90º.

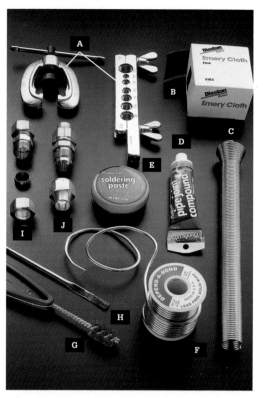

Specialty tools and materials for working with copper include: flaring tools (A), emery cloth (B), coil-spring tubing bender (C), pipe joint compound (D), soldering paste (flux) (E), lead-free solder (F), wire brush (G), flux brush (H), compression fitting (I), flare fitting (J).

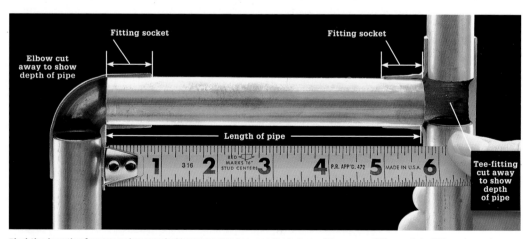

Find the length of copper pipe needed by measuring between the bottom of the copper fitting sockets (fittings shown in cutaway). Mark the length on the pipe with a felt-tipped pen.

Cutting & Soldering Copper

The best way to cut rigid and flexible copper pipe is with a tubing cutter. A tubing cutter makes a smooth, straight cut, an important first step toward making a watertight joint. Remove any metal burrs on the cut edges with a reaming tool or round file.

Copper can be cut with a hacksaw. A hacksaw is useful in tight areas where a tubing cutter will not fit. Take care to make a smooth, straight cut when cutting with a hacksaw.

A soldered pipe joint, also called a sweated joint, is made by heating a copper or brass fitting with a propane torch until the fitting is just hot enough to melt metal solder. The heat draws the solder into the gap between the fitting and pipe to form a watertight seal. A fitting that is overheated or unevenly heated will not draw in solder. Copper pipes and fittings must be clean and dry to form a watertight seal.

Tools & Materials ▸

Tubing cutter
with reaming tip
Wire brush
Flux brush
Propane torch
Spark lighter
Round file
Cloth
Adjustable wrench
Channel-type pliers

Copper pipe
Copper fittings
Emery cloth
Soldering paste (flux)
Sheet metal
Lead-free solder
Rag
Eye and ear
protection
Work gloves

Soldering Tips ▸

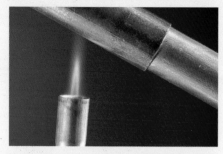

Use caution when soldering copper. Pipes and fittings become very hot and must be allowed to cool before handling.

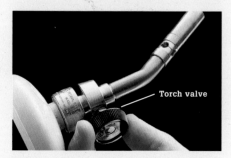

Torch valve

Prevent accidents by shutting off propane torch immediately after use. Make sure valve is closed completely.

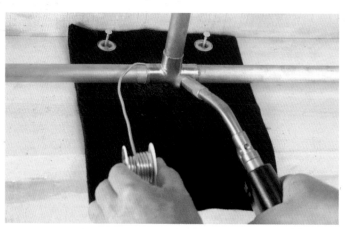

Protect wood from the heat of the torch flame while soldering. Use an old cookie sheet, two sheets of 26-gauge metal, or a fiber shield, as shown.

How to Cut Rigid & Flexible Copper Pipe

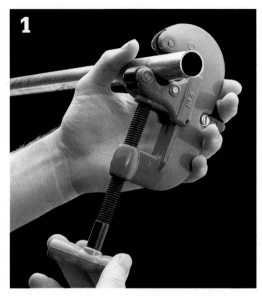

Place the tubing cutter over the pipe and tighten the handle so that the pipe rests on both rollers and the cutting wheel is on the marked line.

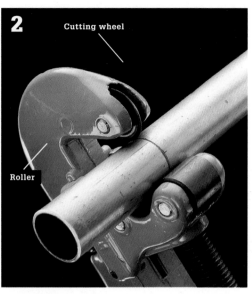

Turn the tubing cutter one rotation so that the cutting wheel scores a continuous straight line around the pipe.

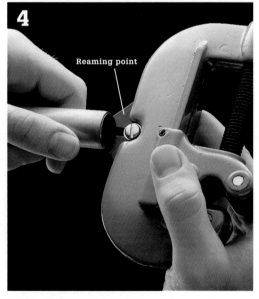

Rotate the cutter in the opposite direction, tightening the handle slightly after every two rotations, until the cut is complete.

Remove sharp metal burrs from the inside edge of the cut pipe, using the reaming point on the tubing cutter, or a round file.

How to Solder Copper Pipes & Fittings

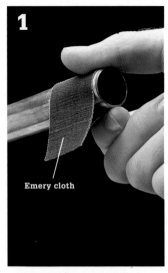

1

Emery cloth

Clean the end of each pipe by sanding with emery cloth. Ends must be free of dirt and grease to ensure that the solder forms a good seal.

2

Clean the inside of each fitting by scouring with a wire brush or emery cloth.

3

Flux brush

Plumbcraft® **soldering paste**

Apply a thin layer of soldering paste (flux) to end of each pipe, using a flux brush. Soldering paste should cover about 1" of pipe end. Don't use too much flux.

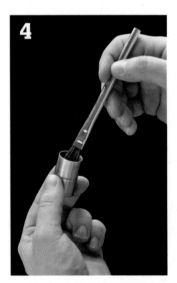

4

Apply a thin layer of flux to the inside of the fitting.

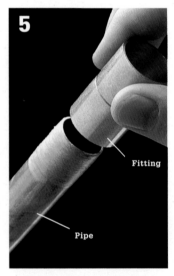

5

Fitting

Pipe

Assemble each joint by inserting the pipe into the fitting so it is tight against the bottom of the fitting sockets. Twist each fitting slightly to spread soldering paste.

6

Use a clean dry cloth to remove excess flux before soldering the assembled fitting.

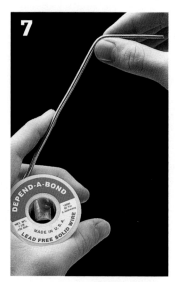

7

Prepare the wire solder by unwinding 8" to 10" of wire from spool. Bend the first 2" of the wire to a 90° angle.

8

Open the gas valve and trigger the spark lighter to ignite the torch. Adjust the torch valve until the inner portion of the flame is 1" to 2" long.

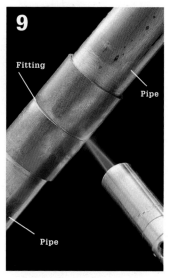

9

Fitting

Pipe

Pipe

Move the torch flame back and forth and around the pipe and the fitting to heat the area evenly.

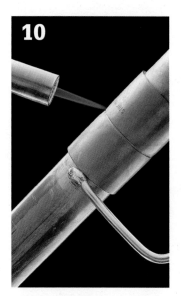

10

Heat the other side of the copper fitting to ensure that heat is distributed evenly. Touch solder to pipe. Solder will melt when the pipe is at the right temperature.

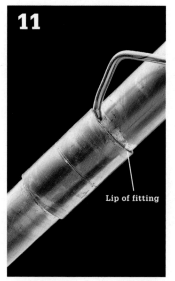

11

Lip of fitting

When solder melts, remove the torch and quickly push ½" to ¾" of solder into each joint. Capillary action fills the joint with liquid solder. A correctly soldered joint should show a thin bead of solder around the lips of the fitting.

12

Allow the joint to cool briefly, then wipe away excess solder with a dry rag. *CAUTION: Pipes will be hot. If joints leak after water is turned on, disassemble and resolder.*

How to Solder Brass Valves

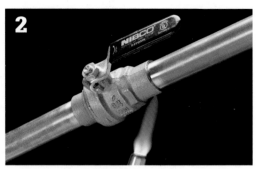

Valves should be fully open during all stages of the soldering process. If a valve has any plastic or rubber parts, remove them prior to soldering.

To prevent valve damage, quickly heat the pipe and the flanges of the valve, not the valve body. After soldering, cool the valve by spraying with water.

How to Take Apart Soldered Joints

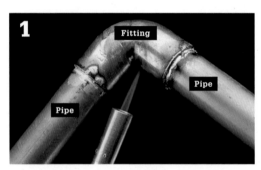

Fitting

Pipe

Pipe

Turn off the water and drain the pipes by opening the highest and lowest faucets in the house. Light your torch. Hold the flame tip to the fitting until the solder becomes shiny and begins to melt.

Use channel-type pliers to separate the pipes from the fitting.

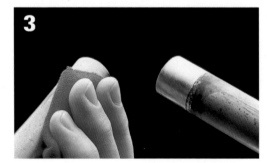

Remove old solder by heating the ends of the pipe with your torch. Use a dry rag to wipe away melted solder quickly. *CAUTION: Pipes will be hot.*

Use emery cloth to polish the ends of the pipe down to bare metal. Never reuse fittings.

Push Fittings ▸

Push fittings make water supply connections about as easy as possible. They are expensive, so you won't want to use them for all connections on a large installation. But even professional plumbers use them in tight spots where sweating or welding would be difficult. They are also an ideal material for making a quick repair.

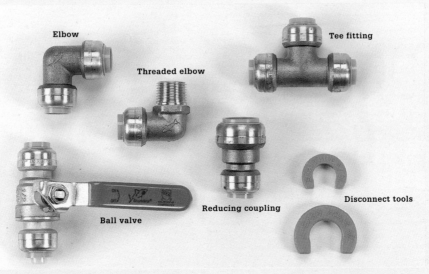

Elbow

Threaded elbow

Tee fitting

Ball valve

Reducing coupling

Disconnect tools

Push fittings are available as couplings tees, elbows, and even shutoff valves. They connect to hard copper, CPVC, and PEX pipe, but not to PVC or galvanized or black steel pipe. In most areas they are approved for use inside covered walls.

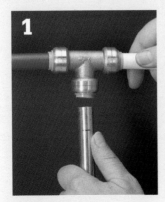

1

Cut the pipe square, and remove any burrs and rough edges. Draw a mark 1" from the cut end.

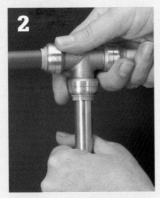

2

Push the pipe into the fitting an inch or so until you hear it click. Tug to make sure you have a strong connection. It may not seem like it, but the connection is indeed watertight and durable. You may rotate it to the desired position.

3

To remove a pipe from a push fitting, slip the disconnect tool over the pipe, slide it over the fitting, and press against the fitting's release collar as you pull the pipe out.

Rigid Plastic Pipe

Cut rigid ABS, PVC, or CPVC plastic pipes with a tubing cutter or with any saw. Cuts must be straight to ensure watertight joints.

Rigid plastics are joined with plastic fittings and solvent cement. Use a solvent cement that is made for the type of plastic pipe you are installing. For example, do not use ABS solvent on PVC pipe. Some solvent cements, called "all-purpose" or "universal" solvents, may be used on all types of plastic pipe.

Solvent cement hardens in about 30 seconds, so test-fit all plastic pipes and fittings before cementing the first joint. For best results, the surfaces of plastic pipes and fittings should be dulled with emery cloth and liquid primer before they are joined.

Liquid solvent cements and primers are toxic and flammable. Provide adequate ventilation when fitting plastics, and store the products away from any source of heat.

Plastic grip fittings can be used to join rigid or flexible plastic pipes to copper plumbing pipes.

Solvent welding is a chemical bonding process used to permanently join PVC pipes and fittings.

Tools & Materials ▸

Tape measure	Plastic pipe
Felt-tipped pen	Fittings
Tubing cutter	Emery cloth
(or miter box	Plastic pipe primer
or hacksaw)	Solvent cement
Utility knife	Rag
Channel-type pliers	Petroleum jelly
Work gloves	Eye and ear protection

Primer and solvent cement are specific to the plumbing material being used. Do not use all-purpose or multipurpose products. Light to medium body cements are appropriate for DIYers as they allow the longest working time and are easiest to use. When working with large pipe, 3 or 4" in diameter, buy a large-size can of cement, which has a larger dauber. If you use the small dauber (which comes with the small can), you may need to apply twice, which will slow you down and make connections difficult. (The smaller can of primer is fine for any other size pipe, since there's no rush in applying primer.) Cement (though not primer) goes bad in the can within a month or two after opening, so you may need to buy a new can for a new project.

How to Cut Rigid Plastic Pipe

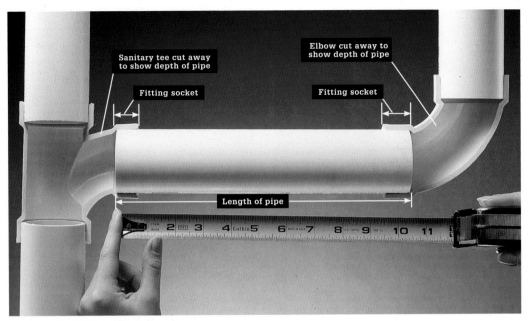

Find the length of plastic pipe needed by measuring between the bottoms of the fitting sockets (fittings shown in cutaway). Mark the length on the pipe with a felt-tipped pen.

Plastic tubing cutters do a fast, neat job of cutting. You'll probably have to go to a professional plumbing supply store to find one, however. They are not interchangeable with metal tubing cutters.

The best cutting tool for plastic pipe is a power miter saw with a fine tooth woodworking blade or a plastic-specific blade.

A ratcheting plastic-pipe cutter can cut smaller diameter PVC and CPVC pipe in a real hurry. They also are sold only at plumbing supply stores.

How to Solvent-Cement Rigid PVC Pipe

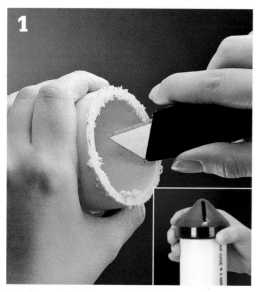

Remove rough burrs on cut ends of plastic pipe, using a utility knife or deburring tool (inset).

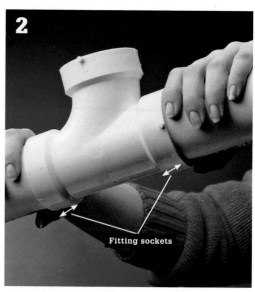

Test-fit all pipes and fittings. Pipes should fit tightly against the bottom of the fitting sockets.

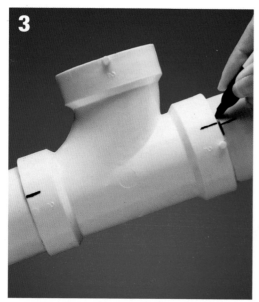

Mark the depth of the fitting sockets on the pipes. Take pipes apart. Clean the ends of the pipes and fitting sockets with emery cloth.

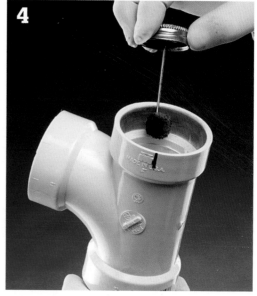

Apply a light coat of plastic pipe primer to the ends of the pipes and to the insides of the fitting sockets. Primer dulls glossy surfaces and ensures a good seal.

5

Solvent-cement each joint by applying a thick coat of solvent cement to the end of the pipe. Apply a thin coat of solvent cement to the inside surface of the fitting socket. Work quickly: solvent cement hardens in about 30 seconds.

6

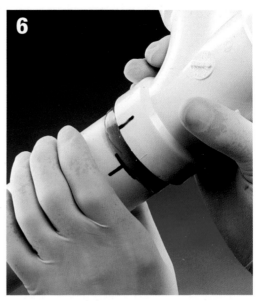

Quickly position the pipe and fitting so that the alignment marks are offset by about 2". Force the pipe into the fitting until the end fits flush against the bottom of the socket.

7

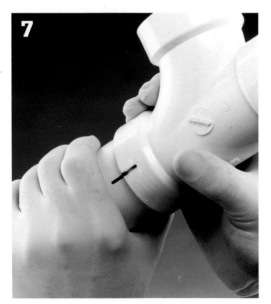

Spread solvent by twisting the pipe until the marks are aligned. Hold the pipe in place for about 20 seconds to prevent the joint from slipping.

8

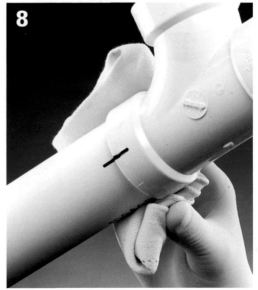

Wipe away excess solvent cement with a rag. Do not disturb the joint for 30 minutes after gluing.

Shutoff Valves

Worn-out shutoff valves or supply tubes can cause water to leak underneath a sink or other fixture. First, try tightening the fittings with an adjustable wrench. If this does not fix the leak, replace the shutoff valves and supply tubes.

Shutoff valves are available in several fitting types. For copper pipes, valves with compression-type fittings are easiest to install. For plastic pipes, use grip-type valves. For galvanized steel pipes, use valves with female threads.

Older plumbing systems often were installed without fixture shutoff valves. When repairing or replacing plumbing fixtures, you may want to install shutoff valves if they are not already present.

Tools & Materials ▸

Hacksaw
Tubing cutter
Adjustable wrench
Tubing bender
Felt-tipped pen

Shutoff valves
Supply tubes
Pipe joint compound
Eye protection

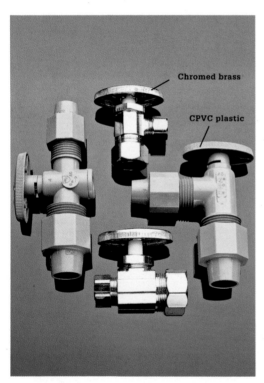

Shutoff valves allow you to shut off the water to an individual fixture so it can be repaired. They can be made from durable chromed brass or lightweight plastic. Shutoff valves come in ½" and ¾" diameters to match common water pipe sizes.

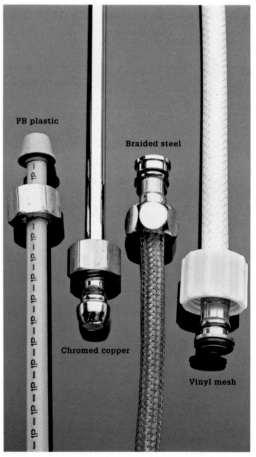

Supply tubes are used to connect water pipes to faucets, toilets, and other fixtures. They come in 12", 20", and 30" lengths. PB plastic and chromed copper tubes are inexpensive. Braided steel and vinyl mesh supply tubes are easy to install.

How to Install Shutoff Valves & Supply Tubes

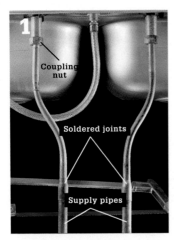

Turn off water at the main shutoff valve. Remove old supply pipes. If pipes are soldered copper, cut them off just below the soldered joint, using a hacksaw or tubing cutter. Make sure the cuts are straight. Unscrew the coupling nuts and discard the old pipes.

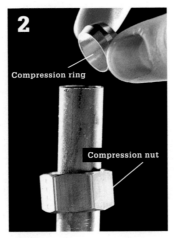

Slide a compression nut and a compression ring over the copper water pipe. Threads of the nut should face the end of the pipe.

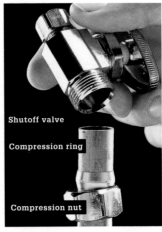

Apply pipe joint compound to the threads of the shutoff valve or compression nut. Screw the compression nut onto the shutoff valve and tighten with an adjustable wrench.

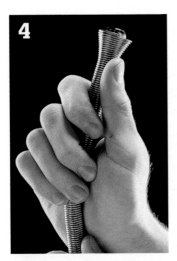

Bend chromed copper supply tube to reach from the tailpiece of the fixture to the shutoff valve, using a tubing bender. Bend the tube slowly to avoid kinking the metal.

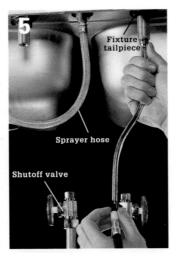

Position the supply tube between fixture tailpiece and the shutoff valve, and mark the tube to length. Cut the supply tube with a tubing cutter.

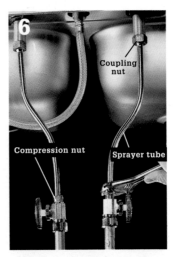

Attach the bell-shaped end of the supply tube to the fixture tailpiece with a coupling nut, then attach the other end to the shutoff valve with compression ring and nut. Tighten all fittings with an adjustable wrench.

Compression Fittings

Compression fittings are used to make connections that may need to be taken apart. Compression fittings are easy to disconnect and are often used to install supply tubes and fixture shutoff valves. Use compression fittings in places where it is unsafe or difficult to solder, such as in crawl spaces.

Compression fittings are used most often with flexible copper pipe. Flexible copper is soft enough to allow the compression ring to seat snugly, creating a watertight seal. Compression fittings also may be used to make connections with Type M rigid copper pipe.

Tools & Materials ▶

Felt-tipped pen
Tubing cutter
  or hacksaw
Adjustable wrenches
Eye protection

Brass compression
  fittings
Pipe joint compound
  or Teflon tape

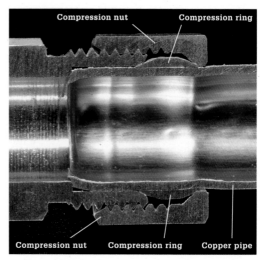

Compression fitting (shown in cutaway) shows how threaded compression nut forms seal by forcing the compression ring against the copper pipe. Compression ring is covered with pipe joint compound before assembling to ensure a perfect seal.

How to Attach Supply Tubes to Fixture Shutoff Valves with Compression Fittings

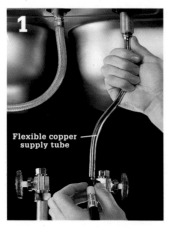

Bend flexible copper supply tube and mark to length. Include ½" for portion that will fit inside valve. Cut tube.

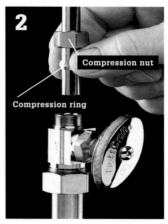

Slide the compression nut and then the compression ring over the end of the pipe. The threads of the nut should face the valve.

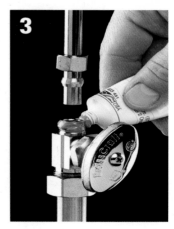

Apply a small amount of pipe joint compound to the threads. This lubricates the threads.

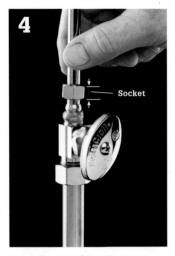

Insert the end of the pipe into the fitting so it fits flush against the bottom of the fitting socket.

Slide the compression ring and nut against the threads of the valve. Hand tighten the nut onto the valve.

Tighten the compression nut with adjustable wrenches. Do not overtighten. Turn on the water and watch for leaks. If the fitting leaks, tighten the nut gently.

How to Join Two Copper Pipes with a Compression Union Fitting

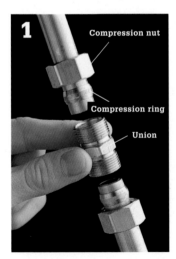

Slide compression nuts and rings over the ends of pipes. Place a threaded union between the pipes.

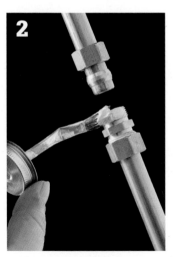

Apply a layer of pipe joint compound or Teflon tape to the union's threads, then screw compression nuts onto the union.

Hold the center of the union fitting with an adjustable wrench and use another wrench to tighten each compression nut one complete turn. Turn on the water. If the fitting leaks, tighten the nuts gently.

Fixing Common Toilet Problems

A clogged toilet is one of the most common plumbing problems. If a toilet overflows or flushes sluggishly, clear the clog with a plunger or closet auger. If the problem persists, the clog may be in a branch drain or a drainage stack (pages 292 to 293).

Most other toilet problems are fixed easily with minor adjustments that require no disassembly or replacement parts. You can make these adjustments in a few minutes, using simple tools (page 299).

If minor adjustments do not fix the problem, further repairs will be needed. The parts of a standard toilet are not difficult to take apart, and most repair projects can be completed in less than an hour.

A recurring puddle of water on the floor around a toilet may be caused by a crack in the toilet base or in the tank. A damaged toilet should be replaced. Installing a new toilet is an easy project that can be finished in three or four hours.

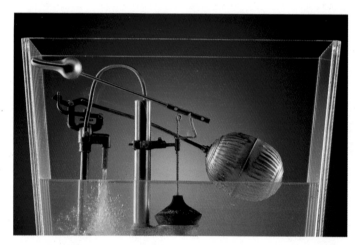

An older toilet may have a tank ball that settles onto the flush valve to stop the flow of water into the bowl. The ball is attached to a lift wire, which is in turn attached to the lift rod. A ballcock valve is usually made of brass, with rubber washers that can wear out. If the ballcock valve malfunctions, you might be able to find old washers to repair it, but replacing both the ballcock and the tank ball with a float-cup assembly and flapper is easier and makes for a more durable repair.

A modern float-cup valve with flapper is inexpensive and made of plastic, but is more reliable than an old ballcock valve and ball.

A pressure-assist toilet has a large vessel that nearly fills the tank. As water enters the vessel, pressure builds up. When the toilet is flushed, this pressure helps push water forcefully down into the bowl. As a result, a pressure-assist toilet provides strong flushing power with minimal water consumption.

Problems & Repairs ▸

PROBLEMS	REPAIRS
Toilet handle sticks or is hard to push.	1. Adjust lift wires (page 320). 2. Clean and adjust handle (page 323).
Handle must be held down for entire flush.	1. Adjust handle (page 323). 2. Shorten lift chain or wires (page 320). 3. Replace waterlogged flapper.
Handle is loose.	1. Adjust handle (page 323). 2. Reattach lift chain or lift wires to lever (page 320).
Toilet will not flush at all.	1. Make sure water is turned on. 2. Adjust lift chain or lift wires (page 320).
Toilet does not flush completely.	1. Adjust lift chain (page 323). 2. Adjust water level in tank (page 322). 3. Increase pressure on pressure-assisted toilet.
Toilet overflows or flushes sluggishly.	1. Clear clogged toilet (pages 334 to 337). 2. Clear clogged branch drain or drainage stack (page 379).
Toilet runs continuously or there are phantom flushes.	1. Adjust lift wires or lift chain (page 320). 2. Replace leaky float ball (pages 324 to 325). 3. Adjust water level in tank (page 322). 4. Adjust and clean flush valve (pages 320 to 323). 5. Replace flush valve (page 326). 6. Replace flapper.
Water on floor around toilet.	1. Tighten tank bolts and water connections (pages 332, 333, and 338). 2. Insulate tank to prevent condensation. 3. Replace wax ring (pages 330 to 331). 4. Replace cracked tank or bowl.
Toilet noisy when filling.	1. Open shutoff valve completely. 2. Replace ballcock and float valve. 3. Refill tube is disconnected.
Weak flush.	1. Clean clogged rim openings. 2. Replace old low-flow toilet.
Toilet rocks.	1. Replace wax ring and bolts (pages 330 to 331). 2. Replace toilet flange (page 331).

Making Minor Adjustments

Many common toilet problems can be fixed by making minor adjustments to the handle and the attached lift chain (or lift wires).

If the handle sticks or is hard to push, remove the tank cover and clean the handle-mounting nut. Make sure the lift wires are straight.

If the toilet will not flush completely unless the handle is held down, you may have to remove excess slack in the lift chain.

If the toilet will not flush at all, the lift chain may be broken or may have to be reattached to the handle lever.

A continuously running toilet (opposite page) can be caused by bent lift wires, kinks in a lift chain, or lime buildup on the handle mounting nut. Clean and adjust the handle and the lift wires or chain to fix the problem.

Tools & Materials ▶

Adjustable wrench	Channel-type pliers	Screwdriver	Hacksaw	Small wire brush	Food coloring
Needlenose pliers	Spud wrench	Scissors	Spray lubricant	Vinegar	Eye protection

How to Adjust a Toilet Handle & Lift Chain (or Lift Wires)

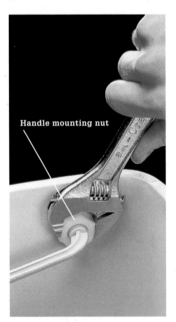

Handle mounting nut

Handle lever

Lift chain

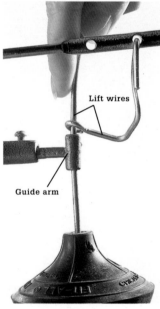

Lift wires

Guide arm

Clean and adjust handle-mounting nut so handle operates smoothly. Mounting nut has reversed threads. Loosen nut by turning clockwise; tighten by turning counterclockwise. Remove lime buildup with a brush dipped in vinegar.

Adjust lift chain so it hangs straight from handle lever, with about ½" of slack. Remove excess slack in chain by hooking the chain in a different hole in the handle lever or by removing links with needlenose pliers. A broken lift chain must be replaced.

Adjust lift wires (found on older toilets without lift chains) so that wires are straight and operate smoothly when handle is pushed. A sticky handle often can be fixed by straightening bent lift wires. You can also buy replacement wires, or replace the whole assembly with a float cup.

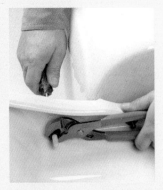

Phantom flushes? Phantom flushes are weak flushes that occur without turning the handle. The flapper may not be completely sealing against the flush valve's seat. Make sure the chain is not tangled, and that the flapper can go all the way down. If that does not solve the problem, shut off water and drain the tank. If the problem persists, the flapper may need to be replaced.

Seat loose? Loose seats are almost always the result of a loose nut on the seat bolts. Tighten the nuts with pliers. If the nut is corroded or stripped, replace the bolts and nuts or replace the whole seat.

Seat uncomfortably low? Instead of going to the trouble of raising the toilet or replacing it with a taller model, you can simply replace the seat with a thicker, extended seat.

Bowl not refilling well? The rim holes may be clogged; many toilets have small holes on the underside of the bowl rim, through which water squirts during a flush. If you notice that some of these holes are clogged, use a stiff-bristled brush to clear out debris. You may need to first apply toilet bowl cleaner or mineral cleaner.

Tank fills too slowly? The first place to check is the shutoff valve where the supply tube for the toilet is connected. Make sure it is fully open. If it is, you may need to replace the shutoff—these fittings are fairly cheap and frequently fail to open fully.

Toilet running? Running toilets are usually caused by faulty or misadjusted fill valves, but sometimes the toilet runs because the tank is leaking water into the bowl. To determine if this is happening with your toilet, add a few drops of food coloring to the tank water. If, after a while, the water in the bowl becomes colored, then you have a leak and probably need to replace the rubber gasket at the base of your flush valve.

Reset Tank Water Level

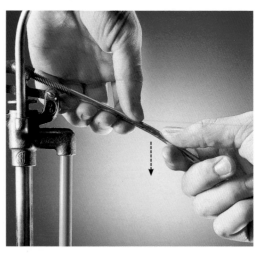

Tank water flowing into the overflow pipe is the sound we hear when a toilet is running. Usually, this is caused by a minor misadjustment that fails to tell the water to shut off when the toilet tank is full. The culprit is a float ball or cup that is adjusted to set a water level in the tank that's higher than the top of the overflow pipe, which serves as a drain for excess tank water. The other photos on this page show how to fix the problem.

A ball float is connected to a float arm that's attached to a plunger on the other end. As the tank fills, the float rises and lifts one end of the float arm. At a certain point, the float arm depresses the plunger and stops the flow of water. By simply bending the float arm downward a bit, you can cause it to depress the plunger at a lower tank water level, solving the problem.

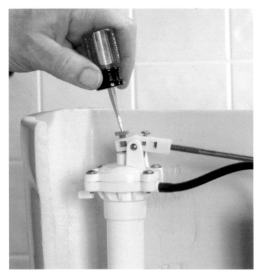

A diaphragm fill valve usually is made of plastic and has a wide bonnet that contains a rubber diaphragm. Turn the adjustment screw clockwise to lower the water level and counterclockwise to raise it.

A float cup fill valve is made of plastic and is easy to adjust. Lower the water level by pinching the spring clip with fingers or pliers and moving the clip and cup down the pull rod and shank. Raise the water level by moving the clip and cup upward.

What If the Flush Stops Too Soon? ▶

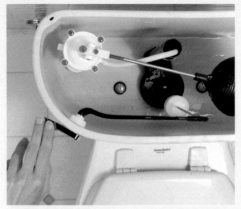

Sometimes there is plenty of water in the tank, but not enough of it makes it to the bowl before the flush valve shuts off the water from the tank. Modern toilets are designed to leave some water in the tank, since the first water that leaves the tank does so with the most force. (It's pressed out by the weight of the water on top.) To increase the duration of the flush, shorten the length of the chain between the flapper and the float (yellow in the model shown).

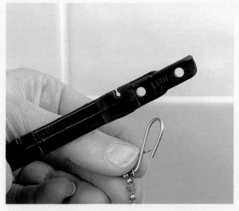

The handle lever should pull straight up on the flapper. If it doesn't, reposition the chain hook on the handle lever. When the flapper is covering the opening, there should be just a little slack in the chain. If there is too much slack, shorten the chain and cut off excess with the cutters on your pliers.

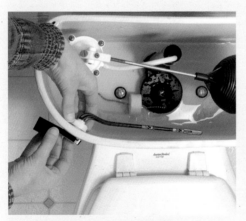

If the toilet is not completing flushes and the lever and chain for the flapper or tank ball are correctly adjusted, the problem could be that the handle mechanism needs cleaning or replacement. Remove the chain/linkage from the handle lever. Remove the nut on the backside of the handle with an adjustable wrench. It unthreads clockwise (the reverse of standard nuts). Remove the old handle from the tank.

Unless the handle parts are visibly broken, try cleaning them with an old toothbrush dipped in white vinegar. Replace the handle and test the action. If it sticks or is hard to operate, replace it. Most replacement handles come with detailed instructions that tell you how to install and adjust them.

How to Replace a Fill Valve

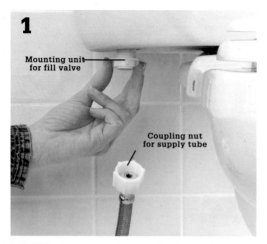

Mounting unit for fill valve

Coupling nut for supply tube

Toilet fill valves wear out eventually. They can be repaired, but it's easier and a better fix to just replace them. Before removing the old fill valve, shut off the water supply at the fixture stop valve located on the tube that supplies water to the tank. Flush the toilet and sponge out the remaining water. Loosen the nut and disconnect the supply tube, then loosen and remove the mounting nut.

If the fill valve spins while you turn the mounting nut, you may need to hold it still with locking pliers. Lift out the fill valve. In the case of an old ballcock valve, the float ball will likely come out as well. When replacing an old valve like this, you will likely also need to replace the flush valve (see page 326).

Critical level mark

The new fill valve must be installed so the critical level ("CL") mark is at least 1" above the overflow pipe (see inset). Slip the shank washer on the threaded shank of the new fill valve and place the valve in the hole so the washer is flat on the tank bottom. Compare the locations of the "CL" mark and the overflow pipe.

Adjust the height of the fill valve shank so the "CL" line and overflow pipe will be correctly related. Different products are adjusted in different ways—the fill valve shown here telescopes when it's twisted.

5

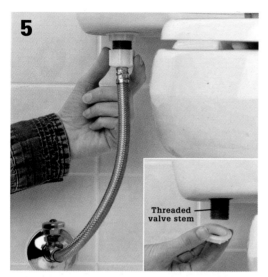

Threaded valve stem

Slip the valve's threaded end down through the tank.
Push down on its shank (not the top) while tightening the
locknut (inset). Hand tighten, then use a wrench to make an
extra ¼ turn. Hook up the water supply tube, and tighten in the
same way.

6

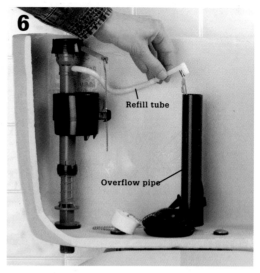

Refill tube

Overflow pipe

If the overflow pipe has a cap, remove it. Attach one
end of the refill tube from the new valve to the plastic angle
adapter and the other end to the refill nipple near the top
of the valve. Attach the angle adapter to the overflow pipe.
Cut off excess tubing with scissors to prevent kinking.
*WARNING: Don't insert the refill tube into the overflow pipe.
The outlet of the refill tube needs to be above the top of the
pipe for it to work properly.*

7

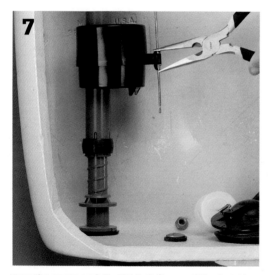

Turn the water on fully. Slightly tighten any fitting that drips
water. Adjust the water level in the tank by squeezing the
spring clip on the float cup with needlenose pliers and moving
the cup up or down on the link bar. Test the flush.

OPTION: Newer diaphragm valves cost a bit more than float
cups, but they boast quieter water flow. Install one the same
way you would a float cup.

How to Replace a Flush Valve

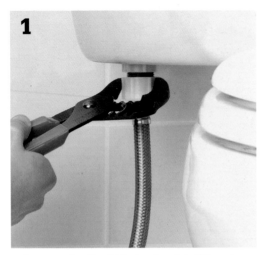

1

Before removing the old flush valve, shut off the water supply at the fixture stop valve located on the tube that supplies water to the tank. Flush the toilet and sponge out the remaining water. To make this repair you'll need to remove the tank from the bowl. Start by unscrewing the water supply coupling nut from the bottom of the tank.

2

Unscrew the bolts holding the toilet tank to the bowl by loosening the nuts from below. If you are having difficulty unscrewing the tank bolts and nuts because they are fused together by rust or corrosion, apply penetrating oil or spray lubricant to the threads, give it a few minutes to penetrate, and then try again. If that fails, slip an open-ended hacksaw (or plain hacksaw blade) between the tank and bowl and saw through the bolt (inset photo).

3

Spud nut

Spud wrench

Unhook the chain from the handle lever arm. Remove the tank and carefully place it upside-down on an old towel. Remove the spud washer and spud nut from the base of the flush valve using a spud wrench or large channel-type pliers. Remove the old flush valve.

4

Place the new flush valve in the valve hole and check to see if the top of the overflow pipe is at least 1" below the critical level line (see page 324) and the tank opening where the handle is installed. If the pipe is too tall, cut it to length with a hacksaw.

5

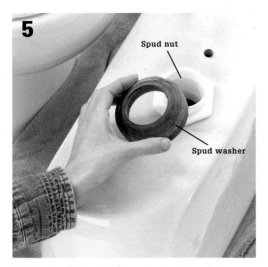

Spud nut

Spud washer

Position the flush valve flapper below the handle lever arm and secure it to the tank from beneath with the spud nut. Tighten the nut one-half turn past hand tight with a spud wrench or large channel-type pliers. Overtightening may cause the tank to break. Put the new spud washer over the spud nut, small side down.

6

Intermediate nut goes between
tank and bowl

With the tank lying on its back, thread a rubber washer onto each tank bolt and insert it into the bolt holes from inside the tank. Then, thread a brass washer and hex nut onto the tank bolts from below and tighten them to a quarter turn past hand tight. Do not overtighten.

7

Intermediate
nut

With the hex nuts tightened against the tank bottom, carefully lower the tank over the bowl and set it down so the spud washer seats neatly over the water inlet in the bowl and the tank bolts fit through the holes in the bowl flange. Secure the tank to the bowl with a rubber washer, brass washer, and nut or wing nut at each bolt end. Press the tank to level as you hand-tighten the nuts. Hook up the water supply at the fill valve inlet.

8

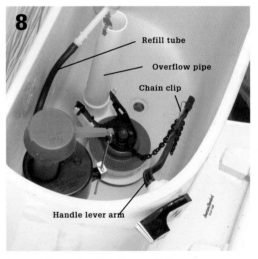

Refill tube

Overflow pipe

Chain clip

Handle lever arm

Connect the chain clip to the handle lever arm and adjust the number of links to allow for a little slack in the chain when the flapper is closed. Leave a little tail on the chain for adjusting, cutting off remaining excess. Attach the refill tube to the top of the overflow pipe the same way it had been attached to the previous refill pipe. Turn on the water supply at the stop valve and test the flush. (Some flush valve flappers are adjustable.)

Installing Toilets

You can replace a poorly functioning or inefficient toilet with a high-efficiency, high-quality new toilet in just a single afternoon. All toilets made since 1994 have been required to use 1.6 gallons or less per flush, which has been a huge challenge for the industry. Today, the most evolved water-saving toilets have wide passages behind the bowl and wide (3") flush valve openings—features that facilitate short, powerful flushes. This means fewer second flushes and fewer clogged toilets. These problems were common complaints of the first generation of 1.6-gallon toilets and continue to beleaguer inferior models today. See which toilets are available at your local home center in your price range, then go online and see what other consumers' experiences with those models have been. New toilets often go through a "de-bugging" stage when problems with leaks and malfunctioning parts are more common. Your criteria should include ease of installation,

good flush performance, and reliability. With a little research, you should be able to purchase and install a high-functioning, economical toilet that will serve you well for years to come.

Tools & Materials ▶

Adjustable wrench	Mineral spirits
Bucket and sponge	Supply tube
Channel-type pliers	Teflon tape
Hacksaw	Toilet seat bolts
Penetrating oil	Toilet seat
Pliers	Towels
Putty knife	Utility knife
Rubber gloves	Wax ring
Screwdriver	Eye protection

Replacing a toilet is simple, and the newer models of water-saving toilets have overcome the performance problems of earlier models.

Gravity-assisted toilets are now designed with taller tanks and steeper bowl walls to increase the effects of gravity.

Choosing a New Toilet

Toilets have changed in recent years. There's a toilet to fit every style. You can even buy a square or stainless-steel toilet, among many other new options. The new designs are efficient, durable, and less susceptible to clogs.

A toilet's style is partly affected by the way it's built. You have a number of options from which to choose:

Two-piece toilets have a separate water tank and bowl.

One-piece toilets have a tank and bowl made of one seamless unit.

Elongated bowls are roughly 2" longer than regular bowls.

Elevated toilets have higher seats, generally 18", rather than the standard 15".

You have a choice of two basic types of flush mechanisms: gravity- and pressure-assisted.

Gravity-assisted toilets allow water to rush down from an elevated tank into the toilet bowl. Federal law mandates that new toilets consume no more than 1.6 gallons of water per flush, less than half the volume used by older styles.

Pressure-assisted toilets rely on either compressed air or water pumps to boost flushing power.

Dual-flush systems feature two flush buttons on the top of the tank, allowing you to select either an 8-ounce flush for liquids or a 1.6-gallon flush for solids.

Two-piece toilets with a separate tank and bowl are much more common than one-piece models, and usually a lot less costly. The cheapest models are compact with a seat that is not as high above the floor as a full-size model. This can create access difficulty for some users. Round-bowl models usually cost less than models with a larger, elongated bowl.

Large-diameter flush valve

Narrow trapway

Some high-end toilets are designed to get maximum pressure out of a small amount of water. Many employ narrower trapways (the path water travels through the bowl) in conjunction with large-diameter flush valves. Some models use as little as 1.2 gallons of water.

Pressure-assisted toilets are relatively expensive, but they can reduce your water usage significantly by eliminating multiple flushes. The flush mechanism of a pressure-assisted toilet boosts the flushing power by using either compressed air or water pumps.

How to Remove a Toilet

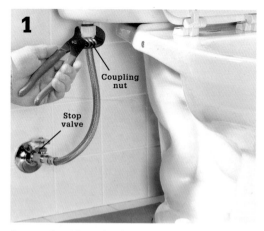

1

2

Remove the old supply tube. First, turn off the water at the stop valve. Flush the toilet, holding the handle down for a long flush, and sponge out the tank. Use a wet/dry vac to clear any remaining water out of the tank and bowl. Unthread the coupling nut for the water supply below the tank using channel-type pliers.

Grip each tank bolt nut with a box wrench or pliers and loosen it as you stabilize each tank bolt from inside the tank with a large slotted screwdriver. If the nuts are stuck, apply penetrating oil to the nut and let it sit before trying to remove them again. You may also cut the tank bolts between the tank and the bowl with an open-ended hacksaw. Remove and discard the tank.

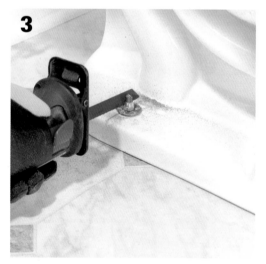

3

Prying Up Wax Rings ▸

Remove the nuts that hold the bowl to the floor. First, pry off the bolt covers with a screwdriver. Use a socket wrench, locking pliers, or your channel-type pliers to loosen the nuts on the tank bolts. Apply penetrating oil and let it sit if the nuts are stuck, then take them off. As a last resort, cut the bolts off with a hacksaw by first cutting down through one side of the nut. Tilt the toilet bowl over and remove it.

Removing an old wax ring is one of the more disgusting jobs you'll encounter in the plumbing universe (the one you see here is actually in relatively good condition). Work a stiff putty knife underneath the plastic flange of the ring (if you can) and start scraping. In many cases the wax ring will come off in chunks. Discard each chunk right away—they stick to everything. If you're left with a lot of residue, scrub with mineral spirits. Once clean, stuff a rag-in-a-bag in the drain opening to block sewer gas.

In photo 1: Coupling nut, Stop valve

How to Install a Toilet

Clean and inspect the old closet flange. Look for breaks or wear. Also inspect the flooring around the flange. If either the flange or floor is worn or damaged, repair the damage. Use a rag and mineral spirits to completely remove residue from the old wax ring. Place a rag-in-a-bag into the opening to block odors.

Installation Tip ▸

If you will be replacing your toilet flange or if your existing flange can be unscrewed and moved, orient the new flange so the slots are parallel to the wall. This allows you to insert bolts under the slotted areas, which are much stronger than the areas at the ends of the curved grooves.

Insert new tank bolts (don't reuse old ones) into the openings in the closet flange. Make sure the heads of the bolts are oriented to catch the maximum amount of flange material. To firmly hold the bolts upright, slide on the plastic washers and press them down.

Remove the wax ring and apply it to the underside of the bowl, around the horn. Remove the protective covering. Do not touch the wax ring. It is very sticky. Remove the rag-in-a-bag. If you have an older 4-inch flange, place the ring on the flange rather than the toilet to make sure it is centered.

(continued)

4

Lower the bowl onto the flange, taking care not to disturb the wax ring. The holes in the bowl base should align perfectly with the tank bolts. Add a washer and tighten a nut onto each bolt. Hand-tighten each nut and then use channel-type pliers to further tighten the nuts. Alternate tightening the nuts until the bowl is secure. Do not overtighten. *NOTE: Some disagreement exists among plumbers as to whether you should seal the joint between the bowl and the floor. Most codes require that you do. The easiest and least visible way to seal it is to apply a thick bead of clear silicone caulk to the bottom rim of the bowl before you set it on the floor. Another option is to apply a bead of caulk between the bowl and the floor after the toilet is installed.*

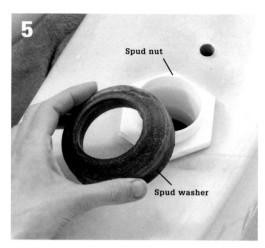

5

Spud nut

Spud washer

Install the flush valve. Some tanks come with a flush valve and a fill valve preinstalled. For models that do not have this, insert the flush valve through the tank opening and tighten a spud nut over the threaded end of the valve. Place a foam spud washer on top of the spud nut.

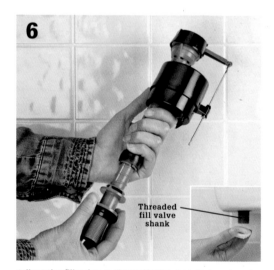

6

Threaded fill valve shank

Adjust the fill valve as directed by the manufacturer to set the correct tank water level height and install the valve inside the tank. Hand tighten the nylon lock nut that secures the valve to the tank (inset photo) and then tighten it further with channel-type pliers.

7

Intermediate nut goes between tank and bowl

With the tank lying on its back, thread a rubber washer onto each tank bolt and insert it into the bolt holes from inside the tank. Then, thread a brass washer and hex nut onto the tank bolts from below and tighten them to a quarter turn past hand tight. Do not overtighten.

8

Intermediate nut

Position the tank on the bowl, spud washer on opening, bolts through bolt holes. Put a rubber washer, followed by a brass washer and a wing nut, on each bolt and tighten these up evenly.

9

You may stabilize the bolts with a large slotted screwdriver from inside the tank, but tighten the nuts, not the bolts. You may press down a little on a side, the front, or the rear of the tank to level it as you tighten the nuts by hand. Do not overtighten and crack the tank. The tank should be level and stable when you're done.

10

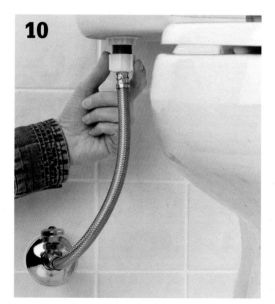

Hook up the water supply by connecting the supply tube to the threaded fill valve with the coupling nut provided. Turn on the water and test for leaks. Do not overtighten.

11

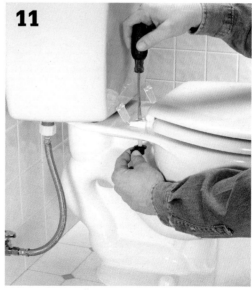

Attach the toilet seat by threading the plastic or brass bolts provided with the seat through the openings on the back of the rim and attaching nuts.

Fixing Clogged Toilets

The toilet is clogged and has overflowed. Have patience. Now is the time for considered action. A second flush is a tempting but unnecessary gamble. First, do damage control. Mop up the water if there's been a spill. Next, consider the nature of the clog. Is it entirely "natural" or might a foreign object be contributing to the congestion? Push a natural blockage down the drain with a plunger. A foreign object should be removed, if possible, with a closet auger. Pushing anything more durable than toilet paper into the sewer may create a more serious blockage in your drain and waste system.

If the tub, sink, and toilet all back up at once, the branch drainline that serves all the bathroom fixtures is probably blocked and your best recourse is to call a drain clearing service.

Tools & Materials ▸

Towels	Plunger with force cup
Closet auger	Eye protection

A blockage in the toilet bowl leaves flush water from the tank nowhere to go but on the floor.

The trap is the most common catching spot for toilet clogs. Once the clog forms, flushing the toilet cannot generate enough water power to clear the trap, so flush water backs up. Traps on modern 1.6-gallon toilets have been redesigned to larger diameters and are less prone to clogs than the first generation of 1.6-gallon toilets.

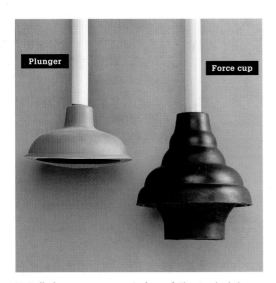

Plunger

Force cup

Not all plungers were created equal. The standard plunger (left) is simply an inverted rubber cup and is used to plunge sinks, tubs, and showers. The flanged plunger, also called a force cup, is designed to get down into the trap of a toilet drain. You can fold the flange up into the flanged plunger cup and use it as a standard plunger.

Drain Clearers ▸

The home repair marketplace is filled with gadgets and gimmicks, as well as well-established products, that are intended to clear drains of all types. Some are caustic chemicals, some are natural enzymes, others are more mechanical in nature. Some help, some are worthless, some can even make the problem worse. Nevertheless, if you are the type of homeowner who is enamored with new products and the latest solutions, you may enjoy testing out new drain cleaners as they become available. In this photo, for example, you'll see a relatively new product that injects blasts of compressed CO_2 directly into your toilet, sink, or tub drain to dislodge clogs. It does not cause any chemicals to enter the waste stream, and the manufacturers claim the CO_2 blast is very gentle and won't damage pipes. As with any new product, use it with caution. But if a plunger or a snake isn't working, it could save you the cost of a house call.

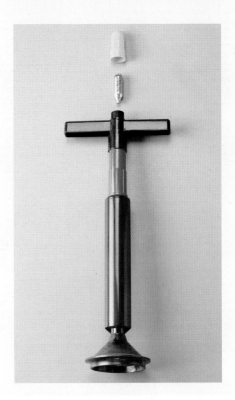

How to Plunge a Clogged Toilet

Plunging is the easiest way to remove "natural" blockages. Take time to lay towels around the base of the toilet and remove other objects to a safe, dry location, since plunging may result in splashing. Often, allowing a very full toilet to sit for 20 or 30 minutes will permit some of the water to drain to a less precarious level.

Force Cups ▸

A flanged plunger (force cup) fits into the mouth of the toilet trap and creates a tight seal so you can build up enough pressure in front of the plunger to dislodge the blockage and send it on its way.

There should be enough water in the bowl to completely cover the plunger. Fold out the skirt from inside the plunger to form a better seal with the opening at the base of the bowl. Pump the plunger vigorously half-a-dozen times, take a rest, and then repeat. Try this for four to five cycles.

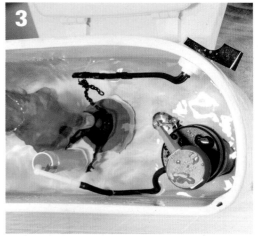

If you force enough water out of the bowl that you are unable to create suction with the plunger, put a controlled amount of water in the bowl by lifting up on the flush valve in the tank. Resume plunging. When you think the drain is clear, you can try a controlled flush, with your hand ready to close the flush valve should the water threaten to spill out of the bowl. Once the blockage has cleared, dump a 5-gallon pail of water into the toilet to blast away any residual debris.

How to Clear Clogs with a Closet Auger

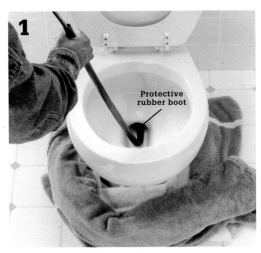

Place the business end of the auger firmly in the bottom of the toilet bowl with the auger tip fully withdrawn. A rubber sleeve will protect the porcelain at the bottom bend of the auger. The tip will be facing back and up, which is the direction the toilet trap takes.

(Label in image: Protective rubber boot)

Closet Augers ▸

A closet auger is a semirigid cable housed in a tube. The tube has a bend at the end so it can be snaked through a toilet trap (without scratching it) to snag blockages.

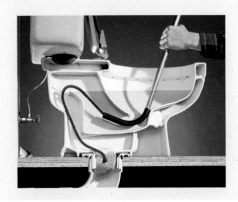

Rotate the handle on the auger housing clockwise as you push down on the rod, advancing the rotating auger tip up into the back part of the trap. You may work the cable backward and forward as needed, but keep the rubber boot of the auger firmly in place in the bowl. When you feel resistance, indicating you've snagged the object, continue rotating the auger counterclockwise as you withdraw the cable and the object.

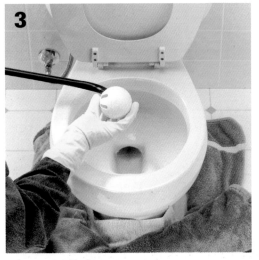

Fully retract the auger until you have recovered the object. This can be frustrating at times, but it is still a much easier task than the alternative—to remove the toilet and go fishing.

Fixing Toilet Flanges

If your toilet rocks, it will eventually leak. The rocking means that the bolts are no longer holding the toilet securely to the floor. If you have tightened the bolts and it still rocks, it is possible that a bolt has broken a piece of the flange off and is no longer able to hold. Rocking might also be because an ongoing leak has weakened the floor and it is now uneven. Whatever the reason, a rocking toilet needs to be fixed.

If your flange is connected to cast-iron piping, use a repair flange. This has a rubber compression ring that will seal the new flange to the cast-iron pipe.

Tools & Materials ▸

Drill	#10 stainless-steel
Wrench	flathead
Internal pipe cutter	wood screws
Solvent-cement	Marker

Use a flange repair kit for a quick fix to a broken flange. The new flange piece from the kit is simply screwed to the floor after it has been oriented correctly over the broken flange.

Toilets that rock often only need to have the nuts on the closet bolts tightened. But if you need to tighten the bolts on an ongoing basis, you very likely have a problem with the closet flange.

Toilet Shims ▸

If the toilet is wobbly because of an uneven floor, shims may solve the problem. (Do not install shims if the toilet leaks at the base; they will not solve that problem.) Slip two or more plastic toilet shims under the toilet until it is stabilized. Press the shims with only medium pressure; don't force them too hard. Cut the exposed portions of the shims with a utility knife.

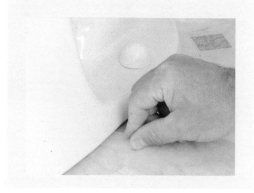

How to Replace a PVC Closet Flange

Begin by removing the toilet and wax ring. Cut the pipe just below the bottom of the flange using an internal pipe cutter (inset, available at plumbing supply stores). Remove the flange.

If your flange is attached to a closet bend, you will need to open up the floor around the toilet to get at the horizontal pipe connecting the bend to the stack to make the repair. If it is connected to a length of vertical plastic pipe, use a repair coupling and a short length of pipe to bring the pipe back up to floor level. Cement the new pipe into the repair coupling first and allow it to set. Clean the old pipe thoroughly before cementing.

Cut the replacement pipe flush with the floor. Dry-fit the new flange into the pipe. Turn the flange until the side cut-out screw slots are parallel to the wall. (Do not use the curved keyhole slots, as they are not as strong.) Draw lines to mark the location of the slots on the floor.

Prime and solvent-cement the pipe and flange, inserting the flange slightly off the marks and twisting it to proper alignment. Secure the flange to the floor with #10 stainless-steel flathead wood screws.

Fixing Sink Faucets

It's not surprising that sink faucets leak and drip. Any fitting that contains moving mechanical parts is susceptible to failure. But add to the equation the persistent force of water pressure working against the parts, and the real surprise is that faucets don't fail more quickly or often. It would be a bit unfair to say that the inner workings of a faucet are regarded as disposable by manufacturers, but it is safe to say that these parts have become more easy to remove and replace.

The older your faucet, the more likely you can repair it by replacing small parts like washers and O-rings. Many newer faucets can be repaired only by replacing the major inner components, like a ceramic disk or a cartridge that encapsulates all the washers and O-rings that could possibly wear out.

The most important aspect of sink faucet repair is identifying which type of faucet you own. In this chapter we show all of the common types and provide instructions on repairing them. In every case, the easiest and most reliable repair method is to purchase a replacement kit with brand-new internal working parts for the model and brand of faucet you own.

Tools & Materials ▸

Pliers
Needlenose pliers
Heatproof grease
Channel-type pliers
Utility knife
White vinegar
Old toothbrush
Tape measure

Repair kit (exact
    type varies)
Teflon tape
Screwdrivers
Pipe joint compound
Plumber's putty
Rag
Eye protection

Eventually, just about every faucet develops leaks and drips. Repairs can usually be accomplished simply by replacing the mechanical parts inside the faucet body (the main trick is figuring out which kind of parts your faucet has).

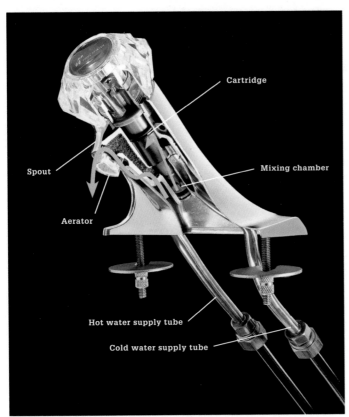

All faucets, no matter the type, have valves that move many thousands of times to open and close hot- and cold-water ports. These valves—or the rubber or plastic parts that rub against other parts when the faucet is being adjusted—wear out in time. Depending on the faucet, you may be able to fix the leak by cleaning or replacing small parts, such as washers or O-rings; or you may need to buy a repair kit and replace a number of parts; or the only solution may be to replace a self-enclosed "cartridge" that contains all the moving parts.

Cartridge

Spout

Mixing chamber

Aerator

Hot water supply tube

Cold water supply tube

Common Problems and Repairs ▶

PROBLEMS

Faucet drips from the end of the spout directions on the or leaks around the base.

Old worn-out faucet continues to leak after repairs are made.

Water pressure at spout seems low, or water flow is partially blocked.

Water pressure from sprayer seems low, or sprayer leaks from handle.

Water leaks onto floor underneath faucet.

Hose bib or valve drips from spout or leaks around handle.

REPAIRS

1. Identify the faucet design (pages 342 to 349), then install replacement parts, using following pages.

1. Replace the old faucet (page 354).

1. Clean faucet aerator (page pages 342 and 356).
2. Replace corroded galvanized pipes with copper or PEX.

1. Clean sprayer head (page 351).
2. Fix diverter valve (pages 351 to 352).

1. Replace cracked sprayer hose (page 353).
2. Tighten water connections, or replace supply tubes and shutoff valves.
3. Fix leaky sink strainer.

1. Take valve apart and replace washers and O-rings.

Identifying Your Faucet and the Parts You Need

A leaky faucet is the most common home plumbing problem. Fortunately, repair parts are available for almost every type of faucet, from the oldest to the newest, and installing these parts is usually easy. But if you don't know your make and model, the hardest part of fixing a leak may be identifying your faucet and finding the right parts. Don't make the common mistake of thinking that any similar-looking parts will do the job; you've got to get exact replacements.

There are so many faucet types that even experts have trouble classifying them into neat categories. Two-handle faucets are either compression (stem) or washerless two-handle. Single-handle faucets are classified as mixing cartridge; ball; disc; or disc/cartridge.

A single-handle faucet with a rounded, dome-shaped cap is often a ball type. If a single-handle faucet has a flat top, it is likely a cartridge or a ceramic disc type. An older two-handle faucet is likely of the compression type; newer two-handle models use washerless cartridges. Shut off the water, and test to verify that the water is off. Dismantle the faucet carefully. Look for a brand name: it may be clearly visible on the baseplate, or may be printed on an inner part, or it may not be printed anywhere. Put all the parts into a reliable plastic bag and take them to your home center or plumbing supply store. A knowledgeable salesperson can help you identify the parts you need.

If you cannot find what you are looking for at a local store, check online faucet sites or the manufacturers' sites; they often have step-by-step instruction for identifying what you need. Note that manufacturers' terminology may not match the terms we use here. For example, the word "cartridge" may refer to a ceramic-disc unit.

Most faucets have repair kits, which include all the parts you need, and sometimes a small tool as well. Even if some of the parts in your faucet look fine, it's a good idea to install the parts provided by the kit, to ensure against future wear.

Repair Tips ▶

If water flow is weak, unscrew the aerator at the tip of the spout. If there is sediment, then dirty water is entering the faucet, which could damage the faucet's inner workings.

To remove handles and spouts, work carefully and look for small screw heads. You often need to first pry off a cap on top, but not always. Parts may be held in place with small setscrews.

Cleaning and removing debris can sometimes solve the problem of low water flow, and occasionally can solve a leak as well.

Apply plumber's grease (also known as faucet grease or valve grease), to new parts before installing them. Be especially sure to coat rubber parts like O-rings and washers.

Compression Faucets

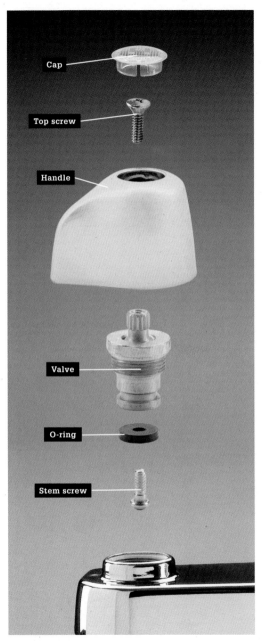

Cap

Top screw

Handle

Valve

O-ring

Stem screw

A compression faucet has a stem assembly that includes a retaining nut, threaded spindle, O-ring, stem washer, and stem screw. Dripping at the spout occurs when the washer becomes worn. Leaks around the handle are caused by a worn O-ring.

Pry off the cap on top of the handle and remove the screw that holds the cap onto the stem. Pull the handle up and out. Use an adjustable wrench or pliers to unscrew the stem and pull it out.

If the handle is stuck, try applying mineral cleaner from above. If that doesn't work, you may need to buy a handle puller. With the cap and the hold-down screw removed, position the wings of the puller under the handle and tighten the puller to slowly pull the handle up.

Remove the screw that holds the rubber washer in place, and pry out the washer. Replace a worn washer with an exact replacement—one that is the same diameter, thickness, and shape.

Replace any O-rings. A worn O-ring can cause water to leak out the handle. Gently pry out the old O-ring and reinstall an exact replacement. Apply plumber's grease to the rubber parts before reinstalling the stem.

If washers wear out quickly, the seat is likely worn. Use a seat wrench to unscrew the seat from inside the faucet. Replace it with an exact duplicate. If replacing the washer and O-ring doesn't solve the problem, you may need to replace the entire stem.

Washerless Two-handle Faucet

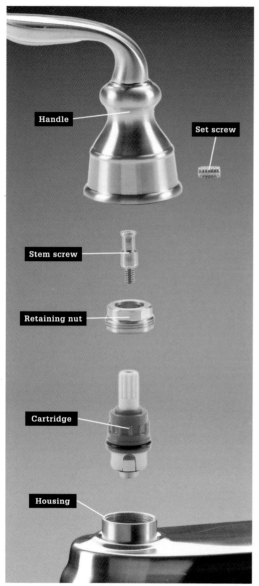

Remove the faucet handle and withdraw the old cartridge. Make a note of how the cartridge is oriented before you remove it. Purchase a replacement cartridge.

Almost all two-handle faucets made today are "washerless." Instead of an older-type compression stem, there is a cartridge, usually with a plastic casing. Many of these cartridges contain ceramic discs, while others have metal or plastic pathways. No matter the type of cartridge, the repair is the same; instead of replacing small parts, you simply replace the entire cartridge.

Install the replacement cartridge. Clean the valve seat first and coat the valve seat and O-rings with faucet grease. Be sure the new cartridge is in the correct position, with its tabs seated in the slotted body of the faucet. Re-assemble the valve and handles.

One-Handle Cartridge Faucets

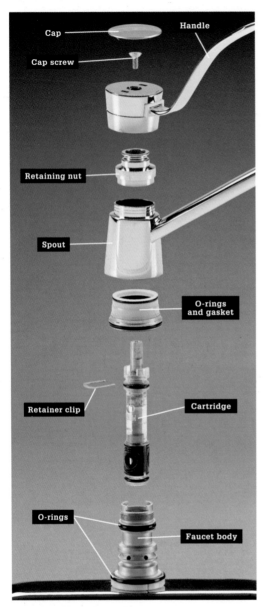

Cap

Handle

Cap screw

Retaining nut

Spout

O-rings and gasket

Retainer clip

Cartridge

O-rings

Faucet body

To remove the spout, pry off the handle's cap and remove the screw below it. Pull the handle up and off. Use a crescent wrench to remove the pivot nut.

Single-handle cartridge faucets like this work by moving the cartridge up and down and side to side, which opens up pathways to direct varying amounts of hot and cold water to the spout. Moen, Price-Pfister, Delta, Peerless, Kohler, and others make many types of cartridges, some of which look very different from this one.

Lift out the spout. If the faucet has a diverter valve, remove it as well. Use a screwdriver to pary out the retainer clip, which holds the cartridge in place.

Remove the cartridge. If you simply pull up with pliers, you may leave part of the stem in the faucet body. If that happens, replace the cartridge and buy a stem puller made for your model.

Gently pry out and replace all O-rings on the faucet body. Smear plumber's grease onto the new replacement cartridge and the new O-rings, and reassemble the faucet.

Here is one of many other types of single-handle cartridges. In this model, all the parts are plastic except for the stem, and it's important to note the direction in which the cartridge is aligned. If you test the faucet and the hot and cold are reversed, disassemble and realign the cartridge.

Ball Faucets

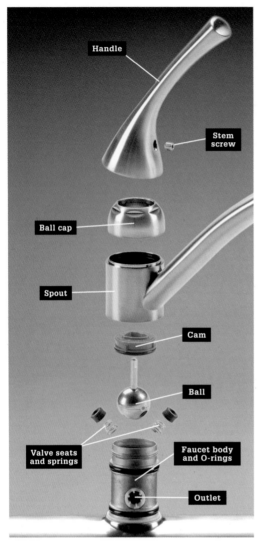

Remove the old ball and cam after removing the faucet handle and ball cap. Some faucets may require a ball faucet tool to remove the handle. Otherwise, simply use a pair of channel-type pliers to twist off the ball cap.

The ball-type faucet is used by Delta, Peerless, and a few others. The ball fits into the faucet body and is constructed with three holes (not visible here)—a hot inlet, a cold inlet, and the outlet, which fills the valve body with water that then flows to the spout or sprayer. Depending on the position of the ball, each inlet hole is open, closed, or somewhere in-between. The inlet holes are sealed to the ball with valve seats, which are pressed tight against the ball with springs. If water drips from the spout, replace the seats and springs. Or go ahead and purchase an entire replacement kit and replace all or most of the working parts.

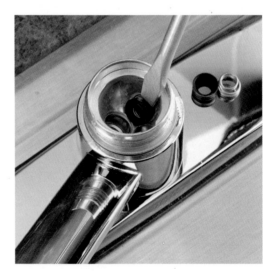

Pry out the neoprene valve seals and springs. Place thick towels around the faucet. Slowly turn on the water to flush out any debris in the faucet body. Replace the seals and springs with new parts. Also replace the O-rings on the valve body. You may want to replace the ball and cam, too, especially if you're purchasing a repair kit. Coat all rubber parts in faucet grease, and reassemble the faucet.

Disc Faucets

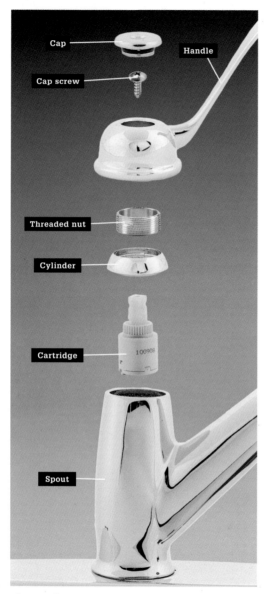

Cap

Handle

Cap screw

Threaded nut

Cylinder

Cartridge

1 00908

Spout

Other Cartridges ▶

Many modern cartridges do not have seals or O-rings that can be replaced, and some have a ball rather than a ceramic disk inside. For the repair, the cartridge's innards do not matter; just replace the whole cartridge.

Disc-type faucets are the most common single-handle faucets currently being made. A pair of ceramic discs encased in a cylinder often referred to as a "cartridge" rub together as they rotate to open ports for hot and cold water. The ceramic discs do wear out in time, causing leaks, and there is only one solution—replace the disc unit (or "cartridge"). This makes for an easy—through comparatively expensive—repair.

Replace the cylinder with a new one, coating the rubber parts with faucet grease before installing the new cylinder. Make sure the rubber seals fit correctly in the cylinder openings before you install the cylinder. Assemble the faucet handle.

Replacing Kitchen Sink Sprayers

If water pressure from a sink sprayer seems low, or if water leaks from the handle, it is usually because lime buildup and sediment have blocked small openings inside the sprayer head. To fix the problem, first take the sprayer head apart and clean the parts. If cleaning the sprayer head does not help, the problem may be caused by a faulty diverter valve. The diverter valve inside the faucet body shifts water flow from the faucet spout to the sprayer when the sprayer handle is pressed. Cleaning or replacing the diverter valve may fix water pressure problems.

Whenever making repairs to a sink sprayer, check the sprayer hose for kinks or cracks. A damaged hose should be replaced.

If water pressure from a faucet spout seems low, or if the flow is partially blocked, take the spout aerator apart and clean the parts. The aerator is a screw-on attachment with a small wire screen that mixes tiny air bubbles into the water flow. Make sure the wire screen is not clogged with sediment and lime buildup. If water pressure is low throughout the house, it may be because galvanized steel water pipes are corroded. Corroded pipes should be replaced with copper.

Tools & Materials ▸

Screwdriver	Penetrating oil
Channel-type pliers	Putty knife
Needlenose pliers	Universal washer kit
Small brush	Heatproof grease
Vinegar	Replacement sprayer hose
Faucet grease	Eye protection
Plumber's putty	

Kitchen sprayers are very convenient and, in theory, quite simple. Yet, they break down with surprising regularity. Fixing or replacing one is an easy job, however.

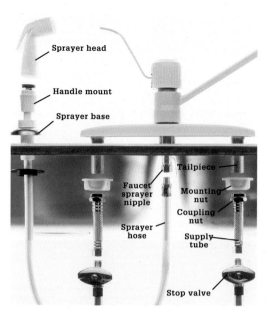

- **Sprayer head**
- **Handle mount**
- **Sprayer base**
- **Tailpiece**
- **Faucet sprayer nipple**
- **Mounting nut**
- **Coupling nut**
- **Sprayer hose**
- **Supply tube**
- **Stop valve**

The standard sprayer hose attachment is connected to a nipple at the bottom of the faucet valve. When the lever of the sprayer is depressed, water flows from a diverter valve in the faucet body out to the sprayer. If your sprayer stream is weak or doesn't work at all, the chances are good that the problem lies in the diverter valve.

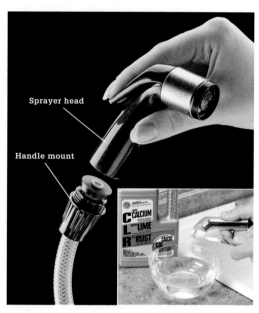

- **Sprayer head**
- **Handle mount**

Sprayer heads can be removed from the sprayer hose, usually by loosening a retaining nut. A sprayer's head can get clogged with minerals. Unscrew the sprayer from the hose and remove any parts at its tip. Soak it in mineral cleaner, and use a small brush to open any clogged orifices.

How to Repair a Sprayer

1

Shut off the water at the stop valves and remove the faucet handle to gain access to the faucet parts. Disassemble the faucet handle and body to expose the diverter valve. Ball-type faucets like the one shown here require that you also remove the spout to get at the diverter.

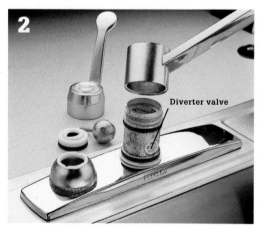

2

- **Diverter valve**

Locate the diverter valve, seen here at the base of the valve body. Because different types and brands of faucets have differently configured diverters, do a little investigating beforehand to try and locate information about your faucet. The above faucet is a ball type.

(continued)

3

Pull the diverter valve from the faucet body with needlenose pliers. Use a toothbrush dipped in white vinegar to clean any lime buildup from the valve. If the valve is in poor condition, bring it to the hardware store and purchase a replacement.

4

Diverter valve washer

Diverter valve

Coat the washer or O-ring on the new or cleaned diverter valve with faucet grease. Insert the diverter valve back into the faucet body. Reassemble the faucet. Turn on the water and test the sprayer. If it still isn't functioning to your satisfaction, remove the sprayer tip and run the sprayer without the filter and aerator in case any debris has made its way into the sprayer line during repairs.

Finding the Diverter on a Two-Handle Faucet ▸

On a two-handle faucet, the diverter is usually located in a vertical position just under the spout. Remove the spout. You may need to use longnose pliers to pull out the diverter. Try cleaning out any debris. If that does not restore operation, replace the valve.

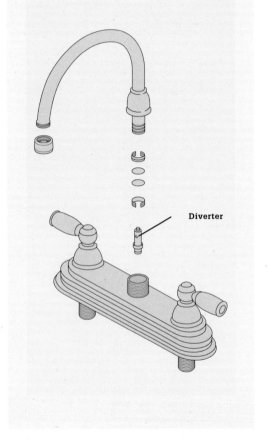

Diverter

How to Replace a Kitchen Sprayer

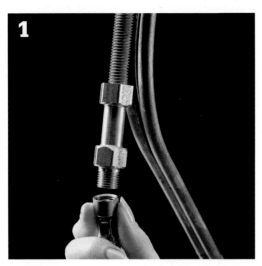

To replace a sprayer hose, start by shutting off the water at the shutoff valves. Clear out the cabinet under your sink and put on eye protection. Unthread the coupling nut that attaches the old hose to a nipple or tube below the faucet spout. Use a basin wrench if you can't get your channel-type pliers on the nut.

Unscrew the mounting nut of the old sprayer from below and remove the old sprayer body. Clean the sink deck and then apply plumber's putty to the base of the new sprayer. Insert the new sprayer tailpiece into the opening in the sink deck.

From below, slip the friction washer up over the sprayer tailpiece. Screw the mounting nut onto the tailpiece and tighten with a basin wrench or channel-type pliers. Do not overtighten. Wipe away any excess plumber's putty.

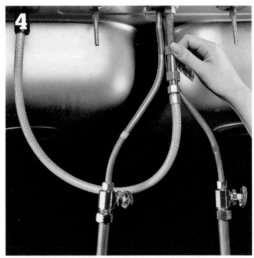

Screw the coupling for the sprayer hose onto the hose nipple underneath the faucet body. For a good seal, apply pipe joint compound to the nipple threads first. Tighten the coupling with a basin wrench, turn on the water supply at the shutoff valves, and test the new sprayer.

How to Remove an Old Faucet

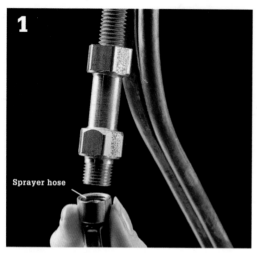

To remove the old faucet, start by clearing out the cabinet under the sink and laying down towels. Turn off the hot and cold stop valves and open the faucet to make sure the water is off. Detach the sprayer hose from the faucet sprayer nipple and unscrew the retaining nut that secures the sprayer base to the sink deck. Pull the sprayer hose out through the sink deck opening.

Spray the mounting nuts that hold the faucet or faucet handles (on the underside of the sink deck) with penetrating oil for easier removal. Let the oil soak in for a few minutes. If the nut is rusted and stubbornly stuck, you may need to drill a hole in its side, then tap the hole with a hammer and screwdriver to loosen it.

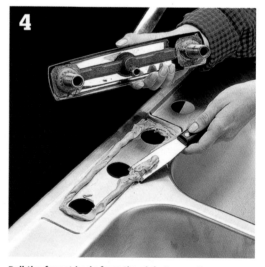

Unhook the supply tubes at the stop valves. Don't reuse old chrome supply tubes. If the stops are missing or unworkable, replace them. Then remove the coupling nuts and the mounting nuts on the tailpieces of the faucet with a basin wrench or channel-type pliers.

Pull the faucet body from the sink. Remove the sprayer base if you wish to replace it. Scrape off any putty or caulk with a putty knife and clean off the sink with a scouring pad and a nonabrasive cleaner.

How to Install a Pullout Kitchen Sink Faucet

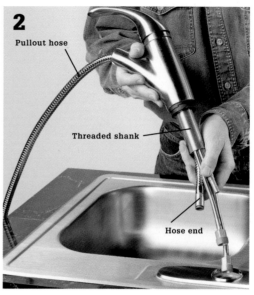

Install the base plate (if your faucet has one) onto the sink flange so it is centered. Have a helper hold it straight from above as you tighten the mounting nuts that secure the base plate from below. Make sure the plastic gasket is centered under the base plate. These nuts can be adequately tightened by hand.

Retract the pullout hose by drawing it out through the faucet body until the fitting at the end of the hose is flush with the bottom of the threaded faucet shank. Insert the shank and the supply tubes down through the top of the deck plate.

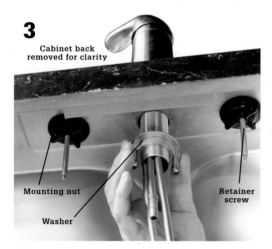

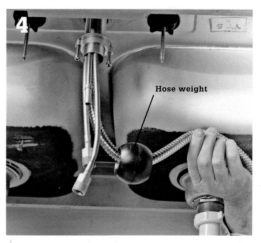

Slip the mounting nut and washer over the free ends of the supply tubes and pullout hose, then thread the nut onto the threaded faucet shank. Hand tighten. Tighten the retainer screws with a screwdriver to secure the faucet.

Slide the hose weight onto the pullout hose (the weight helps keep the hose from tangling and it makes it easier to retract).

(continued)

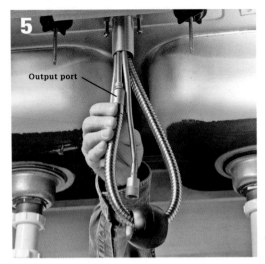

Connect the end of the pullout hose to the outlet port on the faucet body using a quick connector fitting.

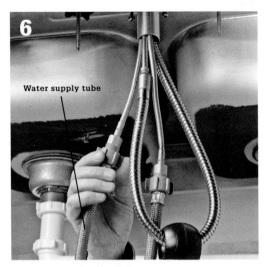

Hook up the water supply tubes to the faucet inlets. Make sure the tubes are long enough to reach the supply risers without stretching or kinking.

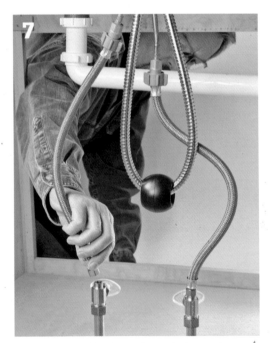

Connect the supply tubes to the supply risers at the stop valves. Make sure to get the hot lines and cold lines attached correctly.

Attach the spray head to the end of the pullout hose and turn the fitting to secure the connection. Turn on the water supply and test. *TIP: Remove the aerator in the tip of the spray head and run hot and cold water to flush out any debris.*

Variation: One-Piece Faucet with Sprayer ▸

1

Thoroughly clean the area around the sink's holes. Slip the faucet's plastic washer onto the underside of the base plate. Press the faucet in place, and have a helper hold it in place while you work from below.

2

Friction washer

Mounting nut

Slip a friction washer onto each tailpiece and then hand tighten a mounting nut. Tighten the mounting nut with channel-type pliers or a basin wrench.

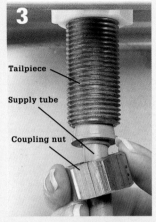

3

Tailpiece

Supply tube

Coupling nut

Connect supply tubes to the faucet tailpieces. Make sure the tubes you buy are long enough to reach the stop valves and that the coupling nuts will fit the tubes and tailpieces.

4

Sprayer tailpiece

Apply a ¼" bead of plumber's putty to the underside of the sprayer base. With the base threaded onto the sprayer hose, insert the tailpiece of the sprayer through the opening in the sink deck.

5

Plumber's putty

Friction washer

Mounting nut

From beneath, slip the friction washer over the sprayer tailpiece and then screw the mounting nut onto the tailpiece. Tighten with channel-type pliers or a basin wrench. Clean up any excess putty or caulk.

6

Screw the sprayer hose onto the hose nipple on the bottom of the faucet. Hand tighten and then give the nut one quarter turn with channel-type pliers or a basin wrench. Turn on the water supply at the shutoff, remove the aerator, and flush debris from the faucet.

Fixing Kitchen Drains & Traps

Kitchen traps, also called sink drains or trap assemblies, are made of 1½-inch pipes (also called tubes), slip washers, and nuts, so they can be easily assembled and disassembled. Most plastic types can be tightened by hand, with no wrench required. Pipes made of chromed brass will corrode in time, and rubber washers will crumble, meaning they need to be replaced. Plastic pipes and plastic washers last virtually forever. All traps are liable to get bumped out of alignment; when this happens, they should be taken apart and reassembled.

A trap's configuration depends on how many bowls the sink has, whether or not you have a food disposer and/or a dishwasher drain line, and local codes. On this page we show three of the most common assembly types. Tee fittings on these traps often have a baffle, which reduces the water flow somewhat. Check local codes to make sure your trap is compliant.

Tools & Materials ▸

Flat screwdriver	Washers
Spud wrench	Waste tee fitting
Trap arm	P-trap
Mineral spirits	Saw
Cloth	Miter box
Strainer kit	Eye protection
Plumber's putty	Work gloves
Teflon tape	

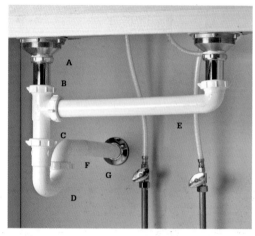

Kitchen sink drains include a strainer body (A), tailpiece (B), waste tee (C), P-trap (D), outlet drain line (E), trap arm (F), and wall stubout with coupling (G).

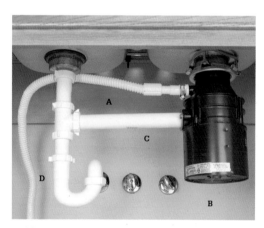

In this arrangement, the dishwasher drain hose (A) attaches to the food disposer (B), and a trap arm (C) leads from the disposer to the P-trap (D).

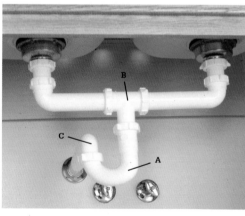

A "center tee" arrangement has a single P-trap (A) that is connected to a waste tee (B) and the trap arm (C).

Drain Kits ▶

Kits for installing a new sink drain include all the pipes, slip fittings, and washers you'll need to get from the sink tailpieces (most kits are equipped for a double bowl kitchen sink) to the trap arm that enters the wall or floor. For wall trap arms, you'll need a kit with a P-trap. Both drains normally are plumbed to share a trap. Chromed brass or PVC with slip fittings let you adjust the drain more easily and pull it apart and then reassemble if there is a clog. Some pipes have fittings on their ends that eliminate the need for a washer. Kitchen sink drains and traps should be 1½" o.d. pipe—the 1¼" pipe is for lavatories and doesn't have enough capacity for a kitchen sink.

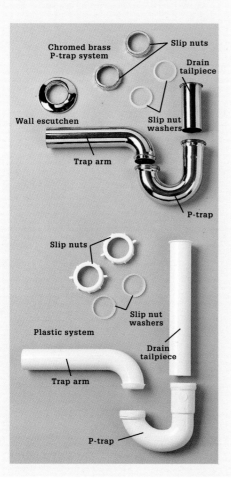

Tips for Choosing Drains ▶

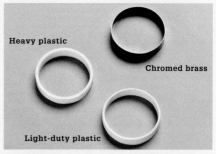

Heavy plastic
Chromed brass
Light-duty plastic

Wall thickness varies in sink drain pipes. The thinner plastic material is cheaper and more difficult to obtain a good seal with than the thicker, more expensive tubing. The thin product is best reserved for lavatory drains, which are far less demanding.

Slip joints are formed by tightening a male-threaded slip nut over a female-threaded fitting, trapping and compressing a beveled nylon washer to seal the joint.

Use a spud wrench to tighten the strainer body against the underside of the sink bowl. Normally, the strainer flange has a layer of plumber's putty to seal beneath it above the sink drain, and a pair of washers (one rubber, one fibrous) to seal below.

How to Hook Up a Kitchen Sink Drain

Slip nut washer

Threaded outlet

Tailpiece

If you are replacing the sink strainer body, remove the old one and clean the top and bottom of the sink deck around the drain opening with mineral spirits. Attach the drain tailpiece to the threaded outlet of the strainer body, inserting a nonbeveled washer between the parts if your strainer kits include one. Lubricate the threads or apply Teflon tape so you can get a good, snug fit.

Apply plumber's putty around the perimeter of the drain opening and seat the strainer assembly into it. Add washers below as directed and tighten the strainer locknut with a spud wrench (see photo, previous page) or by striking the mounting nubs at the top of the body with a flat screwdriver.

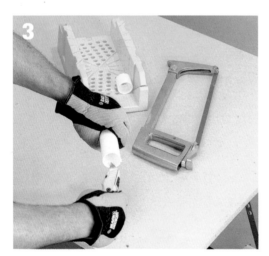

You may need to cut a trap arm or drain tailpiece to length. Cut metal tubing with a hacksaw. Cut plastic tubing with a handsaw, power miter saw, or a hand miter box and a backsaw or hacksaw. You can use a tubing cutter for any material. Deburr the cut end of plastic tubing with a utility knife.

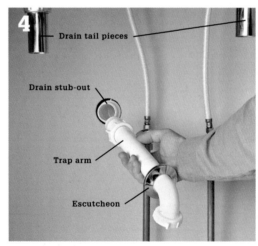

Drain tail pieces

Drain stub-out

Trap arm

Escutcheon

Attach the trap arm to the male-threaded drain stubout in the wall, using a slip nut and beveled compression washer. The outlet for the trap arm should point downward. *NOTE: The trap arm must be lower on the wall than any of the horizontal lines in the set-up, including lines to dishwasher, disposer, or the outlet line to the second sink bowl.*

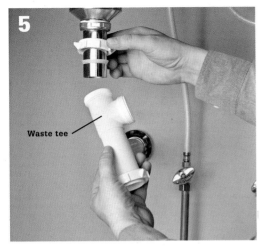

5

Attach a waste tee fitting to the drain tailpiece, orienting the opening in the fitting side so it will accept the outlet drain line from the other sink bowl. If the waste tee is higher than the top of the trap arm, remove it and trim the drain tailpiece.

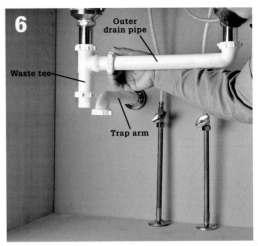

6

Join the short end of the outlet drain pipe to the tailpiece for the other sink bowl and then attach the end of the long run to the opening in the waste tee. The outlet tube should extend into the tee ½"—make sure it does not extend in far enough to block water flow from above.

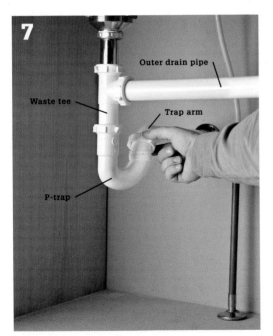

7

Attach the long leg of a P-trap to the waste tee and attach the shorter leg to the downward-facing opening of the trap arm. Adjust as necessary and test all joints to make sure they are still tight, and then test the system.

Variation: Drain in Floor ▸

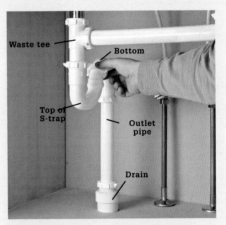

If your drain stubout comes up out of the floor or cabinet base instead of the wall, you probably have a two-part S-trap instead of a P-trap in your drain line. This arrangement is illegal in some areas, because a heavy surge of waterflow from a nearby fixture can siphon the trap dry, rendering it unable to block gases. Check with your local plumbing inspector to learn if S-traps are allowed in your area.

Fixing Tub/Shower Faucets & Showerheads

Tub and shower faucets have the same basic designs as sink faucets, and the techniques for repairing leaks are the same as described in the faucet repair section of this book (pages 340 to 349). To identify your faucet design, you may have to take off the handle and disassemble the faucet.

When a tub and shower are combined, the showerhead and the tub spout share the same hot and cold water supply lines and handles. Combination faucets are available as three-handle, two-handle, or single-handle types (next page). The number of handles gives clues as to the design of the faucets and the kinds of repairs that may be necessary.

With combination faucets, a diverter valve or gate diverter is used to direct water flow to the tub spout or the showerhead. On three-handle faucet types, the middle handle controls a diverter valve. If water does not shift easily from tub to showerhead, or if water continues to run out the spout when the shower is on,

the diverter valve probably needs to be cleaned and repaired (pages 351 to 352).

Two-handle and single-handle types use a gate diverter that is operated by a pull lever or knob on the tub spout. Although gate diverters rarely need repair, the lever occasionally may break, come loose, or refuse to stay in the up position. To repair a gate diverter set in a tub spout, replace the entire spout.

Tub and shower faucets and diverter valves may be set inside wall cavities. Removing them may require a deep-set ratchet wrench.

If spray from the showerhead is uneven, clean the spray holes. If the showerhead does not stay in an upright position, remove the head and replace the O-ring.

To add a shower to an existing tub, install a flexible shower adapter. Several manufacturers make complete conversion kits that allow a shower to be installed in less than one hour.

Tub/shower plumbing is notorious for developing drips from the tub spout and the showerhead. In most cases, the leak can be traced to the valves controlled by the faucet handles.

Tub & Shower Combination Faucets

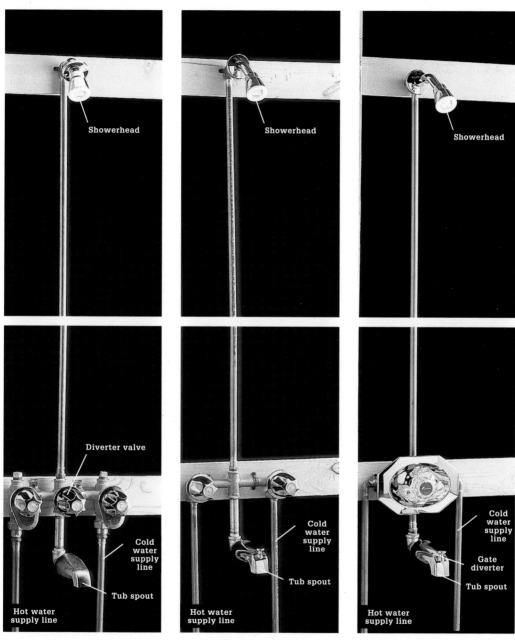

Showerhead

Showerhead

Showerhead

Diverter valve

Cold water supply line

Tub spout

Hot water supply line

Cold water supply line

Tub spout

Hot water supply line

Cold water supply line

Gate diverter

Tub spout

Hot water supply line

Three-handle faucet (page 364) has valves that are either compression or cartridge design.

Two-handle faucet (page 366) has valves that are either compression or cartridge design.

Single-handle faucet (page 368) has valves that are cartridge, ball-type, or disc design.

Fixing Three-handle Tub & Shower Faucets

A three-handle faucet type has two handles to control hot and cold water, and a third handle to control the diverter valve and direct water to either a tub spout or a shower head. The separate hot and cold handles indicate cartridge or compression faucet designs.

If a diverter valve sticks, if water flow is weak, or if water runs out of the tub spout when the flow is directed to the showerhead, the diverter needs to be repaired or replaced. Most diverter valves are similar to either compression or cartridge faucet valves. Compression-type diverters can be repaired, but cartridge types should be replaced.

Remember to turn off the water before beginning work.

Tools & Materials ▸

Screwdriver
Adjustable wrench
   or channel-type
   pliers
Deep-set
   ratchet wrench
Small wire brush
Replacement
   diverter cartridge
   or universal
   washer kit

Faucet grease
Vinegar
Eye protection

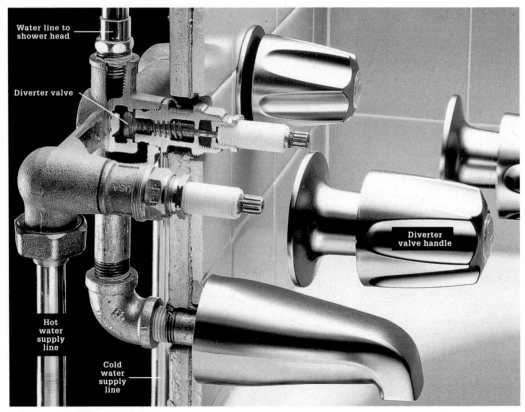

Water line to shower head

Diverter valve

Hot water supply line

Cold water supply line

Diverter valve handle

A three-handle tub/shower faucet has individual controls for hot and cold water plus a third handle that operates the diverter valve.

How to Repair a Compression Diverter Valve

1 Escutcheon

Diverter handle

Remove the diverter valve handle with a screwdriver. Unscrew or pry off the escutcheon.

2 Bonnet nut

Remove bonnet nut with an adjustable wrench or channel-type pliers.

3

Unscrew the stem assembly, using a deep-set ratchet wrench. If necessary, chip away any mortar surrounding the bonnet nut.

4

Stem washer

Stem screw

Remove brass stem screw. Replace stem washer with an exact duplicate. If stem screw is worn, replace it.

5 Retaining nut

Threaded spindle

Unscrew the threaded spindle from the retaining nut.

6

Clean sediment and lime buildup from nut, using a small wire brush dipped in vinegar. Coat all parts with faucet grease and reassemble diverter valve.

Fixing Two-handle Tub & Shower Faucets

Two-handle tub and shower faucets are either cartridge or compression design. Because the valves of two-handle tub and shower faucets may be set inside the wall cavity, a deep-set socket wrench may be required to remove the valve stem.

Two-handle tub and shower designs have a gate diverter. A gate diverter is a simple mechanism located in the tub spout. A gate diverter closes the supply of water to the tub spout and redirects the flow to the shower head. Gate diverters seldom need repair. Occasionally, the lever may break, come loose, or refuse to stay in the up position.

If the diverter fails to work properly, replace the tub spout. Tub spouts are inexpensive and easy to replace.

Remember to turn off the water before beginning any work.

Tools & Materials ▶

Screwdriver	Ball-peen hammer
Allen wrench	Masking tape
Pipe wrench	or cloth
Channel-type pliers	Pipe joint compound
Small cold chisel	Replacement faucet
Deep-set	parts, as needed
ratchet wrench	Eye protection

A two-handle tub/shower faucet can operate with compression valves, but more often these days they contain cartridges that can be replaced. Unlike a three-handled model, the diverter is a simple gate valve that is operated by a lever.

Spout nipple

Allen wrench

Check underneath tub spout for a small access slot. The slot indicates the spout is held in place with an Allen screw. Remove the screw, using an Allen wrench. Spout will slide off.

Unscrew faucet spout. Use a pipe wrench, or insert a large screwdriver or hammer handle into the spout opening and turn spout counterclockwise.

Spread pipe joint compound on threads of spout nipple before replacing spout. If you have a copper pipe or a short pipe, buy a spout retrofit kit, which can attach a spout to most any pipe.

How to Remove a Deep-set Faucet Valve

1 Escutcheon

Masking tape

Stem nipple

2

Bonnet nut

3

Remove handle and unscrew the escutcheon with channel-type pliers. Pad the jaws of the pliers with masking tape to prevent scratching the escutcheon.

Chip away any mortar surrounding the bonnet nut using a ball-peen hammer and a small cold chisel.

Unscrew the bonnet nut with a deep-set ratchet wrench. Remove the bonnet nut and stem from the faucet body.

Fixing Single-handle Tub & Shower Faucets

A single-handle tub and shower faucet has one valve that controls both water flow and temperature. Single-handle faucets may be ball-type, cartridge, or disc designs.

If a single-handle control valve leaks or does not function properly, disassemble the faucet, clean the valve, and replace any worn parts. Repairing a single-handle cartridge faucet is shown on the opposite page.

Direction of the water flow to either the tub spout or the showerhead is controlled by a gate diverter. Gate diverters seldom need repair. Occasionally, the lever may break, come loose, or refuse to stay in the up position. Remember to turn off the water before beginning any work; the shower faucet shown here has built-in shutoff valves, but many other valves do not. Open an access panel in an adjoining room or closet, behind the valve, and look for two shutoffs. If you can't find them there, you may have to shut off intermediate valves or the main shutoff valve.

Tools & Materials ▸

Screwdriver
Adjustable wrench
Channel-type pliers

Replacement faucet
   parts, as needed
Eye protection

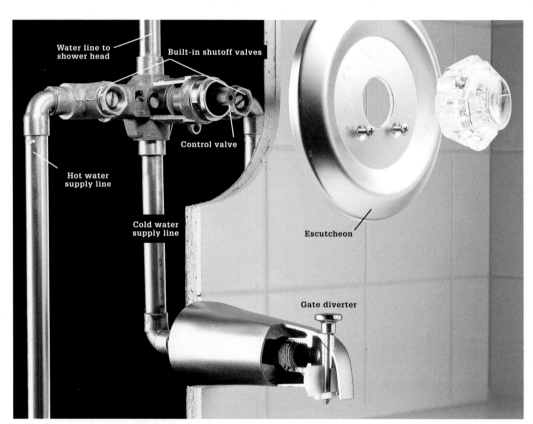

A single-handle tub/shower faucet is the simplest type to operate and to maintain. The handle controls the mixing ratio of both hot and cold water, and the diverter is a simple gate valve.

How to Repair a Single-handle Cartridge Tub & Shower Faucet

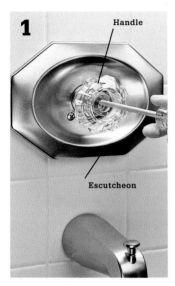

Use a screwdriver to remove the handle and escutcheon.

Turn off water supply at the built-in shutoff valves or the main shutoff valve.

Unscrew and remove the retaining ring or bonnet nut using adjustable wrench.

Remove the cartridge assembly by grasping the end of the valve with channel-type pliers and pulling gently.

Flush the valve body with clean water to remove sediment. Replace any worn O-rings. Reinstall the cartridge and test the valve. If the faucet fails to work properly, replace the cartridge.

Single-Handle Tub & Shower Faucet with Scald Control

In many plumbing systems, if someone flushes a nearby toilet or turns on the cold water of a nearby faucet while someone else is taking a shower, the shower water temperature can suddenly rise precipitously. This is not only uncomfortable; it can actually scald you. For that reason, many one-handle shower valves have a device, called a "balancing valve" or an "anti-scald valve," that keeps the water from getting too hot.

The temperature of your shower may drastically rise to dangerous scalding levels if a nearby toilet is flushed. A shower fixture equipped with an anti-scald valve prevents this sometimes dangerous situation.

How to Adjust the Shower's Temperature

1

To reduce or raise the maximum temperature, remove the handle and escutcheon. Some models have an adjustment screw, others have a handle that can be turned by hand.

2

To remove a balancing valve, you may need to buy a removal tool made for your faucet. Before replacing, slowly turn on water to flush out any debris; use a towel or bucket to keep water from entering inside the wall.

Fixing & Replacing Showerheads

If spray from the showerhead is uneven, clean the spray holes. The outlet or inlet holes of the showerhead may get clogged with mineral deposits. Showerheads pivot into different positions. If a showerhead does not stay in position, or if it leaks, replace the O-ring that seals against the swivel ball.

A tub can be equipped with a shower by installing a flexible shower adapter kit. Complete kits are available at hardware stores and home centers.

Tools & Materials ▸

Adjustable wrench or channel-type pliers	Thin wire (paper clip)
Pipe wrench	Faucet grease
Drill	Rag
Glass and tile bit	Replacement O-rings
Mallet	Masonry anchors
Screwdriver	Flexible shower adapter kit (optional)
Masking tape	Eye protection

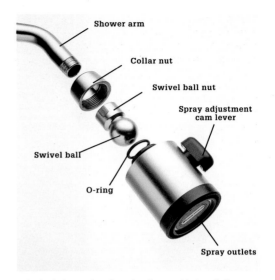

A typical showerhead can be disassembled easily for cleaning and repair. Some showerheads include a spray adjustment cam lever that is used to change the force of the spray.

How to Clean & Repair a Showerhead

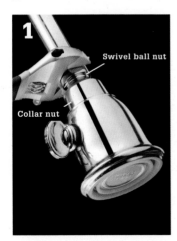

Unscrew the swivel ball nut, using an adjustable wrench or channel-type pliers. Wrap jaws of the tool with masking tape to prevent marring the finish. Unscrew collar nut from the showerhead.

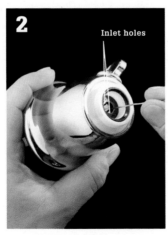

Clean outlet and inlet holes of showerhead with a thin wire. Flush the head with clean water.

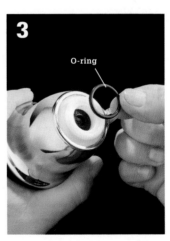

Replace the O-ring, if necessary. Lubricate the O-ring with faucet grease before installing.

Fixing Tub/Shower Drains

Tub or shower not draining? First, make sure it's only the tub or shower. If your sink is plugged, too, it may be a coincidence or it may be that a common branch line is plugged. A sure sign of this is when water drains from the sink into the tub. This could require the help of a drain cleaning service.

If the toilet also can't flush (or worse, water comes into the tub when you flush the toilet), then the common drain to all your bathroom fixtures is plugged. Call a drain cleaning service. If you suspect the problem is only with your tub or shower, then read on. We'll show you how to clear drainlines and clean and adjust two types of tub stopper mechanisms. Adjusting the mechanism can also help with the opposite problem: a tub that drains when you're trying to take a bath.

As with bathroom sinks, tub and shower drain pipes may become clogged with soap and hair. The drain stopping mechanisms can also require cleaning and adjustment.

Tools & Materials ▸

Phillips screwdriver
Plunger
Scrub brush
White vinegar
Hand auger
Toothbrush

Needlenose pliers
Dishwashing brush
Faucet grease
Eye protection
Work gloves

Maintenance Tip ▸

Like bathroom sinks, tubs and showers face an ongoing onslaught from soap and hair. When paired, this pesky combination is a sure-fire source of clogs. The soap scum coagulates as it is washed down the drain and binds the hair together in a mass that grows larger with every shower or bath. To nip these clogs in the bud, simply pour boiling hot clean water down the drain from time to time to melt the soapy mass and wash the binder away.

Using Hand Augers ▶

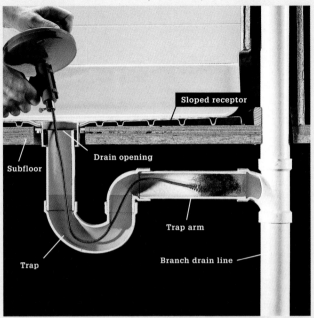

On shower drains, feed the head of a hand-crank or drill-powered auger in through the drain opening after removing the strainer. Crank the handle of the auger to extend the cable and the auger head down into the trap and, if the clog is farther downline, toward the branch drain. When clearing any drain, it is always better to retrieve the clog than to push it farther downline.

Sloped receptor

Drain opening

Subfloor

Trap arm

Trap

Branch drain line

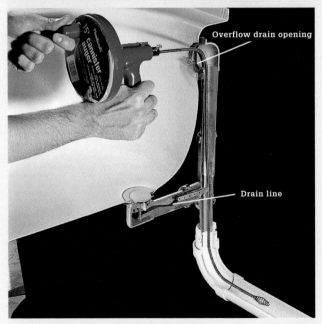

On combination tub/showers, it's generally easiest to insert the auger through the overflow opening after removing the coverplate and lifting out the drain linkage. Crank the handle of the auger to extend the cable and the auger head down into the trap and, if the clog is farther downline, toward the branch drain. When clearing any drain, it is always better to retrieve the clog than to push it farther downline.

Overflow drain opening

Drain line

How to Fix a Plunger-Type Drain

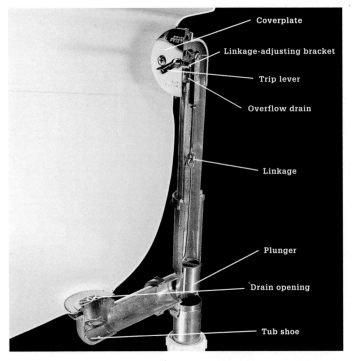

- Coverplate
- Linkage-adjusting bracket
- Trip lever
- Overflow drain
- Linkage
- Plunger
- Drain opening
- Tub shoe

1

A plunger-type tub drain has a simple grate over the drain opening and a behind-the-scenes plunger stopper. Remove the screws on the overflow coverplate with a slotted or Phillips screwdriver. Pull the coverplate, linkage, and plunger from the overflow opening.

2

Clean hair and soap off the plunger with a scrub brush. Mineral buildup is best tackled with white vinegar and a toothbrush or a small wire brush.

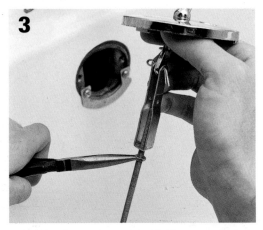

3

Adjust the plunger. If your tub isn't holding water with the plunger down, it's possible the plunger is hanging too high to fully block water from the tub shoe. Loosen the locknut with needlenose pliers, then screw the rod down about ⅛". Tighten the locknut down. If your tub drains poorly, the plunger may be set too low. Loosen the locknut and screw the rod in ⅛" before retightening the locknut.

How to Fix a Pop-up Drain

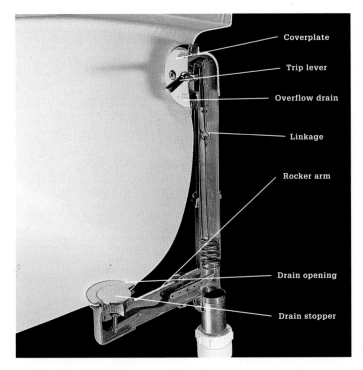

- Coverplate
- Trip lever
- Overflow drain
- Linkage
- Rocker arm
- Drain opening
- Drain stopper

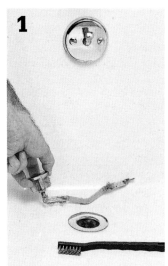

1

Raise the trip lever to the open position. Pull the stopper and rocker arm assembly from the drain. Clean off soap and hair with a dishwashing brush in a basin of hot water. Clean off mineral deposits with a toothbrush or small wire brush and white vinegar.

2

Remove the screws from the cover plate. Pull the trip lever and the linkage from the overflow opening. Clean off soap and hair with a brush in a basin of hot water. Remove mineral buildup with white vinegar and a wire brush. Lubricate moving parts of the linkage and rocker arm mechanism with faucet grease.

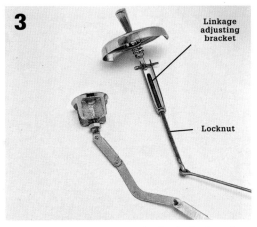

3

- Linkage adjusting bracket
- Locknut

Adjust the pop-up stopper mechanism by first loosening the locknut on the lift rod. If the stopper doesn't close all the way, shorten the linkage by screwing the rod ⅛" farther into the linkage-adjusting bracket. If the stopper doesn't open wide enough, extend the linkage by unscrewing the rod ⅛". Tighten the locknut before replacing the mechanism and testing your adjustment.

Unclogging Sink Drains

Every sink has a drain trap and a fixture drain line. Sink clogs usually are caused by a buildup of soap and hair in the trap or fixture drain line. Remove clogs by using a plunger, disconnecting and cleaning the trap (this page), or using a hand auger (page 373).

Many sinks hold water with a mechanical plug called a pop-up stopper. If the sink will not hold standing water, or if water in the sink drains too slowly, the pop-up stopper must be cleaned and adjusted.

Tools & Materials ▸

Plunger
Channel-type pliers
Small wire brush
Screwdriver
Flashlight
Rag

Bucket
Replacement gaskets
Teflon tape
Eye protection
Work gloves

Clogged lavatory sinks can be cleared with a plunger (not to be confused with a flanged force-cup). Remove the pop-up drain plug and strainer first, and plug the overflow hole by stuffing a wet rag into it, allowing you to create air pressure with the plunger.

How to Clear a Sink Trap

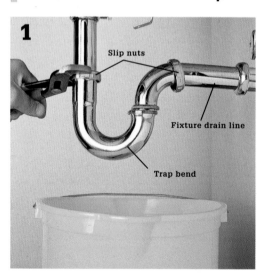

1

Slip nuts

Fixture drain line

Trap bend

Place bucket under trap to catch water and debris.
Loosen slip nuts on trap bend with channel-type pliers. Unscrew nuts by hand and slide away from connections. Pull off trap bend.

2

Dump out debris. Clean trap bend with a small wire brush. Inspect slip nut washers for wear and replace if necessary. Reinstall trap bend and tighten slip nuts.

How to Clear a Kitchen Sink

Drainline from dishwasher

Plunging a kitchen sink is not difficult, but you need to create an uninterrupted pressure lock between the plunger and the clog. If you have a dishwasher, the drain tube needs to be clamped shut and sealed off at the disposer or drainline. The pads on the clamp should be large enough to flatten the tube across its full diameter (or you can clamp the tube ends between small boards).

If there is a second basin, have a helper hold a basket strainer plug in its drain or put a large pot or bucket full of water on top of it. Unfold the skirt within the plunger and place this in the drain of the sink you are plunging. There should be enough water in the sink to cover the plunger head. Plunge rhythmically for six repetitions with increasing vigor, pulling up hard on the last repitition. Repeat this sequence until the clog is removed. Flush out a cleared clog with plenty of hot water.

How to Use a Hand Auger at the Trap Arm

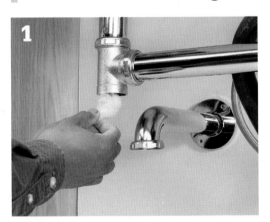

If plunging doesn't work, remove the trap and clean it out (see previous page). With the trap off, see if water flows freely from both sinks (if you have two). Sometimes clogs will lodge in the tee fitting or one of the waste pipes feeding it. These may be pulled out manually or cleared with a bottlebrush or wire. When reassembling the trap, apply Teflon tape clockwise to the male threads of metal waste pieces. Tighten with your channel-type pliers. Plastic pieces need no tape and should be hand tightened only.

If you suspect the clog is downstream of the trap, remove the trap arm from the fitting at the wall. Look in the fixture drain with a flashlight. If you see water, that means the fixture drain is plugged. Clear it with a hand-crank or drill-powered auger (see page 380).

Unclogging Branch & Main Drains

If using a plunger or a hand auger does not clear a clog in a fixture drain line, it means that the blockage may be in a branch line, the main waste-vent stack, or the sewer service line.

First, use a hand-crank or drill-powered auger to clear the branch drain line closest to any stopped-up fixtures. Branch drain lines may be serviced through the cleanout fittings located at the end of the branch. Because waste water may be backed up in the drain lines, always open a cleanout with caution. Place a bucket and rags under the opening to catch waste water. Never position yourself directly under a cleanout opening while unscrewing the plug or cover.

If using an auger on the branch line does not solve the problem, then the clog may be located in a main drainage stack. To clear the stack, run an auger cable down through the roof vent. Make sure that the cable of your auger is long enough to reach down the entire length of the stack. If it is not, you may want to rent or borrow another auger. Always use extreme caution when working on a ladder or on a roof.

If no clog is present in the main stack, the problem may be in the sewer service line. Locate the main cleanout, usually a wye-shaped fitting at the bottom of the main stack. Remove the plug and push the cable of a hand auger into the opening.

Some sewer service lines in older homes have a house trap. The house trap is a U-shaped fitting located at the point where the sewer line exits the house. Most of the fitting will be beneath the floor surface, but it can be identified by its two openings. Use a hand auger to clean a house trap.

If the auger meets solid resistance in the sewer line, retrieve the cable and inspect the bit. Fine, hair-like roots on the bit indicate the line is clogged with tree roots. Dirt on the bit indicates a collapsed line.

Use a power auger to clear sewer service lines that are clogged with tree roots. Power augers (page 380) are available at rental centers. However, a power auger is a large, heavy piece of equipment. Before renting, consider the cost of rental and the level of your do-it-yourself skills versus the price of a professional sewer cleaning service. If you rent a power auger, ask the rental dealer for complete instructions.

Always consult a professional sewer cleaning service if you suspect a collapsed line.

Tools & Materials ▸

Adjustable wrench or pipe wrench	Penetrating oil
Hand auger	Cleanout plug (if needed)
Cold chisel	Pipe joint compound
Ball-peen hammer	Electrical drum auger
Bucket	Gloves
Ladder	Teflon Tape
Phillips screwdriver	Eye and ear protection
Rags	Work gloves

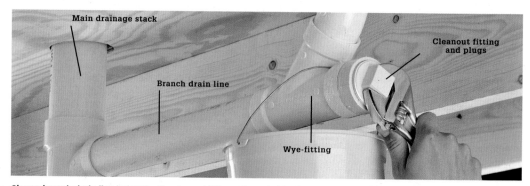

Main drainage stack

Cleanout fitting and plugs

Branch drain line

Wye-fitting

Clear a branch drain line by locating the cleanout fitting at the end of the line. Place a bucket underneath the opening to catch waste water, then slowly unscrew the cleanout plug with an adjustable wrench. Clear clogs in the branch drain line with a hand auger.

How to Clear a Branch Drain Line

Clear the house trap in a sewer service line using a hand auger. Slowly remove only the plug on the "street side" of the trap. If water seeps out the opening as the plug is removed, the clog is in the sewer line beyond the trap. If no water seeps out, auger the trap. If no clog is present in the trap, replace the street-side plug and remove the house-side plug. Use the auger to clear clogs located between the house trap and main stack.

If all else fails, you can try to clear the main drainage stack by running the cable of a hand-crank or drill-powered auger down through the roof vent. Always use extreme caution while working on a ladder or roof.

How to Replace a Main Drain Cleanout Plug

Remove the cleanout plug, using a large wrench. If the plug does not turn out, apply penetrating oil around the edge of the plug, wait 10 minutes, and try again. Place rags and a bucket under fitting opening to catch any water that may be backed up in the line.

Remove stubborn plugs by placing the cutting edge of a cold chisel on the edge of the plug. Strike the chisel with a ball-peen hammer to move plug counterclockwise. If the plug does not turn out, break it into pieces with the chisel and hammer. Remove all broken pieces.

Replace the old plug with a new plug. Apply pipe joint compound to the threads of the replacement plug and screw into the cleanout fitting.

ALTERNATE: Replace the old plug with an expandable rubber plug. A wing nut squeezes the rubber core between two metal plates. The rubber bulges slightly to create a watertight seal.

How to Power-Auger a Floor Drain

Remove the cover from the floor drain using a slotted or Phillips screwdriver. On one wall of the drain bowl you'll see a cleanout plug. Remove the cleanout plug from the drain bowl with your largest channel-type pliers. This cleanout allows you to bypass the trap. If it's stuck, apply penetrating oil to the threads and let it sit a half an hour before trying to free it again. If the wrench won't free it, rent a large pipe wrench from your home center or hardware store. You can also auger through the trap if you have to.

Power Auger Large Lines ▸

If you choose to auger a larger line, you may find yourself opening a cleanout with 10 or 20 vertical feet of waste water behind it. Be careful. The cap may unexpectedly burst open when it's loose enough, spewing noxious waste water uncontrollably over anything in its path, including you! Here are some precautions:

Whenever possible, remove a trap or cleanout close to the top of the backed-up water level. Run your auger through this. Make sure the auger and its electric connections will not get wet should waste water spew forcefully from the cleanout opening. Use the spear tool on the power auger first, to let the water drain out through a smaller hole before widening it with a larger cutting tool. If you are augering through a 3" or 4" cleanout, use three bits: the spear, a small cutter, and then a larger cutter to do the best job.

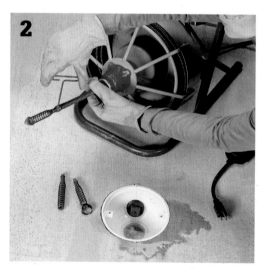

Rent an electric drum auger with at least 50 ft. of ½" cable. The rental company should provide a properly sized, grounded extension cord, heavy leather gloves, and eye protection. The auger should come with a spear tool, cutter tool, and possibly a spring tool suitable for a 2" drainline. Attach the spearhead first (with the machine unplugged).

Wear close-fitting clothing and contain long hair. Place the power auger machine in a dry location within 3 ft. of the drain opening. Plug the tool into a grounded, GFI-protected circuit. Wear eye protection and gloves. Position the footswitch where it is easy to actuate. Make sure the FOR/REV switch is in the Forward position (inset photo). Hand feed the cleaning tool and some cable into the drain or cleanout before turning the machine on.

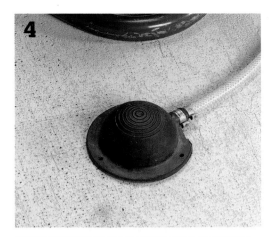

Stationary power augers (as opposed to pistol-grip types) are controlled by a foot pedal called an actuator so you can turn the power on and off hands-free.

With both gloved hands on the cable, depress the foot actuator to start the machine. Gradually push the rotating cable into the drain opening. If the rotation slows or you cannot feed more cable into the drain, pull back on the cable before pushing it forward again. Don't force it. The cable needs to be rotating whenever the motor is running or it can kink and buckle. If the cleaning tool becomes stuck, reverse it, back the tool off the obstruction, and switch back to Forward.

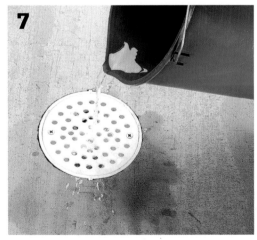

Gradually work through the clog by pulling back on the cable whenever the machine starts to bog down and push it forward again when it gains new momentum. Never let the cable stop turning when the motor is running. When you have broken through the clog or snagged an object, withdraw the cable from the line. Manually pull the cable from the drain line while continuing to run the drum Forward. When the cleaning tool is close to the drain opening, release the foot actuator and let the cable come to a stop before feeding the last 2 or 3 ft. of cable into the drum by hand.

After clearing the drain pipe, run the auger through the trap. Finish cleaning the auger. Wrap Teflon tape clockwise onto the plug threads and replace the plug. Run hot water through a hose from the laundry sink or use a bucket to flush remaining debris through the trap and down the line.

Tips for Replacing Supply Pipes

When replacing old water supply pipes, we recommend that you use Type M rigid copper or PEX. Use ¾" pipe for the main distribution pipes and ½" pipes for the branch lines running to individual fixtures.

For convenience, run parallel hot and cold water pipes, between 3" and 6" apart. Use the straightest, most direct routes possible when planning the layout, because too many bends in the pipe runs can cause significant resistance and reduce water flow.

It is best to remove old pipes that are exposed, but pipes hidden in walls can be left in place unless they interfere with the new supply pipes.

Tools & Materials ▶

Male-threaded adapter	Tee fittings
Full-bone control valve	Eye and ear protection
Copper pipes	Work gloves

Support copper supply pipes at least every 10 ft. along vertical runs and 6 ft. along horizontal runs (check local codes). Always use copper or plastic support materials with copper; never use steel, which can interact with copper and cause corrosion.

How to Replace Water Supply Pipes

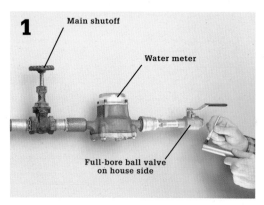

Shut off the water on the street side of the water meter, then disconnect and remove the old water pipes from the house side. Solder a ¾" male-threaded adapter and full-bore control valve to a short length of ¾" copper pipe, then attach this assembly to the house side of the water meter. Extend the ¾" cold-water distribution pipe toward the nearest fixture, which is usually the water heater.

At the water heater, install a ¾" tee fitting in the cold-water distribution pipe. Use two lengths of ¾" copper pipe and a full-bore control valve to run a branch pipe to the water heater. From the outlet opening on the water heater, extend a ¾" hot water distribution pipe. Continue the hot and cold supply lines on parallel routes toward the next group of fixtures in your house.

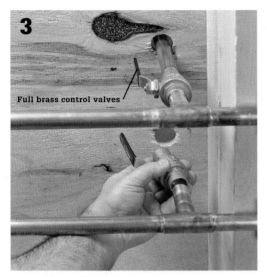

3

Full brass control valves

Establish routes for branch supply lines by drilling holes located in stud cavities. Install tee fittings, then begin the branch lines by installing brass control valves. Branch lines should be made with ¾" pipe if they are supplying more than one fixture; ½" if they are supplying only one fixture.

4

Extend the branch lines to the fixtures. In our project, we ran ¾" vertical branch lines up through the framed chase to the bathroom. Route pipes around obstacles, such as a main waste-vent stack, by using 45° and 90° elbows and short lengths of pipe.

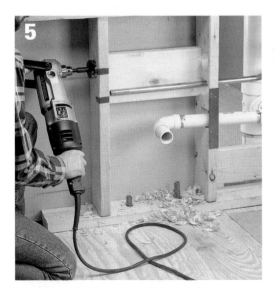

5

Where branch lines run through studs or floor joists, drill holes or cut notches in the framing members, then insert the pipes. For long runs of pipe, you may need to join two or more shorter lengths of pipe, using couplings as you create the runs.

6

Install ¾" to ½" reducing tee fittings and elbows to extend the branch lines to individual fixtures. In our bathroom, we installed a hot and cold stubout for the bathtub and sink, and a cold-water stubout for the toilet. Cap each stubout until your work has been inspected and the wall surfaces have been completed.

Quieting Noisy Pipes

Pipes can make a loud banging noise when faucets are turned off or when valves on washing machines (or other automatic appliances) shut abruptly. The sudden stop of flowing water traps air and creates a shock wave, called water hammer, that slams through the water supply system. Some pipes may knock against wall studs or joists, creating additional noise.

Water hammer can be more than an annoyance. The shockwave can cause damage and eventually failure in pipes and fittings. If a pressure-relief valve on your water heater leaks, it may not be a faulty valve, but a pressure surge in the supply system.

You can eliminate water hammer by installing a simple device called a water hammer arrester in the supply line. Inexpensive point-of-use arresters are small enough to be installed easily near the noisy valve or appliance (the closer the better). They can be positioned horizontally or vertically or at an angle without any change in effectiveness. Unlike with

old-style air chambers, water cannot fill a water hammer arrester, so they should be effective for the life of the system.

Pipes that bang against studs or joists can be quieted by cushioning them with pieces of pipe insulation. Make sure pipe hangers are snug and that pipes are well supported.

Tools & Materials ▸

Reciprocating saw, tubing cutter, or hacksaw	Foam rubber pipe insulation
Propane torch	Utility knife
Pipe wrenches	Teflon tape
Adjustable wrench	Eye and ear protection
Pipe and fittings	Work gloves

Clattering pipes can be a major annoyance, but they also should alert you of a problem with the supply system.

Loose pipes may bang or rub against joist hangers, creating noise. Use pieces of foam rubber pipe insulation to cushion pipes.

A "Sioux strap" holds pipe away from a framing member. Just snap the strap on and drive a nail.

How to Install a Water Hammer Arrester

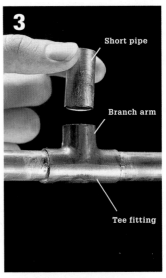

Shut off the water supply and drain the pipes. Use a tubing cutter or reciprocating saw to cut out a section of horizontal pipe long enough for a tee fitting.

Install a tee fitting as close to the valve as possible.

Install a short piece of pipe in the branch arm of the tee fitting. This short pipe will be used to attach a threaded fitting.

Short pipe

Branch arm

Tee fitting

Install a threaded fitting. Use a fitting recommended by the manufacturer of your arrester.

Wrap the threads of the arrester in Teflon tape. Thread the arrester onto the fitting by hand. Tighten by holding the fitting with one adjustable wrench and turning the arrester with the other. Do not overtighten. Turn the water on and check for leaks.

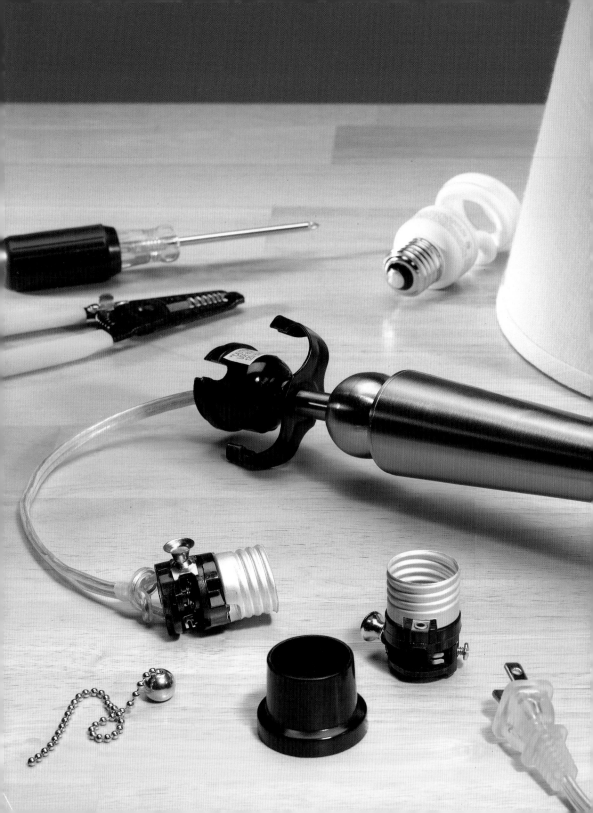

Wiring

In this chapter:

Wiring Tools

To complete the wiring projects shown in this book, you need a few specialty electrical tools as well as a collection of basic hand tools. As with any tool purchase, invest in quality products when you buy tools for electrical work. Keep your tools clean, and sharpen or replace any cutting tools that have dull edges.

The materials used for electrical wiring have changed dramatically in the last 20 years, making it much easier for homeowners to do their own electrical work. The following pages show how to work with the following components for your projects.

Hand tools you'll need for home wiring projects include: Stud finder/laser level (A) for locating framing members and aligning electrical boxes; tape measure (B); a cable ripper (C) for scoring NM sheathing; standard (D) and Phillips (E) screwdrivers; a utility knife (F); side cutters (G) for cutting wires; channel-type pliers (H) for general gripping and crimping; linesman pliers (I) that combine side cutter and gripping jaws; needlenose pliers (J); wire strippers (K) for removing insulation from conductors.

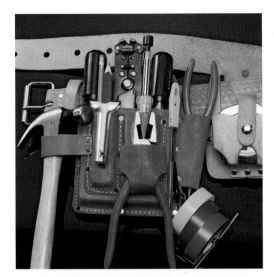

Use a tool belt to keep frequently used tools within easy reach. Electrical tapes in a variety of colors are used for marking wires and for attaching cables to a fish tape.

A fish tape is useful for installing cables in finished wall cavities and for pulling wires through conduit. Products designed for lubrication reduce friction and make it easier to pull cables and wires.

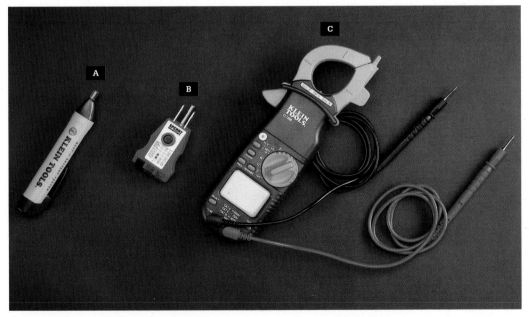

Diagnostic tools for home wiring use include: A touchless circuit tester (A) to safely check wires for current and confirm that circuits are dead; a plug-in tester (B) to check receptacles for correct polarity, grounding, and circuit protection; a multimeter (C) to measure AC/DC voltage, AC/DC current, resistance, capacitance, frequency, and duty cycle (model shown is an auto-ranging digital multimeter with clamp-on jaws that measure through sheathing and wire insulation).

Wiring Safety

Safety should be the primary concern of anyone working with electricity. Although most household electrical repairs are simple and straightforward, always use caution and good judgment when working with electrical wiring or devices. Common sense can prevent accidents.

The basic rule of electrical safety is: Always turn off power to the area or device you are working on. At the main service panel, remove the fuse or shut off the circuit breaker that controls the circuit you are servicing. Then check to make sure the power is off by testing for power with a voltage tester. *TIP: Test a live circuit with the voltage tester to verify that it is working before you rely on it.* Restore power only when the repair or replacement project is complete.

Follow the safety tips shown on these pages. Never attempt an electrical project beyond your skill or confidence level.

Shut power OFF at the main service panel or the main fuse box before beginning any work.

Create a circuit index and affix it to the inside of the door to your main service panel. Update it as needed.

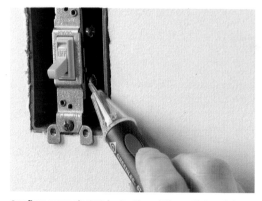

Confirm power is OFF by testing at the outlet, switch, or fixture with a voltage tester.

Use only UL-approved electrical parts or devices. These devices have been tested for safety by Underwriters Laboratories.

Wear rubber-soled shoes while working on electrical projects. On damp floors, stand on a rubber mat or dry wooden boards.

Use fiberglass or wood ladders when making routine household repairs near the service mast.

Extension cords are for temporary use only. Cords must be rated for the intended usage.

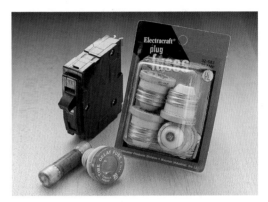

Breakers and fuses must be compatible with the panel manufacturer and match the circuit capacity.

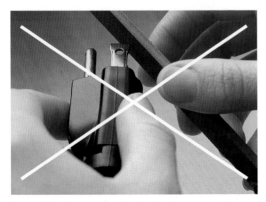

Never alter the prongs of a plug to fit a receptacle. If possible, install a new grounded receptacle.

Do not penetrate walls or ceilings without first shutting off electrical power to the circuits that may be hidden.

Wire & Cable

Wires are made of copper, aluminum, or aluminum covered with a thin layer of copper. Solid copper wires are the best conductors of electricity and are the most widely used. Aluminum and copper-covered aluminum wires require special installation techniques.

A group of two or more wires enclosed in a metal, rubber, or plastic sheath is called a cable (see photo, opposite page). The sheath protects the wires from damage. Conduit also protects wires, but it is not considered a cable.

Individual wires are covered with rubber or plastic vinyl insulation. An exception is a bare copper grounding wire, which does not need an insulation cover. The insulation is color coded (see chart, below left) to identify the wire as a hot wire, a neutral wire, or a grounding wire. New cable sheathing is also color coded to indicate the size of the wires inside. White means #14 wire, yellow means #12 wire, and red means #10 wire.

In most wiring systems installed after 1965, the wires and cables are insulated with plastic vinyl. This type of insulation is very durable and can last as long as the house itself.

Before 1965, wires and cables were insulated with rubber. Rubber insulation has a life expectancy of about 25 years. Old insulation that is cracked or damaged can be reinforced temporarily by wrapping the wire with plastic electrical tape. However, old wiring with cracked or damaged insulation should be inspected by a qualified electrician to make sure it is safe.

Wires must be large enough for the amperage rating of the circuit (see chart, below right). A wire that is too small can become dangerously hot. Wire sizes are categorized according to the American Wire Gauge (AWG) system. To check the size of a wire, use the wire stripper openings of a combination tool (see page 396) as a guide.

Wire Color Chart ▶

WIRE COLOR		FUNCTION
	White or gray	Neutral wire carrying current at zero voltage
	Black	Hot wire carrying current at full voltage
	Red	Hot wire carrying current at full voltage
	White, black markings	Hot wire carrying current at full voltage
	Green	Serves as a bonding pathway
	Bare copper	Serves as a bonding pathway

Individual wires are color-coded to identify their function. In some circuit installations, the white wire serves as a hot wire that carries voltage. If so, this white wire may be labeled with black tape or paint to identify it as a hot wire.

Wire Size Chart ▶

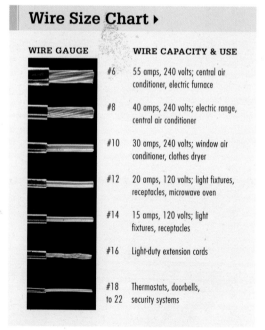

WIRE GAUGE		WIRE CAPACITY & USE
	#6	55 amps, 240 volts; central air conditioner, electric furnace
	#8	40 amps, 240 volts; electric range, central air conditioner
	#10	30 amps, 240 volts; window air conditioner, clothes dryer
	#12	20 amps, 120 volts; light fixtures, receptacles, microwave oven
	#14	15 amps, 120 volts; light fixtures, receptacles
	#16	Light-duty extension cords
	#18 to 22	Thermostats, doorbells, security systems

Wire sizes are categorized by the American Wire Gauge system. The larger the wire size, the smaller the AWG number. The ampacities in this table are for copper wires in NM cable. The ampacity for the same wire in conduit is usually more. The ampacity for aluminum wire is less.

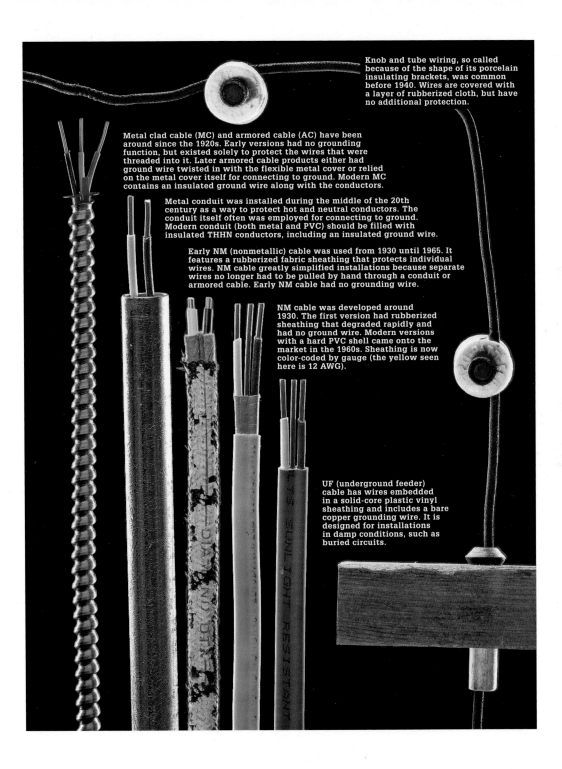

Knob and tube wiring, so called because of the shape of its porcelain insulating brackets, was common before 1940. Wires are covered with a layer of rubberized cloth, but have no additional protection.

Metal clad cable (MC) and armored cable (AC) have been around since the 1920s. Early versions had no grounding function, but existed solely to protect the wires that were threaded into it. Later armored cable products either had ground wire twisted in with the flexible metal cover or relied on the metal cover itself for connecting to ground. Modern MC contains an insulated ground wire along with the conductors.

Metal conduit was installed during the middle of the 20th century as a way to protect hot and neutral conductors. The conduit itself often was employed for connecting to ground. Modern conduit (both metal and PVC) should be filled with insulated THHN conductors, including an insulated ground wire.

Early NM (nonmetallic) cable was used from 1930 until 1965. It features a rubberized fabric sheathing that protects individual wires. NM cable greatly simplified installations because separate wires no longer had to be pulled by hand through a conduit or armored cable. Early NM cable had no grounding wire.

NM cable was developed around 1930. The first version had rubberized sheathing that degraded rapidly and had no ground wire. Modern versions with a hard PVC shell came onto the market in the 1960s. Sheathing is now color-coded by gauge (the yellow seen here is 12 AWG).

UF (underground feeder) cable has wires embedded in a solid-core plastic vinyl sheathing and includes a bare copper grounding wire. It is designed for installations in damp conditions, such as buried circuits.

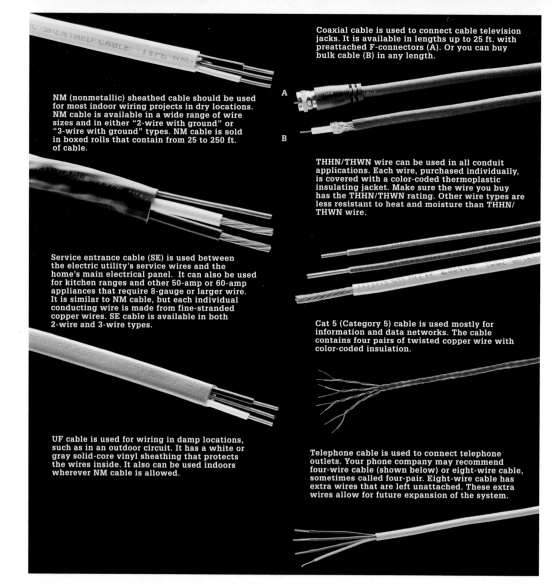

NM (nonmetallic) sheathed cable should be used for most indoor wiring projects in dry locations. NM cable is available in a wide range of wire sizes and in either "2-wire with ground" or "3-wire with ground" types. NM cable is sold in boxed rolls that contain from 25 to 250 ft. of cable.

Service entrance cable (SE) is used between the electric utility's service wires and the home's main electrical panel. It can also be used for kitchen ranges and other 50-amp or 60-amp appliances that require 8-gauge or larger wire. It is similar to NM cable, but each individual conducting wire is made from fine-stranded copper wires. SE cable is available in both 2-wire and 3-wire types.

UF cable is used for wiring in damp locations, such as in an outdoor circuit. It has a white or gray solid-core vinyl sheathing that protects the wires inside. It also can be used indoors wherever NM cable is allowed.

Coaxial cable is used to connect cable television jacks. It is available in lengths up to 25 ft. with preattached F-connectors (A). Or you can buy bulk cable (B) in any length.

A

B

THHN/THWN wire can be used in all conduit applications. Each wire, purchased individually, is covered with a color-coded thermoplastic insulating jacket. Make sure the wire you buy has the THHN/THWN rating. Other wire types are less resistant to heat and moisture than THHN/THWN wire.

Cat 5 (Category 5) cable is used mostly for information and data networks. The cable contains four pairs of twisted copper wire with color-coded insulation.

Telephone cable is used to connect telephone outlets. Your phone company may recommend four-wire cable (shown below) or eight-wire cable, sometimes called four-pair. Eight-wire cable has extra wires that are left unattached. These extra wires allow for future expansion of the system.

▌NM Sheathing Colors

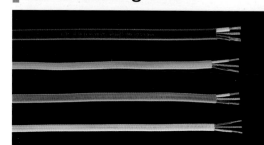

The PVC sheathing for NM cable is coded by color so wiring inspectors can tell what the capacity of the cable is at a glance.

- Black = 6 or 8 AWG conductors
- Yellow = 12 AWG conductors
- Orange = 10 AWG conductors
- White = 14 AWG conductors
- Gray = UF cable (see photo above)

Reading NM (Nonmetallic) Cable

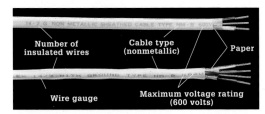

Number of insulated wires — **Cable type (nonmetallic)** — **Paper**

Wire gauge — **Maximum voltage rating (600 volts)**

NM cable is labeled with the number of insulated wires it contains. The bare grounding wire is not counted. For example, a cable marked 14/2 G (or 14/2 WITH GROUND) contains two insulated 14-gauge wires, plus a bare copper grounding wire. Cable marked 14/3 WITH GROUND has three 14-gauge wires plus a grounding wire. NM cable also is stamped with a maximum voltage rating, as determined by Underwriters Laboratories (UL).

Reading Unsheathed, Individual Wire

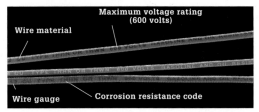

Maximum voltage rating (600 volts)

Wire material

Wire gauge — **Corrosion resistance code**

Unsheathed, individual wires are used for conduit and raceway installations. Wire insulation is coded with letters to indicate resistance to moisture, heat, and gas or oil. Code requires certain letter combinations for certain applications. T indicates thermoplastic insulation. H stands for heat resistance, and two Hs indicate high resistance (up to 194° F). W denotes wire suitable for wet locations. Wire coded with an N is impervious to damage from oil or gas.

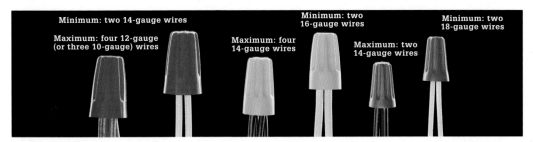

Minimum: two 14-gauge wires
Maximum: four 12-gauge (or three 10-gauge) wires

Minimum: two 16-gauge wires
Maximum: four 14-gauge wires

Maximum: two 14-gauge wires

Minimum: two 18-gauge wires

Use wire connectors rated for the wires you are connecting. Wire connectors are color-coded by size, but the coding scheme varies according to manufacturer. The wire connectors shown above come from one major manufacturer. To ensure safe connections, each connector is rated for both minimum and maximum wire capacity. These connectors can be used to connect both conducting wires and grounding wires. Green wire connectors are used only for grounding wires.

Tips for Working with Wire ▸

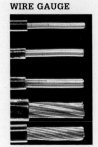

WIRE GAUGE		AMPACITY	MAXIMUM WATTAGE LOAD
	14-gauge	15 amps	1,440 watts (120 volts)
	12-gauge	20 amps	1,920 watts (120 volts)
			3,840 watts (240 volts)
	10-gauge	30 amps	2,880 watts (120 volts)
			5760 watts (240 volts)
	8-gauge	40 amps	7,680 watts (240 volts)
	6-gauge	55 amps	10,560 watts (240 volts)

Wire "ampacity" is a measurement of how much current a wire can carry safely. Ampacity varies by the size of the wires. When installing a new circuit, choose wire with an ampacity rating matching the circuit size. For dedicated appliance circuits, check the wattage rating of the appliance and make sure it does not exceed the maximum wattage load of the circuit. The ampacities in this table are for copper wires in NM cable. The ampacity for the same wire in conduit is usually more. The ampacity for aluminum wire is less.

How to Strip NM Sheathing & Insulation

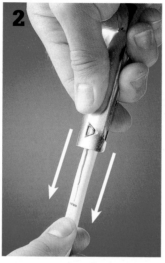

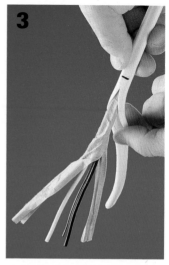

Measure and mark the cable 8 to 10" from the end. Slide the cable ripper onto the cable, and squeeze tool firmly to force the cutting point through the plastic sheathing.

Grip the cable tightly with one hand, and pull the cable ripper toward the end of the cable to cut open the plastic sheathing.

Peel back the plastic sheathing and the paper wrapping from the individual wires.

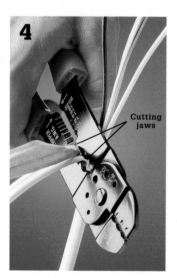

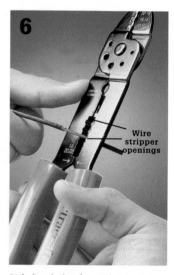

Cut away the excess plastic sheathing and paper wrapping using the cutting jaws of a combination tool.

Cut individual wires as needed using the cutting jaws of the combination tool. Leave a minimum of 3" of wire running past the edge of the box.

Strip insulation for each wire using the stripper openings. Choose the opening that matches the gauge of the wire, and take care not to nick or scratch the ends of the wires.

How to Connect Wires to Screw Terminals

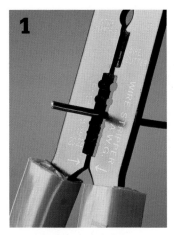

1

Strip about ¾" of insulation from each wire using a combination tool. Choose the stripper opening that matches the gauge of the wire, and then clamp the wire in the tool. Pull the wire firmly to remove plastic insulation.

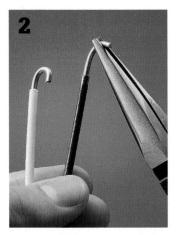

2

Form a C-shaped loop in the end of each wire using a needlenose pliers or the hole of the correct gauge in a pair of wire strippers. The wire should have no scratches or nicks.

3

Hook each wire around the screw terminal so it forms a clockwise loop. Tighten the screw firmly. Insulation should just touch head of screw. Never place the ends of two wires under a single screw terminal. Instead, use a pigtail wire (see page 399).

Cable Staples ▶

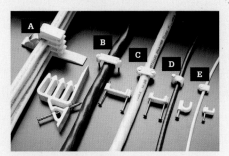

Use plastic cable staples to fasten cables. Choose staples sized to match the cables. Stack-It® staples (A) hold up to four 2-wire cables; ¾" staples (B) for 12/2, 12/3, and all 10-gauge cables; ½" staples (C) for 14/2, 14/3, or 12/2 cables; coaxial staples (D) for anchoring television cables; bell wire staples (E) for attaching telephone cables.

Push-in connectors ▶

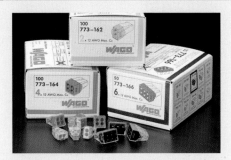

Push-in connectors are a relatively new product for joining wires. Instead of twisting the bare wire ends together, you strip off about ¾" of insulation and insert them into a hole in the connector. The connectors come with two to four holes sized for various gauge wires. These connectors are perfect for inexperienced DIYers, because they do not pull apart like a sloppy twisted connection can.

How to Join Wires with a Wire Connector

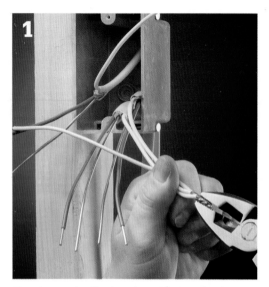

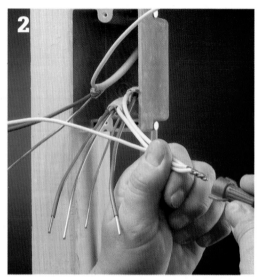

Ensure power is off and test for power. Grasp the wires to be joined in the jaws of a pair of linesman's pliers. The ends of the wires should be flush and they should be parallel and touching. Rotate the pliers clockwise two or three turns to twist the wire ends together.

Twist a wire connector over the ends of the wires. Make sure the connector is the right size (see page 395). Hand-twist the connector as far onto the wires as you can. There should be no bare wire exposed beneath the collar of the connector.

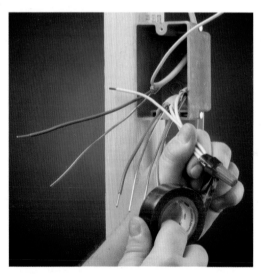

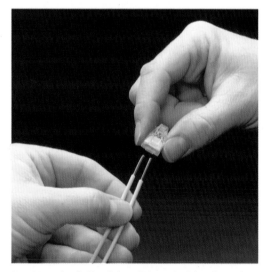

OPTION: Reinforce the joint by wrapping it with electrician's tape. By code, you cannot bind the wire joint with tape only, but it can be used as insurance. Few professional electricians use tape for purposes other than tagging wires for identification.

OPTION: Strip ¾" of insulation off the ends of the wires to be joined, and insert each wire into a push-in connector. Gently tug on each wire to make sure it is secure.

How to Pigtail Wires

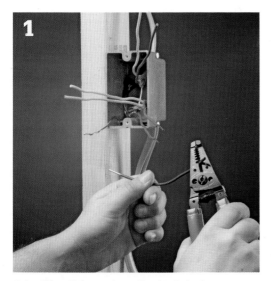

1

Cut a 6" length from a piece of insulated wire the same gauge and color as the wires it will be joining. Strip ¾" of insulation from each end of the insulated wire. *NOTE: Pigtailing is done mainly to avoid connecting multiple wires to one terminal, which is a code violation.*

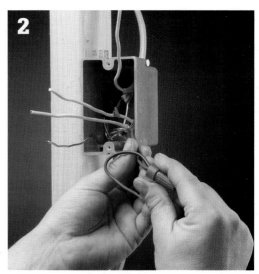

2

Join one end of the pigtail to the wires that will share the connection using a wire nut.

ALTERNATIVE: If you are pigtailing to a grounding screw or grounding clip in a metal box, you may find it easier to attach one end of the wire to the grounding screw before you attach the other end to the other wires.

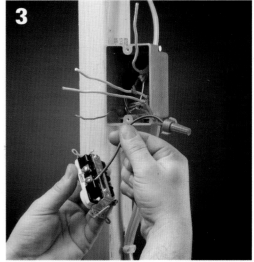

3

Connect the pigtail to the appropriate terminal on the receptacle or switch. Fold the wires neatly and press the fitting into the box.

Electrical Boxes

The National Electrical Code requires that wire connections and cable splices be contained inside an approved metal or plastic box. The box shields framing members and other flammable materials from electrical sparks and protects people from being shocked.

Electrical boxes come in several shapes. Rectangular and square boxes are used for switches and receptacles. Rectangular (2 × 3") boxes are used for single switches or duplex receptacles. Square (4 × 4") boxes are used any time it is convenient for two switches or receptacles to be wired, or "ganged," in one box. Octagonal electrical boxes contain wire connections for ceiling fixtures.

Electrical boxes are available in different depths. A box must be deep enough so a switch or receptacle can be removed or installed easily without crimping and damaging the circuit wires. The box must also be large enough to safely dissipate the heat from wires, switches, and receptacles. This is an important fire safety rule. Replace an undersized box with a larger box using the Electrical Box Fill Chart (right) as a guide. In addition to the maximum box fill allowed by the chart, the area of all wires, taps, and splices should not exceed 75% of the box area. The NEC also says that all electrical boxes must remain accessible. Never cover an electrical box with drywall, paneling, or wallcoverings.

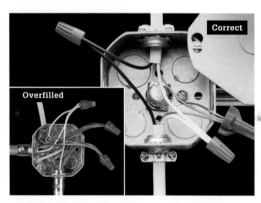

Octagonal boxes usually contain wire connections for ceiling fixtures. Because the ceiling fixture attaches directly to the box, the box should be anchored firmly to a framing member. A properly installed octagonal box can support a ceiling fixture weighing up to 35 pounds. Any box must be covered with a tightly fitting cover plate, and the box must not have open knockouts. Do not overfill the box (inset).

Electrical Box Fill Chart ▸

BOX SIZE AND SHAPE	MAXIMUM NUMBER OF CONDUCTORS PERMITTED (SEE NOTES BELOW)			
Wire Size	10 AWG	8 AWG	14 AWG	12 AWG
Junction Boxes				
4 × 1¼" R or O	5	5	6	5
4 × 1½" R or O	6	5	7	6
4 × 2⅛" R or O	8	7	10	9
4 × 1¼" S	7	6	9	8
4 × 1½" S	8	7	10	9
4 × 2⅛" S	12	10	15	13
4¹¹⁄₁₆ × 1¼" S	10	8	12	11
4¹¹⁄₁₆ × 1½" S	11	9	14	13
4¹¹⁄₁₆ × 2⅛" S	16	14	21	18
Device Boxes				
3 × 2 × 1½"	3	2	3	3
3 × 2 × 2"	4	3	5	4
3 × 2 × 2¼"	4	3	5	4
3 × 2 × 2½"	5	4	6	5
3 × 2 × 2¾"	5	4	7	6
3 × 2 × 3½"	7	6	9	8
4 × 2⅛ × 1½"	4	3	5	4
4 × 2⅛ × 1⅞"	5	4	6	5
4 × 2⅛ × 2⅛"	5	4	7	6

NOTES:
- R = Round; O = Octagonal; S = Square or rectangular
- Each hot or neutral wire entering the box is counted as one conductor.
- Grounding wires are counted as one conductor in total—do not count each one individually.
- Raceway fittings and external cable clamps do not count. Internal cable connectors and straps count as either half or one conductor, depending on type.
- Devices (switches and receptacles mainly) each count as two conductors.
- When calculating total conductors, any nonwire components should be assigned the gauge of the largest wire in the box.
- For wire gauges not shown here, contact your local electrical inspections office.

Common Electrical Boxes

Detachable side

Adapter cover

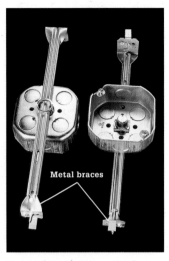

Metal braces

Rectangular boxes are used with wall switches and duplex receptacles. Single-size rectangular boxes (shown above) may have detachable sides that allow them to be ganged together to form double-size boxes.

Square 4 × 4" boxes are large enough for most wiring applications. They are used for cable splices and ganged receptacles or switches. To install one switch or receptacle in a square box, use an adapter cover.

Braced octagonal boxes fit between ceiling joists. The metal braces extend to fit any joist spacing and are nailed or screwed to framing members.

Foam gasket

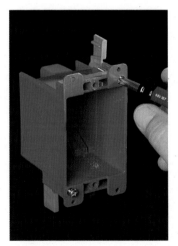

Outdoor boxes have sealed seams and foam gaskets to guard a switch or receptacle against moisture. Corrosion-resistant coatings protect all metal parts. Code-compliant models include a watertight hood that protects even when the outlet is in use.

Old work boxes can be installed to upgrade older boxes or to allow you to add new additional receptacles and switches. One type (above) has built-in clamps that tighten against the inside of a wall and hold the box in place.

Plastic boxes are common in new construction. The box may include preattached nails for anchoring it to framing members. Wall switches must have grounding screws if installed in plastic boxes.

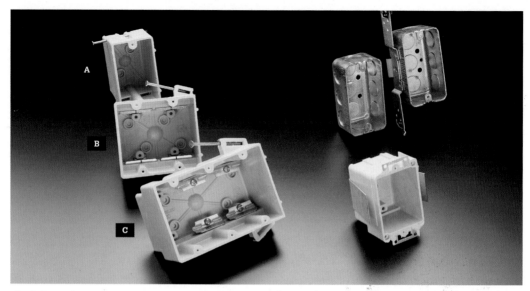

Plastic boxes 3½"-deep with preattached mounting nails are used for any wiring project protected by finished walls. Common styles include single-gang (A), double-gang (B), and triple-gang (C). Double-gang and triple-gang boxes require internal cable clamps. Metal boxes should be used for exposed indoor wiring, such as conduit installations in an unfinished basement. Metal boxes also can be used for wiring that will be covered by finished walls. Plastic retrofit boxes are used when a new switch or receptacle must fit inside a finished wall. Use internal cable clamps.

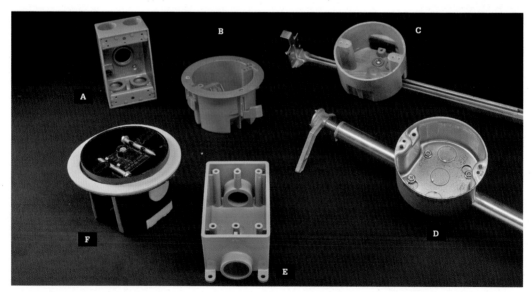

Additional electrical boxes include cast aluminum box (A) for use with outdoor fixtures, including receptacles that are wired through metal conduit (these must have in-use covers if they house receptacles); old work ceiling box (B) used for light fixtures; light-duty ceiling fan box (C) with brace that spans ceiling joists; heavy-duty retrofit ceiling fan box (D) designed for retrofit; PVC box (E) for use with PVC conduit in indoor or outdoor setting; and vapor-proof ceiling box with foam gasket (F).

Box Specifications ▸

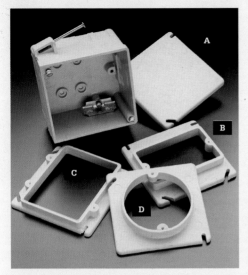

High-quality nonmetallic boxes are rigid and don't contort easily. A variety of adapter plates are available, including junction box cover plate (A), single-gang (B), double-gang (C), and light fixture (D). Adapter plates come in several thicknesses to match different wall constructions.

Boxes larger than 2 × 4" and all retrofit boxes must have internal cable clamps. After installing cables in the box, tighten the cable clamps over the cables so they are gripped firmly, but not so tightly that the cable sheathing is crushed.

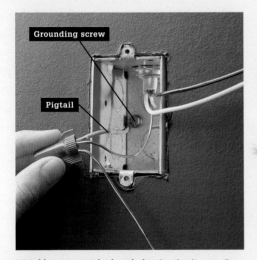

Grounding screw

Pigtail

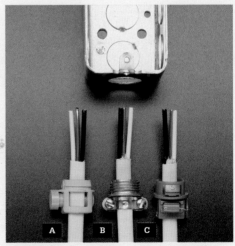

A   B   C

Metal boxes must be bonded to the circuit grounding system. Connect the circuit grounding wires to the box with a green insulated pigtail wire and wire connector (as shown) or with a grounding clip.

Cables entering a metal box must be clamped. A variety of clamps are available, including plastic clamps (A, C) and threaded metal clamps (B).

Nonmetallic Boxes

Nonmetallic electrical boxes have taken over much of the do-it-yourself market. Most are sold prefitted with installation hardware—from metal wings to 10d common nails attached at the perfect angle for a nail-in box. The bulk of the nonmetallic boxes sold today are inexpensive blue PVC. You can also purchase heavier-duty fiberglass or thermoset plastic models that provide a nonmetallic option for installing heavier fixtures such as ceiling fans and chandeliers.

In addition to cost and availability, nonmetallic boxes hold a big advantage over metal boxes in that their resistance to conducting electricity will prevent a sparking short circuit if a hot wire contacts the box. Nonmetallic boxes generally are not approved for exposed areas, where they may be susceptible to damage. Their lack of rigidity also allows them to compress or distort, which can reduce the interior capacity beyond code minimums or make outlets difficult to attach.

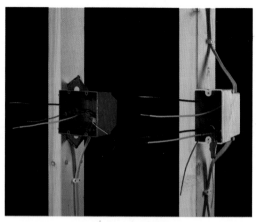

Low cost is the primary reason that blue PVC nail-in boxes are so popular. Not only are they inexpensive, they also feature built-in cable clamps so you may not need to buy extra hardware to install them. The standard PVC nail-in box is prefitted with a pair of 10d common nails for attaching to exposed wall studs. These boxes, often called handy boxes, are too small to be of much use (see fill chart, page 400).

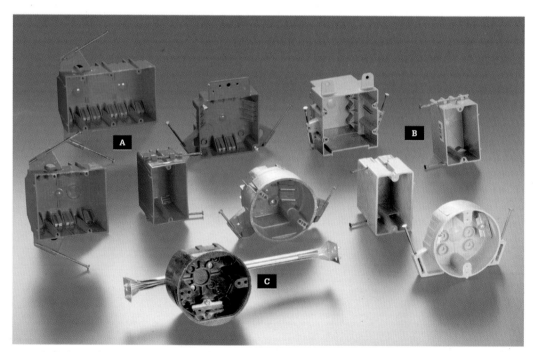

Nonmetallic boxes for home use include: Single-gang, double-gang, triple gang, and quad boxes (A); thermoset and fiberglass boxes for heavier duty (B); and round fixture boxes (C) for ceiling installation (nail-in and with integral metal bracket).

Working With Nonmetallic Boxes

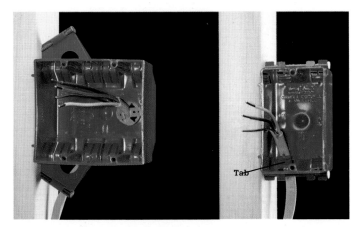

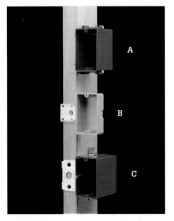

Do not break off the tabs that cover cable entry holes in plastic boxes. These are not knockouts as you would find in metal boxes. In single-gang boxes (right), the pressure from the tab is sufficient to secure the cable as long as it enters with sheathing intact and is stapled no more than 8" from the box. On larger boxes (left), you will find traditional knockouts intended to be used with plastic cable clamps that resemble metal cable clamps. Use these for heavier gauge cable and cable with more than three wires.

Nail-in boxes (A) are prefitted with 10d nails that are attached perpendicular to the face of single-gang boxes and at an inward angle for better gripping power on larger boxes. Side-mount boxes (B) feature a nailing plate that is attached to the front of the stud to automatically create the correct setback; adjustable side-mount boxes (C) are installed the same way but can be moved on the bracket.

Distortion can occur in nonmetallic boxes when nails or other fasteners are overdriven or installed at improper angles, or when the semiflexible boxes are compressed into improperly sized or shaped openings. This can reduce the box capacity and prevent devices and faceplates from fitting.

Integral ribs cast into many nonmetallic boxes are used to register the box against the wall studs so the front edges of the box will be flush with the wall surface after drywall is installed. Most are set for ½" drywall, but if your wall will be a different thickness you may be able to find a box with corresponding ribs. Otherwise, use a piece of the wallcovering material as a reference.

Installing Pop-in Retrofit Boxes

Attaching an electrical box to a wall stud during new construction is relatively easy. The task becomes complicated, however, when you're working in finished walls during remodeling or repair. In most cases, it's best to use an electronic stud finder, make a large cutout in the wall, and attach a new box directly to a framing member or bracing (and then replace and refinish the wall materials). But there are occasions when this isn't possible or practical and you just need to retrofit an electrical box without making a large hole in the wall. You also may find that an older switch or receptacle box is too shallow to accommodate a new dimmer or GFCI safely. These situations call for a pop-in retrofit box (sometimes called an "old work" box).

A pop-in box typically has wings, tabs, or brackets that are drawn tight against the wall surface on the wall cavity side, holding the box in place. It can be made either of metal or plastic.

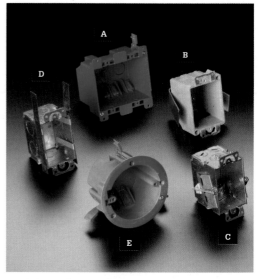

Pop-in boxes for remodeling come in a variety of styles. For walls, they include plastic retrofit boxes with flip-out wings (A), metal or plastic boxes with compression tabs or brackets (B), metal retrofit boxes with flip-out wings (C), and metal boxes with bendable brackets, also known as F-straps, (D). For ceilings, plastic fixture boxes with flip-out wings (E) are available.

Tools & Materials ▸

Screwdriver	Reciprocating saw or hacksaw
Pencil	Template (if provided)
String	Plastic or metal pop-in box
Electrical tape	Eye protection

How to Replace an Electrical Box

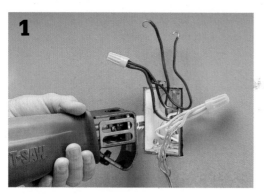

To install a dimmer switch or GFCI receptacle, you may have to replace an old, overcrowded box. Shut off power and remove the old switch or receptacle. Identify the location of nails holding the box to the framing member and cut the nails with a hacksaw or reciprocating saw with a metal blade inserted between the box and the stud.

Bind the cable ends together and attach string in case they fall into the wall cavity when the old box is removed. Disconnect the cable clamps and slide the old box out. Install a new pop-in box (see next page).

How to Install a Pop-in Box

1

Use a template to trace a cutout for the box at the intended location. If no template is provided, press the pop-in box against the wall surface and trace its front edges (but not the tabs on the top and bottom).

2

Puncture the wallboard with the tip of a wallboard saw or by drilling a small hole inside the lines, and make the cutout for the box.

3

Pull NM cable through a knockout in the box (no cable clamp is required with a plastic box; just be sure not to break the pressure tab that holds the cable in place).

4

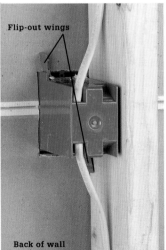

Flip-out wings

Back of wall

Insert the box into the cutout so the tabs are flush against the wall surface. Tighten the screws that cause the flip-out wings to pivot (right) until the box is held firmly in place. Connect the switch or receptacle that the box will house.

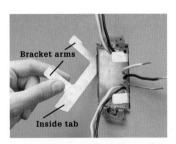

Bracket arms

Inside tab

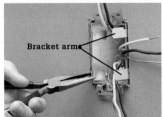

Bracket arm

VARIATION: Feed cable into the new box and secure it in the opening after clamping the cables. With this pop-in box, bracket arms are inserted at the sides of the box (top) and then bent around the front edges to secure the box in the opening (bottom).

Electrical Panels

Every home has a main panel that distributes electrical current to the individual circuits. The main panel may be found in the basement, garage, utility area, or on an exterior wall and can be identified by its metal casing. Before making any repair to your electrical system, you must shut off power to the correct circuit at the main panel or at the subpanel where the circuit begins. Every circuit in every panel should be labeled (see page 390) so circuits can be identified easily.

Panels vary in appearance, depending on the age of the system. Very old wiring may operate on 30-amp service that has only two circuits. New homes can have up to 400-amp service with 30 or more circuits. Find the size of the service by reading the amperage rating printed on the main fuse block or main circuit breakers.

Regardless of age, all panels have fuses or circuit breakers (see page 412) that protect each circuit from overloads. In general, older service panels use fuses, while newer panels use circuit breakers.

In addition to the main panel, your electrical system may have one or more subpanels that protect some of the circuits in the home. A subpanel has its own circuit breakers or fuses.

The subpanel resembles the main service panel but is usually smaller. It may be located near the main panel, or it may be found near the areas served by the new circuits. Garages and basements that have been updated often have their own subpanels. If your home has subpanels, make sure that their circuits are indexed correctly.

When handling fuses or circuit breakers, make sure the area around the panel is dry. Never remove the protective cover on the panel. After turning off a circuit to make electrical repairs, remember to always test the circuit for power before touching any wires.

200-amp Service Panel

The main panel is the heart of your wiring system. As our demand for household energy has increased, the panels have also grown in capacity. Today, a 200-amp panel is often installed in new construction. Many homebuilders are installing dual 200-amp panels to deliver 400 amps to larger houses. A pair of 200-amp panels is much cheaper than one 400-amp panel.

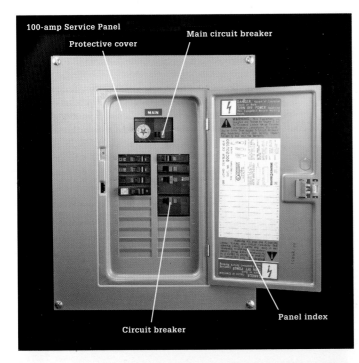

100-amp Service Panel

Protective cover

Main circuit breaker

MAIN

Circuit breaker

Panel index

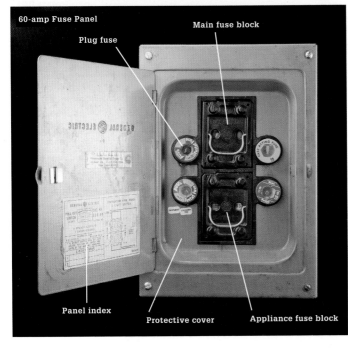

60-amp Fuse Panel

Plug fuse

Main fuse block

GENERAL ELECTRIC

Panel index

Protective cover

Appliance fuse block

A circuit breaker panel providing 100 amps or more of current is common in wiring systems installed during the 1960s and later. A circuit breaker panel is housed in a gray metal cabinet that contains two rows of individual circuit breakers. You can determine service size by reading the amperage rating of the main circuit breakers. In systems rated 200 amps and below, the main breaker is often located in the main panel, but it may be in a separate cabinet located elsewhere.

Larger new homes may have 300- or 400-amp service. These systems usually have two main circuit breakers in the main panel and at least one subpanel.

A 100-amp service panel is now the minimum standard for all new housing. It is adequate for a medium-sized house with no more than three major electric appliances. However, larger houses with more electrical appliances require a service panel that provides 150 amps or more.

To shut off power to individual circuits in a circuit breaker panel, flip the lever on the appropriate circuit breaker to the OFF position. To shut off the power to the entire house, turn the main circuit breakers to the OFF position.

Some older homes may still have a 60-amp fuse panel. It usually is housed in a gray metal cabinet that contains four individual plug fuses, plus one or two pull-out fuse blocks that hold cartridge fuses. A 60-amp panel is considered undersized by current standards. The system should be upgraded for both convenience and safety. Insurance companies and mortgage lenders may require a complete electrical system upgrade before issuing a homeowner insurance policy or approving mortgage financing.

To shut off power to a circuit, carefully unscrew the plug fuse, touching only its insulated rim. To shut off power to the entire house, hold the handle of the main fuse block and pull sharply to remove it. Major appliance circuits are controlled with another cartridge fuse block. Shut off the appliance circuit by pulling out this fuse block.

Fuses & Circuit Breakers

Fuses and circuit breakers are safety devices designed to protect the electrical system from short circuits and overloads. Fuses and circuit breakers are located in the main service panel and in subpanels.

Most service panels installed before 1965 rely on fuses to protect individual circuits. Screw-in plug fuses protect 120-volt circuits that power lights and receptacles. Cartridge fuses protect 240-volt appliance circuits and the main shutoff of the service panel.

Inside each fuse is a current-carrying metal alloy ribbon. If a circuit is overloaded, the metal ribbon melts and stops the current flow. A fuse must match the amperage rating of the circuit. Never replace a fuse with one that has a larger amperage rating.

In most service panels installed after 1965, circuit breakers protect individual circuits. Single-pole circuit breakers protect 120-volt circuits, and double-pole circuit breakers protect 240-volt circuits. Amperage ratings for circuit breakers range from 15 to 100 amps.

Each circuit breaker has a permanent metal strip that heats up and bends when current passes through it. If a circuit is overloaded, the metal strip inside the breaker bends enough to "trip" the switch and stop the flow of power. Circuit breakers are listed to trip twice. After the second trip they weaken and tend to nuisance trip at lower currents. Replace breakers that have tripped more than twice—they may fail.

When a fuse blows or a circuit breaker trips, it is usually because there are too many light fixtures and plug-in appliances drawing power through the circuit. Move some of the plug-in appliances to another circuit, and then replace the fuse or reset the breaker. If the fuse blows or the breaker trips again immediately, there may be a short circuit in the system. Call a licensed electrician if you suspect a short circuit.

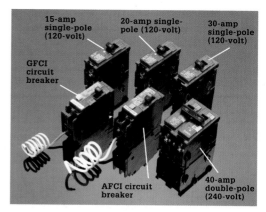

Circuit breakers are found in the majority of panels installed since the 1960s. Single-pole breakers control 120-volt circuits. Double-pole breakers rated for 20 to 60 amps control 240-volt circuits. Ground-fault circuit interrupter (GFCI) provides protection from shocks. Arc-fault circuit interrupter (AFCI) breakers provide protection from fire-causing arcs for the entire circuit.

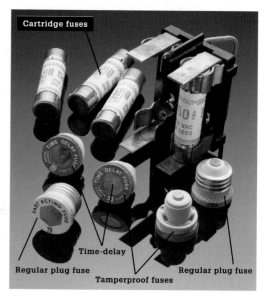

Fuses are used in older panels. Plug fuses usually control 120-volt circuits rated for 15, 20, or 30 amps. Tamper-proof plug fuses have threads that fit only matching sockets, making it impossible to install a wrong-sized fuse. Time-delay fuses absorb temporary heavy power loads without blowing. Cartridge fuses control 240-volt circuits and range from 30 to 100 amps.

Old-style fuse boxes can accept modern "s" type fuses if you use an Edison adapter. Be sure to screw the fuse into the adapter first, and then screw the assembly into the socket.

How to Identify & Replace a Blown Plug Fuse

Locate the blown fuse at the panel. If the metal ribbon inside is cleanly melted (left), the circuit was overloaded. If window is discolored (right), there was a short circuit.

Unscrew the fuse, being careful to touch only the insulated rim of the fuse. Replace it with a fuse that has the same amperage rating.

How to Remove, Test & Replace a Cartridge Fuse

Remove cartridge fuses by gripping the handle of the fuse block and pulling sharply.

Remove the individual cartridge fuses from the block using a fuse puller.

Test each fuse using a continuity tester. If the tester glows, the fuse is good. If not, install a new fuse with the same amperage rating.

How to Reset a Circuit Breaker

Open the service panel and locate the tripped breaker. The lever on the tripped breaker will be either in the OFF position or in a position between ON and OFF.

Reset the tripped circuit breaker by pressing the circuit breaker lever all the way to the OFF position and then pressing it to the ON position.

Test AFCI and GFCI circuit breakers by pushing the TEST button. The breaker should trip to the OFF position. If not, the breaker is faulty and must be replaced.

Connecting Circuit Breakers

The last step in a wiring project is connecting circuits at the breaker panel. After this is done, the work is ready for the final inspection.

Circuits are connected at the main panel, if it has enough open slots, or at a circuit breaker subpanel (see pages 410 to 411). When working at a subpanel, make sure the feeder breaker at the main panel has been turned off, and test for power (see photo, right) before touching any parts in the subpanel.

Make sure the circuit breaker amperage does not exceed the ampacity of the circuit wires you are connecting to it. Also be aware that circuit breaker styles and installation techniques vary according to manufacturer. Use breakers made by the panel manufacturer. You should install AFCI circuit breakers for most 15- and 20-amp, 120-volt circuits inside the home.

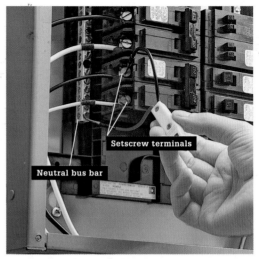

Setscrew terminals

Neutral bus bar

Tools & Materials ▸

Screwdriver	Circuit tester
Hammer	Pliers
Pencil	Cable clamps
Combination tool	Single- and double-pole
Cable ripper	AFCI circuit breakers

Test for current before touching any parts inside a circuit breaker panel. With the main breaker turned off but all other breakers turned on, touch one probe of a neon tester to the neutral bus bar, and touch the other probe to each setscrew on one of the double-pole breakers (not the main breaker). If the tester does not light for either setscrew, it is safe to work in the panel. *NOTE: Touchless circuit testers are preferred in most situations where you are testing for current because they're safer. But in some instances you'll need a tester with individual probes to properly check for current.*

How to Connect Circuit Breakers

1

Shut off the main circuit breaker in the main circuit breaker panel (if you are working in a subpanel, shut off the feeder breaker in the main panel). Remove the panel cover plate, taking care not to touch the parts inside the panel. Test for power (photo, top).

2

Open a knockout in the side of the circuit breaker panel using a screwdriver and hammer. Attach a cable clamp to the knockout.

3

Hold the cable across the front of the panel near the knockout, and mark the sheathing about ½" inside the edge of the panel. Strip the cable from the marked line to the end using a cable ripper. (There should be 18" to 24" of excess cable.) Insert the cable through the clamp and into the service panel, and then tighten the clamp.

Bend the bare copper grounding wire around the inside edge of the panel to an open setscrew terminal on the grounding bus bar. Insert the wire into the opening on the bus bar, and tighten the setscrew. Fold excess wire around the inside edge of the panel.

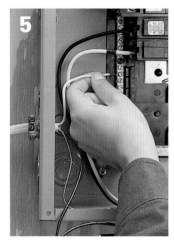

For 120-volt circuits, bend the white circuit wire around the outside of the panel to an open setscrew terminal on the neutral bus bar. Clip away excess wire, and then strip ½" of insulation from the wire using a combination tool. Insert the wire into the terminal opening, and tighten the setscrew.

Strip ½" of insulation from the end of the black circuit wire. Insert the wire into the setscrew terminal on a new single-pole circuit breaker, and tighten the setscrew.

Slide one end of the circuit breaker onto the guide hook, and then press it firmly against the bus bar until it snaps into place. (Breaker installation may vary, depending on the manufacturer.) Fold excess black wire around the inside edge of the panel.

120/240-volt circuits (top): Connect red and black wires to the double-pole breaker. Connect white wire to the neutral bus bar, and the grounding wire to grounding bus bar. For 240-volt circuits (bottom), attach white and black wires to the double-pole breaker, tagging white wire with black tape. There is no neutral bus bar connection on this circuit.

Remove the appropriate breaker tab on the panel cover plate to make room for the new circuit breaker. A single-pole breaker requires one tab, while a double-pole breaker requires two tabs. Reattach the cover plate, and label the new circuit on the panel index.

Wall Switches

An average wall switch is turned on and off more than 1,000 times each year. Because switches receive constant use, wire connections can loosen and switch parts gradually wear out. If a switch no longer operates smoothly, it must be replaced.

The methods for replacing a switch vary slightly, depending on the switch type and its location along an electrical circuit. When working on a switch, use the photographs on pages 418 to 429 to identify your switch type and its wiring configuration. Individual switch styles may vary from manufacturer to manufacturer, but the basic switch types are universal.

It is possible to replace most ordinary wall switches with a specialty switch, such as a timer switch or an electronic switch. When installing a specialty switch, make sure it is compatible with the wiring configuration and size of the switch box. Notice: Two changes in the NEC affect how new switch wiring should be installed. These changes do not affect existing switch wiring. The pictures and instructions in this book about replacing

existing switches show wiring that does not comply with these new requirements. This is because you will probably see non-compliant wiring for many years to come. Pictures and instructions about installing new switch wiring show wiring that complies with these new requirements.

One change requires that a wire with white insulation should not supply current to a light or receptacle, even when the wire is marked as hot. A black or red colored wire should supply current to the device. A white colored wire, marked as hot, may supply current to the switch.

The other change requires that a neutral wire be available at switch boxes. An exception allows you to ignore this requirement if the switch box is accessible from above or below, such as from a basement, crawlspace, or attic. This new requirement is intended to allow easier installation of devices, such as intelligent switch controllers, that need power for controller operation.

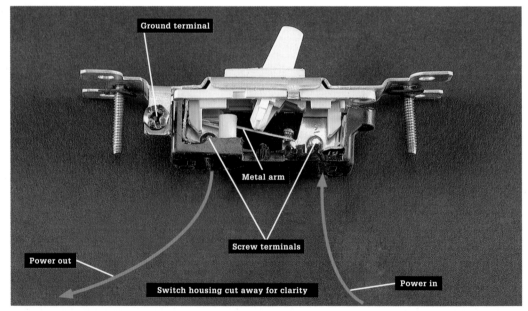

A typical wall switch has a movable metal arm that opens and closes the electrical circuit. When the switch is ON, the arm completes the circuit and power flows between the screw terminals and through the black hot wire to the light fixture. When the switch is OFF, the arm lifts away to interrupt the circuit, and no power flows. Switch problems can occur if the screw terminals are not tight or if the metal arm inside the switch wears out. *NOTE: The switch above has had part of its housing removed so the interior workings can be seen. Switches or fixtures that are not in original condition should never be installed.*

Rotary snap switches are found in many installations completed between 1900 and 1920. The handle is twisted clockwise to turn light on and off. The switch is enclosed in a ceramic housing.

Push-button switches were widely used from 1920 until about 1940. Many switches of this type are still in operation. Reproductions of this switch type are available for restoration projects.

Toggle switches were introduced in the 1930s. This early design has a switch mechanism that is mounted in a ceramic housing sealed with a layer of insulating paper.

Toggle switches were improved during the 1950s and are now the most commonly used type. This switch type was the first to use a sealed plastic housing that protects the inner switch mechanism from dust and moisture.

Mercury switches became common in the early 1960s. They conduct electrical current by means of a sealed vial of mercury. No longer manufactured for home use, old mercury switches are considered a hazardous waste.

Electronic motion-sensor switches have an infrared eye that senses movement and automatically turns on lights when a person enters a room. Motion-sensor switches can provide added security against intruders.

Types of Wall Switches

Wall switches are available in three general types. To reconnect or replace a switch, it is important to identify its type.

Single-pole switches are used to control a set of lights from one location. Three-way switches are used to control a set of lights from two different locations and are always installed in pairs. Four-way switches are used in combination with a pair of three-way switches to control a set of lights from three or more locations.

Identify switch types by counting the terminals. Single-pole switches have two screw terminals, three-way switches have three screw terminals, and four-way switches have four. Most switches include a grounding screw terminal, which is identified by its green color.

When replacing a switch, choose a new switch that has the same number of screw terminals as the old one. The location of the screws on the switch body varies depending on the manufacturer, but these differences will not affect the switch operation.

Whenever possible, connect switches using the screw terminals rather than push-in fittings. Some specialty switches (pages 94 to 97) have wire leads instead of screw terminals. They are connected to circuit wires with wire connectors.

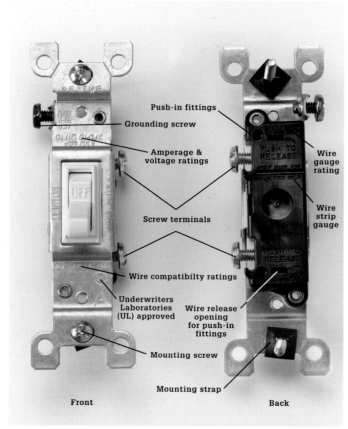

Push-in fittings
Grounding screw
Amperage & voltage ratings
Screw terminals
Wire compatibilty ratings
Underwriters Laboratories (UL) approved
Wire release opening for push-in fittings
Mounting screw
Mounting strap

Wire gauge rating
Wire strip gauge

Front

Back

A wall switch is connected to circuit wires with screw terminals or with push-in fittings on the back of the switch. A switch may have a stamped strip gauge that indicates how much insulation must be stripped from the circuit wires to make the connections.

The switch body is attached to a metal mounting strap that allows it to be mounted in an electrical box. Several rating stamps are found on the strap and on the back of the switch. The abbreviation UL or UND. LAB. INC. LIST means that the switch meets the safety standards of the Underwriters Laboratories. Switches also are stamped with maximum voltage and amperage ratings. Standard wall switches are rated 15A or 125V. Voltage ratings of 110, 120, and 125 are considered to be identical for purposes of identification.

For standard wall switch installations, choose a switch that has a wire gauge rating of #12 or #14. For wire systems with solid-core copper wiring, use only switches marked COPPER, CU, or CO/ALR. For aluminum wiring, use only switches marked CO/ALR. Note that while CO/ALR switches and receptacles are approved by the National Electrical Code for use with aluminum wiring, the Consumer Products Safety Commission does not recommend using these. Switches and receptacles marked AL/CU can no longer be used with aluminum wiring, according to the National Electrical Code.

Single-Pole Wall Switches

A single-pole switch is the most common type of wall switch. It has ON-OFF markings on the switch lever and is used to control a set of lights, an appliance, or a receptacle from a single location. A single-pole switch has two screw terminals and a grounding screw. When installing a single-pole switch, check to make sure the ON marking shows when the switch lever is in the up position.

In a correctly wired single-pole switch, a hot circuit wire is attached to each screw terminal. However, the color and number of wires inside the switch box will vary, depending on the location of the switch along the electrical circuit.

If two cables enter the box, then the switch lies in the middle of the circuit. In this installation, both of the hot wires attached to the switch are black.

If only one cable enters the box, then the switch lies at the end of the circuit. In this installation (sometimes called a switch loop), one of the hot wires is black, but the other hot wire usually is white. A white hot wire should be coded with black tape or paint.

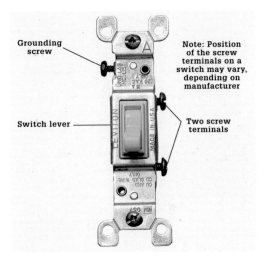

Grounding screw

Switch lever

Note: Position of the screw terminals on a switch may vary, depending on manufacturer

Two screw terminals

A single-pole switch is essentially an interruption in the black power supply wire that is opened or closed with the toggle. Single-pole switches are the simplest of all home wiring switches.

Typical Single-Pole Switch Installations

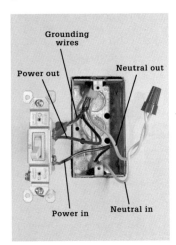

Grounding wires

Power out

Neutral out

Power in

Neutral in

Grounding wire

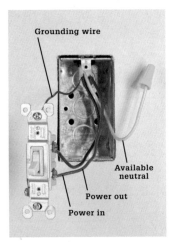

Grounding wire

Available neutral

Power out

Power in

Two cables enter the box when a switch is located in the middle of a circuit. Each cable has a white and a black insulated wire, plus a bare copper grounding wire. The black wires are hot and are connected to the screw terminals on the switch. The white wires are neutral and are joined together with a wire connector. Grounding wires are pigtailed to the switch.

Old method: One cable enters the box when a switch is located at the end of a circuit. In this installation, both of the insulated wires are hot. The white wire should be labeled with black tape or paint to identify it as a hot wire. The grounding wire is connected to the switch grounding screw.

Code change: In new switch wiring, the white wire should not supply current to the switched device and a separate neutral wire should be available in the switch box.

Three-Way Wall Switches

Three-way switches have three screw terminals and do not have ON-OFF markings. Three-way switches are always installed in pairs and are used to control a set of lights from two locations.

One of the screw terminals on a three-way switch is darker than the others. This screw is the common screw terminal. The position of the common screw terminal on the switch body may vary, depending on the manufacturer. Before disconnecting a three-way switch, always label the wire that is connected to the common screw terminal. It must be reconnected to the common screw terminal on the new switch.

The two lighter-colored screw terminals on a three-way switch are called the traveler screw terminals. The traveler terminals are interchangeable, so there is no need to label the wires attached to them.

Because three-way switches are installed in pairs, it sometimes is difficult to determine which of the switches is causing a problem. The switch that receives greater use is more likely to fail, but you may need to inspect both switches to find the source of the problem.

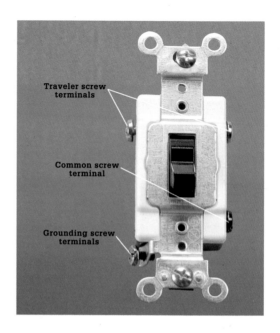

Traveler screw terminals

Common screw terminal

Grounding screw terminals

Typical Three-Way Switch Installation

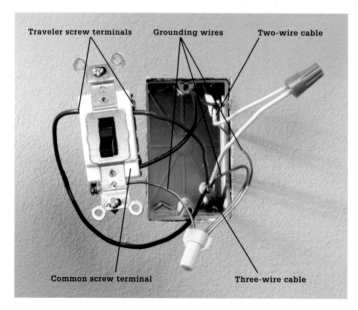

Traveler screw terminals   Grounding wires   Two-wire cable

Common screw terminal   Three-wire cable

Two cables enter the box: one cable has two wires, plus a bare copper grounding wire; the other cable has three wires, plus a ground. The black wire from the two-wire cable is connected to the dark common screw terminal. The red and black wires from the three-wire cable are connected to the traveler screw terminals. The white neutral wires are joined together with a wire connector, and the grounding wires are pigtailed to the grounded metal box.

How to Replace a Three-Way Wall Switch

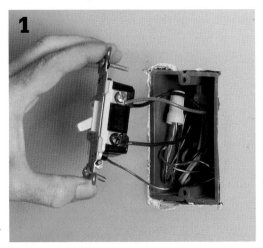

1

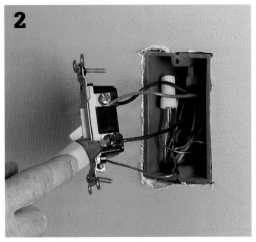

2

Turn off the power to the switch at the panel, and then remove the switch cover plate and mounting screws. Holding the mounting strap carefully, pull the switch from the box. Be careful not to touch the bare wires or screw terminals until they have been tested for power. *NOTE: If you are installing a new switch circuit, you must provide a neutral conductor at the switch.*

Test for power by touching one probe of the circuit tester to the grounded metal box or to the bare copper grounding wire and touching the other probe to each screw terminal. Tester should not glow. If it does, there is still power entering the box. Return to the panel, and turn off the correct circuit.

3

Common screw terminal

4

Common screw terminal

5

Locate the dark common screw terminal, and use masking tape to label the "common" wire attached to it. Disconnect wires and remove switch. Test the switch for continuity. If it tests faulty, buy a replacement. Inspect wires for nicks and scratches. If necessary, clip damaged wires and strip them.

Connect the common wire to the dark common screw terminal on the switch. On most three-way switches, the common screw terminal is black. Or it may be labeled with the word COMMON stamped on the back of the switch. Reconnect the grounding screw, and connect it to the circuit grounding wires with a pigtail.

Connect the remaining two circuit wires to the screw terminals. These wires are interchangeable and can be connected to either screw terminal. Carefully tuck the wires into the box. Remount the switch, and attach the cover plate. Turn on the power at the panel.

Four-Way Wall Switches

Four-way switches have four screw terminals and do not have ON-OFF markings. Four-way switches are always installed between a pair of three-way switches. This switch combination makes it possible to control a set of lights from three or more locations. Four-way switches are common in homes where large rooms contain multiple living areas, such as a kitchen opening into a dining room. Switch problems in a four-way installation can be caused by loose connections or worn parts in a four-way switch or in one of the three-way switches (previous page).

In a typical installation, there will be a pair of three-wire cables that enter the box for the four-way switch. With most switches, the white and red wires from one cable should be attached to the bottom or top pair of screw terminals, and the white and red wires from the other cable should be attached to the remaining pair of screw terminals. However, not all switches are configured the same way, and wiring configurations in the box may vary, so always study the wiring diagram that comes with the switch.

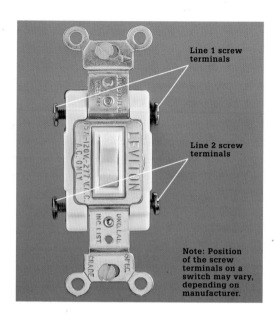

Line 1 screw terminals

Line 2 screw terminals

Note: Position of the screw terminals on a switch may vary, depending on manufacturer.

Typical Four-Way Switch Installation

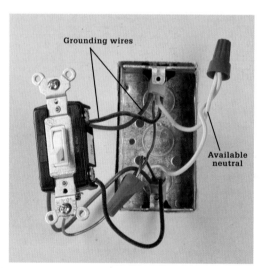

Grounding wires

Available neutral

Four wires are connected to a four-way switch. The red and white wires from one cable are attached to the top pair of screw terminals, while the red and white wires from the other cable are attached to the bottom screw terminals. In new switch wiring, the white wire should not supply current to the switched device, and a separate neutral wire should be available in the switch box.

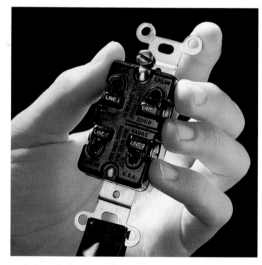

Switch variation: Some four-way switches have a wiring guide stamped on the back to help simplify installation. For the switch shown above, one pair of color-matched circuit wires will be connected to the screw terminals marked LINE 1, while the other pair of wires will be attached to the screw terminals marked LINE 2.

How to Replace a Four-Way Wall Switch

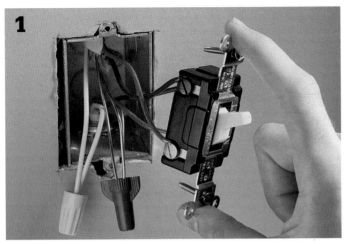

1

Turn off the power to the switch at the panel, and then remove the switch cover plate and mounting screws. Holding the mounting strap carefully, pull the switch from the box. Be careful not to touch any bare wires or screw terminals until they have been tested for power. Test for power by touching one probe of the neon circuit tester to the grounded metal box or bare copper grounding wire and touching the other probe to each of the screw terminals. The tester should not glow. If it does, there is still power entering the box. Return to the panel, and turn off the correct circuit.

2

Disconnect the wires and inspect them for nicks and scratches. If necessary, clip damaged wires and strip them. Test the switch for continuity (pages 430 to 431). Buy a replacement if the switch tests faulty.

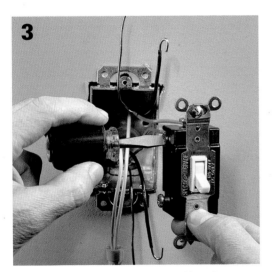

3

Connect two wires from one incoming cable to the top set of screw terminals.

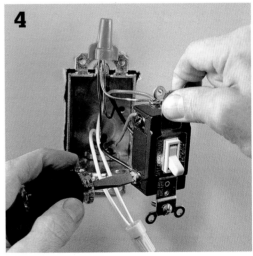

4

Attach remaining wires to the other set of screw terminals. Pigtail the grounding wires to the grounding screw. Carefully tuck the wires inside the switch box, and then remount the switch and cover plate. Turn on power at the panel.

Double Switches

A double switch has two switch levers in a single housing. It is used to control two light fixtures or appliances from the same switch box.

In most installations, both halves of the switch are powered by the same circuit. In these single-circuit installations, three wires are connected to the double switch. One wire, called the feed wire (which is hot), supplies power to both halves of the switch. The other wires, called the switch leg, carry power out to the individual light fixtures or appliances.

In rare installations, each half of the switch is powered by a separate circuit. In these separate-circuit installations, four wires are connected to the switch, and the metal connecting tab joining two of the screw terminals is removed (see photo below).

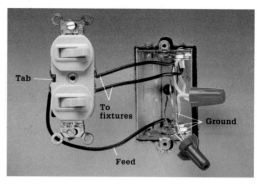

Single-circuit wiring: Three black wires are attached to the switch. The black feed wire bringing power into the box is connected to the side of the switch that has a connecting tab. The wires carrying power out to the light fixtures or appliances are connected to the side of the switch that does not have a connecting tab. The white neutral wires are connected together with a wire connector.

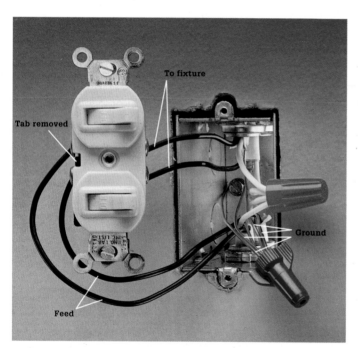

Separate-circuit wiring: Four black wires are attached to the switch. Feed wires from the power source are attached to the side of the switch that has a connecting tab, and the connecting tab is removed (photo, right). Wires carrying power from the switch to light fixtures or appliances are connected to the side of the switch that does not have a connecting tab. White neutral wires are connected together with a wire connector.

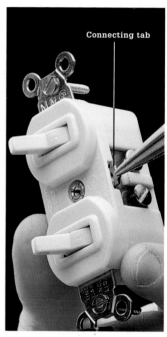

Remove the connecting tab on a double switch when wired in a separate-circuit installation. The tab can be removed with needlenose pliers or a screwdriver.

Pilot-Light Switches

A pilot-light switch has a built-in bulb that glows when power flows through the switch to a light fixture or appliance. Pilot-light switches often are installed for convenience if a light fixture or appliance cannot be seen from the switch location. Basement lights, garage lights, and attic exhaust fans frequently are controlled by pilot-light switches.

A pilot-light switch requires a neutral wire connection. A switch box that contains a single two-wire cable has only hot wires and cannot be fitted with a pilot-light switch.

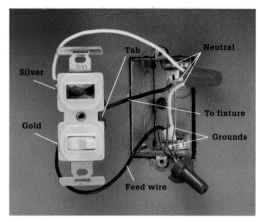

Pilot-light switch wiring: Three wires are connected to the switch. One black wire is the feed wire that brings power into the box. It is connected to the brass (gold) screw terminal on the side of the switch that does not have a connecting tab. The white neutral wires are pigtailed to the silver screw terminal. The black wire carrying power out to a light fixture or appliance is connected to the screw terminal on the side of the switch that has a connecting tab.

Switch/Receptacles

A switch/receptacle combines a grounded receptacle with a single-pole wall switch. In a room that does not have enough wall receptacles, electrical service can be improved by replacing a single-pole switch with a switch/receptacle.

A switch/receptacle requires a neutral wire connection. A switch box that contains a single two-wire cable has only hot wires and cannot be fitted with a switch/receptacle.

A switch/receptacle can be installed in one of two ways. In the most common installations, the receptacle is hot even when the switch is off (photo, right).

In rare installations, a switch/receptacle is wired so the receptacle is hot only when the switch is on. In this installation, the hot wires are reversed, so that the feed wire is attached to the brass screw terminal on the side of the switch that does not have a connecting tab.

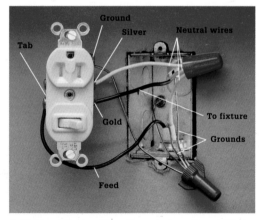

Switch/receptacle wiring: Three wires are connected to the switch/receptacle. One of the hot wires is the feed wire that brings power into the box. It is connected to the side of the switch that has a connecting tab. The other hot wire carries power out to the light fixture or appliance. It is connected to the brass screw terminal on the side that does not have a connecting tab. The white neutral wire is pigtailed to the silver screw terminal. The grounding wires must be pigtailed to the green grounding screw on the switch/receptacle and to the grounded metal box.

Specialty Switches

Your house may have several types of specialty switches. Dimmer switches (pages 428 to 429) are used frequently to control light intensity in dining and recreation areas. Timer switches and time-delay switches (below) are used to control light fixtures and exhaust fans automatically. Electronic switches provide added convenience and home security, and they are easy to install. Electronic switches are durable, and they rarely need replacement.

Most specialty switches have preattached wire leads instead of screw terminals and are connected to circuit wires with wire connectors. Some motor-driven

timer switches require a neutral wire connection and cannot be installed in switch boxes that have only one cable with two hot wires. It is precisely due to the rise in popularity of "smart" switches that the NEC Code was changed in 2014 to require an available neutral wire in newly installed switch boxes.

If a specialty switch is not operating correctly, you may be able to test it with a continuity tester. Timer switches and time-delay switches can be tested for continuity, but dimmer switches cannot be tested. With electronic switches, the manual switch can be tested for continuity, but the automatic features cannot be tested.

Timer Switches

Countdown timer switches can be set to turn lights or fans on and off automatically once each day. They are commonly used to control outdoor light fixtures.

Timer switches have three preattached wire leads. The black wire lead is connected to the hot feed wire that brings power into the box, and the red lead is connected to the wire carrying power out

to the light fixture. The remaining wire lead is the neutral lead. It must be connected to any neutral circuit wires. A switch box that contains only one cable has no neutral wires, so it cannot be fitted with a timer switch.

After a power failure, the dial on a timer switch must be reset to the proper time.

Countdown timer switch. This rocker-type switch gives you the option to easily program the switch to shut off after a specified time: from 5 to 60 minutes. Garage lights or basement lights are good applications: anywhere you want the light to stay on long enough to allow you to exit, but not to stay on indefinitely. These switches often are used to control vent fans.

Occupancy sensor. Many smart switches incorporate a motion detector that will switch the lights on if they sense movement in the room and will also shut them off when no movement is detected for a period of time. The model shown above also has a dimmer function for further energy savings.

Programmable timer switch. A dial-type timer allows you to program the switch to turn on for specific time periods at designated times of day within a 24-hour cycle. Security lights, space heaters, towel warmers, and radiant floors are typical applications.

Preset timer switch. This lets you turn on lights, heat lamps, and other loads for a designated amount of time (10 to 60 minutes) with one easy push of a button. The green LED at the bottom of this unit provides a readout of how much time is left before the switch shuts off. The model shown is not compatible with fluorescent ballasts.

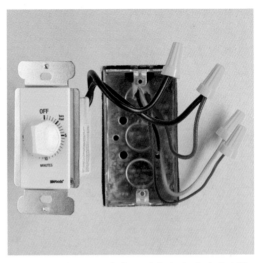

Spring-wound timer switch. A relatively simple device, this timer switch functions exactly like a kitchen timer, employing a hand-turned dial to and spring mechanism to shut the switch off in increments up to 15 minutes.

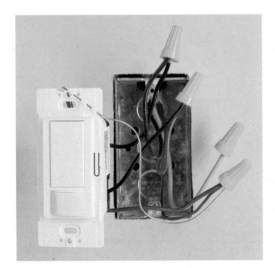

Daylight sensor switch. This switch automatically turns on when light levels drop below a proscribed level. It can also be programmed as an occupancy sensor to shut off when the room is vacant and turn on when the room is entered.

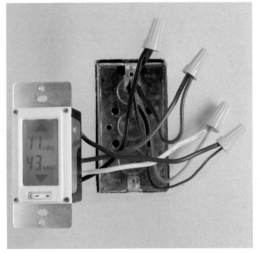

Backlit countdown timer. This digital switch lets you program lights or other devices to stay on for up to 24 hours and then shut off automatically. The backlit, LED readout gives a countdown, in minutes, of the amount of time left in the "on" cycle. Up and down buttons let you raise or lower the remaining time easily, and a manual override button will shut off the switch until it is turned back on.

Dimmer Switches

A dimmer switch makes it possible to vary the brightness of a light fixture. Dimmers are often installed in dining rooms, recreation areas, or bedrooms.

Any standard single-pole switch can be replaced with a dimmer, as long as the switch box is of adequate size. Dimmer switches have larger bodies than standard switches. They also generate a small amount of heat that must dissipate. For these reasons, dimmers should not be installed in undersized electrical boxes or in boxes that are crowded with circuit wires. Always follow the manufacturer's specifications for installation.

In lighting configurations that use three-way switches (pages 420 to 421), buy a packaged pair of three-way dimmers designed to work together.

Dimmer switches are available in several styles (see photo, right). All types have wire leads instead of screw terminals, and they are connected to circuit wires using wire connectors. Some types have a green grounding lead that should be connected to the grounded metal box or to the bare copper grounding wires. Until very recently, dimmers were designed to work only with incandescent lamps. They may not work well, or may not work at all, with CFL and LED lamps. When replacing incandescent lamps with CFL and LED lamps, make sure the new lamps are designed to work with older dimmers. When replacing dimmers, make sure the new dimmers are designed to work with CFL and LED lamps.

Tools & Materials ▸

Screwdriver   Wire connectors
Circuit tester   Masking tape
Needlenose pliers   Eye protection

Tip: Automatic dimmers ▸

An automatic dimmer has an electronic sensor that adjusts the light fixture to compensate for the changing levels of natural light. An automatic dimmer also can be operated manually.

Switch Action Options

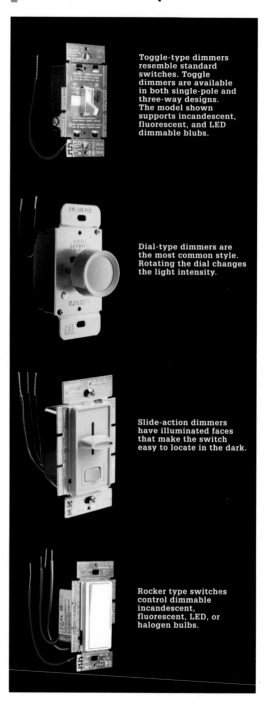

Toggle-type dimmers resemble standard switches. Toggle dimmers are available in both single-pole and three-way designs. The model shown supports incandescent, fluorescent, and LED dimmable blubs.

Dial-type dimmers are the most common style. Rotating the dial changes the light intensity.

Slide-action dimmers have illuminated faces that make the switch easy to locate in the dark.

Rocker type switches control dimmable incandescent, fluorescent, LED, or halogen bulbs.

How to Install a Dimmer Switch

1

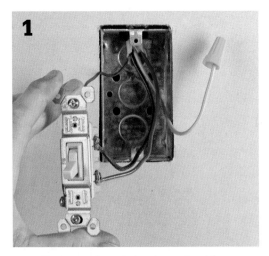

Turn off power to the switch at the panel, and then remove the cover plate and mounting screws. Holding the mounting straps carefully, pull the switch from the box. Be careful not to touch bare wires or screw terminals until they have been tested for power. In new switch wiring, the white wire should not supply current to the switched device, and a separate neutral wire should be available in the switch box.

2

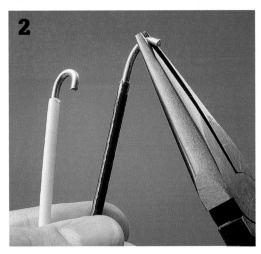

Disconnect the circuit wires and remove the switch. Straighten the circuit wires, and clip the ends, leaving about ½" of the bare wire end exposed.

3

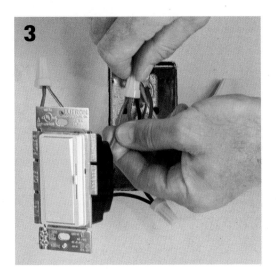

Connect the wire leads on the dimmer switch to the circuit wires using wire connectors. The switch leads are interchangeable and can be attached to either of the two circuit wires.

4

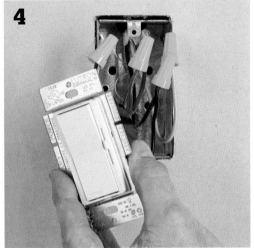

A three-way dimmer has an additional wire lead. This "common" lead is connected to the common circuit wire. When replacing a standard three-way switch with a dimmer, the common circuit wire is attached to the darkest screw terminal on the old switch. In new switch wiring, the white wire should not supply current to the switched device, and a separate neutral wire should be available in the switch box.

Testing Switches

A switch that does not work properly may have worn or broken internal parts. Test switches with a battery-operated continuity tester. The continuity tester detects any break in the metal pathway inside the switch. Replace the switch if the continuity tester shows the switch to be faulty.

Never use a continuity tester on wires that might carry live current. Always shut off the power and disconnect the switch before testing for continuity.

Some specialty switches, such as dimmers, cannot be tested for continuity. Electronic switches can be tested for manual operation using a continuity tester, but the automatic operation of these switches cannot be tested.

How to Test a Single-Pole Wall Switch

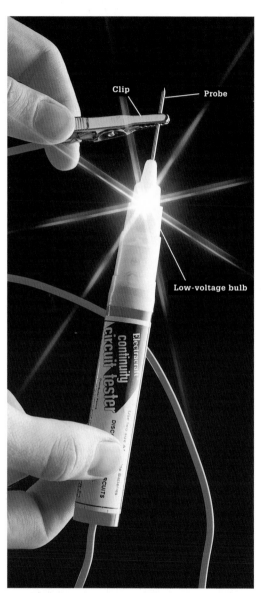

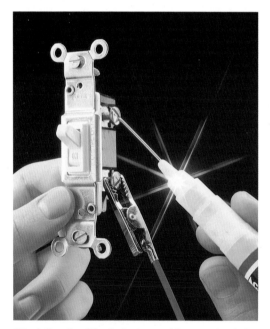

Attach the clip of the tester to one of the screw terminals. Touch the tester probe to the other screw terminal. Flip the switch lever from ON to OFF. If the switch is good, the tester glows when the lever is ON but not when it's OFF.

A continuity tester uses battery-generated current to test the metal pathways running through switches and other electrical fixtures. Always "test" the tester before use. Touch the tester clip to the metal probe. The tester should glow. If not, then the battery or lightbulb is dead and must be replaced.

How to Test a Three-Way Wall Switch

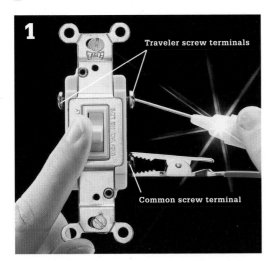

Traveler screw terminals

Common screw terminal

Attach the tester clip to the dark common screw terminal. Touch the tester probe to one of the traveler screw terminals, and flip the switch lever back and forth. If the switch is good, the tester should glow when the lever is in one position, but not both.

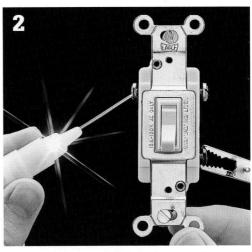

Touch the probe to the other traveler screw terminal, and flip the switch lever back and forth. If the switch is good, the tester will glow only when the switch lever is in the position opposite from the positive test in step 1.

How to Test a Four-Way Wall Switch

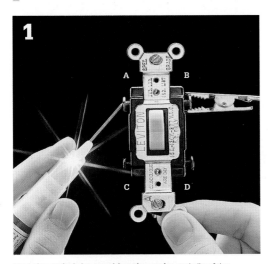

Test the switch by touching the probe and clip of the continuity tester to each pair of screw terminals (A-B, C-D, A-D, B-C, A-C, B-D). The test should show continuous pathways between the two different pairs of screw terminals. Flip the lever to the opposite position, and repeat the test. It should show continuous pathways between two different pairs of screw terminals.

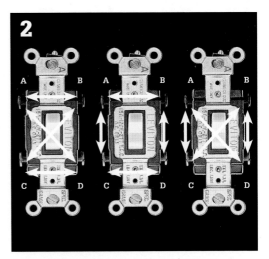

If the switch is good, the test will show a total of four continuous pathways between screw terminals—two pathways for each lever position. If not, then the switch is faulty and must be replaced. (The arrangement of the pathways may differ, depending on the switch manufacturer. The photo above shows the three possible pathway arrangements.)

How to Test a Pilot-Light Switch

Test the pilot light by flipping the switch lever to the ON position. Check to see if the light fixture or appliance is working. If the pilot light does not glow even though the switch operates the light fixture or appliance, then the pilot light is defective and the unit must be replaced.

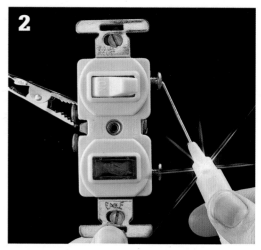

Test the switch by disconnecting the unit. With the switch lever in the ON position, attach the tester clip to the top screw terminal on one side of the switch. Touch the tester probe to the top screw terminal on the opposite side of the switch. If the switch is good, the tester will glow when switch is ON but not when OFF.

How to Test a Timer Switch

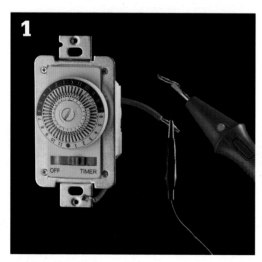

Attach the tester clip to the red wire lead on the timer switch, and touch the tester probe to the black hot lead. Rotate the timer dial clockwise until the ON tab passes the arrow marker. The tester should glow. If it does not, the switch is faulty and must be replaced.

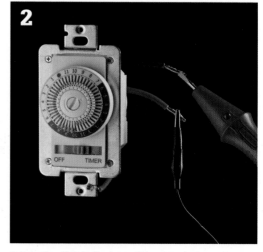

Rotate the dial clockwise until the OFF tab passes the arrow marker. The tester should not glow. If it does, the switch is faulty and must be replaced.

How to Test a Switch/Receptacle

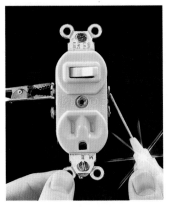

Attach the tester clip to one of the top screw terminals. Touch the tester probe to the top screw terminal on the opposite side. Flip the switch lever from ON to OFF position. If the switch is working correctly, the tester will glow when the switch lever is ON but not when it's OFF.

How to Test a Double Switch

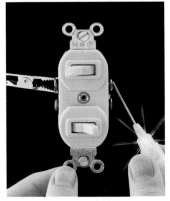

Test each half of the switch by attaching the tester clip to one screw terminal and touching the probe to the opposite side. Flip the switch lever from ON to OFF position. If the switch is good, the tester glows when the switch lever is ON but not when it's OFF. Repeat the test with the remaining pair of screw terminals. If either half tests faulty, replace the unit.

How to Test a Time-Delay Switch

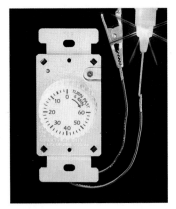

Attach the tester clip to one of the wire leads, and touch the tester probe to the other lead. Set the timer for a few minutes. If the switch is working correctly, the tester will glow until the time expires.

How to Test Manual Operation of Electronic Switches

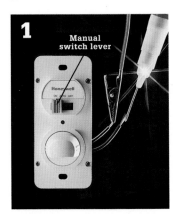

Automatic switch: Attach the tester clip to a black wire lead, and touch the tester probe to the other black lead. Flip the manual switch lever from ON to OFF position. If the switch is working correctly, the tester will glow when the switch lever is ON but not when it's OFF.

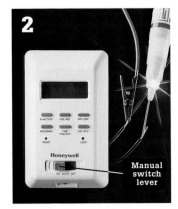

Programmable switch: Attach the tester clip to a wire lead, and touch the tester probe to the other lead. Flip the manual switch lever from ON to OFF position. If the switch is working correctly, the tester will glow when the switch lever is ON but not when it's OFF.

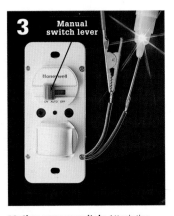

Motion-sensor switch: Attach the tester clip to a wire lead, and touch the tester probe to the other lead. Flip the manual switch lever from ON to OFF position. If the switch is working correctly, the tester will glow when the switch lever is ON but not when it's OFF.

Receptacles

Several different types of receptacles are found in the typical home. Each has a unique arrangement of slots that accepts only a certain kind of plug, and each is designed for a specific job.

Household receptacles provide two types of voltage: normal and high. Although voltage ratings have changed slightly over the years, normal receptacles should be rated for 110, 115, 120, or 125 volts. For purposes of replacement, these ratings are considered identical. High-voltage receptacles are rated at 220, 240, or 250 volts. These ratings are considered identical.

When replacing a receptacle, check the amperage rating of the circuit at the main service panel, and buy a receptacle with the correct amperage rating.

15 amps, 120 volts. Polarized two-slot receptacles are common in homes built before 1960. Slots are different sizes to accept polarized plugs.

15 amps, 120 volts. Three-slot grounded receptacles have two different-sized slots and a U-shaped hole for grounding which is required in all new wiring installations.

20 amps, 120 volts. This three-slot grounded receptacle features a special T-shaped slot. It is installed for use with large appliances or portable tools that require 20 amps of current.

15 amps, 240 volts. This receptacle is used primarily for window air conditioners. It is available as a single unit or as half of a duplex receptacle, with the other half wired for 120 volts.

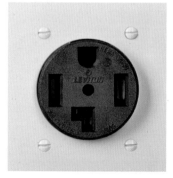

30 amps, 120/240 volts. This grounded receptacle is used for clothes dryers. It provides high-voltage current for heating coils and 120-volts to run lights and timers.

50 amps, 120/240 volts. This new, grounded receptacle is used for ranges. The high voltage powers heating coils, and the 120-volts run clocks and lights.

Older Receptacles

Older receptacles may look different from more modern types, but most will stay in good working order. Follow these simple guidelines for evaluating or replacing older receptacles:

- Never replace a receptacle with one of a different voltage or higher amperage rating.

- Do not replace a two-slot receptacle with a three-slot receptacle. Replace the two-slot receptacle with a polarized two-slot receptacle or with a GFCI receptacle.
- If in doubt, contact an electrician.
- Never alter the prongs of a plug to fit an older receptacle. Altering the prongs may remove the grounding or polarizing features of the plug.

The earliest receptacles were modifications of the screw-in light bulb. This receptacle was used in the early 1900s.

Unpolarized receptacles have same-length slots. Modern plugs may not fit these receptacles. Never modify the prongs of a polarized plug to fit the slots of an unpolarized receptacle.

Surface-mounted receptacles were popular in the 1940s and 1950s for their ease of installation. Wiring ran behind hollowed-out base moldings. These receptacles are usually ungrounded.

Ceramic duplex receptacles were manufactured in the 1930s. They are polarized but ungrounded, and they are wired for 120 volts.

Twist-lock receptacles are designed to be used with plugs that are inserted and rotated. A small tab on the end of one of the prongs prevents the plug from being pulled from the receptacle.

This ceramic duplex receptacle has a unique hourglass shape. It is rated for 250 volts but only 5 amps and would not be allowed by today's electrical codes.

High-Voltage Receptacles

High-voltage receptacles provide current to large appliances such as clothes dryers, ranges, and air conditioners. The slot configuration of a high-voltage receptacle (page 434) will not accept a plug rated for 120 volts.

A high-voltage receptacle can be wired in one of two ways. In one type of high-voltage receptacle, voltage is brought to the receptacle with two hot wires, each carrying a maximum of 120 volts. No white neutral wire is necessary, but a grounding wire should be attached to the receptacle and to the metal receptacle box. Conduit may also act as a grounding conductor from the metal receptacle box back to the panel in old circuits without a grounding wire. This method is not allowed today.

A clothes dryer or range also may require 120 volts to run lights, timers, and clocks. If so, a white neutral wire will be attached to the receptacle. The appliance itself will split the incoming electricity into a 120-volt circuit and a 240-volt circuit.

It is important to identify and tag all wires on the existing receptacle so that the new receptacle will be properly wired.

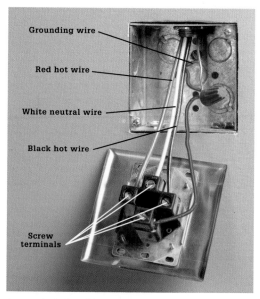

A receptacle rated for 120/240 volts has two incoming hot wires, each carrying 120 volts, a white neutral wire, and a copper grounding wire. Connections are made with setscrew terminals at the back of the receptacle.

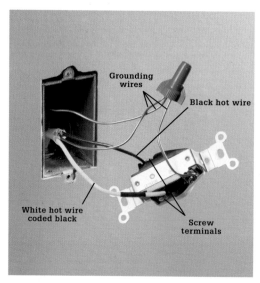

One type of receptacle rated for 240 volts has two incoming hot wires and no neutral wire. A grounding wire is pigtailed to the receptacle and to the metal receptacle box.

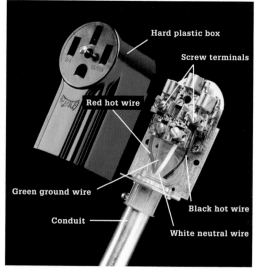

This surface-mounted receptacle rated for 240 volts has a hard plastic box that can be installed on concrete or block walls. Surface-mounted receptacles are often found in basements and utility rooms.

Childproofing

Childproof your receptacles or adapt them for special uses by adding receptacle accessories. Before installing an accessory, be sure to read the manufacturer's instructions.

Homeowners with small children should add inexpensive caps or covers to guard against accidental electric shocks.

Plastic caps do not conduct electricity and are virtually impossible for small children to remove. A receptacle cover attaches directly to the receptacle and fits over plugs, preventing the cords from being removed. Tamper-resistant receptacles are now required in all new residential installations.

Standard receptacles present a real shock hazard to small children. Fortunately there are many products that make receptacles safer without making them less convenient.

Protect electronic equipment, such as a home computer or stereo, with a surge protector. The surge protector reduces the chance of any damage to sensitive equipment caused by sudden drops or surges in power.

A recessed wall receptacle permits a plug-in clock to be hung flush against a wall surface.

Snap protective caps over sockets to prevent children from having access to the slots.

Duplex Receptacles

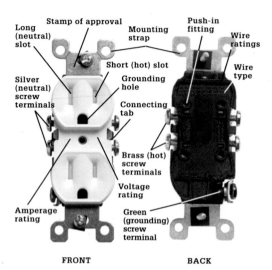

Long (neutral) slot

Stamp of approval

Mounting strap

Push-in fitting

Wire ratings

Silver (neutral) screw terminals

Short (hot) slot

Grounding hole

Connecting tab

Wire type

Amperage rating

Brass (hot) screw terminals

Voltage rating

Green (grounding) screw terminal

FRONT

BACK

The standard duplex receptacle has two halves for receiving plugs. Each half has a long (neutral) slot, a short (hot) slot, and a U-shaped grounding hole. The slots fit the wide prong, narrow prong, and grounding prong of a three-prong plug. This ensures that the connection between receptacle and plug will be polarized and grounded for safety.

Wires are attached to the receptacle at screw terminals or push-in fittings. A connecting tab between the screw terminals allows a variety of different wiring configurations. Receptacles also include mounting straps for attaching to electrical boxes.

Stamps of approval from testing agencies are found on the front and back of the receptacle. Look for the symbol UL or UND. LAB. INC. LIST to make sure the receptacle meets the strict standards of Underwriters Laboratories.

The receptacle is marked with ratings for maximum volts and amps. The common receptacle is marked 15A, 125V. Receptacles marked CU or COPPER are used with solid copper wire. Those marked CU-CLAD ONLY are used with copper-coated aluminum wire. Only receptacles marked CO/ALR may be used with solid aluminum wiring. Receptacles marked AL/CU no longer may be used with aluminum wire, according to code.

AFCI receptacles have integral protection against arc faults and may be required in some remodeling situations where AFCI protection cannot be provided at the service panel.

The ground-fault circuit-interrupter, or GFCI, receptacle is a modern safety device. When it detects slight changes in current, it instantly shuts off power. The larger picture shows a modern GFCI with an alert bulb that lights when the device is tripped. The older but more familiar style is seen in the inset photo.

Common Receptacle Problems ▸

Household receptacles, also called outlets, have no moving parts to wear out and usually last for many years without servicing. Most problems associated with receptacles are actually caused by faulty lamps and appliances or their plugs and cords. However, the constant plugging in and removal of appliance cords can wear out the metal contacts inside a receptacle. Any receptacle that does not hold plugs firmly should be replaced. In addition, older receptacles made of hard plastic may harden and crack with age. They must be replaced when this happens.

A loose wire connection with the receptacle box is another possible problem. A loose connection can spark (called arcing), trip a circuit breaker, or cause heat to build up in the receptacle box, creating a potential fire hazard.

Wires can come loose for a number of reasons. Everyday vibrations caused by walking across floors, or from nearby street traffic, may cause a connection to shake loose. In addition, because wires heat and cool with normal use, the ends of the wires will expand and contract slightly. This movement also may cause the wires to come loose from the screw terminal connections.

Not all receptacles are created equally. When replacing, make sure to buy one with the same amp rating as the old one. Inadvertently installing a 20-amp receptacle in replacement of a 15-amp receptacle is a very common error.

PROBLEM	REPAIR
Circuit breaker trips repeatedly, or fuse burns out immediately after being replaced.	1. Repair or replace worn or damaged lamp or appliance cord. 2. Move lamps or appliances to other circuits to prevent overloads. 3. Tighten any loose wire connections. 4. Clean dirty or oxidized wire ends.
Lamp or appliance does not work.	1. Make sure the lamp or appliance is plugged in. 2. Replace burned-out bulbs. 3. Repair or replace a worn or damaged lamp or appliance cord. 4. Tighten any loose wire connections. 5. Clean dirty or oxidized wire ends. 6. Replace any faulty receptacle.
Receptacle does not hold plugs firmly.	1. Repair or replace worn or damaged plugs. 2. Replace the faulty receptacle.
Receptacle is warm to the touch, buzzes, or sparks when plugs are inserted or removed.	1. Move lamps or appliances to other circuits to prevent overloads. 2. Tighten any loose wire connections. 3. Clean dirty or oxidized wire ends. 4. Replace the faulty receptacle.

Receptacle Wiring Configurations

A 120-volt duplex receptacle can be wired to the electrical system in several ways. The most common are shown on these pages.

Wiring configurations may vary slightly from these photographs, depending on the kind of receptacles used, the type of cable, or the technique of the electrician who installed the wiring. To make dependable repairs or replacements, use masking tape and label each wire according to its location on the terminals of the existing receptacle.

Receptacles are wired as either end-of-run or middle-of-run. These two basic configurations are easily identified by counting the number of cables entering the receptacle box. End-of-run wiring has only one cable, indicating that the circuit ends. Middle-of-run wiring has two cables, indicating that the circuit continues on to other receptacles, switches, or fixtures.

A split-circuit receptacle is shown on the next page. Each half of a split-circuit receptacle is wired to a separate circuit. This allows two appliances of high wattage to be plugged into the same receptacle without blowing a fuse or tripping a breaker. This wiring configuration is similar to a receptacle that is controlled by a wall switch. Code requires a switch-controlled receptacle in most rooms that do not have a built-in light fixture operated by a wall switch.

Split-circuit and switch-controlled receptacles are connected to two hot wires, so use caution during repairs or replacements. Make sure the connecting tab between the hot screw terminals is removed.

Two-slot receptacles are common in older homes. There is no grounding wire attached to the receptacle, but the metal box may be grounded with armored cable or metal conduit. Tamper-resistant receptacles are now required in all new residential installations.

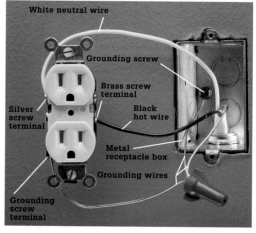

A single cable entering the box indicates end-of-run wiring. The black hot wire is attached to a brass screw terminal, and the white neutral wire is connected to a silver screw terminal. If the box is metal, the grounding wire is pigtailed to the grounding screws of the receptacle and the box. In a plastic box, the grounding wire is attached directly to the grounding screw terminal of the receptacle.

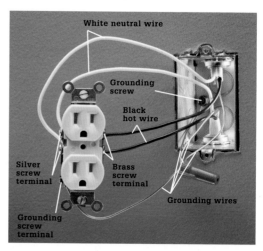

Two cables entering the box indicate middle-of-run wiring. Black hot wires are connected to brass screw terminals and white neutral wires to silver screw terminals. The grounding wire is pigtailed to the grounding screws of the receptacle and the box.

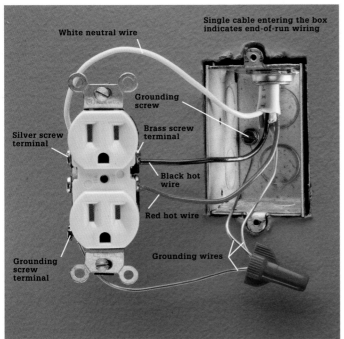

White neutral wire

Single cable entering the box
indicates end-of-run wiring

Grounding
screw

Silver screw
terminal

Brass screw
terminal

Black hot
wire

Red hot wire

Grounding
screw
terminal

Grounding wires

A split-circuit receptacle (technically a multi-wire branch circuit) is attached to a black hot wire, a red hot wire, a white neutral wire, and a bare grounding wire. The wiring is similar to a switch-controlled receptacle. The hot wires are attached to the brass screw terminals, and the connecting tab or fin between the brass terminals is removed. The white wire is attached to a silver screw terminal, and the connecting tab on the neutral side remains intact. The grounding wire is pigtailed to the grounding screw terminal of the receptacle and to the grounding screw attached to the box.

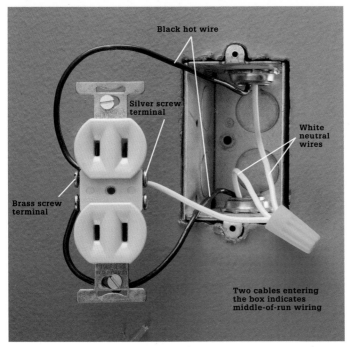

Black hot wire

Silver screw
terminal

White
neutral
wires

Brass screw
terminal

Two cables entering
the box indicates
middle-of-run wiring

A two-slot receptacle is often found in older homes. The black hot wires are connected to the brass screw terminals, and the white neutral wires are pigtailed to a silver screw terminal. Two-slot receptacles may be replaced with three-slot types, but only if a means of grounding exists at the receptacle box. In some municipalities, you may replace a two-slot receptacle with a GFCI receptacle as long as the receptacle has a sticker that reads "No equipment ground."

How to Install a New Receptacle

1

Position the new old work box on the wall and trace around it. Consider the location of hidden utilities within the wall before you cut.

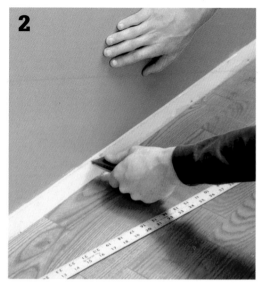

2

Remove baseboard between the new and existing receptacle. Cut away the drywall about 1" below the baseboard with a jigsaw, wallboard saw, or utility knife.

3

Drill a ⅝" hole in the center of each stud along the opening between the two receptacles. A drill bit extender or a flexible drill bit will allow you a better angle and make drilling the holes easier.

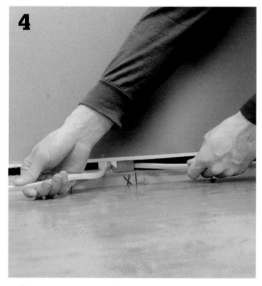

4

Run the branch cable through the holes from the new location to the existing receptacle. Staple the cable to the stud below the box. Install a metal nail plate on the front edge of each stud that the cable routes through.

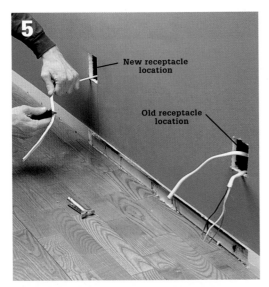

Turn off the power at the panel and test for power.
Remove the old receptacle and its box, and pull the new branch cable up through the hole. Remove sheathing and insulation from both ends of the new cable.

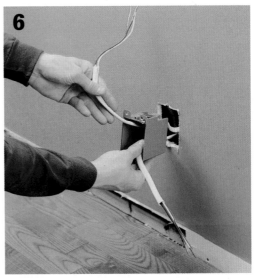

Thread the new and old cables into an old work box large enough to contain the added wires and clamp the cables. Fit the box into the old hole and attach it.

Reconnect the old receptacle by connecting its neutral, hot, and grounding screws to the new branch cable and the old cable from the panel with pigtails.

Pull the cable through another old work box for the new receptacle. Secure the cable and install the box. Connect the new receptacle to the new branch cable. Insert the receptacle into the box and attach the receptacle and cover plate with screws. Patch the opening with ½"-thick wood strips or drywall. Reattach the baseboard to the studs.

GFCI Receptacles

The ground-fault circuit interrupter (GFCI) protects against electrical shock caused by a faulty appliance or a worn cord or plug. It senses small changes in current flow and can shut off power in as little as $\frac{1}{40}$ of a second. GFCIs can be a circuit breaker and protect the circuit from the panel. Often, however, they are receptacles that protect one receptacle and may protect other receptacles and light fixtures downstream.

GFCIs are now required in bathrooms, kitchens, garages, crawl spaces, unfinished basements, and outdoor receptacle locations. Consult your local codes for any requirements regarding the installation of GFCIs. Most GFCI receptacles use standard screw terminal connections, but some have wire leads and are attached with wire connectors. Because the body of a GFCI receptacle is larger than a standard receptacle, small, crowded electrical boxes may need to be replaced with more spacious boxes.

Because the GFCI is so sensitive, it is most effective when wired to protect a single location. The more receptacles any one GFCI protects, the more susceptible it is to "phantom tripping," shutting off power because of tiny, normal fluctuations in current flow. GFCI receptacles installed in outdoor locations must be rated for outdoor use and weather resistance (WR) along with ground fault protection.

Tools & Materials ▸

Circuit tester   Wire connectors
Screwdriver   Masking tape

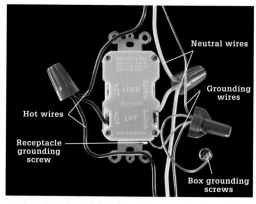

A GFCI wired for single-location protection (shown from the back) has hot and neutral wires connected only to the screw terminals marked LINE. A GFCI connected for single-location protection may be wired as either an end-of-run or middle-of-run configuration.

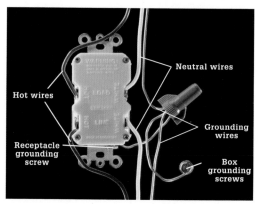

A GFCI wired for multiple-location protection (shown from the back) has one set of hot and neutral wires connected to the LINE pair of screw terminals and the other set connected to the LOAD pair of screw terminals. A GFCI receptacle connected for multiple-location protection may be wired only as a middle-of-run configuration.

Modern GFCI receptacles have tamper-resistant slots. Look for a model that's rated "WR" (for weather resistance) if you'll be installing it outdoors or in a wet location.

How to Install a GFCI for Single-Location Protection

1

Shut off power to the receptacle at the panel. Test for power with a neon circuit tester. Be sure to check both halves of the receptacle.

2

Remove the cover plate. Loosen mounting screws, and gently pull the receptacle from the box. Do not touch wires. Confirm power is off with a circuit tester.

3

Disconnect all white neutral wires from the silver screw terminals of the old receptacle.

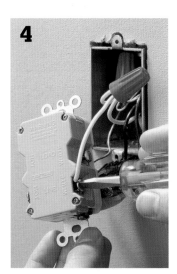

4

Pigtail all the white neutral wires together, and connect the pigtail to the terminal marked WHITE LINE on the GFCI (see photo on opposite page).

5

Disconnect all black hot wires from the brass screw terminals of the old receptacle. Pigtail these wires together, and connect them to the terminal marked HOT LINE on the GFCI.

6

If a grounding wire is available, connect it to the green grounding screw terminal of the GFCI. Mount the GFCI in the receptacle box, and reattach the cover plate. Restore power, and test the GFCI according to the manufacturer's instructions. If a grounding wire is not available, label the receptacle cover plate: "NO EQUIPMENT GROUND".

How to Install a GFCI for Multiple-Location Protection

1

Use a map of your house circuits to determine a location for your GFCI. Indicate all receptacles that will be protected by the GFCI installation.

2

Turn off power to the correct circuit at the panel. Test all the receptacles in the circuit with a neon circuit tester to make sure the power is off. Always check both halves of each duplex receptacle.

3

Remove the cover plate from the receptacle that will be replaced with the GFCI. Loosen the mounting screws and gently pull the receptacle from its box. Take care not to touch any bare wires. Confirm the power is off with a neon circuit tester.

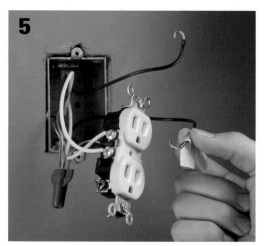

Disconnect all black hot wires. Carefully separate the hot wires and position them so that the bare ends do not touch anything. Restore power to the circuit at the panel. Determine which black wire is the feed wire by testing for hot wires. The feed wire brings power to the receptacle from the service panel. *Use caution: This is a live wire test, during which the power is turned on temporarily.*

When you have found the hot feed wire, turn off power at the panel. Identify the feed wire by marking it with masking tape.

6

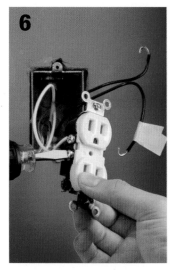

Disconnect the white neutral wires from the old receptacle. Identify the white feed wire and label it with masking tape. The white feed wire will be the one that shares the same cable as the black feed wire.

7

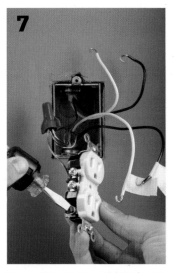

Disconnect the grounding wire from the grounding screw terminal of the old receptacle. Remove the old receptacle. Connect the grounding wire to the grounding screw terminal of the GFCI.

8

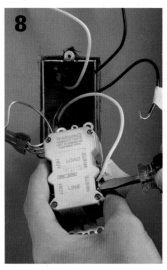

Connect the white feed wire to the terminal marked WHITE LINE on the GFCI. Connect the black feed wire to the terminal marked HOT LINE on the GFCI.

9

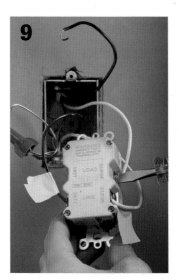

Connect the other white neutral wire to the terminal marked WHITE LOAD on the GFCI.

10

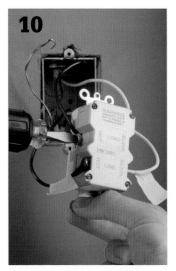

Connect the other black hot wire to the terminal marked HOT LOAD on the GFCI.

11

Carefully tuck all wires into the receptacle box. Mount the GFCI in the box and attach the cover plate. Turn on power to the circuit at the panel. Test the GFCI according to the manufacturer's instructions.

GFCI & AFCI Breakers

Understanding the difference between GFCI (ground-fault circuit interrupter) and AFCI (arc fault circuit interrupter) is tricky for most homeowners. Essentially it comes down to this: Arc-fault interrupters keep your house from burning down; ground-fault interrupters keep people from being electrocuted.

The National Electric Code (NEC) requires that an AFCI breaker be installed on most branch circuits that supply outlets or fixtures in newly constructed homes. The NEC also requires adding AFCI protection to these circuits when you add new circuits and modify or extend existing circuits. They're a prudent precaution in any home, especially if it has older wiring. AFCI breakers will not interfere with the operation of GFCI receptacles, so it is safe to install an AFCI breaker on a circuit that contains GFCI receptacles.

GROUND-FAULT CIRCUIT-INTERRUPTERS

A GFCI is an important safety device that disconnects a circuit in the event of a ground fault (when current takes a path other than the neutral back to the panel).

On new construction, GFCI protection is required for receptacles in these locations: kitchen counter tops, bathrooms, garages, unfinished basements, crawlspaces, outdoors, within six feet of sinks, and in unfinished accessory buildings such as storage and work sheds. In general it is a good practice to protect all receptacle and fixture locations that could encounter damp or wet circumstances.

Tools & Materials ▸

Insulated
  screwdriver
Circuit tester

Combination tool
AFCI or
  GFCI breaker

ARC-FAULT CIRCUIT INTERRUPTERS

AFCIs detect arcing (sparks) that can cause fires between and along damaged wires. AFCI protection is required for 15- and 20-amp, 120-volt circuits that serve living rooms, family rooms, dens, parlors, libraries, dining rooms, bedrooms, sun rooms, kitchens, laundry areas, closets, and hallways. AFCI protection is not required for circuits serving bathrooms, garages, the exterior of the home, appliances such as furnaces and air handlers.

The easiest way to provide AFCI protection for a circuit is to install an AFCI circuit breaker labeled as a "combination" device in the electrical panel. The 2014 NEC allows several alternate methods of providing AFCI protection, but you should consult an electrician before using these alternate methods. You should install combination AFCI circuit breakers when installing new circuits that require AFCI protection. You should install either combination AFCI circuit breakers or AFCI receptacles when you modify, replace, or extend an existing circuit that requires AFCI protection.

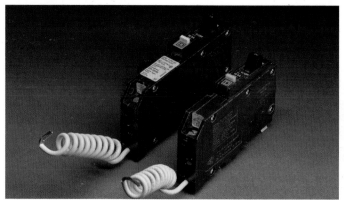

AFCI breakers (left) are similar in appearance to GFCI breakers (right), but they function differently. AFCI breakers trip when they sense an arc fault. GFCI breakers trip when they sense fault between the hot wire and the ground.

An AFCI-protected receptacle

How to Install an AFCI or GFCI Breaker

Locate the breaker for the circuit you'd like to protect. Turn off the main circuit breaker. Remove the cover from the panel, and test to ensure that power is off (see page 390). Remove the breaker you want to replace from the panel. Remove the black wire from the LOAD terminal of the breaker.

Find the white wire on the circuit you want to protect, and remove it from the neutral bus bar.

Flip the handle of the new AFCI or GFCI breaker to OFF. Loosen both of the breaker's terminal screws. Connect the white circuit wire to the breaker terminal labeled PANEL NEUTRAL. Connect the black circuit wire to the breaker terminal labeled LOAD POWER.

Connect the new breaker's coiled white wire to the neutral bus bar on the service panel.

Make sure all the connections are tight. Snap the new breaker into the bus bar.

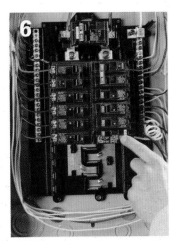

Turn the main breaker on. Turn off and unplug all fixtures and appliances on the AFCI or GFCI breaker circuit. Turn the AFCI or GFCI breaker on. Press the test button. If the breaker is wired correctly, the breaker trips open. If it doesn't trip, check all connections or consult an electrician. Replace the panel cover.

Testing Receptacles

For testing receptacles and other devices for power, grounding, and polarity, neon circuit testers are inexpensive and easy to use. But they are less sensitive than auto-ranging multimeters. In some cases, neon testers won't detect the presence of lower voltage in a circuit. This can lead you to believe that a circuit is shut off when it is not—a dangerous mistake. The small probes on a neon circuit tester also force you to get too close to live terminals and wires. For a quick check and confirmation, a neon circuit tester (or a plug-in tester) is adequate. But for the most reliable readings, buy and learn to use a multimeter.

The best multimeters are auto-ranging models with a digital readout. Unlike manual multimeters, auto-ranging models do not require you to preset the voltage range to get an accurate reading. Unlike neon testers, multimeters may be used for a host of additional diagnostic functions such as testing fuses, measuring battery voltage, testing internal wiring in appliances, and checking light fixtures to determine if they're functional.

Auto-ranging multimeter

Metal probes

Tools & Materials ▶

Multimeter
Touchless circuit tester
Plug-in tester
Screwdriver

How to Use a Plug-in Tester

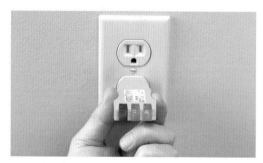

Use a plug-in tester to test a three-slot receptacle. With the power on, insert the tester into the suspect outlet. The face of the tester has three colored lights that will light up in different combinations, according to the outlet's problem. A reference chart is provided with the tester, and there may be a chart on the tester itself. These testers are useful, but they do not test for all wiring errors.

How to Test Quickly for Power

Use a touchless circuit tester to verify that power is not flowing to a receptacle. Using either a no-touch sensor or a probe-style circuit tester, test the receptacle for current before you remove the cover plate. Once the plate is removed, double-check at the terminals to make sure there is no current.

How to Test a Receptacle with a Multimeter

1

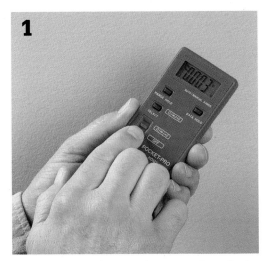

Set the selector dial for alternating-current voltage. Plug the black probe lead into the common jack (labeled COM) on the multimeter. Plug the red probe lead into the V-labeled jack.

2

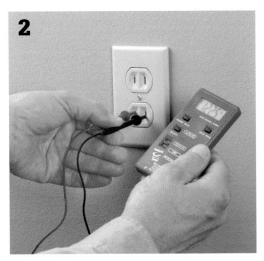

Insert the test ends of the probe into the receptacle slots. It does not make a difference which probe goes into which slot as long as they're in the same receptacle. If power is present and flowing normally, you will see a voltage reading on the readout screen.

3

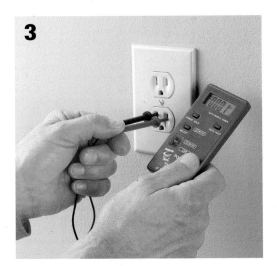

If the multimeter reads 0 or gives a very low reading (less than 1 or 2 volts), power is not present in the receptacle and it is safe to remove the cover plate and work on the fixture (although it's always a good idea to confirm your reading by touching the probes directly to the screw terminals on the receptacles).

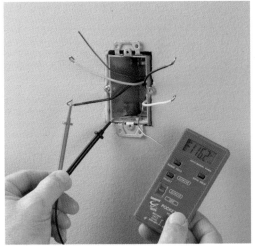

Option: When a receptacle or switch is in the middle of a circuit, it is difficult to tell which wires are carrying current. Use a multimeter to check. With power off, remove the receptacle and separate the wires. Restore power. Touch one probe to the bare ground or the grounded metal box and touch the other probe to the end of each wire. The wire that shows current on the meter is hot.

Replacing Ceiling Lights

Ceiling fixtures don't have any moving parts, and their wiring is very simple, so, other than changing bulbs, you're likely to get decades of trouble-free service from a fixture. This sounds like a good thing, but it also means that the fixture probably won't fail and give you an excuse to update a room's look with a new one. Fortunately you don't need an excuse. Upgrading a fixture is easy and can make a dramatic impact on a room. You can substantially increase the light in a room by replacing a globe-style fixture with one with separate spot lights, or you can simply install a new fixture that matches the room's décor. Check the weight rating of the box to which you will attach your fixture. Older boxes may not handle a heavy fixture.

Tools & Materials ▸

Replacement light fixture
Wire stripper
Voltage sensor
Insulated screwdrivers
Wire connectors
Eye protection

If you are unsure how much weight the existing box can handle, consider changing the box. New light fixture boxes should handle fixtures up to 50 pounds. Support the fixture independently from the box if the fixture weighs more than 50 pounds.

Installing a new ceiling fixture can provide more light to a space, not to mention an aesthetic lift. It's one of the easiest upgrades you can do.

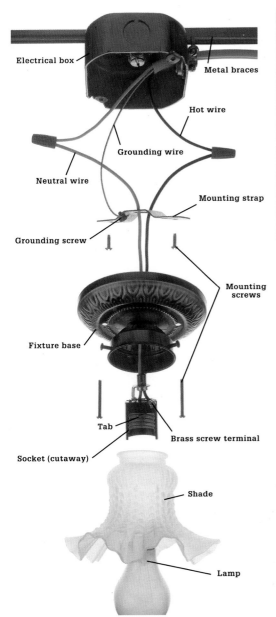

Electrical box

Metal braces

Hot wire

Grounding wire

Neutral wire

Mounting strap

Grounding screw

Mounting screws

Fixture base

Tab

Brass screw terminal

Socket (cutaway)

Shade

Lamp

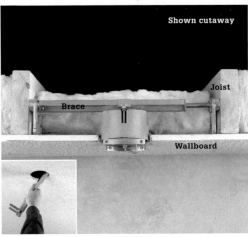

Shown cutaway

Joist

Brace

Wallboard

If the new fixture is much heavier than the original fixture, it will require additional bracing in the ceiling to support the electrical box and the fixture. The manufacturer's instructions should specify the size and type of box. If the ceiling is finished and there is no access from above, you can remove the old box and use an adjustable remodeling brace appropriate for your fixture (shown). The brace fits into a small hole in the ceiling (inset). Once the bracing is in place, install a new electrical box specified for the new fixture.

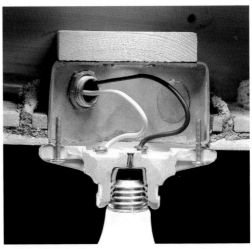

No matter what a ceiling light fixture looks like on the outside, they all attach in basically the same way. An electrical box in the ceiling is fitted with a mounting strap, which holds the fixture in place. The bare wire from the ceiling typically connects to the mounting strap. The two wires coming from the fixture connect to the black and the white wires from the ceiling.

Inexpensive light fixtures have screw terminals mounted directly to the backside of the fixture plate. Often, as seen here, they have no grounding terminal. Some codes do not allow this type of fixture, but even if your hometown does approve them, it is a good idea to replace them with a better quality, safer fixture that is UL-approved.

How to Replace a Ceiling Light

1

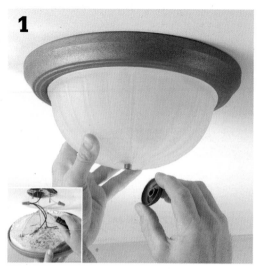

Shut off power to the ceiling light, and remove the shade or diffuser. Loosen the mounting screws and carefully lower the fixture, supporting it as you work (do not let light fixtures hang by their electrical wires alone). Test with a voltage sensor to make sure no power is reaching the connections.

2

Remove the twist connectors from the fixture wires or unscrew the screw terminals and remove the white neutral wire and the black lead wire (inset).

3

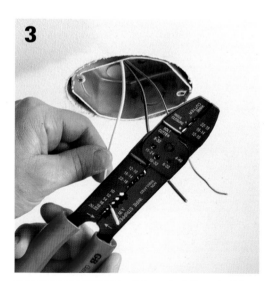

Before you install the new fixture, check the ends of the wires coming from the ceiling electrical box. They should be clean and free of nicks or scorch marks. If they're dirty or worn, clip off the stripped portion with your combination tool. Then strip away about ¾" of insulation from the end of each wire.

4

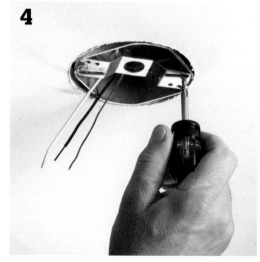

Attach a mounting strap to the ceiling fixture box if there is not one already present. Your new light may come equipped with a strap; otherwise you can find one for purchase at any hardware store.

5

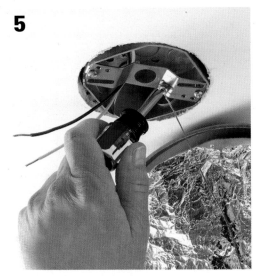

Lift the new fixture up to the ceiling (you may want a helper for this), and attach the bare copper ground wire from the power supply cable to the grounding screw or clip on the mounting strap. Also attach the ground wire from the fixture to the screw or clip.

6

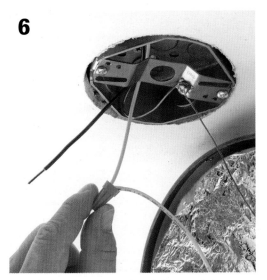

With the fixture supported by a ladder or a helper, join the white wire lead and the white fixture wire with a wire connector (often supplied with the fixture).

7

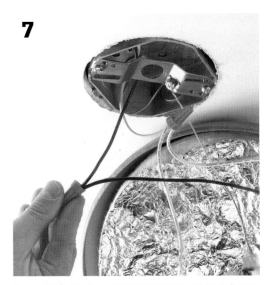

Connect the black power supply wire to the black fixture wire with a wire connector.

8

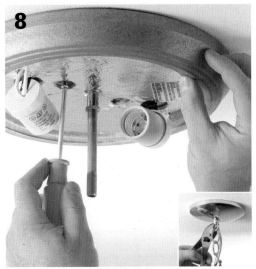

Position the new fixture mounting plate over the box so the mounting screw holes align. Drive the screws until the fixture is secure against the ceiling. *NOTE: Some fixtures are supported by a threaded rod or nipple in the center that screws into a female threaded opening in the mounting strap (inset).*

Replacing Vanity Lights

Many bathrooms have a single fixture positioned above the vanity, but a light source in this position casts shadows on the face and makes grooming more difficult. Light fixtures on either side of the mirror is a better arrangement.

For a remodel, mark the mirror location, run cable, and position boxes before drywall installation. You can also retrofit by installing new boxes and drawing power from the existing fixture.

The light sources should be at eye level; 66" is typical. The size of your mirror and its location on the wall may affect how far apart you can place the sconces, but 36" to 40" apart is a good guideline.

Tools & Materials ▸

Drywall saw	Cable protector plates
Drill	Electrical boxes
Combination tool	and braces
Circuit tester	Vanity light fixtures
Screwdrivers	NM cable
Hammer	Wire connectors
Cable clamps	Eye protection

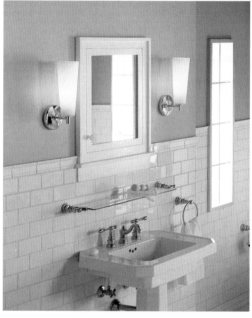

Vanity lights on the sides of the mirror provide good lighting.

How to Replace Vanity Lights in a Finished Bathroom

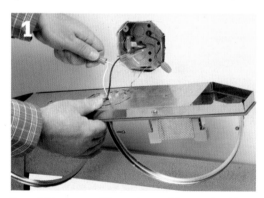

Turn off the power at the service panel. Remove the old fixture from the wall, and test to make sure that the power is off. Then remove a strip of drywall from around the old fixture to the first studs beyond the approximate location of the new fixtures. Make the opening large enough that you have room to route cable from the existing fixture to the boxes.

Mark the location for the fixtures, and install new boxes. Install the boxes about 66" above the floor and 18" to 20" from the centerline of the mirror (the mounting base of some fixtures is above or below the bulb, so adjust the height of the bracing accordingly). If the correct location is on or next to a stud, you can attach the box directly to the stud; otherwise you'll need to install blocking or use boxes with adjustable braces (shown).

3

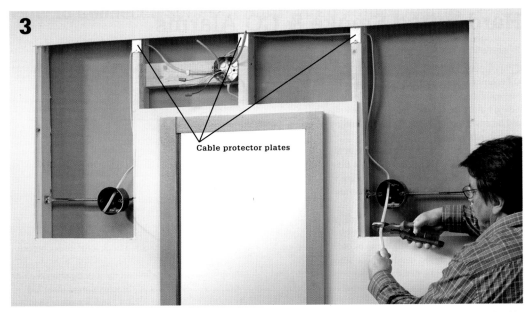

Cable protector plates

Open the side knockouts on the electrical box above the vanity. Then drill ⅝" holes in the centers of any studs between the old fixture and the new ones. Run two NM cables from the new boxes for the fixtures to the box above the vanity. Protect the cable with metal protector plates. Secure the cables with cable clamps, leaving 11" of extra cable for making the connection to the new fixtures. Remove sheathing, and strip insulation from the ends of the wires.

4

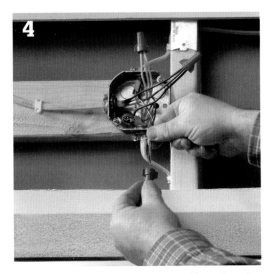

5

Connect the white wires from the new cables to the white wire from the old cable, and connect the black wires from the new cables to the black wire from the old cable. Connect the ground wires. Cover all open boxes, and then replace the drywall, leaving openings for the fixture and the old box. (Cover the old box with a solid junction box cover plate.)

Install the fixture mounting braces on the boxes. Attach the fixtures by connecting the black circuit wire to the black fixture wire and connecting the white circuit wire to the white fixture wire. Connect the ground wires. Position each fixture over each box, and attach with the mounting screws. Restore power, and test the circuit.

Doorbells

Most doorbell problems are caused by loose wire connections or worn-out switches. Reconnecting loose wires or replacing a switch requires only a few minutes. Doorbell problems also can occur if the chime unit becomes dirty or worn or if the low-voltage transformer burns out. Both parts are easy to replace. Because doorbells operate at low voltage, the switches and the chime unit can be serviced without turning off power to the system. However, when replacing a transformer, always turn off the power at the main service panel.

Some older houses have other low-voltage transformers in addition to the doorbell transformer. These transformers control heating and air-conditioning thermostats (see pages 464 to 467) or other low-voltage systems. When testing and repairing a doorbell system, it is important to identify the correct transformer. A doorbell transformer has a rating of 24 volts or less. This rating is printed on the face of the transformer. The location of your doorbell transformer is based on local custom and the age of your home. It may be near or attached to the service panel. It may be in the attic, basement, crawlspace, or garage.

In most modern heating and air-conditioning systems, the transformer serving the system is inside the furnace cabinet. In older systems, it may be located near the furnace.

Occasionally, a doorbell problem is caused by a broken low-voltage wire somewhere in the system. You can test for wire breaks with a battery-operated multitester. If the test indicates a break, new low-voltage wires must be installed between the transformer and the switches or between the switches and chime unit. Replacing low-voltage wires is not a difficult job, but it can be time-consuming. You may choose to have an electrician do this work.

Tools & Materials ▸

Continuity tester	Replacement doorbell
Screwdriver	switch (if needed)
Multimeter	Masking tape
Needlenose pliers	Replacement chime
Cotton swab	unit (if needed)
Rubbing alcohol	Eye protection

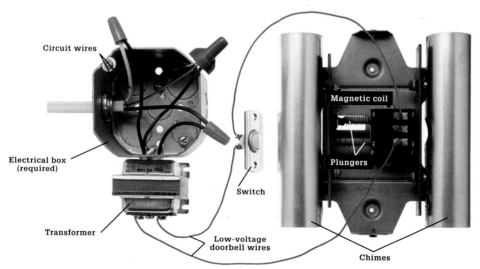

Circuit wires

Electrical box (required)

Transformer

Switch

Low-voltage doorbell wires

Magnetic coil

Plungers

Chimes

A home doorbell system is powered by a transformer that reduces 120-volts to 24 volts or less. Current flows from the transformer to one or more push-button switches. When pushed, the switch activates a magnetic coil inside the chime unit, causing a plunger to strike a musical tuning bar.

How to Test a Nonfunctional Doorbell System

1

Remove the mounting screws holding the doorbell switch to the siding.

2

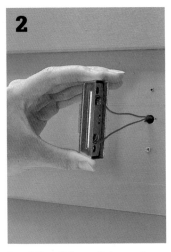

Carefully pull the switch away from the wall.

3

Inspect wire connections on the switch. If wires are loose, reconnect them to the screw terminals. Test the doorbell by pressing the button. If the doorbell still does not work, disconnect the switch and test it with a continuity tester.

4

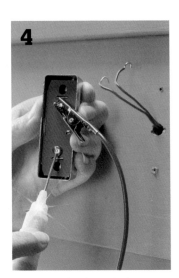

Attach the clip of a continuity tester to one screw terminal and touch the probe to the other screw terminal. Press the switch button. The tester should glow. If not, then the switch is faulty and must be replaced.

5

Twist the doorbell switch wires together temporarily to test the other parts of the doorbell system.

6

Transformer

Locate the doorbell transformer. If it's not near the service panel, look in the garage, crawlspace, and attic.

(continued)

Identify the doorbell transformer by reading its voltage rating. Doorbell transformers have a voltage rating of 24 volts or less. Turn off power to the transformer at the main service panel. Remove the cover on the electrical box, and test wires for power. Reconnect any loose wires. Replace taped connections with wire connectors.

Reattach the cover plate. Inspect the low-voltage wire connections, and reconnect any loose wires using needlenose pliers or a screwdriver. Turn on power to the transformer at the main service panel.

Touch the probes of the multitester to the low-voltage screw terminals on the transformer. If the transformer is operating properly, the meter will detect power within 2 volts of the transformer's rating. If not, the transformer is faulty and must be replaced.

Test the chime unit. Remove the cover plate on the doorbell chime unit. Inspect the low-voltage wire connections, and reconnect any loose wires.

Test that the chime unit is receiving current. Touch probes of a multimeter to screw terminals. If the multimeter detects power within 2 volts of the transformer rating, then the unit is receiving proper current. If it detects no power or very low power, there is a break in the low-voltage wiring, and new wires must be installed.

Clean the chime plungers (some models) with a cotton swab dipped in rubbing alcohol. Reassemble doorbell switches, and then test the system by pushing one of the switches. If the doorbell still does not work, then the chime unit is faulty and must be replaced (see opposite page).

How to Replace a Doorbell Switch

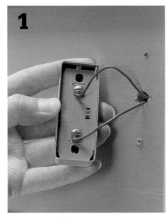

1

Remove the doorbell switch mounting screws, and carefully pull the switch away from the wall.

2

Disconnect wires from the switch. Tape wires to the wall to prevent them from slipping into the wall cavity.

3

Purchase a new doorbell switch, and connect the wires to the screw terminals on the new switch. (Wires are interchangeable and can be connected to either terminal.) Anchor the switch to the wall.

How to Replace a Doorbell Chime Unit

1

Turn off power to the doorbell at the main panel. Remove the cover plate from the old chime. Label the low-voltage wires FRONT, REAR, or TRANS to identify their screw terminal locations. Disconnect the wires. Remove the old chime unit.

2

Purchase a new chime unit that matches the voltage rating of the old unit. Thread the low-voltage wires through the base of the new chime unit. Attach the chime unit to the wall using the mounting screws included with the installation kit.

3

Connect the low-voltage wires to the screw terminals on the new chime unit. Attach the cover plate, and turn on the power at the main service panel.

Replacing Thermostats

A thermostat is a temperature-sensitive switch that automatically controls home heating and air-conditioning systems. There are two types of thermostats. Low-voltage thermostats control whole-house heating and air conditioning from one central location. Line-voltage thermostats are used in zone heating systems, where each room has its own heating unit and thermostat.

A low-voltage thermostat is powered by a transformer (usually located inside the furnace) that reduces 120-volt current to about 24 volts. A low-voltage thermostat is very durable, but failures can occur if wire connections become loose or dirty, if thermostat parts become corroded, or if a transformer wears out. Some thermostat systems have two transformers. One transformer controls the heating unit, and the other controls the air-conditioning unit.

Line-voltage thermostats are powered by the same circuit as the heating unit, usually a 240-volt circuit. Always make sure to turn off the power before servicing a line-voltage thermostat (typically, these are found in electric heaters).

A thermostat can be replaced in about one hour. Many homeowners choose to replace standard low-voltage or line-voltage thermostats with programmable setback thermostats. These programmable thermostats can cut energy use by up to 35 percent.

When buying a new thermostat, make sure the new unit is compatible with your heating/air-conditioning system. For example, a thermostat intended for a furnace and air conditioner may not work with a heat pump. For reference, take along the brand name and model number of the old thermostat and of your heating/air-conditioning units. When buying a new low-voltage transformer, choose a replacement with voltage and amperage ratings that match the old thermostat.

Tools & Materials ›

Screwdriver
Masking tape

New thermostat
Eye protection

A programmable thermostat allows you to significantly reduce your energy consumption by taking greater control over your heating and cooling system.

Traditional Low-Voltage Thermostats

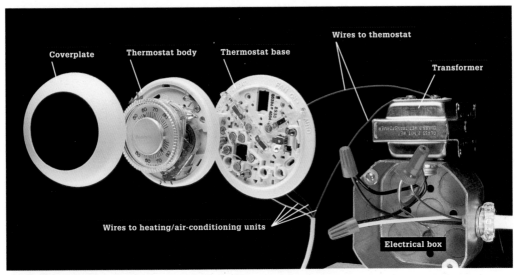

Coverplate   Thermostat body   Thermostat base

Wires to themostat

Transformer

Wires to heating/air-conditioning units

Electrical box

Low-voltage thermostat systems have a transformer that is either connected to an electrical junction box or mounted inside a furnace access panel. Very thin wires (18 to 22 gauge) send current to the thermostat. The thermostat constantly monitors room temperatures and sends electrical signals to the heating/cooling unit through additional wires. The number of wires connected to the thermostat varies from two to six, depending on the type of heating/air-conditioning system. In the common four-wire system shown above, power is supplied to the thermostat through a single wire attached to screw terminal R. Wires attached to other screw terminals relay signals to the furnace heating unit, the air-conditioning unit, and the blower unit. Before removing a thermostat, make sure to label each wire to identify its screw terminal location.

Programmable Thermostats

Programmable thermostats contain sophisticated circuitry that allows you to set the heating and cooling systems in your house to adjust automatically at set times of the day. Replacing a manual thermostat with a programmable model is a relatively simple job that can have big payback on heating and cooling energy savings.

How to Upgrade to a Programmable Thermostat

Start by removing the existing thermostat. Turn off the power to the furnace at the main service panel, and test for power. Then remove the thermostat cover.

The body of the thermostat is held to a wall plate with screws. Remove these screws, and pull the body away from the wall plate. Set the body aside.

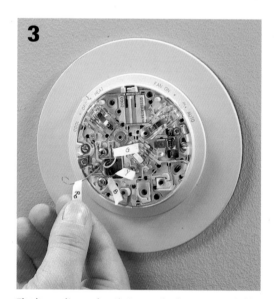

The low-voltage wires that power the thermostat are held by screw terminals to the mounting plate. Do not remove the wires until you label them with tape according to the letter printed on the terminal to which each wire is attached.

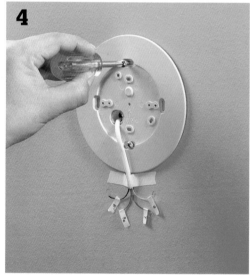

Once all the wires are labeled and removed from the mounting plate, tape the cable that holds these wires to the wall to keep it from falling back into the wall. Then unscrew the mounting plate and set it aside.

5

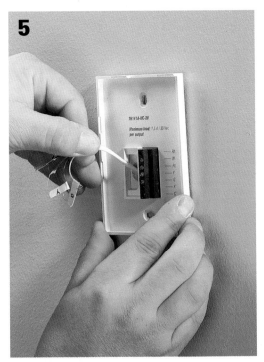

Position the new thermostat base on the wall, and guide the wires through the central opening. Screw the base to the wall using wall anchors if necessary.

6

Check the manufacturer's instructions to establish the correct terminal for each low-voltage wire. Then connect the wires to these terminals, making sure each screw is secure.

7

Programmable thermostats require batteries to store the programs so they won't disappear if the power goes out in a storm. Make sure to install batteries before you snap the thermostat cover in place. Program the new unit to fit your needs, and then turn on the power to the furnace.

Mercury Thermostats ▶

Older model thermostats (and even a few still being made today) often contained one or more small vials of mercury totaling 3 to 4 grams in weight. Because mercury is a highly toxic metal that can cause nerve damage in humans, along with other environmental problems, DO NOT dispose of an old mercury thermostat with your household waste. Instead, bring it to a hazardous waste disposal site or a mercury recycling site if your area has one (check with your local solid waste disposal agency). The best way to determine if your old thermostat contains mercury is simply to remove the cover and look for the small glass vials or ampules containing the silverfish mercury substance. If you are unsure, it is always better to be safe and keep the device in question out of the normal waste stream.

Installing Motion-sensing Floodlights

Most houses and garages have floodlights on their exteriors. You can easily upgrade these fixtures so that they provide additional security by replacing them with motion-sensing floodlights. Motion-sensing floods can be set up to detect motion in a specific area—like a walkway or driveway—and then cast light into that area. And there are few things intruders like less than the spotlight. These lights typically have timers that allow you to control how long the light stays on and photosensors that prevent the light from coming on during the day.

A motion-sensing light fixture provides inexpensive and effective protection against intruders. It has an infrared eye that triggers the light fixture when a moving object crosses its path. Choose a light fixture with a photo cell to prevent the light from turning on in daylight; an adjustable timer to control how long the light stays on; and range control to adjust the reach of the motion-sensor eye.

Tools & Materials ▶

Circuit tester
Jigsaw
Fish tape
Screwdrivers
Wire cutter
Cable ripper
Wire stripper

Caulk gun
Motion-sensing floodlight fixture
Electrical box
NM cable
Wire connectors
Eye and ear protection
Work gloves

An exterior floodlight with a motion sensor is an effective security measure. Keep the motion sensor adjusted to cover only the area you wish to secure—if the coverage area is too large, the light will turn on frequently.

How to Install a New Exterior Fixture Box

1

On the outside of the house, make the cutout for the motion-sensor light fixture. Outline the light fixture box on the wall, drill a pilot hole, and complete the cutout with a wallboard saw or jigsaw.

2

Estimate the distance between the indoor switch box and the outdoor motion-sensor box, and cut a length of NM cable about 2 ft. longer than this distance. Use a fish tape to pull the cable from the switch box to the motion-sensor box.

3

Mounting bracket

Retrofit box

Strip about 10" of outer insulation from the end of the cable using a cable ripper. Open a knockout in the retrofit light fixture box with a screwdriver. Insert the cable into the box so that at least ¼" of outer sheathing reaches into the box. Apply a heavy bead of silicone or polyurethane caulk to the flange of the electrical box before attaching it to the wall.

4

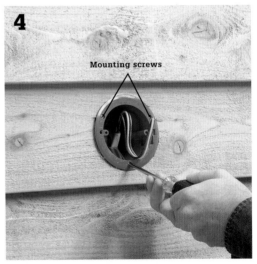

Mounting screws

Insert the box into the cutout opening, and tighten the mounting screws until the brackets draw the outside flange firmly against the siding.

How to Replace a Floodlight with a Motion-Sensor Light

1

Turn off power to the old fixture. To remove it, unscrew the mounting screws on the part of the fixture attached to the wall. There will probably be four of them. Carefully pull the fixture away from the wall, exposing the wires. Don't touch the wires yet.

2

Before you touch any wires, use a voltage sensor to verify that the circuit is dead. With the light switch turned on, insert the sensor's probe into the electrical box and hold the probe within ½" of the wires inside to confirm that there is no voltage. Disconnect the wire connectors, and remove the old fixture.

3

Examine the ends of the three wires coming from the box (one white, one black, and one bare copper). They should be clean and free of corrosion. If the ends are in poor condition, clip them off and then strip ¾" of wire insulation with a combination tool.

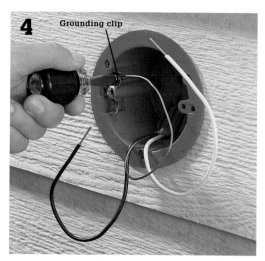

4 Grounding clip

If the electrical box is nonmetallic and does not have a metal grounding clip, install a grounding clip or replace the box with one that does have a clip, and make sure the ground wire is attached to it securely. Some light fixtures have a grounding terminal on the base. If yours has one, attach the grounding wire from the house directly to the terminal.

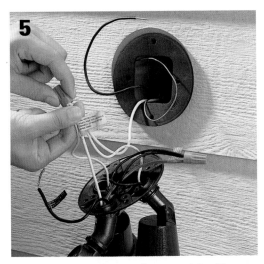

5

Now you can attach the new fixture. Begin by sliding a rubber or foam gasket (usually provided with the fixture) over the wires and onto the flange of the electrical box. Set the new fixture on top of a ladder or have a helper hold it while you make the wiring connections. There may be as many as three white wires coming from the fixture. Join all white wires, including the feed wire from the house, using a wire connector.

6

Next, join the black wire from the box and the single black wire from the fixture with a wire connector. You may see a couple of black wires and a red wire already joined on the fixture. You can ignore these in your installation.

7

Neatly tuck all the wires into the box so they are behind the gasket. Align the holes in the gasket with the holes in the box, and then position the fixture over the gasket so its mounting holes are also aligned with the gasket. Press the fixture against the gasket, and drive the four mounting screws into the box. Install floodlights (exterior rated) and restore power.

8

Test the fixture. You will still be able to turn it on and off with the light switch inside. Flip the switch on and pass your hand in front of the motion sensor. The light should come on. Adjust the motion sensor to cover the traffic areas, and pivot the light head to illuminate the intended area.

Troubleshooting Light Fixtures

Light fixtures are attached permanently to ceilings or walls. They include wall-hung sconces, ceiling-hung globe fixtures, recessed light fixtures, and chandeliers. Most light fixtures are easy to repair using basic tools and inexpensive parts.

If a light fixture fails, always make sure the light bulb is screwed in tightly and is not burned out. A faulty light bulb is the most common cause of light fixture failure. If the light fixture is controlled by a wall switch, also check the switch as a possible source of problems.

Light fixtures can fail because the sockets or built-in switches wear out. Some fixtures have sockets and switches that can be removed for minor repairs. These parts are held to the base of the fixture with mounting screws or clips. Other fixtures have sockets and switches that are joined permanently to the base. If this type of fixture fails, purchase and install a new light fixture.

Damage to light fixtures often occurs because homeowners install light bulbs with wattage ratings that are too high. Prevent overheating and light fixture failures by using only light bulbs that match the wattage ratings printed on the fixtures.

Techniques for repairing fluorescent lights are different from those for incandescent lights. Refer to pages 482 to 487 to repair or replace a fluorescent light fixture.

Tools & Materials ▸

Circuit tester
Screwdriver
Continuity tester
Combination tool

Replacement parts,
as needed
Eye protection

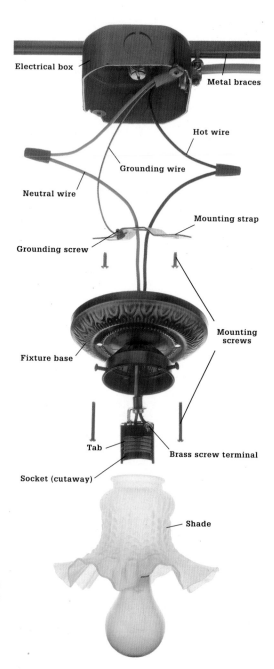

Electrical box

Metal braces

Hot wire

Grounding wire

Neutral wire

Mounting strap

Grounding screw

Mounting screws

Fixture base

Tab

Brass screw terminal

Socket (cutaway)

Shade

In a typical incandescent light fixture, a black hot wire is connected to a brass screw terminal on the socket. Power flows to a small tab at the bottom of the metal socket and through a metal filament inside the bulb. The power heats the filament and causes it to glow. The current then flows through the threaded portion of the socket and through the white neutral wire back to the main service panel.

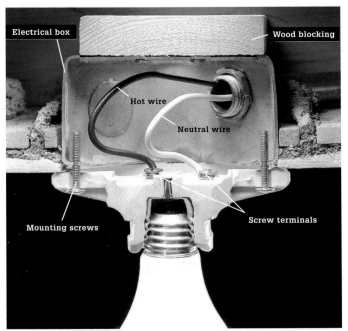

Electrical box

Wood blocking

Hot wire

Neutral wire

Mounting screws

Screw terminals

Before 1959, incandescent light fixtures (shown cutaway) often were mounted directly to an electrical box or to plaster lath. Electrical codes now require that fixtures be attached to mounting straps that are anchored to the electrical boxes. If you have a light fixture attached to plaster lath, install an approved electrical box with a mounting strap to support the fixture.

PROBLEM	REPAIR
Wall- or ceiling-mounted fixture flickers or does not light.	1. Check for faulty light bulb. 2. Check wall switch and replace, if needed. 3. Check for loose wire connections in electrical box. 4. Test socket and replace, if needed (page 475). 5. Replace light fixture.
Built-in switch on fixture does not work.	1. Check for faulty light bulb. 2. Check for loose wire connections on switch. 3. Replace switch. 4. Replace light fixture.
Chandelier flickers or does not light.	1. Check for faulty light bulb. 2. Check wall switch and replace, if needed. 3. Check for loose wire connections in electrical box. 4. Test sockets and fixture wires, and replace, if needed.
Recessed fixture flickers or does not light.	1. Check for faulty light bulb. 2. Check wall switch, and replace, if needed. 3. Check for loose wire connections in electrical box. 4. Test fixture, and replace, if needed.

How to Remove a Light Fixture & Test a Socket

1

Turn off the power to the light fixture at the main panel. Remove the light bulb and any shade or globe, then remove the mounting screws holding the fixture base and the electrical box or mounting strap. Carefully pull the fixture base away from the box.

2

Grounding screw

Test for power with a circuit tester. The tester should not glow. If it does, there is still power entering the box. Return to the panel and turn off power to the correct circuit.

3

Disconnect the light fixture base by loosening the screw terminals. If the fixture has wire leads instead of screw terminals, remove the light fixture base by unscrewing the wire connectors.

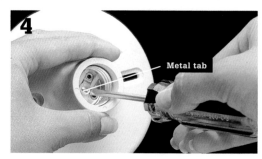

4

Metal tab

Adjust the metal tab at the bottom of the fixture socket by prying it up slightly with a small screwdriver. This adjustment will improve the contact between the socket and the light bulb.

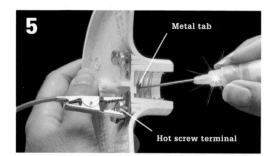

5

Metal tab

Hot screw terminal

Test the socket (shown cutaway) by attaching the clip of a continuity tester to the hot screw terminal (or black wire lead) and touching probe of the tester to the metal tab in the bottom of the socket. The tester should glow. If not, the socket is faulty and must be replaced.

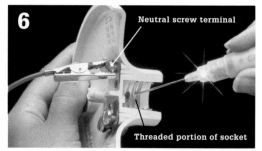

6

Neutral screw terminal

Threaded portion of socket

Attach the tester clip to the neutral screw terminal (or white wire lead), and touch the probe to the threaded portion of the socket. The tester should glow. If not, the socket is faulty and must be replaced. If the socket is permanently attached, replace the fixture.

How to Replace a Socket

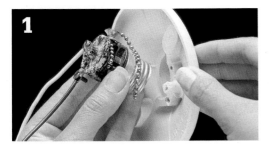

Remove the old light fixture. Remove the socket from the fixture. The socket may be held by a screw, clip, or retaining ring. Disconnect wires attached to the socket.

Purchase an identical replacement socket. Connect the white wire to the silver screw terminal on the socket, and connect the black wire to the brass screw terminal. Attach the socket to the fixture base, and reinstall the fixture.

How to Test & Replace a Built-in Light Switch

Retaining ring

Remove the light fixture. Unscrew the retaining ring holding the switch.

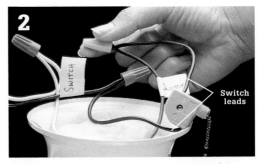

Switch leads

Label the wires connected to the switch leads. Disconnect the switch leads, and remove the switch.

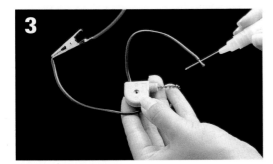

Test the switch by attaching the clip of the continuity tester to one of the switch leads and holding the tester probe to the other lead. Operate the switch control. If the switch is good, the tester will glow when the switch is in one position but not both.

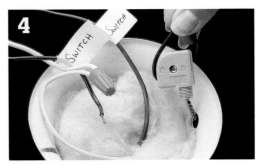

If the switch is faulty, purchase and install a duplicate switch. Remount the light fixture, and turn on the power at the main service panel.

Repairing Chandeliers

Repairing a chandelier requires special care. Because chandeliers are heavy, it is a good idea to work with a helper when removing a chandelier. Support the fixture to prevent its weight from pulling against the wires.

Chandeliers have two fixture wires that are threaded through the support chain from the electrical box to the hollow base of the chandelier. The socket wires connect to the fixture wires inside this base.

Fixture wires are identified as hot and neutral. Look closely for a raised stripe on one of the wires. This is the neutral wire that is connected to the white circuit wire and white socket wire. The other smooth fixture wire is hot and is connected to the black wires.

If you have a new chandelier, it may have a grounding wire that runs through the support chain to the electrical box. If this wire is present, make sure it is connected to the grounding wires in the electrical box.

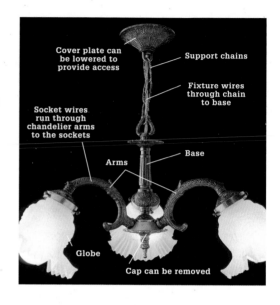

Cover plate can be lowered to provide access

Support chains

Fixture wires through chain to base

Socket wires run through chandelier arms to the sockets

Arms

Base

Globe

Cap can be removed

How to Repair a Chandelier

Label any lights that are not working using masking tape. Turn off power to the fixture at the main service panel. Remove light bulbs and all shades or globes.

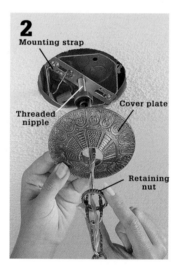

2

Mounting strap

Threaded nipple

Cover plate

Retaining nut

Unscrew the retaining nut, and lower the decorative coverplate away from the electrical box. Most chandeliers are supported by a threaded nipple attached to a mounting strap.

Mounting strap

Mounting bolt

Bolt cap nut

Mounting variation: Some chandeliers are supported only by the cover plate that is bolted to the electrical box mounting strap. These types do not have a threaded nipple.

3

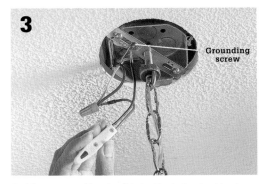

Grounding screw

Test for power with a circuit tester. The tester should not glow. If it does, turn off power to the correct circuit at the panel.

4

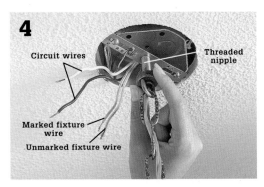

Circuit wires

Threaded nipple

Marked fixture wire

Unmarked fixture wire

Disconnect fixture wires by removing the wire connectors. Unscrew the threaded nipple and carefully place the chandelier on a flat surface.

5

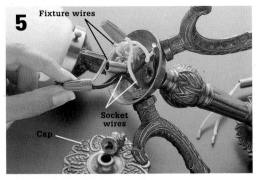

Fixture wires

Socket wires

Cap

Remove the cap from the bottom of the chandelier, exposing the wire connections inside the hollow base. Disconnect the socket wires and fixture wires.

6

Test the socket by attaching the clip of the continuity tester to the black socket wire and touching the probe to the tab in the socket. Repeat with the socket threads and the white socket wire. If the tester does not glow, the socket must be replaced.

7

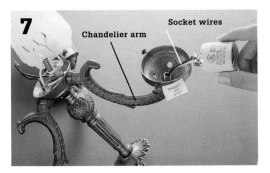

Socket wires

Chandelier arm

Remove a faulty socket by loosening any mounting screws or clips and pulling the socket and socket wires out of the fixture arm. Purchase and install a new chandelier socket, threading the socket wires through the fixture arm.

8

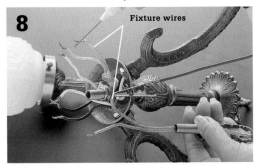

Fixture wires

Test each fixture wire by attaching the clip of the continuity tester to one end of the wire and touching the probe to other end. If the tester does not glow, the wire must be replaced. Install new wires, if needed, then reassemble and rehang the chandelier.

Repairing Ceiling Fans

Ceiling fans contain rapidly moving parts, making them more susceptible to trouble than many other electrical fixtures. Installation is a relatively simple matter, but repairing a ceiling fan can be very frustrating. The most common problems you'll encounter are balance and noise issues and switch failure, usually precipitated by the pull chain breaking. In most cases, both problems can be corrected without removing the fan from the ceiling. But if you have difficulty on ladders or simply don't care to work overhead, consider removing the fan when replacing the switch.

Ceiling fans are subject to a great deal of vibration and stress, so it's not uncommon for switches and motors to fail. Minimize wear and tear by making sure blades are in balance so the fan doesn't wobble.

Tools & Materials ▸

Screwdriver
Combination tool
Replacement switch
Voltage sensor
Eye protection

How to Troubleshoot Blade Wobble

1

Start by checking and tightening all hardware used to attach the blades to the mounting arms and the mounting arms to the motor. Hardware tends to loosen over time, and this is frequently the cause of wobble.

2

If wobble persists, try switching around two of the blades. Often this is all it takes to get the fan back into balance. If a blade is damaged or warped, replace it.

3

If the blades are tight and you still have wobble, turn the power off at the panel, remove the fan canopy, and inspect the mounting brace and the connection between the mounting pole and the fan motor. If any connections are loose, tighten them, and then replace the canopy.

How to Fix a Loose Wire Connection

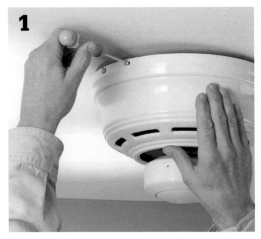

1

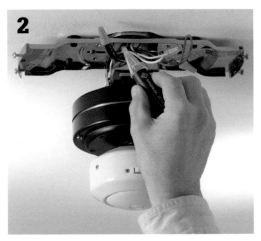

2

A leading cause of fan failure is loose wire connections. To inspect these connections, first shut off the power to the fan. Remove the fan blades to gain access, and then remove the canopy that covers the ceiling box and fan mounting bracket. Most canopies are secured with screws on the outside shell. Have a helper hold the fan body while you remove the screws so it won't fall.

Once the canopy is lowered, you'll see black, white, green, copper, and possibly blue wires. Hold a voltage sensor within ½" of these wires with the wall switch that controls the fan in the ON position. The black and blue wires should cause the sensor to beep if power is present.

3

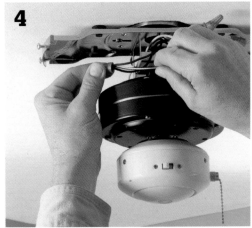

4

Shut off power, and test the wires by placing a voltage sensor within ½" of the wires. If the sensor beeps or lights up, then the circuit is still live and is not safe to work on. When the sensor does not beep or light up, the circuit is dead and may be worked upon.

When you have confirmed that there is no power, check all the wire connections to make certain each is tight and making good contact. You may be able to see that a connection has come apart and needs to be remade. But even if you see one bad connection, check them all by gently tugging on the wire connectors. If the wires pull out of the wire connector or the connection feels loose, unscrew the wire connector from the wires. Turn the power back on and see if the problem has been solved.

How to Replace a Ceiling Fan Pull-Chain Switch

1

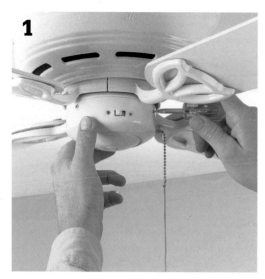

Turn off the power at the panel. Use a screwdriver to remove the three to four screws that secure the bottom cap on the fan switch housing. Lower the cap to expose the wires that supply power to the pull-chain switch.

2

Test the wires by placing a voltage sensor within ½" of the wires. If the sensor beeps or lights up, then the circuit is still live and is not safe to work on. When the sensor does not beep or light up, the circuit is dead and may be worked upon.

3

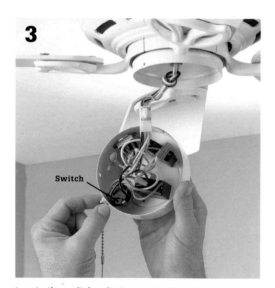

Switch

Locate the switch unit (the part that the pull chain used to be attached to if it broke off); it's probably made of plastic. You'll need to replace the whole switch. Fan switches are connected with three to eight wires, depending on the number of speed settings.

4

Attach a small piece of tape to each wire that enters the switch, and write an identifying number on the tape. Start at one side of the switch, and label the wires in the order they're attached.

5

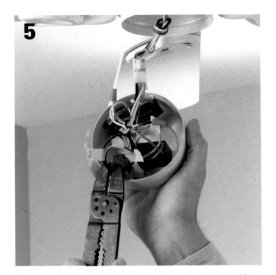

Disconnect the old switch wires, in most cases by cutting the wires off as close to the old switch as possible. Unscrew the retaining nut that secures the switch to the switch housing.

6

Remove the switch. There may be one or two screws that hold it in place or it may be secured to the outside of the fan with a small knurled nut, which you can loosen with needlenose pliers. Purchase an identical new switch.

7

Connect the new switch using the same wiring configuration as on the old model. To make connections, first use a wire stripper to strip ¾" of insulation from the ends of each of the wires coming from the fan motor (the ones you cut in step 5). Attach the wires to the new switch in the same order and configuraion as they were attached to the old switch. Secure the new switch in the housing, and make sure all wires are tucked neatly inside. Reattach the bottom cap. Restore power to the fan. Test all the fan's speeds to make sure all the connections are good.

Repairing Fluorescent Lights

Fluorescent lights are relatively trouble free and use less energy than incandescent lights. A typical fluorescent tube lasts about three years and produces two to four times as much light per watt as a standard incandescent light bulb.

The most frequent problem with a fluorescent light fixture is a worn-out tube. If a fluorescent light fixture begins to flicker or does not light fully, remove and examine the tube. If the tube has bent or broken pins or black discoloration near the ends, replace it. Light gray discoloration is normal in working fluorescent tubes. When replacing an old tube, read the wattage rating and the color temperature rating printed on the tube, and buy a new tube with matching ratings. The color temperature rating is a measure of the color of the light produced by the tube. Most people prefer a "warm" light in the 2,700K range. Never dispose of old tubes by

breaking them. Fluorescent tubes contain a small amount of hazardous mercury. Check with your local environmental control agency or health department for disposal guidelines.

Fluorescent light fixtures also can malfunction if the sockets are cracked or worn. Inexpensive replacement sockets are available at any hardware store and can be installed in a few minutes.

If a fixture does not work even after the tube and sockets have been serviced, the ballast probably is defective. Faulty ballasts may leak a black, oily substance and can cause a fluorescent light fixture to make a loud humming sound. Although ballasts can be replaced, always check prices before buying a new ballast. It may be cheaper to purchase and install a new fluorescent fixture rather than to replace the ballast in an old fluorescent light fixture.

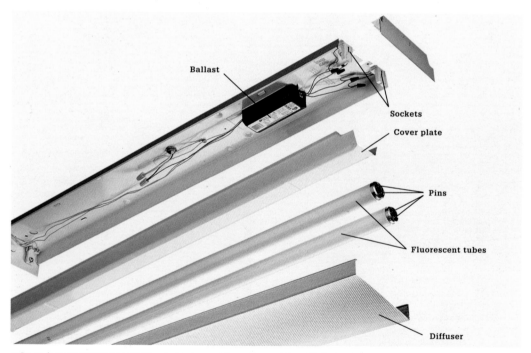

Ballast

Sockets

Cover plate

Pins

Fluorescent tubes

Diffuser

A fluorescent light works by directing electrical current through a special gas-filled tube that glows when energized. A white translucent diffuser protects the fluorescent tube and softens the light. A cover plate protects a special transformer, called a ballast. The ballast regulates the flow of 120-volt household current to the sockets. The sockets transfer power to metal pins that extend into the tube.

PROBLEM	REPAIR
Tube flickers, or lights partially.	1. Rotate tube to make sure it is seated properly in the sockets.
	2. Replace tube and the starter (where present) if tube is discolored or if pins are bent or broken.
	3. Replace the ballast if replacement cost is reasonable. Otherwise, replace the entire fixture.
Tube does not light.	1. Check wall switch and replace, if needed.
	2. Rotate the tube to make sure it is seated properly in sockets.
	3. Replace tube and the starter (where present) if tube is discolored or if pins are bent or broken.
	4. Replace sockets if they are chipped or if tube does not seat properly.
	5. Replace the ballast or the entire fixture.
Noticeable black substance around ballast.	Replace ballast if replacement cost is reasonable. Otherwise, replace the entire fixture.
Fixture hums.	Replace ballast if replacement cost is reasonable. Otherwise, replace the entire fixture.

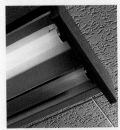
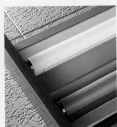

Tools & Materials ▶

Screwdriver
Ratchet wrench
Combination tool
Circuit tester
Replacement tubes
Starters, or ballast
    (if needed)
Replacement fluorescent light fixture
    (if needed)
Eye protection

Older fluorescent lights may have a small cylindrical device, called a starter, located near one of the sockets. When a tube begins to flicker, replace both the tube and the starter. Turn off the power, and then remove the starter by pushing it slightly and turning it counterclockwise. Install a replacement that matches the old starter.

How to Replace a Fluorescent Tube

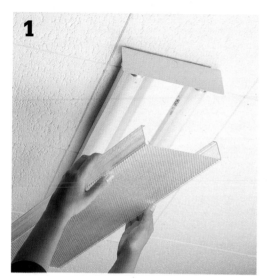

Turn off power to the light fixture at the switch. Remove the diffuser to expose the fluorescent tube.

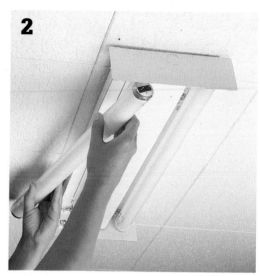

Remove the fluorescent tube by rotating it ¼ turn in either direction and sliding the tube out of the sockets. Inspect the pins at the end of the tube. Tubes with bent or broken pins should be replaced.

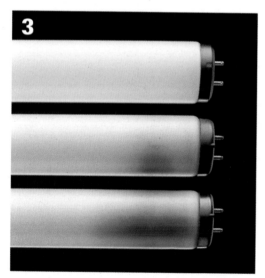

Inspect the ends of the fluorescent tube for discoloration. The new tube in good working order (top) shows no discoloration. The normal, working tube (middle) may have gray color. A worn-out tube (bottom) shows black discoloration.

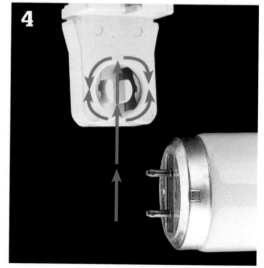

Install a new tube with the same wattage rating as the old tube. Insert the tube so that pins slide fully into sockets, and then twist tube ¼ turn in either direction until it is locked securely. Reattach the diffuser, and turn on the power at the switch.

How to Replace a Socket

1

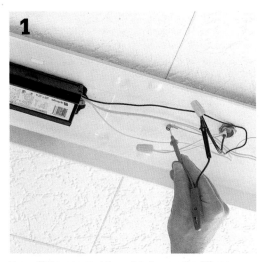

Turn off the power at the switch. Remove the diffuser, fluorescent tube, and the cover plate. Test for power by touching one probe of a neon circuit tester to the grounding screw and inserting the other probe into the hot wire connector. If the tester glows, return to the panel and turn off the correct circuit.

2

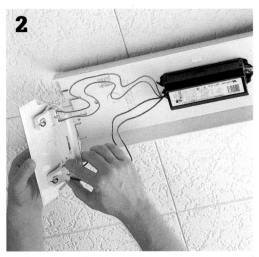

Remove the faulty socket from the fixture housing. Some sockets slide out, while others must be unscrewed.

3

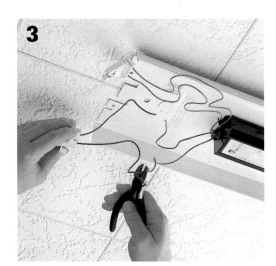

Disconnect wires attached to the socket. For push-in fittings (above) remove the wires by inserting a small screwdriver into the release openings. Some sockets have screw terminal connections, while others have preattached wires that must be cut before the socket can be removed.

4

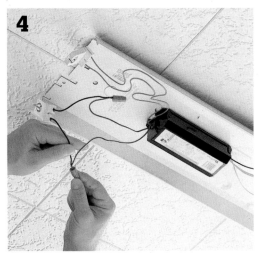

Purchase and install a new socket. If the socket has preattached wire leads, connect the leads to the ballast wires using wire connectors. Replace the cover plate and then the fluorescent tube, making sure that it seats properly. Replace the diffuser. Restore power to the fixture at the panel, and test.

How to Replace a Ballast

1

Turn off the power at the panel, and then remove the diffuser, fluorescent tube, and cover plate. Test for power using a circuit tester (page 302, step 3).

2

Remove the sockets from the fixture housing by sliding them out or by removing the mounting screws and lifting the sockets out.

3

Disconnect the wires attached to the sockets by pushing a small screwdriver into the release openings (above), by loosening the screw terminals, or by cutting wires to within 2" of sockets.

4

Remove the old ballast using a ratchet wrench or screwdriver. Make sure to support the ballast so it does not fall.

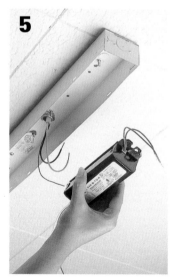

5

Install a new ballast that has the same ratings as the old ballast.

6

Attach the ballast wires to the socket wires using wire connectors, screw terminal connections, or push-in fittings. Reinstall the cover plate, fluorescent tube, and diffuser. Turn on power to the light fixture at the panel.

How to Replace a Fluorescent Light Fixture

1

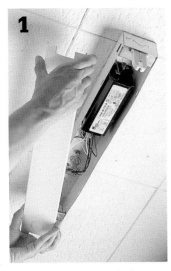

Turn off power to the light fixture at the panel. Remove the diffuser, tube, and cover plate. Test for power using a circuit tester.

2

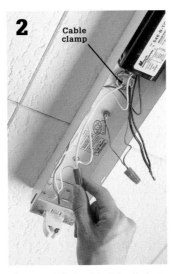

Cable clamp

Disconnect the insulated circuit wires and the bare copper grounding wire from the light fixture. Loosen the cable clamp holding the circuit wires.

3

Unscrew the fixture from the wall or ceiling and carefully remove it. Make sure to support the fixture so it does not fall.

4

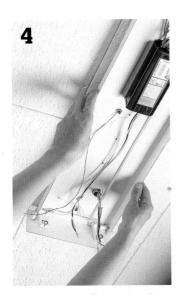

Position the new fixture, threading the circuit wires through the knockout opening in the back of the fixture. Screw the fixture in place so it is firmly anchored to framing members.

5

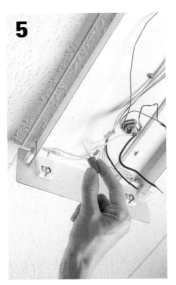

Connect the circuit wires to the fixture wires using wire connectors. Follow the wiring diagram included with the new fixture. Tighten the cable clamp holding the circuit wires.

6

Attach the fixture cover plate, and then install the fluorescent tubes and attach the diffuser. Turn on power to the fixture at the panel, and test.

Replacing Plugs & Cords

Replace an electrical plug whenever you notice bent or loose prongs, a cracked or damaged casing, or a missing insulating faceplate. A damaged plug poses a shock and fire hazard.

Replacement plugs are available in different styles to match common appliance cords. Always choose a replacement that is similar to the original plug. Flat-cord and quick-connect plugs are used with light-duty appliances, such as lamps and radios. Round-cord plugs are used with larger appliances, including those that have three-prong grounding plugs.

Some tools and appliances use polarized plugs. A polarized plug has one wide prong and one narrow prong, corresponding to the hot and neutral slots found in a standard receptacle.

If there is room in the plug body, tie the individual wires in an underwriter's knot to secure the plug to the cord (see photo, right).

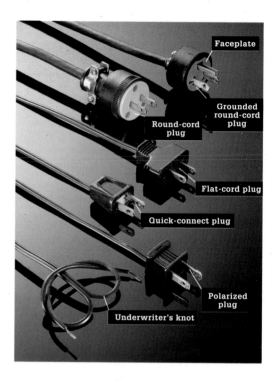

Faceplate

Grounded round-cord plug

Round-cord plug

Flat-cord plug

Quick-connect plug

Polarized plug

Underwriter's knot

Tools & Materials ▶

Combination tool
Needlenose pliers

Screwdriver
Replacement plug

How to Install a Quick-Connect Plug

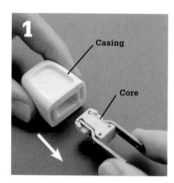

Casing

Core

Squeeze the prongs of the new quick-connect plug together slightly, and pull the plug core from the casing. Cut the old plug from the flat-cord wire with a combination tool, leaving a clean cut end.

Feed unstripped wire through the rear of the plug casing. Spread the prongs, and then insert the wire into the opening in the rear of the core. Squeeze the prongs together; spikes inside the core penetrate the cord. Slide the casing over the core until it snaps into place.

Ridged half

Wide prong

When replacing a polarized plug, make sure that the ridged half of the cord lines up with the wider (neutral) prong of the plug.

How to Replace a Round-Cord Plug

Cut off the round cord near the old plug using a combination tool. Remove the insulating faceplate on the new plug and feed the cord through the rear of the plug. Strip about 3" of outer insulation from the round cord. Strip ¾" insulation from the individual wires.

Tie an underwriter's knot with the black and the white wires. Make sure the knot is located close to the edge of the stripped outer insulation. Pull the cord so that the knot slides into the plug body.

Hook the end of the black wire clockwise around the brass screw and the white wire around the silver screw. On a three-prong plug, attach the third wire to the grounding screw. If necessary, excess grounding wire can be cut away.

Tighten the screws securely, making sure the copper wires do not touch each other. Replace the insulating faceplate.

How to Replace a Flat-Cord Plug

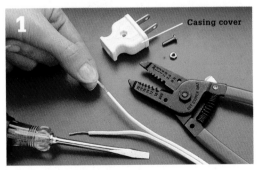

Cut the old plug from cord using a combination tool. Pull apart the two halves of the flat cord so that about 2" of wire are separated. Strip ¾" insulation from each half. Remove the casing cover on the new plug.

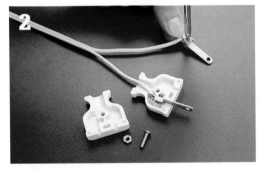

Hook the ends of the wires clockwise around the screw terminals, and tighten the screw terminals securely. Reassemble the plug casing. Some plugs may have an insulating faceplate that must be installed.

How to Replace a Lamp Cord

With the lamp unplugged, the shade off, and the bulb out, you can remove the socket. Squeeze the outer shell of the socket just above the base, and pull the shell out of the base. The shell is often marked "Press" at some point along its perimeter. Press there, and then pull.

Under the outer shell there is a cardboard insulating sleeve. Pull this off and you'll reveal the socket attached to the end of the cord.

With the shell and insulation set aside, pull the socket away from the lamp (it will still be connected to the cord). Unscrew the two screws to completely disconnect the socket from the cord. Set the socket aside with its shell (you'll need them to reassemble the lamp).

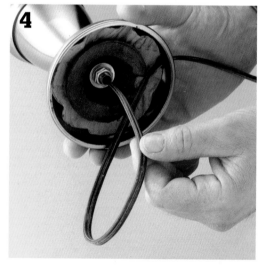

Remove the old cord from the lamp by grasping the cord near the base and pulling the cord through the lamp.

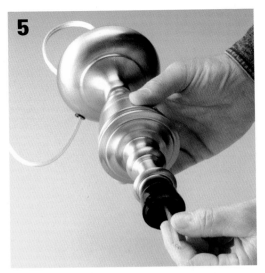

5

Bring your damaged cord to a hardware store or home center and purchase a similar cord set. (A cord set is simply a replacement cord with a plug already attached.) Snake the end of the cord up from the base of the lamp through the top so that about 3" of cord is visible above the top.

6

Carefully separate the two halves of the cord. If the halves won't pull apart, you can carefully make a cut in the middle with a knife. Strip away about ¾" of insulation from the end of each wire.

7

Connect the ends of the new cord to the two screws on the side of the socket (one of which will be silver in color, the other brass-colored). One half of the cord will have ribbing or markings along its length; wrap that wire clockwise around the silver screw, and tighten the screw. The other half of the cord will be smooth; wrap it around the copper screw, and tighten the screw.

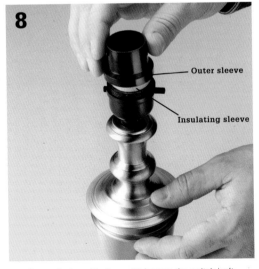

8

Outer sleeve

Insulating sleeve

Set the socket on the base. Make sure the switch isn't blocked by the harp—the part that holds the shade on some lamps. Slide the cardboard insulating sleeve over the socket so the sleeve's notch aligns with the switch. Now slide the outer sleeve over the socket, aligning the notch with the switch. It should snap into the base securely. Screw in a light bulb, plug the lamp in, and test it.

Replacing a Lamp Socket

Next to the cord plug, the most common source of trouble in a lamp is a worn lightbulb socket. When a lamp socket assembly fails, the problem is usually with the socket-switch unit, although replacement sockets may include other parts you do not need.

Lamp failure is not always caused by a bad socket. You can avoid unnecessary repairs by checking the lamp cord, plug, and light bulb before replacing the socket.

Tools & Materials ▸

Replacement socket
Continuity tester
Screwdriver

Socket-mounted switch types are usually interchangeable: choose a replacement you prefer. Clockwise from top left: twist knob, remote switch, pull chain, push lever.

Tip ▸

When replacing a lamp socket, you can improve a standard ON-OFF lamp by installing a three-way socket.

How to Repair or Replace a Lamp Socket

1 Contact tab

Unplug the lamp. Remove the shade, light bulb, and harp (shade bracket). Scrape the contact tab clean with a small screwdriver. Pry the contact tab up slightly if flattened inside the socket. Replace the bulb, plug in the lamp, and test. If the lamp does not work, unplug, remove the bulb, and continue with the next step.

2 Outer shell

Insulating sleeve

Squeeze the outer shell of the socket near the "Press" marking, and lift it off. On older lamps, the socket may be held by screws found at the base of the screw socket. Slip off the cardboard insulating sleeve. If the sleeve is damaged, replace the entire socket.

3

Check for loose wire connections on the screw terminals. Refasten any loose connections, and then reassemble the lamp, and test. If connections are not loose, remove the wires, lift out the socket, and continue with the next step.

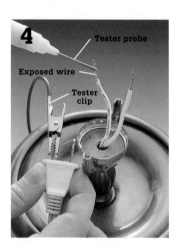

4 Tester probe

Exposed wire

Tester clip

Test for lamp cord problems with a continuity tester. Place the clip of the tester on one prong of the plug. Touch the probe to one exposed wire, and then to the other wire. Repeat the test with the other prong of the plug. If the tester fails to light for either prong, then replace the cord and plug. Retest the lamp.

5 Silver screw

Ridged insulation   Smooth insulation

If cord and plug are functional, then choose a replacement socket marked with the same amp and volt ratings as the old socket. One half of flat-cord lamp wire is covered by insulation that is ridged or marked: attach this wire to the silver screw terminal. Connect the other wire to the brass screw.

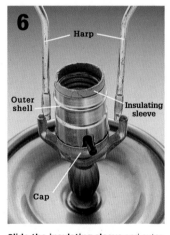

6 Harp

Outer shell   Insulating sleeve

Cap

Slide the insulating sleeve and outer shell over the socket so that the socket and screw terminals are fully covered and the switch fits into the sleeve slot. Press the socket assembly down into the cap until the socket locks into place. Replace the harp, light bulb, and shade.

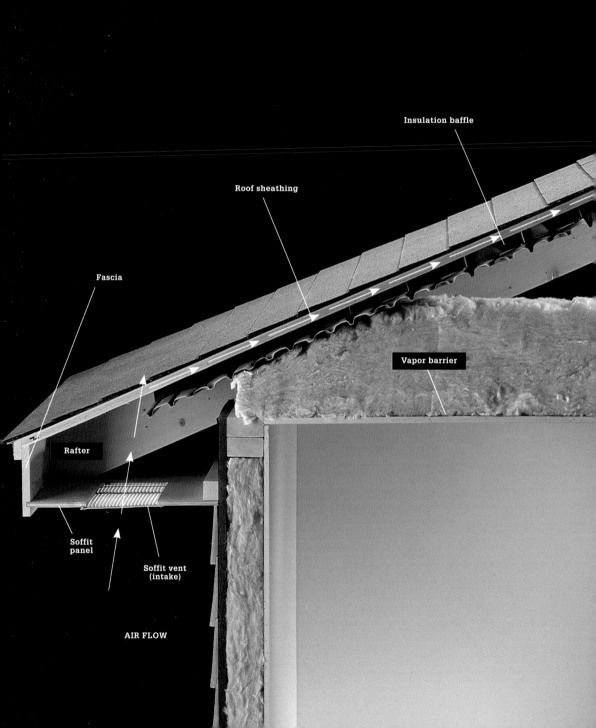

Insulation baffle

Roof sheathing

Fascia

Vapor barrier

Rafter

Soffit
panel

Soffit vent
(intake)

AIR FLOW

Roof vent
(outtake)

Unheated
attic space

Attic insulation blanket
(between ceiling joists)

Heated room space

Shown cutaway for clarity

HVAC & Appliances

In this chapter:

- Maintaining Gas Forced-air Heat Systems
- Maintaining Hot Water & Steam Heat Systems
- Replacing Dishwashers
- Replacing Food Disposers
- Replacing Water Heaters
- Servicing Thermostats

Maintaining Gas Forced-air Heat Systems

Gas forced-air systems are widely used in cool climates worldwide. A gas forced-air furnace—running on natural gas or liquid propane (LP)—draws in surrounding air, channels it across a set of heated plates, known as a heat exchanger, and then uses a blower to circulate the air throughout the house (illustration). A chamber on top of the furnace, known as a plenum, leads the warmed air from the furnace to a network of ducts that carry the warm air to heat registers or vents mounted on walls or ceilings. To keep the cycle going, return ducts carry cooled air from each room back to the furnace so it can be reheated and recirculated. Older systems use gravity to carry warm air throughout the house and cool air back to the furnace.

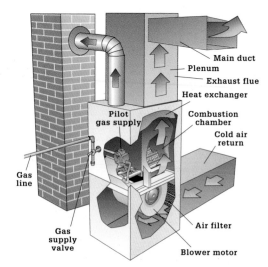

Identifying the plenum and cold air return, as well as the main duct leading to the rooms in your home, is a good way to begin familiarizing yourself with your forced-air system.

Balancing a Forced-air System

Most forced-air systems have dampers within the ducts that let you control how much air flows to various parts of the house. These are separate from the registers used to manage airflow within each room. Adjusting the dampers is called balancing the system.

Start by locating the dampers (illustration). When a damper handle or wing nut is parallel to the duct, it is wide open, allowing maximum airflow. When the handle is perpendicular to the duct, it is closed.

To balance your system, start by setting the thermostat as you would for the times when you're at home. Close the dampers that lead to the room with the thermostat. Wait a few hours, and go to the rooms that are farthest from the furnace. If those rooms are too warm, leave them until later, when more dampers are open. Check the other rooms for comfort. After each damper adjustment, wait a few hours for the air temperature to stabilize.

Once you're satisfied with the heat each room receives, use a permanent marker on each duct to

indicate the correct setting for each damper (photo 1). Repeat the process in the summer for air conditioning, making a second set of marks to indicate the correct damper settings for cooling.

Mark damper positions on each duct, and indicate which room is affected by the settings. Open or close the damper using a screwdriver or by turning the wing nut (inset).

Maintaining a Forced-air System

You can handle most routine furnace maintenance yourself. Generally, the newer the furnace, the simpler the maintenance, since a number of heavy-maintenance components have been eliminated on newer models.

Most furnaces installed since the 1980s do not have a thermocouple-controlled pilot light. In fact, the standing pilot light found on older furnaces has been eliminated completely. In most cases, it's been replaced with either an intermittent pilot light that's lit only when there's a call for heat from the thermostat, or a glowing element, known as a hot-surface igniter. An intermittent pilot light must be repaired by a professional technician, should it fail. You can replace a hot-surface igniter yourself.

Use this section to identify and complete the maintenance procedures that apply to the furnace in your home.

Before doing any maintenance, always turn off the furnace's main gas supply and the pilot gas supply, if your furnace has a separate one. Then, switch off the furnace's main power switch and the power to the furnace at the main service panel. Check your owner's manual for any warnings or special instructions concerning your furnace. Then, clear the area, so you have a safe work space.

Start with the most important and simplest furnace maintenance procedure—inspecting the air filter. There are many types of filters. Read the section below to find out how to clean yours and how often it must be changed.

Tools & Materials ▸

Standard screwdriver	Parts brush
Ratchet wrench	Mild liquid detergent
Nut driver	Light machine oil
Open-end wrench set	Thermometer
Straightedge	Garden hose
Channel-type pliers	Protective gloves
Pilot jet tool	Eye and ear protection

Replacing the Air Filter

The air filter on your forced-air furnace is designed to capture dust, pollen, and other airborne particles. The filter must be cleaned regularly, according to the manufacturer's specifications, and should be inspected once a month. Locate the filter compartment and remove the access cover (photo 1). The location of the compartment depends on the furnace type and the style of filter. Many filters fit in a slot between the return air duct and blower. A few styles are located inside the main furnace compartment. An electrostatic filter is installed in a separate unit attached to the furnace.

Slide the filter out of its compartment, taking care not to catch it on the sides of the blower housing. Hold the filter up to a light (photo 2). If the filter blocks much of the light, replace it. Electrostatic filters can be reused after cleaning.

Many filters are located between the return air duct and the blower, and rest in a slot or bracket.

Hold the filter up to a bright light for inspection.

Maintaining the Blower Motor

Inspect the blower motor before the start of the heating season. Inspect it again before the start of the cooling season if your central air conditioning uses the same blower.

Turn off the power to the furnace. Remove the access panel to the blower housing and inspect the motor (photo 1). Some motors have oil ports and an adjustable, replaceable drive belt. Others are self-lubricating and have a direct-drive mechanism. Wipe the motor clean with a damp cloth and check for oil fill ports. The access panel may include a diagram indicating their location. Remove the covers to the ports (if equipped) and add a few drops of light machine oil (photo 2). Place the covers on the ports.

With the power still off, inspect the drive belt. If it is cracked, worn, glazed, or brittle, replace it. Check the belt tension by pushing down gently midway between the pulleys (photo 3). The belt should flex about 1". To tighten or loosen the belt, locate the pulley tension adjustment nut on the blower motor (photo 4). Loosen the locknut, and turn the adjustment nut slightly. Check the belt tension, and readjust as required until the tension is correct.

If the belt is out of alignment or the bearings are worn, adjusting the tension will not solve the problem. With the power off, hold a straightedge so it's flush with the edge of both pulleys (photo 5). To align the belt, locate the mounting bolts on the motor's sliding bracket (photo 6). Loosen the bolts, and move the motor carefully until the pulleys are aligned. Tighten the bolts and check the tension and alignment again. Repeat until the pulley is aligned and the tension adjusted. Replace the furnace access panels. Restore power and switch on the furnace.

Remove the access panel to the blower housing and inspect the motor.

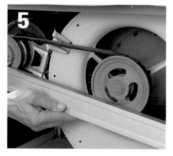

Remove the covers to the oil ports and add a few drops to each port.

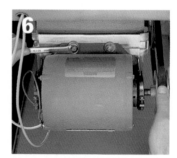

Check the tension by pushing down on the middle of the belt.

Loosen the pulley tension adjustment nut slightly to tighten the belt.

Check the pulley alignment, using a straightedge.

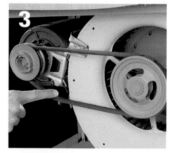

Loosen the bolts that hold the motor on its sliding bracket, and move the motor carefully until the pulleys are aligned.

Inspecting the Pilot & Thermocouple

The pilot light (it's actually a flame used to ignite gas flowing through the burners) plays a large role in the efficiency of the entire system, and a clean-burning pilot saves money, improves indoor air quality, and extends furnace life.

If your furnace has a standing pilot light, always check the flame before the start of the heating season to ensure that it's burning cleanly and with the proper mix of air and fuel. Start by removing the main furnace access panel. If you can't see the pilot flame clearly, turn off the gas supply (photo 1) and the pilot gas shutoff switch (if equipped). Wait 10 minutes for the pilot to cool, and remove the pilot cover. Relight the pilot, following the instructions on the control housing or access cover. If the pilot won't stay lit, shut off the gas supply once again and inspect the thermocouple.

Inspect the flame (photo 2). If the flame is too weak (left flame), it will be blue and may barely touch the thermocouple. If the flame is too strong (center flame), it will also be blue, but may be noisy and lift off the pilot. A well-adjusted flame (right flame) will be blue with a yellow tip, and cover ½" at the end of the thermocouple. Turn the pilot adjustment screw (photo 3) on the control housing or gas valve to reduce the pressure. If it's weak, turn the screw in the other direction to increase the pressure. If the flame appears weak and yellow even after adjustment, remove the pilot jet and clean the orifice (page 500).

If the pilot in your furnace or boiler goes out quickly, and you have made sure the gas supply is sufficient, you may need to replace the thermocouple. Turn off the gas supply. Using an open-end wrench, loosen the thermocouple tube fitting from the control housing or gas valve. Unscrew the thermocouple from the pilot housing and install a new one (photo 4). Tighten it with a wrench just until it's snug.

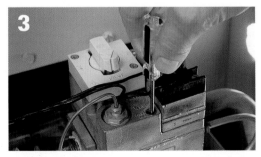

Turn off the main gas supply and the pilot gas supply (if your furnace has a separate one).

Adjust the flame so it is steady, has a yellow tip, and covers the thermocouple's tip (right).

Turn the screw to adjust the height of the flame so it covers the top of the thermocouple.

Remove the thermocouple from the control housing and install a new one.

Cleaning & Adjusting the Pilot Light

If the thermocouple and burners in your furnace or boiler appear to be working correctly, but the pilot flame is inconsistent or weak, remove the pilot jet and clean or replace it. Turn off the power and close the gas supply, including the gas supply to the pilot if your unit has a separate one. Wait at least 30 minutes for the parts to cool. Using an open-end wrench, remove the thermocouple from the pilot housing (photo 1).

Use two wrenches to hold the gas line in place, then loosen the nut that connects it to the control housing. Unscrew and remove the pilot housing, then carefully remove the pilot jet from the housing (photo 2).

Clean the outside of the pilot jet with a parts brush, and carefully clean the inside with a pilot jet tool. Take care not to scratch the inside of the jet, as this will affect its performance. If the pilot jet is severely corroded or difficult to clean, replace it.

Thread the pilot jet back into the pilot housing, and reinstall the housing. Reattach the gas line, turning the connecting nut while holding the line steady. Reinstall the thermocouple. Reopen the gas supply and turn the power back on, then light the pilot.

Loosen the connecting nut on the gas line with an open-end wrench.

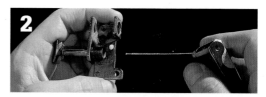

Remove the pilot jet from the housing and clean it with a pilot jet tool.

Inspecting the Burner Flame

Once you've set the pilot flame, check the burner flame. The burner flame should be blue, with a bluish green flame at the center and occasional streaks of yellow (photo 1). If it appears too blue or too yellow, adjust the air shutter at the end of the burner tube (photo 2). Start by setting the thermostat high

so that the furnace continues to burn. Wearing protective gloves, loosen the air shutter locking screw. Open the shutter wide, then close it slowly until the flame color is right. Retighten the locking screw. Repeat the procedure for each remaining burner. Reset the thermostat.

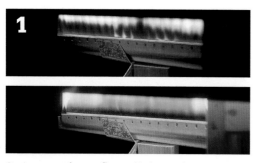

Compare your burner flame with the two above. Yours should be blue-green, with streaks of yellow (top).

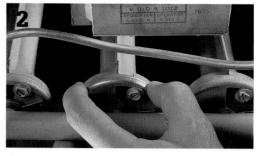

If the shutters are adjustable, you can set them yourself. Otherwise, call a professional for service.

Cleaning the Burners

Burners work by mixing together gas and air that is then ignited by a pilot flame or a heated element. Gas is delivered by a manifold and enters each burner tube through a small orifice, known as a spud. Burners and spuds gradually become encrusted with soot and other products of the combustion process and must be cleaned occasionally to keep them working efficiently.

To clean the burners, turn off the furnace's main shutoff, and switch off the power to the furnace at the main service panel. Shut off the gas supply, including the pilot gas supply if your unit has a separate one. Wait at least 30 minutes for the parts to cool. Remove the burner tubes by unscrewing them from their retaining brackets (photo 1), by pulling out the metal pan that holds them, or by loosening the screws that attach the gas manifold to the furnace. On some furnaces, you need to remove the pilot housing to reach the burners.

Twist each burner carefully to remove it from its spud (photo 2). Fill a laundry tub with water and soak the burners. Carefully clean the outside of the burner tubes and the burner ports with a soft-bristled brush. Replace any tubes that are cracked, bent, or severely corroded.

Inspect the spuds: clean burners won't work effectively if the spuds are dirty or damaged. Use a ratchet wrench to loosen and remove each spud (photo 3). Clean the outside of each spud with a soft-bristled brush. Then, use a pilot jet tool to clean the inside of each spud (photo 4). The tool is designed for cleaning small orifices, but take special care to avoid scratching or enlarging a spud's opening. Reinstall the spuds in the manifold. Tighten them just until they're snug. Once the burner tubes are dry, install them on the spuds, and attach them to the burner tube brackets or burner pan. Connect the pilot housing, if equipped. Turn the power and gas supply back on. On furnaces with a standing pilot, relight the pilot flame.

Remove the screws holding the burners to their brackets or to a slide-out pan.

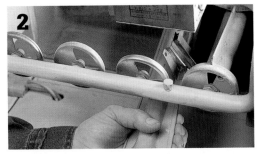

If a burner is difficult to remove, twist it carefully from side to side while lifting and pulling.

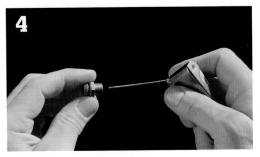

To avoid bending or damaging the spud threads, hold the manifold steady with one hand as you remove each spud.

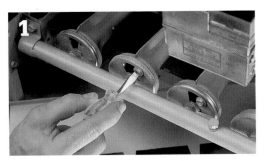

Clean each spud orifice carefully with a pilot jet tool, taking care not to scratch or enlarge the orifice.

Servicing Electronic Ignition Furnaces

Newer furnaces include an intermittent pilot light or hot-surface igniter as well as an electronic control center, with warning lights to help you recognize problems.

On some newer models, the temperature difference between the supply and return ducts needs to be within a narrow range to avoid damaging the heat exchanger. To find out whether this applies to your furnace, check the information plate on the burner compartment—it may include an indication of the acceptable range.

Each season, check the differential by slipping the probe of a pocket thermometer into a slit in an expansion joint in the supply duct (photo 1). Record the reading and compare it with the temperature in the return air duct. Call a professional technician if the difference between the two numbers falls outside the recommended range.

Your furnace may contain an intermittent pilot, which is lighted with a spark when signaled by the thermostat. An intermittent pilot consumes gas only when necessary, reducing home fuel costs. If the electronic ignition fails to spark, call a technician for service.

Some furnace models ignite the gas with a glowing element, known as a hot-surface igniter. If the igniter fails, replace it. Remove the main furnace panel and locate the igniter just beyond the ignition end of the burner tubes. Disconnect the igniter plug and remove the nut on the mounting bracket with a nut driver or ratchet wrench (photo 2). Replace the igniter.

If the igniter still doesn't function properly, check with the manufacturer: you may need to replace the control center. Detach the wires from the old control center one at a time and attach them to the replacement (photo 3). Then, disconnect the old control center, using a screwdriver, and connect the new one (photo 4).

Remove the control center wires one at a time and switch them over to the new control center.

Check the temperature inside the supply duct and compare it with the temperature in the return duct.

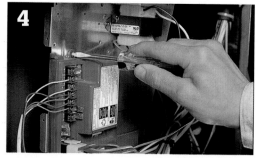

Disconnect the faulty hot-surface igniter from the mounting bracket.

Unscrew the control center's mounting screws and install the replacement unit.

Maintaining a High-efficiency Gas Furnace

A high-efficiency gas furnace is defined as a furnace that's at least 90% "efficient," as determined by an annual fuel utilization efficiency (AFUE) rating.

Furnaces made as late as 1992 can have ratings as low as 60%. A standard, mid-efficient unit sold today is about 80% percent, while high-efficiency units can be as high as 96% efficient.

Like other furnaces, high-efficiency gas furnaces require maintenance. The air filters must be cleaned regularly—electronic filters need to be cleaned on a monthly basis, and disposable filters should be changed every three months (photo 1).

If the drain line cannot drain properly, moisture can build up inside the heat exchanger and restrict gas flow. Inspect the drain line to make sure it's free of kinks. Some furnaces have several drain connections that should be inspected.

Clean the drain line once a year by disconnecting it from the furnace and forcing water from a garden hose through the line (photo 2). If the drain line is black plastic, remove it at a connection point, then reattach once it's clean. If the line is white, then it's PVC, and you'll need to reconnect it to the unit with a coupling after cleaning it.

Some furnaces have a removable condensate trap. If your unit has one, remove it at the beginning of the winter season and clean it out with water. Check the trap periodically throughout the season and dump the water as necessary.

Check the vent pipes and furnace unit for signs of corrosion (photo 3). The water produced by the furnace is acidic and will corrode metal quickly. If pipes are leaking, they must be replaced.

Make sure the areas around the air intake and exhaust are unobstructed. Plants, bushes, and other materials that block the intake and exhaust can cause the furnace to shut down (photo 4).

Clean electronic filters every month, then reinsert them in your furnace.

Clean the drain line once a year by running water through it from a garden hose.

Inspect the areas around vent pipes for signs of corrosion. Corroded pipes will need to be replaced.

Remove any debris and materials that could block the air intake and exhaust.

Maintaining Hot Water & Steam Heat Systems

Hot water and steam systems, also known as hydronic systems, feature a boiler that heats water and circulates it through a closed network of pipes to a set of radiators or convectors. Because water expands and contracts as it heats and cools, these systems include expansion tanks to ensure a constant volume of water circulating through the pipes.

Hot water and steam systems warm the surrounding air through a process called convection. Hot water radiators (photo 1) are linked to the system by pipes connected near the bottom of the radiator. As water cools inside the radiator, it is drawn back to the boiler for reheating. The radiators in steam systems (photo 2) have pipes connected near the top of the radiator. These radiators can be very hot to the touch. Convectors (photo 3) are smaller and lighter and may be used to replace hot water radiators, or to extend an existing hot water system.

Although the delivery of hot water or steam to the rooms in your house is considered a closed system, some air will make its way into the system. Steam radiators have an automatic release valve that periodically releases hot, moist air. Hot water radiators contain a bleed valve that must periodically be opened to release trapped air. It is usually necessary to bleed convector systems using a valve near the boiler.

Today's hot water and steam systems are often fueled by natural gas. Older systems may use fuel oil. Fuel oil systems require more frequent maintenance of the filter (page 529) and blower (page 530).

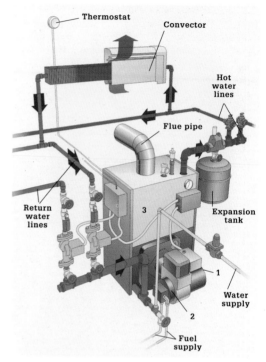

A blower draws in air through the air intake (1) while a fuel pump (2) maintains a constant supply of fuel oil. The mixture is ignited by a high-voltage spark as it enters the combustion chamber (3) and heats water.

Hot-water radiators circulate heated water through pipes. As it cools, water is drawn back to the boiler for reheating.

Steam radiators operate at a higher temperature. Steam cools in the radiators, returns to a liquid state, and then flows back to the boiler.

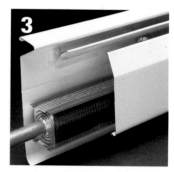

Space-saving hot water convectors work on the same principle as radiators, but use thin sheet-metal fins to transfer heat to the air.

Servicing the Oil Filter & Strainer

Replacing the oil filter is the best routine maintenance you can do for your hot water or steam heating system.

Surround the base of the boiler with a drop cloth and newspaper. Shut off the power to the boiler at the main service panel and at the boiler shutoff switch, usually located near the boiler. Then, close the fuel line supply valve and wait 30 minutes for all parts to cool.

Wearing disposable gloves, unscrew the top of the filter cartridge (photo 1). Remove the cartridge with a twisting motion and turn it over to dump the old filter into a plastic bag (photo 2). Remove the gasket from the cartridge and wipe out the inside, first with a cloth dipped in solvent, then with a dry cloth. Install a new filter and gasket (photo 3). Position the cartridge under the cover and screw it back in place.

Use an open-end wrench to remove the bolts from the pump cover (photo 4). Leave the oil line attached, and remove the gasket and mesh strainer from the cover (photo 5). Clean the strainer with solvent and a parts brush. If it's badly worn or damaged, replace it. Wipe the cover with a clean cloth. Place the clean strainer or replacement strainer in the cover and install a new gasket. Fasten the cover bolts in place. Restart the boiler.

Tools & Materials ›

Open-end wrench set
Parts brush
Gloves
Drop cloth
Solvent

Replacement oil filter
  and cartridge gasket
Strainer gasket
Cloth
Eye protection

Have a disposable plastic bag ready, and unscrew the top of the filter cartridge.

Twist the cartridge to remove it from the oil supply line. Ask your waste removal company for disposal instructions.

Wipe the edge of the cartridge, first with a solvent-dipped rag and then with a dry rag.

Leave the pump cover attached to the fuel line when you remove it.

Remove the mesh strainer carefully. Even a heavily soiled one can often be reused after a good cleaning.

Cleaning & Lubricating the Blower

Clean fuel and a reliable air supply are critical to your boiler's performance. Clean the air intake on your boiler every month and lubricate the motor every two months during the heating season.

Turn off the power to the boiler. Brush any dust and debris from the air intake with a narrow, medium-bristle brush (photo 1). Use an open-end wrench or screwdriver, as required, to loosen the transformer. With the transformer still attached, move it aside to reach the blower fan (photo 2). Use the brush and a damp cloth to remove dirt and debris from the fan blades (photo 3).

Most boiler blowers have a port on top or cups at each end for adding lubricating oil. Check your owner's manual or consult the manufacturer on the best lubricating oil for your blower. Before removing the plugs or opening the cups, clean the outside of the motor with a damp cloth (photo 4) to keep dirt and debris from getting into the motor. Remove the plug from the opening or the lid from each cup, using a wrench or screwdriver, as required. Add a few drops of lubricating oil (photo 5).

If the motor doesn't have oil ports or cups, it's probably a self-lubricating type (photo 6). Check your owner's manual to be sure.

Tools & Materials ▸

Open-end wrench set
Screwdrivers
 (standard
 and Phillips)
Medium-bristle brush

Drop cloth
Boiler lubricating oil
Cloth
Eye protection
Work gloves

To clean the air intake, use a brush designed for cleaning the condensing coils on a refrigerator.

If the transformer attaches to the blower housing with a hinge, simply swing it out of the way. If it comes loose, be careful not to strain the wire connections.

The blades on most blower fans are thin and hard to reach, so use a long brush carefully: a bent fan blade makes much more noise than a dirty one.

To prevent dust or dirt from getting in the motor while you add oil, clean off the surface with a damp cloth before opening the ports or cups.

Add lubricating oil to the ports or cups. The motor housing may indicate what kind of oil to use.

If the motor doesn't have cups or openings for adding lubricating oil, it's probably sealed and may not need extra lubrication.

Draining & Filling a System

Sediment gradually accumulates in any water-based system, reducing the system's efficiency and damaging internal parts. Draining the boiler every season reduces the accumulation of sediment. Be aware that draining the system can take a long time, and the water often has an unpleasant odor. This doesn't indicate a problem. Drain the system during warm weather, and open the windows and run a fan to reduce any odor.

Start by shutting off the boiler and allowing the hot system to cool. Attach a garden hose to the drain at the bottom of the boiler (photo 1), and place the other end in a floor drain or utility sink. Open a bleed valve on the highest radiator in the house (page 508).

When water stops draining, open a bleed valve on a radiator closer to the boiler. When the flow stops, locate the valve or gauge on top of the boiler, and remove it with a wrench (photo 2).

Make sure the system is cool before you add water. Close the drain valve on the boiler. Insert a funnel into the gauge fitting and add rust inhibitor, available from heating supply dealers (photo 3). Check the container for special instructions. Reinstall the valve or gauge in the top of the boiler, close all radiator bleed valves, and slowly reopen the water supply to the boiler.

When the water pressure gauge reads 5 psi, bleed the air from the radiators on the first floor, then do the same on the upper floors. Let the boiler reach 20 psi before you turn the power on (photo 4). Allow 12 hours for water to circulate fully, then bleed the radiators again.

Tools & Materials ▸

Open-end wrench set	Drop cloth
Pipe wrenches	Boiler rust inhibitor
Garden hose	Eye protection
Funnel	Work gloves
Plastic bucket	

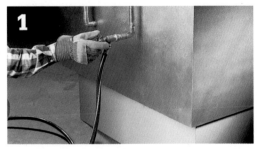

Use a garden hose to drain water from the boiler. Keep the drain end of the hose lower than the drain cock on the boiler.

If the valve or gauge on top of the boiler is attached to a separate fitting, hold the fitting still with one wrench while removing the valve or gauge with another.

Using a funnel, add a recommended rust inhibitor to the boiler through the valve or gauge fitting.

The boiler should reach a pressure of 20 psi before you turn the power back on.

Bleeding a Hot Water System

Hot water systems operate more quietly and efficiently if you bleed them of trapped air once a year. To bleed a hot water system, the boiler must be on. Start with the radiator that's highest in the house and farthest from the boiler. Place a cloth under the bleed valve, and open the valve slowly (photo 1). Close it as soon as water squirts out. Some bleed valves have knobs, which open with a half turn; others must be opened with a screwdriver or valve key, available at hardware stores.

Steam radiators have automatic bleed valves. To clear a clogged valve, close the shutoff at the radiator and let unit cool. Unscrew the bleed valve and clear the orifice with a fine wire or needle (photo 2).

Older hot water convector systems may have bleed valves on or near the convectors. Bleed these convectors as you would radiators.

Most convector systems today don't have bleed valves. For these, locate the hose bib where the return water line reaches the boiler. Close the gate valve between the bib and the boiler. Attach a short section of hose to the bib and immerse the other end in a bucket of water. Open the bib while adding water to the boiler by opening the supply valve. The supply valve is located on the supply pipe, usually the smallest pipe in the system. Flush the system until no air bubbles come out of the hose in the bucket (photo 3). Open the gate valve to bleed any remaining air. Close the hose bib before restarting the boiler.

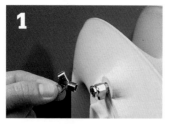

If you can't find a key for your radiators, a local hardware store or home center may have a replacement.

If the radiator isn't heating, clear the orifice with a fine wire or needle.

A convector-based heating system is usually bled at the boiler by holding a hose underwater and flushing the system until there are no more air bubbles coming from the hose.

Replace Radiator Control Valves ▸

A radiator control valve that won't operate should be replaced. To replace the valve, you'll first need to drain the system (page 507). Then use a pipe wrench to disconnect the nut on the outlet side of the valve, then disconnect the valve body from the supply pipe (photo 1, right). Thread the tailpiece of the new valve into the radiator. Thread the valve body onto the supply pipe. Make sure the arrow on the valve body points in the direction of the water flow. Thread the connecting nut on the tailpiece onto the outlet side of the valve (photo 2). When you recharge the system, open the bleed valve on the radiator until a trickle of water runs out.

Use a pipe wrench to remove the control valve (left). Thread the tailpiece of the new valve into the radiator (right).

Fasten the valve to the supply tube, then secure the connecting nut on the tailpiece to the valve.

Identifying & Repairing Exhaust Leaks

Leaks in the exhaust flue, around the burner mounting flange, combustion chamber cover plate, or fire door are potential sources of carbon monoxide. Any leak that might allow carbon monoxide to enter your home should be repaired immediately.

Holes and rusted portions are visible signs of a damaged flue. Smaller leaks can be found by turning on the burner and holding a lighted candle along the joints in the flue and the seams of the burner mounting flange, combustion chamber cover plate, and fire door. The flame is drawn toward the joint or seam when there is a leak.

Tools & Materials ▸

Wire brush
Putty knife
Long candle
Work gloves
Power drill/screwdriver
Replacement flue sections
Refractory furnace cement
Eye and ear protection

Hold a lighted candle to the joints on the flue and seams around the burner to find leaks.

Sealing an Exhaust Leak

To seal a leak at a seam, turn off the burner and let the boiler cool. Then, use a wire brush to remove any dirt or rust that has accumulated around the leak (photo 1).

Seal the leak by applying refractory furnace cement with a putty knife (photo 2). To stop a mounting flange leak, loosen the retaining bolts located at the edges of the flange. Scrape away the decayed gasket and apply refractory furnace cement at the edge. Then, tighten the bolts.

To test your repair, turn on the boiler and hold a lighted candle to the repair area. The candle flame should not flicker or waver.

Use a wire brush to clean off any rust or dirt deposits that have accumulated on the surface.

With a putty knife, apply refractory furnace cement to seal the leak.

Replacing Dishwashers

A dishwasher that's past its prime may be inefficient in more ways than one. If it's an old model, it probably wasn't designed to be very efficient to begin with. But more significantly, if it no longer cleans effectively, you're probably spending a lot of time and hot water pre-rinsing the dishes. This alone can consume more energy and water than a complete wash cycle on a newer machine. So even if your old dishwasher still runs, replacing it with an efficient new model can be a good green upgrade.

In terms of sizing and utility hookups, dishwashers are generally quite standard. If your old machine is a built-in and your countertops and cabinets are standard sizes, most full-size dishwashers will fit right in. Of course, you should always measure the dimensions of the old unit before shopping for a new one to avoid an unpleasant surprise at installation time. Also be sure to review the manufacturer's instructions before starting any work.

Tools & Materials ▸

Screwdrivers	Cable connector
Adjustable wrench	Teflon tape
2-ft. level	Hose clamps
¾" discharge tube	Wire connectors
½" flexible	Carpet scrap
supply tubing	Bowl
Brackets	Eye protection

Replacing an old, inefficient dishwasher is a straightforward project that usually takes just a few hours. The energy and water savings start with the first load of dishes and continue with every load thereafter.

How to Replace a Dishwasher

1

Start by shutting off the electrical power to the circuit at the main service panel. Also, turn off the water supply at the shutoff valve, usually located directly under the floor or in the cabinet beneath the kitchen sink. *NOTE: Most local codes now require that dishwashers be on a GFCI-protected circuit. If yours is not, it's always a good idea to replace the regular receptacle with a GFCI-protected model, or to replace the circuit breaker at the main panel with a GFCI breaker.*

2 L-fitting

Disconnect old plumbing connections. First unscrew the front access panel. Once the access panel is removed, disconnect the water supply line from the L-fitting on the bottom of the unit. This is usually a brass compression fitting, so just turning the compression nut counterclockwise with an adjustable wrench should do the trick. Use a bowl to catch any water that might leak out when the nut is removed.

3

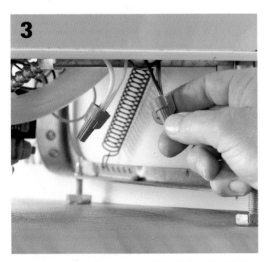

Disconnect old wiring connections. The dishwasher has an integral electrical box at the front of the unit where the power cable is attached to the dishwasher's fixture wires. Take off the box cover and remove the wire connectors that join the wires together.

4

Disconnect the discharge hose, which is usually connected to the dishwasher port on the side of the garbage disposer. To remove it, just loosen the screw on the hose clamp and pull it off. You may need to push this hose back through a hole in the cabinet wall and into the dishwasher compartment so it won't get caught when you pull the dishwasher out.

(continued)

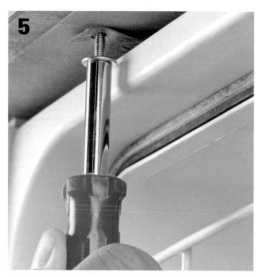

5

Detach the unit from the cabinets before you pull it out. Remove the screws that hold the brackets to the underside of the countertop. Then put a piece of cardboard or old carpet under the front legs to protect the floor from getting scratched, and pull the dishwasher out.

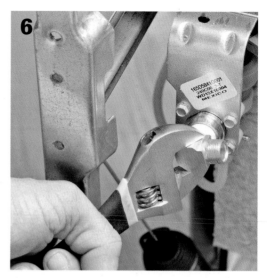

6

First, read the appliance's installation instructions carefully and then prepare the new dishwasher to be installed. Tip it on its back and attach the new L-fitting into the threaded port on the solenoid. Apply some Teflon tape to the fitting threads before tightening to allow the coupling to be tightened fully.

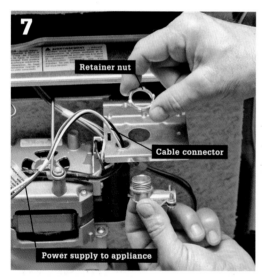

7

Retainer nut

Cable connector

Power supply to appliance

Prepare for the wiring connections. Like the old dishwasher, the new one will have an integral electrical box for making the wiring connections. To gain access to the box, just remove the box cover. Then install a cable connector on the back of the box and bring the power cable from the service panel through this connector. Power should be shut off at the main service panel at all times.

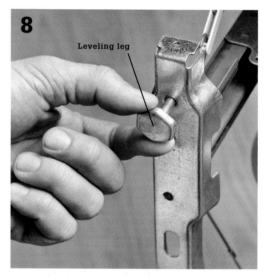

8

Leveling leg

Install a leveling leg at each of the four corners while the new dishwasher is still on its back. Just turn the legs into the threaded holes designed for them. Leave about ½" of each leg projecting from the bottom of the unit. These will have to be adjusted later to level the appliance. Tip the appliance up onto the feet and slide it into the opening. Check for level in both directions and adjust the feet as required.

9

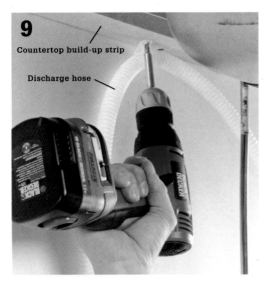

Countertop build-up strip

Discharge hose

10

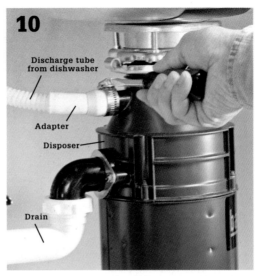

Discharge tube from dishwasher

Adapter

Disposer

Drain

Once the dishwasher is level, attach the brackets to the underside of the countertop to keep the appliance from moving. Then pull the discharge hose into the sink cabinet and install it so there's a loop that is attached with a bracket to the underside of the countertop. This loop prevents waste water from flowing from the disposer back into the dishwasher. *NOTE: Some codes require that you install an air gap fitting for this purpose. Check with your local plumbing inspector.*

Push an adapter over the disposer's discharge nipple and tighten it in place with a hose clamp. If you don't have a disposer, replace one of the drain tailpieces with a dishwasher tailpiece, and clamp the discharge tube to its fitting.

Tube Choices ▸

Codes still allow flexible copper supply tubes like the one shown in the next step, but a flexible dishwasher supply tube, such as reinforced, braided stainless steel, is a better choice in just about any situation. Copper tubes may crimp and either burst or restrict water flow when you move the dishwasher.

11

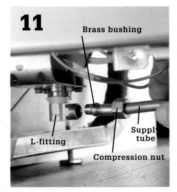

Brass bushing

Supply tube

L-fitting

Compression nut

Adjust the L-fitting on the dishwasher's water inlet valve until it points directly toward the water supply tubing. Then lubricate the threads slightly with a drop of dishwashing liquid and tighten the tubing's compression nut onto the fitting, keeping the brass bushing between the nut and the L-fitting. Use an adjustable wrench and turn the nut clockwise.

12

Complete the electrical connections by clamping the cable and joining the wires with wire nuts, following manufacturer's instructions. Replace the electrical cover, usually by hooking it onto a couple of prongs and driving a screw. Restore power and water, and test. Replace the toe-kick.

Replacing Food Disposers

Food disposers are standard equipment in the modern home, and most of us have come to depend on them to macerate our plate leavings and crumbs so they can exit the house along with waste water from the sink drain. If your existing disposer needs replacing, you'll find that the job is relatively simple, especially if you select a replacement appliance that is the same model as the old one. In that case, you can probably reuse the existing mounting assembly, drain sleeve, and drain plumbing.

Disposers are available with power ratings between ⅓ and 1 HP (horsepower). More powerful models bog down less under load and the motors last longer because they don't have to work as hard. They are also costlier.

Choose a switch option that meets your family's safety needs. A "continuous feed" disposer may be controlled by a standard on-off switch on the wall. Another option is a disposer that stays on only when the switch is actively pressed. A "batch feed" disposer can turn on only when a lid is locked onto it, eliminating the possibility of harming fingers. Some models are controlled at the lid, without a wall switch. Continuous food disposers are the most common.

Tools & Materials ▸

Screwdriver
Channel-type pliers
Spud wrench (optional)
Hammer
Hacksaw or tubing cutter
Kitchen drain supplies
Threaded Wye-fitting
Drain auger

Mallet
Putty knife
Mineral spirits
Plumber's putty
Wire caps
Hose clamps
Electrical tape
Eye protection

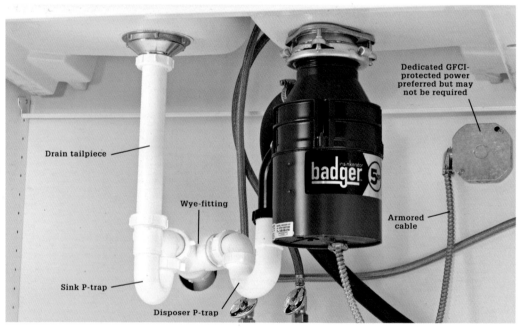

Drain tailpiece

Dedicated GFCI-protected power preferred but may not be required

Wye-fitting

Armored cable

Sink P-trap

Disposer P-trap

A properly functioning food disposer that's used correctly can help reduce clogs. Some plumbers use separate P-traps for the disposer and the drain outlet tube as shown here. Others contend that configuring the drain line with a single P-trap minimizes the chance that a trap will have its water seal broken by suction from the second trap. See page 519, lower left.

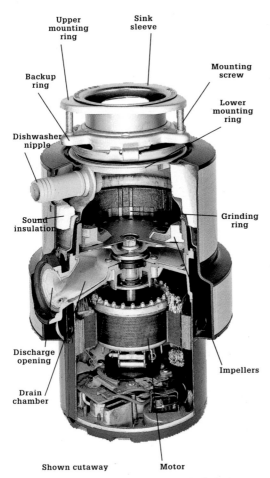

Upper mounting ring

Sink sleeve

Backup ring

Mounting screw

Lower mounting ring

Dishwasher nipple

Sound insulation

Grinding ring

Discharge opening

Impellers

Drain chamber

Shown cutaway

Motor

A food disposer grinds food waste so it can be flushed away through the sink drain system. A quality disposer has a ½–horsepower, or larger, self-reversing motor. Other features to look for include foam sound insulation, a grinding ring, and overload protection that allows the motor to be reset if it overheats. Better food disposers have a 5-year manufacturer's warranty.

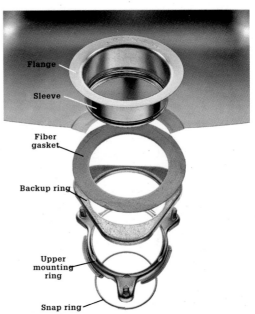

Flange

Sleeve

Fiber gasket

Backup ring

Upper mounting ring

Snap ring

The disposer is attached directly to the sink sleeve, which comes with the disposer and replaces the standard sink strainer. A snap ring fits into a groove around the sleeve of the strainer body to prevent the upper mounting ring and backup ring from sliding down while the upper mounting ring is tightened against the backup ring with mounting screws. Use a fiber gasket compressor when the mounting screws are tightened to create a better seal under the flange.

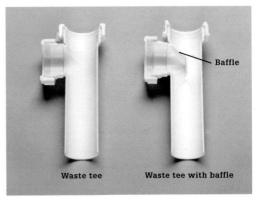

Baffle

Waste tee

Waste tee with baffle

Kitchen and drain tees are required to have a baffle if the tee is connected to a dishwasher or disposer. The baffle is intended to prevent discharge from finding its way up the drain and into the sink.

How to Replace a Food Disposer

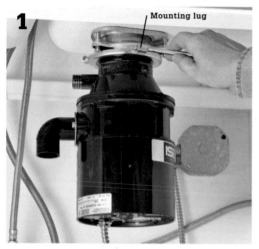

1

Mounting lug

Remove the old disposer if you have one. You'll need to disconnect the drain pipes and traps first. If your old disposer has a special wrench for the mounting lugs, use it to loosen the lugs. Otherwise, use a screwdriver. If you do not have a helper, place a solid object directly beneath the disposer to support it before you begin removal. *IMPORTANT: Shut off electrical power at the main service panel before you begin removal. Disconnect the wire leads, cap them, and stuff them into the electrical box.*

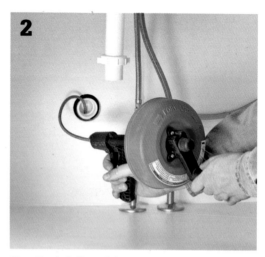

2

Clear the drain lines all the way to the branch drain before you begin the new installation. Remove the trap and trap arm first.

3

Upper mounting ring

Lower mounting ring

Snap ring

Disassemble the mounting assembly and then separate the upper and lower mounting rings and the backup ring. Also remove the snap ring from the sink sleeve. See photo, previous page.

4

Sink sleeve

Press the flange of the sink sleeve for your new disposer into a thin coil of plumber's putty that you have laid around the perimeter of the drain opening. The sleeve should be well-seated in the coil.

5

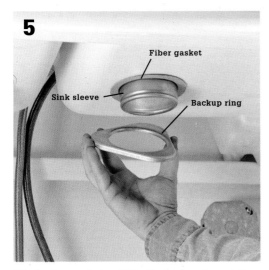

Fiber gasket

Sink sleeve

Backup ring

Slip the fiber gasket and then the backup ring onto the sink sleeve, working from inside the sink base cabinet. Make sure the backup ring is oriented the same way it was before you disassembled the mounting assembly.

6

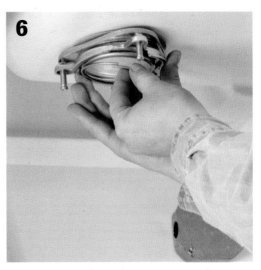

Insert the upper mounting ring onto the sleeve with the slotted ends of the screws facing away from the backup ring so you can access them. Then, holding all three parts at the top of the sleeve, slide the snap ring onto the sleeve until it snaps into the groove.

7

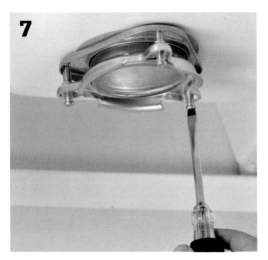

Tighten the three mounting screws on the upper mounting ring until the tips press firmly against the backup ring. It is the tension created by these screws that keeps the disposer steady and minimizes vibrating.

8

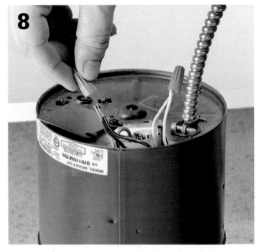

Make electrical connections before you mount the disposer unit on the mounting assembly. Shut off the power at the service panel if you have turned it back on. Remove the access plate from the disposer. Attach the white and black branch circuit wires from the electrical box to the white and black wires (respectively) inside the disposer. Twist a small wire cap onto each connection and wrap it with electrical tape for good measure. Also attach the green ground wire from the box to the grounding terminal on your disposer.

(continued)

9

Knock out the plug in the disposer port if you will be connecting your dishwasher to the disposer. If you have no dishwasher, leave the plug in. Insert a large flathead screwdriver into the port opening and rap it with a mallet. Retrieve the knock-out plug from inside the disposer canister.

10

Hang the disposer from the mounting ring attached to the sink sleeve. To hang it, simply lift it up and position the unit so the three mounting ears are underneath the three mounting screws and then spin the unit so all three ears fit into the mounting assembly. Wait until after the plumbing hookups have been made to lock the unit in place.

11

Attach the discharge tube to the disposer according to the manufacturer's instructions. It is important to get a very good seal here, or the disposer will leak. Go ahead and spin the disposer if it helps you access the discharge port.

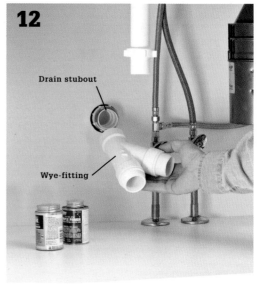

12

Drain stubout

Wye-fitting

Attach a Wye-fitting at the drain stubout. The Wye-fitting should be sized to accept a drain line from the disposer and another from the sink. Adjust the sink drain plumbing as needed to get from the sink P-trap to one opening of the Wye.

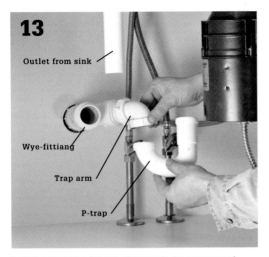

13

Outlet from sink

Wye-fittiang

Trap arm

P-trap

14

P-trap

Install a trap arm for the disposer in the open port of the Wye-fitting at the wall stubout. Then, attach a P-trap or a combination of a tube extension and a P-trap so the trap will align with the bottom of the disposer discharge tube.

Spin the disposer so the end of the discharge tube is lined up over the open end of the P-trap and confirm that they will fit together correctly. If the discharge tube extends down too far, mark a line on it at the top of the P-trap and cut at the line with a hacksaw. If the tube is too short, attach an extension with a slip joint. You may need to further shorten the discharge tube first to create enough room for the slip joint on the extension. Slide a slip nut and beveled compression washer onto the discharge tube and attach the tube to the P-trap.

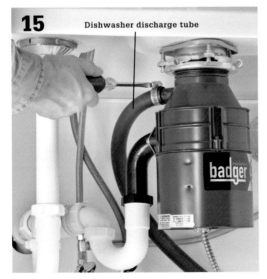

15   Dishwasher discharge tube

16

Connect the dishwasher discharge tube to the inlet port located at the top of the disposer unit. This may require a dishwasher hookup kit. Typically, a hose clamp is used to secure the connection.

Lock the disposer into position on the mounting ring assembly once you have tested to make sure it is functioning correctly and without leaks. Lock it by turning one of the mounting lugs until it makes contact with the locking notch.

Replacing Water Heaters

Replacing a water heater is a relatively easy DIY plumbing task, as long as it is a like-for-like replacement. In an ideal situation, you'd replace the old unit with one of the exact same size and make, and thereby avoid having to move any gas, water, or electrical lines. But if you choose to upgrade or downgrade in size, you'll find that relocating the necessary lines isn't that difficult. Although you can usually realize some energy cost savings in the long run, be aware that replacing an electric water heater with a gas-fueled model requires installing a vent and an approved combustion air source (and usually a permit).

It is a commonly held belief that a water heater should last around 10 years. The longevity depends on many factors, including initial quality, usage levels, maintenance diligence, and other miscellaneous factors such as hardness of water. While it is everyone's goal to get as much use out of our major appliances as possible, it is also undeniable that the best time to replace a water heater is before it leaks and fills your basement with water. It's a bit of a gamble, but once your old heater starts showing signs of wear and perhaps even acting up a bit, go ahead and make the change.

Water heaters for primary duty in residences range in size from 30 gallons to 65 gallons. For a family of four, a 40- or 50-gallon model should be adequate. While you don't want to run out of hot water every morning, you also don't want to pay to heat more water than you use. Base your choice on how well your current water heater is meeting your demand.

Follow local codes when choosing the pipe and fittings for both gas and water. Make sure there is a gas shutoff within 5 feet of the water heater. Also, there should be a union between the shutoff and the water heater, so pipes can be easily dismantled for service.

Water heaters typically last for at least 10 years, but once they start to show signs of aging, it's a good idea to replace them with a new, more efficient appliance.

Tools & Materials ▸

Tubing cutter	Appliance dolly	Pipe thread lubricant	Leak detector solution
Hacksaw	Water heater	Vent pipe elbow	Ball-type water shutoff valve
Pipe wrenches (2)	T & P relief valve	Couplings	Armored cable or conduit
Adjustable wrench	Discharge tube	Gas supply pipe and fittings	Lubricating tape
Channel-type pliers	Garden hose	Copper soldering supplies	
Screwdriver	Drain pan		

The nameplate on the side of a water heater lists tank capacity, insulation R-value, and working pressure (pounds per square inch). More efficient water heaters have an insulation R-value of 7 or higher. The nameplate for an electric water heater includes the voltage and the wattage capacity of the heating elements and thermostats. Water heaters also have a yellow energy guide label that lists typical yearly operating costs.

Use armored cable or wires housed in metal conduit to bring electrical power to electric water heaters. The armored cable or conduit should enter the top of the unit through a conduit clamp.

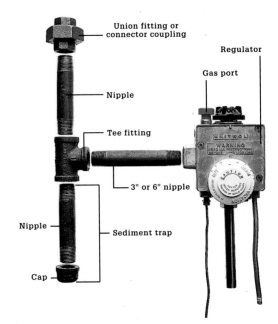

Union fitting or connector coupling

Regulator

Gas port

Nipple

Tee fitting

3" or 6" nipple

Nipple

Sediment trap

Cap

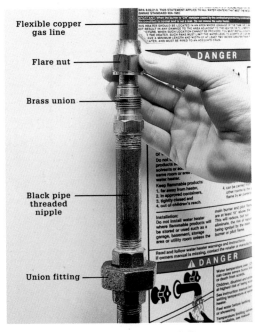

Flexible copper gas line

Flare nut

Brass union

Black pipe threaded nipple

Union fitting

Install a sediment trap between the gascock and the gas port on your gas water heater. A sediment trap is simply a vertical pipe nipple that is installed at the base of the union to allow any impurities in the fuel to collect rather than being drawn into the combustion chamber through the port. In most cases it is easier to locate the sediment trap at the water heater connection point, not the gascock fitting on the supply pipe.

If your house has soft copper gas supply lines, use a flare fitting to connect an additional threaded nipple from the black pipe assembly that connects to the water heater regulator. If you have black pipe supply lines, use a union fitting.

Gas water heater parts include:
(A) Draft hood and vent
(B) Cold water inlet pipe
(C) Tank
(D) Dip tube
(E) Gas burner
(F) Hot water outlet
(G) Temperature/pressure relief valve
(H) Anode rod
(I) Thermostat
(J) Thermocouple
(K) Cold water inlet valve

Electric water heater parts can include:
(A) Cold water inlet pipe
(B) Cold water inlet valve
(C) Insulation
(D) Draincock
(E) Hot water outlet pipe
(F) Temperature/pressure relief valve
(G) Power cable
(H) Upper heating element thermostat
(I) Upper heating element
(J) Bracket
(K) Lower heating thermostat
(L) Lower heating element
(M) Gasket

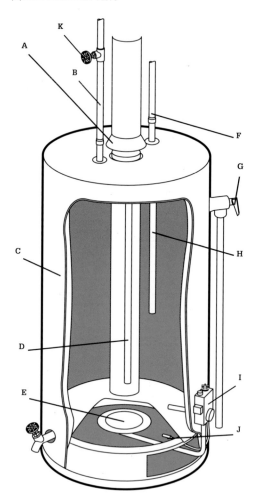

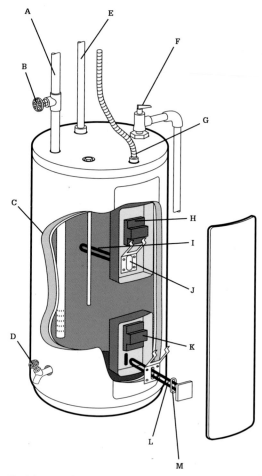

Gas water heaters operate on either propane or natural gas and are generally very economical to run. They do cost a bit more than electric heaters up front. The following installation features a gas water heater. Check with your local building department to find out if homeowners are allowed to install gas appliances in your municipality.

Electric water heaters require 240-volt service, which might overload your service panel if you are replacing a gas heater with an electric model. Their primary advantage is that they are cheaper to purchase (but not to operate) and they do not require that you make gas connections.

How to Remove a Water Heater

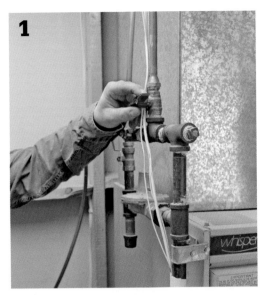

Shut off the gas supply at the stopcock installed in the gas line closest to the water heater. The handle of the stopcock should be perpendicular to the gas supply pipe. Also shut off the water supply.

Drain the water from the old heater by hooking a garden hose up to the sillcock drain and running it to a floor drain. If you don't have a floor drain, drain the water into buckets. For your personal safety, wait until the water heater has been shut off for a couple of hours before draining it.

Disconnect the gas supply from the water heater. To do so, loosen the flare fitting with two wrenches or pliers in a soft copper supply line or loosen the union fitting with two pipe wrenches for black pipe supply lines (right photo).

(continued)

4

Disconnect the vent pipe from the draft hood by withdrawing the sheet metal screws connecting the parts. Also remove vent pipes up to and including the elbow so you may inspect them for corrosion buildup and replace if needed.

5

Cut the water supply lines. Prior to cutting, shut off the cold water supply either at the stop valve downline from the heater or at the water meter. Replace the shutoff valve with a new ball-type shutoff valve.

6

Remove the old water heater and dispose of it properly. Most trash collection companies will haul it away for $20 or $30. Don't simply leave it out at the curb unless you know that is allowed by your municipal waste collection department. A two-wheel truck or appliance dolly is a big help here. Water heaters usually weigh around 150 pounds.

Install a Relief Valve ▸

Prepare the new water heater for installation. Before you put the water heater in place, add a T & P relief valve at the valve opening. Make sure to read the manufacturer's instructions and purchase the recommended valve type. Lubricate the threads and tighten the valve into the valve opening with a pipe wrench.

How to Install a Gas Water Heater

1

Remove the old unit (see previous pages) and position the new unit in the installation area. A drip pan is required if the water heater is installed where a leak could cause damage. This usually means anywhere except a crawlspace or an unfinished basement. If the water heater is not level, level it by shimming under the bottom with a metal or composite shim.

Hose bib

Drip pan

2

Attach a discharge tube to the T & P relief valve. You may use either copper pipe or CPVC drain pipe. Cut the tube so the free end is between 1½ and 6" above the floor. If you have floorcoverings you wish to protect, add a 90-degree elbow and a copper drain tube that leads from the discharge tube to a floor drain.

3

Attach the draft hood for the flue to the top of the unit with the provided hardware. Attach any other connector parts that are not preattached according to the manufacturer's instructions.

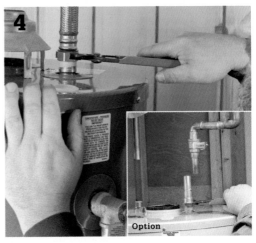

4

Option

Attach approved supply connectors to the inlet and outlet ports at the top of the appliance. Flexible connectors are much easier to work with, but you may use copper tubing if you prefer. If using copper, you'll need a red-coded copper nipple for the outlet port and a blue-coded copper nipple for the inlet port (inset photo).

(continued)

5

Join the supply connectors to the supply tubing with approved couplings. If the supply line feeding the water heater has no shutoff valve nearby, it is recommended that you add one. As long as there is a shutoff on the incoming supply side you do not need one on the outgoing (hot water) line.

6

Assemble the vent and attach the end to the draft hood for the flue.

OPTION: If you are running a new vent, you will most likely need to use an elbow fitting and adjustable fittings to achieve the configuration you need. The new vent should be inspected and approved by your local building department.

7

Begin making the gas connections. Working with gas pipes and tubing is dangerous and you should only attempt it if you have considerable experience in this skill area. If you are not comfortable working with gas pipe, hire a plumber to take on this part of the job. You'll still save plenty of money by doing the rest of the work yourself. Begin by screwing the male-threaded union securely into the gas regulator port. Wrap gas-approved lubricating tape around the threads first. Tighten with channel-type pliers, taking care not to overtighten or cause undue pressure on the regulator.

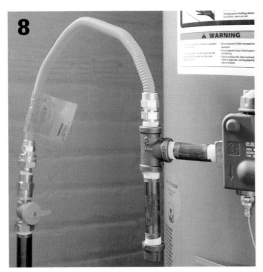

8

Connect a flexible gas supply tube to the port on a shutoff valve on the gas supply line. The shutoff must be within six feet of the appliance. Connect the other end to the union at the regulator. Wrap the threads in each threaded connection with three or four tight courses of gas-rated lubricating tape first. Include a sediment trap in the hook-up (see page 521).

9

Turn on the gas supply and test the gas connections with testing solution (inset photo) to make sure there are no leaks— do not use dish soap or any other products that may contain chlorides. Make sure the tank drain valve is closed, then turn on the water supply and check for water leaks. Once you have determined there are no plumbing leaks, light the pilot light (the instructions are always printed on a label near the pilot light).

Hooking Up Electric Water Heaters ▸

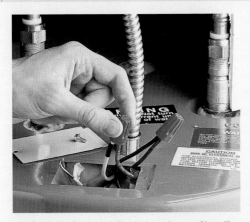

The fuel supply connection is the only part of installing an electric water heater that differs from installing a gas heater, except that electric heaters do not require a vent. The branch circuit wires (240 volts) are twisted together with mating wires in the access panel located at the top of the unit.

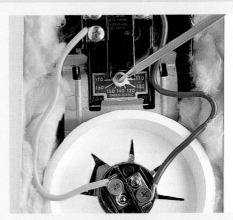

Temperature adjustments on electric water heaters are made by tightening or loosening a thermostat adjustment screw located near the heating element. Always shut off power to the unit before making an adjustment. In this photo you can see how close the live terminals for the heating element are to the thermostat.

Servicing Thermostats

A thermostat is a temperature-sensitive switch that automatically controls home heating and air-conditioning systems. There are two types of thermostats used to control heating and air-conditioning systems. Low-voltage thermostats control whole-house heating and air conditioning from one central location. Line-voltage thermostats are used in zone heating systems, where each room has its own heating unit and thermostat.

A low-voltage thermostat is powered by a transformer that reduces 120-volt current to about 24 volts. A low-voltage thermostat is very durable, but failures can occur if wire connections become loose or dirty, if thermostat parts become corroded, or if a transformer wears out. Some thermostat systems have two transformers. One transformer controls the heating unit, and the other controls the air-conditioning unit.

Line-voltage thermostats are powered by the same circuit as the heating unit, usually a 240-volt circuit. Always make sure to turn off the power before servicing a line-voltage thermostat.

A thermostat can be replaced in about one hour. Many homeowners choose to replace standard low-voltage or line-voltage thermostats with programmable setback thermostats. These programmable thermostats can cut energy use by up to 35%.

When buying a new thermostat, make sure the new unit is compatible with your heating/air-conditioning system. For reference, take along the brand name and model number of the old thermostat and of your heating/air-conditioning units. When buying a new low-voltage transformer, choose a replacement with voltage and amperage ratings that match the old thermostat.

Tools & Materials ▸

Soft-bristled
   paint brush
Multimeter
Screwdriver
Needlenose pliers

Combination tool
Continuity tester
Masking tape
Short piece of wire

Electronic programmable thermostats can be set to make up to four temperature changes each day. They are available in low-voltage designs (right) for central heating/cooling systems and in line-voltage designs (left) for electric baseboard heating. Most electronic programmable thermostats have an internal battery that saves the program in case of a power failure.

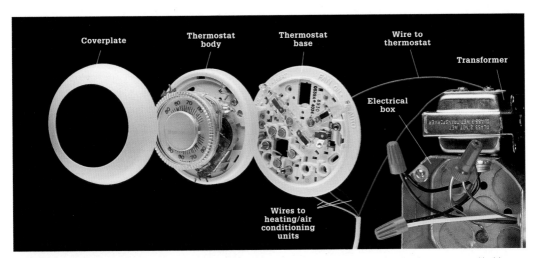

Low-voltage thermostat system has a transformer that is either connected to an electrical junction box or mounted inside a furnace access panel. Very thin wires (18 to 22 gauge) send current to the thermostat. The thermostat constantly monitors room temperatures, and sends electrical signals to the heating/cooling unit through additional wires. The number of wires connected to the thermostat varies from two to six, depending on the type of heating/air conditioning system. In the common four-wire system shown above, power is supplied to the thermostat through a single wire attached to screw terminal R. Wires attached to other screw terminals relay signals to the furnace heating unit, the air-conditioning unit, and the blower unit. Before removing a thermostat, make sure to label each wire to identify its screw terminal location.

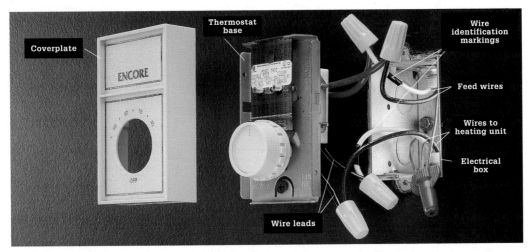

Line-voltage thermostat for 240-volt baseboard heating unit usually has four wire leads, although some models have only two leads. On a four-wire thermostat, the two red wire leads (sometimes marked LINE or L) are attached to the two hot feed wires bringing power into the box from the service panel. The black wire leads (sometimes marked LOAD) are connected to the circuit wires that carry power to the heating unit.

How to Inspect & Test a Low-voltage Thermostat System

1

Coverplate

Turn off power to the heating/air-conditioning system at the main service panel. Remove the thermostat coverplate.

2

Clean dust from the thermostat parts using a small, soft-bristled paint brush.

3

Mounting screws

Remove the thermostat body by loosening the mounting screws with a screwdriver.

4

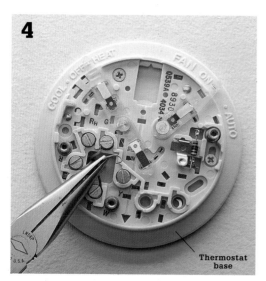

Thermostat base

Inspect the wire connections on the thermostat base. Reattach any loose wires. If wires are broken or corroded, they should be clipped, stripped, and reattached to the screw terminals.

5

Locate the low-voltage transformer that powers the thermostat. This transformer usually is located near the heating/air-conditioning system or inside a furnace access panel. Tighten any loose wire connections.

Set a multimeter to the 50-volt (AC) range. Turn on power to the heating/air-conditioning system at the main service panel.

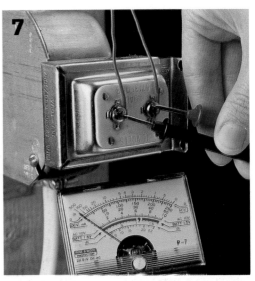

Touch one probe of multimeter to each of the low-voltage screw terminals. If tester does not detect current, then the transformer is defective and must be replaced (page 543).

Turn on power to heating system. Set thermostat control levers to AUTO and HEAT.

Strip ½" from each end of a short piece of insulated wire. Touch one end of the wire to terminal marked W and the other end to terminal marked R. If heating system begins to run, then the thermostat is faulty and must be replaced (pages 464 to 465).

Metric Conversions

Metric Conversions

TO CONVERT:	TO:	MULTIPLY BY:
Inches	Millimeters	25.4
Inches	Centimeters	25.4
Feet	Meters	0.305
Yards	Meters	0.914
Square inches	Square centimeters	6.45
Square feet	Square meters	0.093
Square yards	Square meters	0.836
Ounces	Milliliters	30.0
Pints (U.S.)	Liters	0.473 (Imp. 0.568)
Quarts (U.S.)	Liters	0.946 (Imp. 1.136)
Gallons (U.S.)	Liters	3.785 (Imp. 4.546)
Ounces	Grams	28.4
Pounds	Kilograms	0.454

TO CONVERT:	TO:	MULTIPLY BY:
Millimeters	Inches	0.039
Centimeters	Inches	0.394
Meters	Feet	3.28
Meters	Yards	1.09
Square centimeters	Square inches	0.155
Square meters	Square feet	10.8
Square meters	Square yards	1.2
Milliliters	Ounces	.033
Liters	Pints (U.S.)	2.114 (Imp. 1.76)
Liters	Quarts (U.S.)	1.057 (Imp. 0.88)
Liters	Gallons (U.S.)	0.264 (Imp. 0.22)
Grams	Ounces	0.035
Kilograms	Pounds	2.2

Converting Temperatures

Convert degrees Fahrenheit (F) to degrees Celsius (C) by following this simple formula: Subtract 32 from the Fahrenheit temperature reading. Then, multiply that number by $\frac{5}{9}$. For example, 77°F - 32 = 45. 45 × $\frac{5}{9}$ = 25°C.

To convert degrees Celsius to degrees Fahrenheit, multiply the Celsius temperature reading by $\frac{9}{5}$. Then, add 32. For example, 25°C × $\frac{9}{5}$ = 45. 45 + 32 = 77°F.

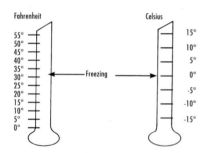

Metric Plywood Panels

Metric plywood panels are commonly available in two sizes: 1,200 mm × 2,400 mm and 1,220 mm × 2,400 mm, which is roughly equivalent to a 4 × 8-ft. sheet. Standard and Select sheathing panels come in standard thicknesses, while Sanded grade panels are available in special thicknesses.

STANDARD SHEATHING GRADE		SANDED GRADE	
7.5 mm	(5/16 in.)	6 mm	(4/17 in.)
9.5 mm	(3/8 in.)	8 mm	(5/16 in.)
12.5 mm	(1/2 in.)	11 mm	(7/16 in.)
15.5 mm	(5/8 in.)	14 mm	(9/16 in.)
18.5 mm	(3/4 in.)	17 mm	(2/3 in.)
20.5 mm	(13/16 in.)	19 mm	(3/4 in.)
22.5 mm	(7/8 in.)	21 mm	(13/16 in.)
25.5 mm	(1 in.)	24 mm	(15/16 in.)

Lumber Dimensions

NOMINAL - U.S.	ACTUAL - U.S. (IN INCHES)	METRIC
1 × 2	3/4 × 1 1/2	19 × 38 mm
1 × 3	3/4 × 2 1/2	19 × 64 mm
1 × 4	3/4 × 3 1/2	19 × 89 mm
1 × 5	3/4 × 4 1/2	19 × 114 mm
1 × 6	3/4 × 5 1/2	19 × 140 mm
1 × 7	3/4 × 6 1/4	19 × 159 mm
1 × 8	3/4 × 7 1/4	19 × 184 mm
1 × 10	3/4 × 9 1/4	19 × 235 mm
1 × 12	3/4 × 11 1/4	19 × 286 mm
1 1/4 × 4	1 × 3 1/2	25 × 89 mm
1 1/4 × 6	1 × 5 1/2	25 × 140 mm
1 1/4 × 8	1 × 7 1/4	25 × 184 mm
1 1/4 × 10	1 × 9 1/4	25 × 235 mm
1 1/4 × 12	1 × 11 1/4	25 × 286 mm
1 1/2 × 4	1 1/4 × 3 1/2	32 × 89 mm
1 1/2 × 6	1 1/4 × 5 1/2	32 × 140 mm
1 1/2 × 8	1 1/4 × 7 1/4	32 × 184 mm
1 1/2 × 10	1 1/4 × 9 1/4	32 × 235 mm
1 1/2 × 12	1 1/4 × 11 1/4	32 × 286 mm
2 × 4	1 1/2 × 3 1/2	38 × 89 mm
2 × 6	1 1/2 × 5 1/2	38 × 140 mm
2 × 8	1 1/2 × 7 1/4	38 × 184 mm
2 × 10	1 1/2 × 9 1/4	38 × 235 mm
2 × 12	1 1/2 × 11 1/4	38 × 286 mm
3 × 6	2 1/2 × 5 1/2	64 × 140 mm
4 × 4	3 1/2 × 3 1/2	89 × 89 mm
4 × 6	3 1/2 × 5 1/2	89 × 140 mm

Liquid Measurement Equivalents

1 Pint	= 16 Fluid Ounces	= 2 Cups
1 Quart	= 32 Fluid Ounces	= 2 Pints
1 Gallon	= 128 Fluid Ounces	= 4 Quarts

Drill Bit Guide

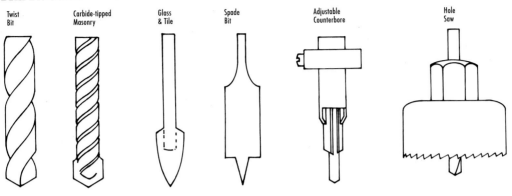

Twist Bit	Carbide-tipped Masonry	Glass & Tile	Spade Bit	Adjustable Counterbore	Hole Saw

Nails

Nail lengths are identified by numbers from 4 to 60 followed by the letter "d," which stands for "penny." For general framing and repair work, use common or box nails. Common nails are best suited to framing work where strength is important. Box nails are smaller in diameter than common nails, which makes them easier to drive and less likely to split wood. Use box nails for light work and thin materials. Most common and box nails have a cement or vinyl coating that improves their holding power.

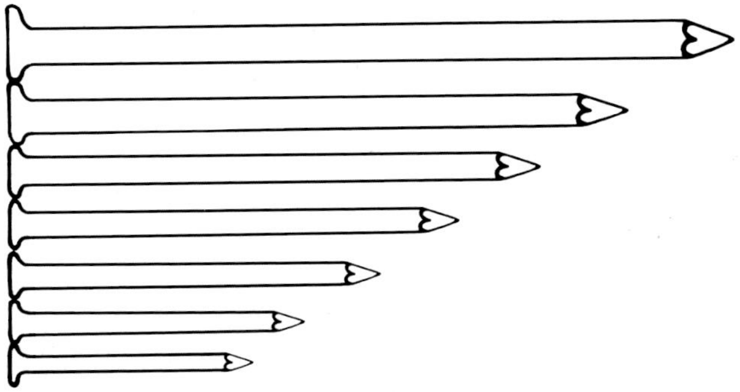

LBS.	MM	IN.
20d	102 mm	4"
16d	89 mm	3½"
10d	76 mm	3"
8d	64 mm	2½"
6d	51 mm	2"
5d	44 mm	1¾"
4d	38 mm	1½"

Counterbore, Shank & Pilot Hole Diameters

SCREW SIZE	COUNTERBORE DIAMETER FOR SCREW HEAD (IN INCHES)	CLEARANCE HOLE FOR SCREW SHANK (IN INCHES)	PILOT HOLE DIAMETER HARD WOOD (IN INCHES)	SOFT WOOD (IN INCHES)
#1	.146 (⁹/₆₄)	⁵/₆₄	³/₆₄	¹/₃₂
#2	¼	³/₃₂	³/₆₄	¹/₃₂
#3	¼	⁷/₆₄	¹/₁₆	³/₆₄
#4	¼	⅛	¹/₁₆	³/₆₄
#5	¼	⅛	⁵/₆₄	¹/₁₆
#6	⁵/₁₆	⁹/₆₄	³/₃₂	⁵/₆₄
#7	⁵/₁₆	⁵/₃₂	³/₃₂	⁵/₆₄
#8	⅜	¹¹/₆₄	⅛	³/₃₂
#9	⅜	¹¹/₆₄	⅛	³/₃₂
#10	⅜	³/₁₆	⅛	⁷/₆₄
#11	½	³/₁₆	⁵/₃₂	⁹/₆₄
#12	½	⁷/₃₂	⁹/₆₄	⅛

Index